COMMON CORE MATHEMATICS

A Story of Units

Grade 5, Module 4: Multiplication and Division of Fractions and Decimal Fractions

COMMON CORE™ consider the source

JB JOSSEY-BASS™

A Wiley Brand

Cover design by Chris Clary

Published by Jossey-Bass
A Wiley Brand
One Montgomery Street, Suite 1200, San Francisco, CA 94104-4594—www.josseybass.com

ISBN: 978-1-118-79354-1

Printed in the United States of America
FIRST EDITION
PB Printing   10 9 8 7 6 5 4 3

WELCOME

Dear Teacher,

Thank you for your interest in Common Core's curriculum in mathematics. Common Core is a non-profit organization based in Washington, DC dedicated to helping K-12 public schoolteachers use the power of high-quality content to improve instruction.[1] We are led by a board of master teachers, scholars, and current and former school, district, and state education leaders. Common Core has responded to the Common Core State Standards' (CCSS) call for "content-rich curriculum"[2] by creating new, CCSS-based curriculum materials in mathematics, English Language Arts, history, and (soon) the arts. All of our materials are written by teachers who are among the nation's foremost experts on the new standards.

In 2012 Common Core won three contracts from the New York State Education Department to create a PreKindergarten–12th grade mathematics curriculum for the teachers of that state, and to conduct associated professional development. The book you hold contains a portion of that work. In order to respond to demand in New York and elsewhere, modules of the curriculum will continue to be published, on a rolling basis, as they are completed. This curriculum is based on New York's version of the CCSS (the CCLS, or Common Core Learning Standards). Common Core will be releasing an enhanced version of the curriculum this summer on our website, commoncore.org. That version also will be published by Jossey-Bass, a Wiley brand.

Common Core's curriculum materials are not merely aligned to the new standards, they take the CCSS as their very foundation. Our work in math takes its shape from the expectations embedded in the new standards— including the instructional shifts and mathematical progressions, and the new expectations for student fluency, deep conceptual understanding, and application to real-life context. Similarly, our ELA and history curricula are deeply informed by the CCSS's new emphasis on close reading, increased use of informational text, and evidence-based writing.

Our curriculum is distinguished not only by its adherence to the CCSS. The math curriculum is based on a theory of teaching math that is proven to work. That theory posits that mathematical knowledge is most coherently and

---

1. Despite the coincidence of name, Common Core and the Common Core State Standards are not affiliated. Common Core was established in 2007, prior to the start of the Common Core State Standards Initiative, which was led by the National Governors Association and the Council for Chief State School Officers.
2. *Common Core State Standards for English Language Arts & Literacy in History/Social Studies, Science, and Technical Subjects* (Washington, DC: Common Core State Standards Initiative), 6.

effectively conveyed when it is taught in a sequence that follows the "story" of mathematics itself. This is why we call the elementary portion of this curriculum "A Story of Units," to be followed by "A Story of Ratios" in middle school, and "A Story of Functions" in high school. Mathematical concepts flow logically, from one to the next, in this curriculum. The sequencing has been joined with methods of instruction that have been proven to work, in this nation and abroad. These methods drive student understanding beyond process, to deep mastery of mathematical concepts. The goal of the curriculum is to produce students who are not merely literate, but fluent, in mathematics.

It is important to note that, as extensive as these curriculum materials are, they are not meant to be prescriptive. Rather, they are intended to provide a basis for teachers to hone their own craft through study, collaboration, training, and the application of their own expertise as professionals. At Common Core we believe deeply in the ability of teachers and in their central and irreplaceable role in shaping the classroom experience. We strive only to support and facilitate their important work.

The teachers and scholars who wrote these materials are listed beginning on the next page. Their deep knowledge of mathematics, of the CCSS, and of what works in classrooms defined this work in every respect. I would like to thank Louisiana State University professor of mathematics Scott Baldridge for the intellectual leadership he provides to this project. Teacher, trainer, and writer Robin Ramos is the most inspired math educator I've ever encountered. It is Robin and Scott's aspirations for what mathematics education in America *should* look like that is spelled out in these pages.

Finally, this work owes a debt to project director Nell McAnelly that is so deep I'm confident it never can be repaid. Nell, who leads LSU's Gordon A. Cain Center for STEM Literacy, oversees all aspects of our work for NYSED. She has spent days, nights, weekends, and many cancelled vacations toiling in her efforts to make it possible for this talented group of teacher-writers to produce their best work against impossible deadlines. I'm confident that in the years to come Scott, Robin, and Nell will be among those who will deserve to be credited with putting math instruction in our nation back on track.

Thank you for taking an interest in our work. Please join us at www.commoncore.org.

Lynne Munson

Lynne Munson
President and Executive Director
Common Core
Washington, DC
October 25, 2013

Common Core's K-5 Math Staff

Scott Baldridge, Lead Mathematician and Writer
Robin Ramos, Lead Writer, PreKindergarten-5
Jill Diniz, Lead Writer, 6-12
Ben McCarty, Mathematician

Nell McAnelly, Project Director
Tiah Alphonso, Associate Director
Jennifer Loftin, Associate Director
Catriona Anderson, Curriculum Manager,
    PreKindergarten-5

Sherri Adler, PreKindergarten
Debbie Andorka-Aceves, PreKindergarten

Kate McGill Austin, Kindergarten
Nancy Diorio, Kindergarten
Lacy Endo-Peery, Kindergarten
Melanie Gutierrez, Kindergarten
Nuhad Jamal, Kindergarten
Cecilia Rudzitis, Kindergarten
Shelly Snow, Kindergarten

Beth Barnes, First Grade
Lily Cavanaugh, First Grade
Ana Estela, First Grade
Kelley Isinger, First Grade
Kelly Spinks, First Grade
Marianne Strayton, First Grade
Hae Jung Yang, First Grade

Wendy Keehfus-Jones, Second Grade
Susan Midlarsky, Second Grade
Jenny Petrosino, Second Grade
Colleen Sheeron, Second Grade
Nancy Sommer, Second Grade
Lisa Watts-Lawton, Second Grade
MaryJo Wieland, Second Grade
Jessa Woods, Second Grade

Eric Angel, Third Grade
Greg Gorman, Third Grade
Susan Lee, Third Grade
Cristina Metcalf, Third Grade
Ann Rose Santoro, Third Grade
Kevin Tougher, Third Grade
Victoria Peacock, Third Grade
Saffron VanGalder, Third Grade

Katrina Abdussalaam, Fourth Grade
Kelly Alsup, Fourth Grade
Patti Dieck, Fourth Grade
Mary Jones, Fourth Grade
Soojin Lu, Fourth Grade
Tricia Salerno, Fourth Grade
Gail Smith, Fourth Grade
Eric Welch, Fourth Grade
Sam Wertheim, Fourth Grade
Erin Wheeler, Fourth Grade

Leslie Arceneaux, Fifth Grade
Adam Baker, Fifth Grade
Janice Fan, Fifth Grade
Peggy Golden, Fifth Grade
Halle Kananak, Fifth Grade
Shauntina Kerrison, Fifth Grade
Pat Mohr, Fifth Grade
Chris Sarlo, Fifth Grade

Additional Writers

Bill Davidson, Fluency Specialist
Robin Hecht, UDL Specialist
Simon Pfeil, Mathematician

Document Management Team

Tam Le, Document Manager
Jennifer Merchan, Copy Editor

Table of Contents

GRADE 5 • MODULE 4

Multiplication and Division of Fractions and Decimal Fractions

Grade 5 • Module 4

Multiplication and Division of Fractions and Decimal Fractions

OVERVIEW

In Module 4, students learn to multiply fractions and decimal fractions and begin work with fraction division.

Topic A begins the 38-day module with an exploration of fractional measurement. Students construct line plots by measuring the same objects using three different rulers accurate to 1/2, 1/4, and 1/8 of an inch (**5.MD.2**).

Students compare the line plots and explain how changing the accuracy of the unit of measure affects the distribution of points. This is foundational to the understanding that measurement is inherently imprecise, as it is limited by the accuracy of the tool at hand. Students use their knowledge of fraction operations to explore questions that arise from the plotted data. The interpretation of a fraction as division is inherent in this exploration. To measure to the quarter inch, one inch must be divided into four equal parts, or 1 ÷ 4. This reminder of the meaning of a fraction as a point on a number line, coupled with the embedded, informal exploration of fractions as division, provides a bridge to Topic B's more formal treatment of fractions as division.

Interpreting fractions as division is the focus of Topic B. Equal sharing with area models (both concrete and pictorial) gives students an opportunity to make sense of division of whole numbers with answers in the form of fractions or mixed numbers (e.g., seven brownies shared by three girls; three pizzas shared by four people). Discussion also includes an interpretation of remainders as a fraction (**5.NF.3**). Tape diagrams provide a linear model of these problems. Moreover, students see that by renaming larger units in terms of smaller units, division resulting in a fraction is just like whole number division.

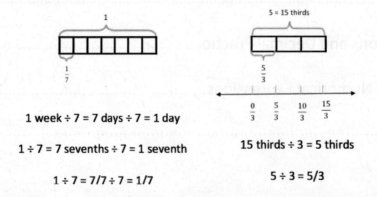

1 week ÷ 7 = 7 days ÷ 7 = 1 day

1 ÷ 7 = 7 sevenths ÷ 7 = 1 seventh

1 ÷ 7 = 7/7 ÷ 7 = 1/7

15 thirds ÷ 3 = 5 thirds

5 ÷ 3 = 5/3

Topic B continues as students solve real world problems (**5.NF.3**) and generate story contexts for visual models. The topic concludes with students making connections between models and equations while reasoning about their results (e.g., between what two whole numbers does the answer lie?).

In Topic C, students interpret finding a fraction of a set (3/4 *of* 24) as multiplication of a whole number by a fraction (3/4 × 24) and use tape diagrams to support their understandings (**5.NF.4a**). This in turn leads students to see division by a whole number as equivalent to multiplication by its reciprocal. That is, division by 2, for example, is the same as multiplication by 1/2. Students also use the commutative property to relate fraction of a set to the Grade 4 repeated addition interpretation of multiplication by a fraction. This opens the door for students to reason about various strategies for multiplying fractions and whole numbers. Students apply their knowledge of fraction of a set and previous conversion experiences (with scaffolding from a conversion chart, if necessary) to find a fraction of a measurement, thus converting a larger unit to an equivalent smaller unit (e.g.,1/3 min = 20 seconds and 2 1/4 feet = 27 inches).

Interpreting numerical expressions opens Topic D as students learn to evaluate expressions with parentheses, such as 3 × (2/3 –1/5) or 2/3 × (7 + 9) (**5.OA.1**). They then learn to interpret numerical expressions such as 3 *times the difference between 2/3 and 1/5* or *two-thirds the sum of 7 and 9* (**5.OA.2**). Students generate word problems that lead to the same calculation (**5.NF.4a**), such as, "Kelly combined 7 ounces of carrot juice and 5 ounces of orange juice in a glass. Jack drank 2/3 of the mixture. How much did Jack drink?" Solving word problems (**5.NF.6**) allows students to apply new knowledge of fraction multiplication in context, and tape diagrams are used to model multi-step problems requiring the use of addition, subtraction, and multiplication of fractions.

Topic E introduces students to multiplication of fractions by fractions—both in fraction and decimal form (**5.NF.4a**, **5.NBT.7**). The topic starts with multiplying a unit fraction by a unit fraction, and progresses to multiplying two non-unit fractions. Students use area models, rectangular arrays, and tape diagrams to model the multiplication. These familiar models help students draw parallels between whole number and fraction multiplication, and solve word problems. This intensive work with fractions positions students to extend their previous work with decimal-by-whole number multiplication to decimal-by-decimal multiplication. Just as students used unit form to multiply fractional units by wholes in Module 2 (e.g., 3.5 × 2 = 35 tenths × 2 ones = 70 tenths), they will connect fraction-by-fraction multiplication to multiply fractional units-by-fractional units (3.5 × 0.2 = 35 tenths × 2 tenths = 70 hundredths). Reasoning about decimal

$\frac{3}{4}$ of a foot = $\frac{3}{4}$ × 12 inches

1 foot = 12 inches

Express $5\frac{3}{4}$ ft as inches.

$5\frac{3}{4}$ ft = (5 × 12) inches + ($\frac{3}{4}$ × 12) inches

= 60 + 9 inches

= 69 inches

$\frac{3}{4}$ × 12

placement is an integral part of these lessons. Finding fractional parts of customary measurements and measurement conversion (**5.MD.1**) concludes Topic E. Students convert smaller units to fractions of a larger unit (e.g., 6 inches = 1/2 ft). The inclusion of customary units provides a meaningful context for many common fractions (1/2 pint = 1 cup, 1/3 yard = 1 foot, 1/4 gallon = 1 quart, etc.). This topic, together with the

fraction concepts and skills learned in Module 3, opens the door to a wide variety of application word problems (**5.NF.6**).

Students interpret multiplication in Grade 3 as equal groups, and in Grade 4 students begin to understand multiplication as comparison. Here, in Topic F, students once again extend their understanding of multiplication to include scaling (**5.NF.5**). Students compare the product to the size of one factor, given the size of the other factor (**5.NF.5a**) without calculation (e.g., 486 × 1,327.45 is twice as large as 243 × 1,327.45, because 486 = 2 × 243). This reasoning, along with the other work of this module, sets the stage for students to reason about the size of products when quantities are multiplied by numbers larger than 1 and smaller than 1. Students relate their previous work with equivalent fractions to interpreting multiplication by *n/n* as multiplication by 1 (**5.NF.5b**). Students build on their new understanding of fraction equivalence as multiplication by *n/n* to convert fractions to decimals and decimals to fractions. For example, 3/25 is easily renamed in hundredths as 12/100 using multiplication of 4/4. The word form of *twelve hundredths* will then be used to notate this quantity as a decimal. Conversions between fractional forms will be limited to fractions whose denominators are factors of 10, 100, or 1,000. Students will apply the concepts of the topic to real world, multi-step problems (**5.NF.6**).

Topic G begins the work of division with fractions, both fractions and decimal fractions. Students use tape diagrams and number lines to reason about the division of a whole number by a unit fraction and a unit fraction by a whole number (**5.NF.7**). Using the same thinking developed in Module 2 to divide whole numbers, students reason about how many *fourths* are in 5 when considering such cases as 5 ÷ 1/4. They also reason about the size of the unit when 1/4 is partitioned into 5 equal parts: 1/4 ÷ 5. Using this thinking as a backdrop, students are introduced to decimal fraction divisors and use equivalent fraction and place value thinking to reason about the size of quotients, calculate quotients, and sensibly place the decimal in quotients (**5.NBT.7**).

The module concludes with Topic H, in which numerical expressions involving fraction-by-fraction multiplication are interpreted and evaluated (**5.OA.1**, **5.OA.2**). Students create and solve word problems involving both multiplication and division of fractions and decimal fractions.

The Mid-Module Assessment is administered after Topic D, and the End-of-Module Assessment follows Topic H.

Distribution of Instructional Minutes

This diagram represents a suggested distribution of instructional minutes based on the emphasis of particular lesson components in different lessons throughout the module.

- ■ Fluency Practice
- □ Concept Development
- ▦ Application Problems
- ■ Student Debrief

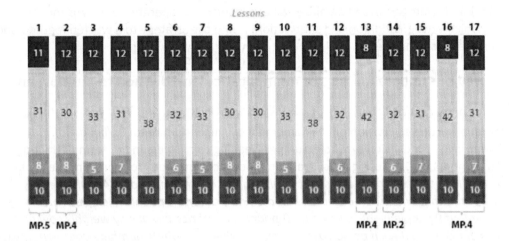

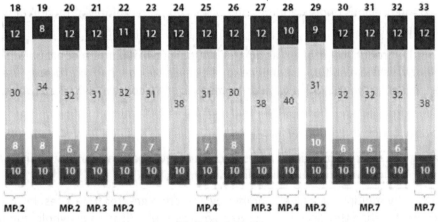

MP = Mathematical Practice

Focus Grade Level Standards

Write and interpret numerical expressions.

5.OA.1   Use parentheses, brackets, or braces in numerical expressions, and evaluate expressions with these symbols.

5.OA.2   Write simple expressions that record calculations with numbers, and interpret numerical expressions without evaluating them. *For example, express the calculation "add 8 and 7, then multiply by 2" as 2 × (8 +7). Recognize that 3 × (18932 + 921) is three times as large as 18932 + 921, without having to calculate the indicated sum or product.*

Perform operations with multi-digit whole numbers and with decimals to hundredths.

5.NBT.7   Add, subtract, multiply, and divide decimals to hundredths, using concrete models or drawings and strategies based on place value, properties of operations, and/or the relationship between addition and subtraction; relate the strategy to a written method and explain the reasoning used.

Apply and extend previous understandings of multiplication and division to multiply and divide fractions.

5.NF.3   Interpret a fraction as division of the numerator by the denominator (*a/b = a ÷ b*). Solve word problems involving division of whole numbers leading to answers in the form of fractions or mixed numbers, e.g., by using visual fraction models or equations to represent the problem. *For example, interpret 3/4 as the result of dividing 3 by 4, noting that 3/4 multiplied by 4 equals 3, and that when 3 wholes are shared equally among 4 people each person has a share of size 3/4. If 9 people want to share a 50-pound sack of rice equally by weight, how many pounds of rice should each person get? Between what two whole numbers does your answer lie?*

5.NF.4   Apply and extend previous understandings of multiplication to multiply a fraction or whole number by a fraction.

    a.   Interpret the product of *(a/b)* × *q* as *a* parts of a partition of *q* into *b* equal parts; equivalently, as the result of a sequence of operations *a* × *q* ÷ *b*. *For example, use a visual fraction model to show (2/3 × 4 = 8/3, and create a story context for this equation. Do the same with (2/3) × (4/5) = 8/15. (In general, (a/b) × (c/d) = ac/bd.)*

5.NF.5   Interpret multiplication as scaling (resizing), by:

    a.   Comparing the size of a product to the size of one factor on the basis of the size of the other factor, without performing the indicated multiplication.

    b.   Explaining why multiplying a given number by a fraction greater than 1 results in a product greater than the given number (recognizing multiplication by whole numbers greater than 1 as a familiar case); explaining why multiplying a given number by a fraction less than 1 results in a product smaller than the given number; and relating the principle of fraction equivalence *a/b = (n×a)/(n×b)* to the effect of multiplying *a/b* by 1.

5.NF.6   Solve real world problems involving multiplication of fractions and mixed numbers, e.g., by using visual fraction models or equations to represent the problem.

5.NF.7   Apply and extend previous understandings of division to divide unit fractions by whole numbers and whole numbers by unit fractions. (Students able to multiple fractions in general can develop strategies to divide fractions in general, by reasoning about the relationship between multiplication and division. But division of a fraction by a fraction is not a

requirement at this grade level.)

a. Interpret division of a unit fraction by a non-zero whole number, and compute such quotients. *For example, create a story context for (1/3) ÷ 4, and use a visual fraction model to show the quotient. Use the relationship between multiplication and division to explain that (1/3) ÷ 4 = 1/12 because (1/12) × 4 = 1/3.*

b. Interpret division of a whole number by a unit fraction, and compute such quotients. *For example, create a story context for 4 ÷ (1/5), and use a visual fraction model to show the quotient. Use the relationship between multiplication and division to explain that 4 ÷ (1/5) = 20 because 20 × (1/5) = 4.*

c. Solve real world problems involving division of unit fractions by non-zero whole numbers and division of whole numbers by unit fractions, e.g., by using visual fraction models and equations to represent the problem. *For example, how much chocolate will each person get if 3 people share 1/2 lb of chocolate equally? How many 1/3-cup servings are in 2 cups of raisins?*

Convert like measurement units within a given measurement system.

5.MD.1 Convert among different-sized standard measurement units within a given measurement system (e.g., convert 5 cm to 0.05 m), and use these conversions in solving multi-step, real world problems.

Represent and interpret data.

5.MD.2 Make a line plot to display a data set of measurements in fractions of a unit (1/2, 1/4, 1/8). Use operations on fractions for this grade to solve problems involving information presented in line plots. *For example, given different measurements of liquid in identical beakers, find the amount of liquid each beaker would contain if the total amount in all the beakers were redistributed equally.*

Foundational Standards

4.NF.1 Explain why a fraction a/b is equivalent to a fraction $(n \times a)/(n \times b)$ by using visual fraction models, with attention to how the number and size of the parts differ even though the two fractions themselves are the same size. Use this principle to recognize and generate equivalent fractions.

4.NF.2 Compare two fractions with different numerators and different denominators, e.g., by creating common denominators or numerators, or by comparing to a benchmark fraction such as 1/2. Recognize that comparisons are valid only when the two fractions refer to the same whole. Record the results of comparisons with symbols >, =, or <, and justify the conclusions, e.g., by using a visual fraction model.

4.NF.3 Understand a fraction a/b with $a > 1$ as a sum of fractions $1/b$.

a. Understand addition and subtraction of fractions as joining and separating parts referring to the same whole.

     b.   Decompose a fraction into a sum of fractions with the same denominator in more than one way, recording each decomposition by an equation. Justify decompositions, e.g., by using a visual fraction model. *Examples: 3/8 = 1/8 + 1/8 + 1/8 ; 3/8 = 1/8 + 2/8 ; 2 1/8 = 1 + 1 + 1/8 = 8/8 + 8/8 + 1/8.*

4.NF.4   Apply and extend previous understandings of multiplication to multiply a fraction by a whole number.

     a.   Understand a fraction *a/b* as a multiple of 1/*b*. *For example, use a visual fraction model to represent 5/4 as the product 5 × (1/4), recording the conclusion by the equation 5/4 = 5 × (1/4).*

     b.   Understand a multiple of *a/b* as a multiple of 1/*b*, and use this understanding to multiply a fraction by a whole number. *For example, use a visual fraction model to express 3 × (2/5) as 6 × (1/5), recognizing this product as 6/5. (In general, n × (a/b) = (n × a)/b.)*

     c.   Solve word problems involving multiplication of a fraction by a whole number, e.g., by using visual fraction models and equations to represent the problem. *For example, if each person at a party will eat 3/8 of a pound of roast beef, and there will be 5 people at the party, how many pounds of roast beef will be needed? Between what two whole numbers does your answer lie?*

4.NF.5   Express a fraction with denominator 10 as an equivalent fraction with denominator 100, and use this technique to add two fractions with respective denominators 10 and 100. (Students who can generate equivalent fractions can develop strategies for adding fractions with unlike denominators in general. But addition and subtraction with unlike denominators in general is not a requirement at this grade.) *For example, express 3/10 as 30/100, and add 3/10 + 4/100 = 34/100.*

4.NF.6   Use decimal notation for fractions with denominators 10 or 100. *For example, rewrite 0.62 as 62/100; describe a length as 0.62 meters; locate 0.62 on a number line diagram.*

Focus Standards for Mathematical Practice

MP.2   **Reason abstractly and quantitatively.** Students reason abstractly and quantitatively as they interpret the size of a product in relation to the size of a factor, interpret terms in a multiplication sentence as a quantity and a scaling factor and then create a coherent representation of the problem at hand while attending to the meaning of the quantities.

MP.4   **Model with mathematics.** Students model with mathematics as they solve word problems involving multiplication and division of fractions and decimals and identify important quantities in a practical situation and map their relationships using diagrams. Students use a line plot to model measurement data and interpret their results in the context of the situation, reflect on whether results make sense, and possibly improve the model if it has not served its purpose.

MP.5   **Use appropriate tools strategically.** Students use rulers to measure objects to the 1/2, 1/4 and 1/8 inch increments recognizing both the insight to be gained and the limitations of this tool as they learn that the actual object may not match the mathematical model precisely.

   Module 4:   Multiplication and Division of Fractions and Decimal Fractions
   Date: 11/10/13

Overview of Module Topics and Lesson Objectives

Standards		Topics and Objectives		Days
5.MD.2	A	**Line Plots of Fraction Measurements**		1
		Lesson 1:	Measure and compare pencil lengths to the nearest 1/2, 1/4, and 1/8 of an inch, and analyze the data through line plots.	
5.NF.3	B	**Fractions as Division**		4
		Lessons 2–3:	Interpret a fraction as division.	
		Lesson 4:	Use tape diagrams to model fractions as division.	
		Lesson 5:	Solve word problems involving the division of whole numbers with answers in the form of fractions or whole numbers.	
5.NF.4a	C	**Multiplication of a Whole Number by a Fraction**		4
		Lesson 6:	Relate fractions as division to fraction of a set.	
		Lesson 7:	Multiply any whole number by a fraction using tape diagrams.	
		Lesson 8:	Relate fraction of a set to the repeated addition interpretation of fraction multiplication.	
		Lesson 9:	Find a fraction of a measurement, and solve word problems.	
5.OA.1 **5.OA.2** **5.NF.4a** **5.NF.6**	D	**Fraction Expressions and Word Problems**		3
		Lesson 10:	Compare and evaluate expressions with parentheses.	
		Lesson 11–12:	Solve and create fraction word problems involving addition, subtraction, and multiplication.	
		Mid-Module Assessment: Topics A–D (assessment ½ day, return ½ day, remediation or further applications 1 day)		2
5.NBT.7 **5.NF.4a** **5.NF.6** **5.MD.1** 5.NF.4b	E	**Multiplication of a Fraction by a Fraction**		8
		Lesson 13:	Multiply unit fractions by unit fractions.	
		Lesson 14:	Multiply unit fractions by non-unit fractions.	
		Lesson 15:	Multiply non-unit fractions by non-unit fractions.	
		Lesson 16:	Solve word problems using tape diagrams and fraction-by-fraction multiplication.	
		Lessons 17–18:	Relate decimal and fraction multiplication.	
		Lesson 19:	Convert measures involving whole numbers, and solve multi-step word problems.	

Standards		Topics and Objectives	Days
		Lesson 20: Convert mixed unit measurements, and solve multi-step word problems.	
5.NF.5 **5.NF.6**	F	**Multiplication with Fractions and Decimals as Scaling and Word Problems**	4
		Lesson 21: Explain the size of the product, and relate fraction and decimal equivalence to multiplying a fraction by 1.	
		Lessons 22–23: Compare the size of the product to the size of the factors.	
		Lesson 24: Solve word problems using fraction and decimal multiplication.	
5.OA.1 **5.NBT.7** **5.NF.7**	G	**Division of Fractions and Decimal Fractions**	7
		Lesson 25: Divide a whole number by a unit fraction.	
		Lesson 26: Divide a unit fraction by a whole number.	
		Lesson 27: Solve problems involving fraction division.	
		Lesson 28: Write equations and word problems corresponding to tape and number line diagrams.	
		Lessons 29: Connect division by a unit fraction to division by 1 tenth and 1 hundredth.	
		Lessons 30–31: Divide decimal dividends by non-unit decimal divisors.	
5.OA.1 **5.OA.2**	H	**Interpretation of Numerical Expressions**	2
		Lesson 32: Interpret and evaluate numerical expressions including the language of scaling and fraction division.	
		Lesson 33: Create story contexts for numerical expressions and tape diagrams, and solve word problems.	
		End-of-Module Assessment: Topics A–H (assessment ½ day, return ½ day, remediation or further applications 2 days)	3
Total Number of Instructional Days			**38**

Terminology

New or Recently Introduced Terms

- Decimal divisor (the number that divides the whole and that has units of tenths, hundredths, thousandths, etc.)
- Simplify (using the largest fractional unit possible to express an equivalent fraction)

Familiar Terms and Symbols[1]

- Denominator (denotes the fractional unit, e.g., fifths in 3 fifths, which is abbreviated to the 5 in $\frac{3}{5}$)
- Decimal fraction
- Conversion factor
- Commutative Property (e.g., $4 \times \frac{1}{2} = \frac{1}{2} \times 4$)
- Distribute (with reference to the distributive property, e.g., in $\frac{2}{3} \times 15 = (1 \times 15) + (\frac{2}{3} \times 15)$)
- Divide, division (partitioning a total into equal groups to show how many units in a whole, e.g., $5 \div \frac{1}{5} = 25$)
- Equation (statement that two expressions are equal, e.g., $3 \times 4 = 6 \times 2$)
- Equivalent fraction
- Expression
- Factors (numbers that are multiplied to obtain a product)
- Feet, mile, yard, inch, gallon, quart, pint, cup, pound, ounce, hour, minute, second
- Fraction greater than or equal to 1 (e.g., $\frac{7}{2}$, $3\frac{1}{2}$, an abbreviation for $3 + \frac{1}{2}$)
- Fraction written in the largest possible unit (e.g., $\frac{3}{6} = \frac{1 \times 3}{2 \times 3} = \frac{1}{2}$ or 1 three out of 2 threes $= \frac{1}{2}$)
- Fractional unit (e.g., the fifth unit in 3 fifths denoted by the denominator 5 in $\frac{3}{5}$)
- Hundredth ($\frac{1}{100}$ or 0.01)
- Line plot
- Mixed number ($3\frac{1}{2}$, an abbreviation for $3 + \frac{1}{2}$)
- Numerator (denotes the count of fractional units, e.g., 3 in 3 fifths or 3 in $\frac{3}{5}$)
- Parentheses (symbols ( ) used around a fact or numbers within an equation)
- Quotient (the answer when one number is divided by another)
- Tape diagram (method for modeling problems)

---

[1] These are terms and symbols students have seen previously.

- Tenth ($\frac{1}{10}$ or 0.1)
- Unit (one segment of a partitioned tape diagram)
- Unknown (the missing factor or quantity in multiplication or division)
- Whole unit (any unit that is partitioned into smaller, equally sized fractional units)

Suggested Tools and Representations

- Area models
- Number lines
- Tape diagrams

Scaffolds[2]

The scaffolds integrated into *A Story of Units* give alternatives for how students access information as well as express and demonstrate their learning. Strategically placed margin notes are provided within each lesson elaborating on the use of specific scaffolds at applicable times. They address many needs presented by English language learners, students with disabilities, students performing above grade level, and students performing below grade level. Many of the suggestions are organized by Universal Design for Learning (UDL) principles and are applicable to more than one population. To read more about the approach to differentiated instruction in *A Story of Units,* please refer to "How to Implement *A Story of Units.*"

---

[2] Students with disabilities may require Braille, large print, audio, or special digital files. Please visit the website, www.p12.nysed.gov/specialed/aim, for specific information on how to obtain student materials that satisfy the National Instructional Materials Accessibility Standard (NIMAS) format.

Assessment Summary

Type	Administered	Format	Standards Addressed
Mid-Module Assessment Task	After Topic D	Constructed response with rubric	5.OA.1 5.OA.2 5.NF.3 5.NF.4a 5.NF.6 5.MD.1 5.MD.2
End-of-Module Assessment Task	After Topic H	Constructed response with rubric	5.OA.1 5.OA.2 5.NBT.7 5.NF.3 5.NF.4a 5.NF.5 5.NF.6 5.NF.7 5.MD.1 5.MD.2

Topic A

Line Plots of Fraction Measurements

5.MD.2

Focus Standard:	5.MD.2	Make a line plot to display a data set of measurements in fractions of a unit (1/2, 1/4, 1/8). Use operations on fractions for this grade to solve problems involving information presented in line plots. *For example, given different measurements of liquid in identical beakers, find the amount of liquid each beaker would contain if the total amount in all the beakers were redistributed equally.*
Instructional Days:	1	
Coherence -Links from:	G4–M5	Fraction Equivalence, Ordering, and Operations
-Links to:	G6–M2	Arithmetic Operations Including Dividing by a Fraction

Topic A begins the 38-day module with an exploration of fractional measurement. Students construct line plots by measuring the same objects using three different rulers accurate to 1/2, 1/4, and 1/8 of an inch (**5.MD.2**). Students compare the line plots and explain how changing the accuracy of the unit of measure affects the distribution of points (see line plots below). This is foundational to the understanding that measurement is inherently imprecise as it is limited by the accuracy of the tool at hand.

Students use their knowledge of fraction operations to explore questions that arise from the plotted data "What is the total length of the five longest pencils in our class? Can the half inch line plot be reconstructed using only data from the quarter inch plot? Why or why not?" The interpretation of a fraction as division is inherent in this exploration. To measure to the quarter inch, one inch must be divided into 4 equal parts, or $1 \div 4$. This reminder of the meaning of a fraction as a point on a number line coupled with the embedded, informal exploration of fractions as division provides a bridge to Topic B's more formal treatment of fractions as division.

Pencils measured to $\frac{1}{2}$ inch

Pencils measured to $\frac{1}{4}$ inch

A Teaching Sequence Towards Mastery of Line Plots of Fraction Measurements

Objective 1: Measure and compare pencil lengths to the nearest 1/2, 1/4, and 1/8 of an inch, and analyze the data through line plots.
(Lesson 1)

Lesson 1

Objective: Measure and compare pencil lengths to the nearest 1/2, 1/4, and 1/8 of an inch and analyze the data through line plots.

Suggested Lesson Structure

■ Fluency Practice   (11 minutes)
▨ Application Problem   (8 minutes)
▨ Concept Development   (31 minutes)
■ Student Debrief   (10 minutes)
   Total Time   **(60 minutes)**

Fluency Practice (11 minutes)

▪ Compare Fractions **4.NF.2**   (4 minutes)
▪ Decompose Fractions **4.NF.3**   (4 minutes)
▪ Equivalent Fractions **4.NF.1**   (3 minutes)

Compare Fractions (4 minutes)

Materials: (S) Personal white boards

Note: This fluency review prepares students for this lesson's Concept Development.

T: (Project a tape diagram labeled as one whole and partitioned into 2 equal parts. Shade 1 of the parts.) Say the fraction.

S: 1 half.

T: (Write $\frac{1}{2}$ to the right of the tape diagram. Directly below the tape diagram, project another tape diagram partitioned into 4 equal parts. Shade 1 of the parts.) Say this fraction.

S: 1 fourth.

T: (Write $\frac{1}{2}$ _____ $\frac{1}{4}$ to the right of the tape diagrams.) On your boards, use the greater than, less than, or equal sign to compare.

S: (Write $\frac{1}{2} > \frac{1}{4}$.)

Continue with the following possible suggestions: $\frac{1}{2} - \frac{1}{8}$, $\frac{1}{8} - \frac{1}{4}$, $\frac{1}{2} - \frac{1}{4}$, $\frac{1}{3} - \frac{1}{4}$, $\frac{2}{4} - \frac{3}{6}$, $\frac{3}{4} - \frac{3}{8}$, $\frac{2}{5} - \frac{2}{3}$, $\frac{3}{10} - \frac{3}{8}$, and $\frac{2}{3} - \frac{6}{9}$.

Lesson 1:   Measure and compare pencil lengths to the nearest 1/2, 1/4, and 1/8
            of an inch and analyze the data through line plots.
Date: 11/10/13

4.A.3

Decompose Fractions (4 minutes)

Materials: (S) Personal white boards

Note: This fluency review prepares students for this lesson's Concept Development.

T: (Write a number bond with $\frac{2}{3}$ as the whole and $\frac{1}{3}$ as the part.) Say the whole.

S: 2 thirds.

T: Say the given part.

S: 1 third.

T: On your boards, write the number bond. Fill in the missing part.

S: (Write $\frac{1}{3}$ as the missing part.)

T: Write an addition sentence to match the number bond.

S: $\frac{1}{3} + \frac{1}{3} = \frac{2}{3}$.

T: Write a multiplication sentence to match the number bond.

S: $2 \times \frac{1}{3} = \frac{2}{3}$.

Continue with the following possible suggestions: $\frac{1}{5} + \frac{1}{5} = \frac{2}{5}$, $\frac{1}{4} + \frac{1}{4} + \frac{1}{4} = \frac{3}{4}$, and $\frac{1}{8} + \frac{1}{8} + \frac{1}{8} = \frac{3}{8}$.

Equivalent Fractions (3 minutes)

T: (Write $\frac{1}{2}$.)

T: Say the fraction.

S: 1 half.

T: (Write $\frac{1}{2} = \frac{}{4}$.)

T: 1 half is how many fourths?

S: 2 fourths.

Continue with the following possible sequence: $\frac{1}{2} = \frac{}{6}$, $\frac{1}{3} = \frac{}{6}$, $\frac{2}{3} = \frac{}{12}$, $\frac{3}{4} = \frac{}{16}$, and $\frac{3}{5} = \frac{}{25}$.

T: (Write $\frac{1}{2}$.)

T: Say the fraction.

S: 1 half.

T: (Write $\frac{1}{2} = \frac{2}{}$.)

T: 1 half, or 1 part of 2, is the same as 2 parts of what unit?

S: Fourths.

Continue with the following possible sequence: $\frac{1}{2} = \frac{2}{}$, $\frac{1}{5} = \frac{2}{}$, $\frac{2}{5} = \frac{8}{}$, $\frac{3}{4} = \frac{9}{}$, and $\frac{4}{5} = \frac{16}{}$.

Lesson 1:	Measure and compare pencil lengths to the nearest 1/2, 1/4, and 1/8 of an inch and analyze the data through line plots.
Date:	11/10/13

4.A.4

Application Problem (8 minutes)

The following line plot shows the growth of 10 bean plants on their second week after sprouting.

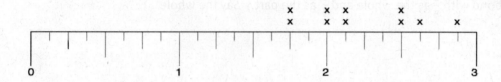

a. What was the measurement of the shortest plant?

b. How many plants measure $2\frac{1}{2}$ inches?

c. What is the measure of the tallest plant?

d. What is the difference between the longest and shortest measurement?

Note: This Application Problem provides an opportunity for a quick, formative assessment of student ability to read a customary ruler and a simple line plot. As today's lesson is time-intensive, the analysis of this plot data is necessarily simple.

Concept Development (31 minutes)

Materials: (S) Inch ruler, Problem Set, 8½" × 1" strip of paper (with straight edges) per student

Note: Before beginning the lesson, draw three number lines, one beneath the other, on the board. The lines should be marked 0–8 with increments of halves, fourths, and eighths, respectively. Leave plenty of room to put the three line plots directly beneath each other.

Students will compare these line plots later in the lesson.

T: Cut the strip of paper so that it is the same length as your pencil.

S: (Measure and cut.)

T: Estimate the length of your pencil strip to the nearest inch and record your estimate on the first line in your Problem Set.

T: If I ask you to measure your pencil strip to the nearest half inch, what do I mean?

S: I should measure my pencil and see which half-inch or whole-inch mark is closest to the length of my strip. → When I look at the ruler, I have to pay attention to the marks that split the inches into 2 equal parts. Then look for the one that is closest to the length of my strip. → I know that I will give a measurement that is either a whole number or a measurement that has a half in it.

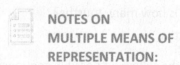

NOTES ON MULTIPLE MEANS OF REPRESENTATION:

Use colored paper for the pencil measurements to help students see where their pencil paper lines up on the rulers.

Lesson 1: Measure and compare pencil lengths to the nearest 1/2, 1/4, and 1/8 of an inch and analyze the data through line plots.

Date: 11/10/13

4.A.5

Discuss with students what they should do if their pencil strip is between two marks (e.g., 6 and $6\frac{1}{2}$). Remind students that any measurement that is more than halfway should be rounded up.

T: Use your ruler to measure your strip to the nearest half inch. Record your measurement by placing an X on the picture of the ruler in Problem 2 on your Problem Set.

T: Was the measurement to the nearest half inch accurate? Let's find out. Raise your hand if your actual length was on or very close to one of the half-inch marking on your ruler.

T: It seems that most of us had to round our measurement in order to mark it on the sheet. Let's record everyone's measurements on a line plot. As each person calls out his or her measurement, I'll record on the board as you record on your sheet. (Poll the students.)

A typical class line plot might look like this:

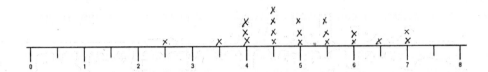

T: Which pencil measurement is the most common, or frequent, in our class? Turn and talk.

Answers will vary by class. In the plot above, $4\frac{1}{2}$ inches is most frequent.

T: Are all of the pencils used for these measurements *exactly* the same length? (Point to the X's above the most frequent data point—$4\frac{1}{2}$ inches on the exemplar line plot.) Are they exactly $4\frac{1}{2}$ inches long?

S: No, these measurements are to the nearest half inch. → The pencils are different sizes. We had to round the measurement of some of them. → My partner and I had pencils that were different lengths, but they were close to the same mark. We had to put our marks on the same place on the sheet even though they weren't really the same length.

MP.5

T: Now let's measure our strips to the nearest quarter inch. How is measuring to the quarter inch different from measuring to the half inch? Turn and talk.

S: The whole is divided into 4 equal parts instead of just 2 equal parts. → Quarter inches are smaller than half inches. → Measuring to the nearest quarter inch gives us more choices about where to put our X's on the ruler.

Follow the same sequence of measuring and recording the strips to the nearest quarter inch. Your line plot might look something like this:

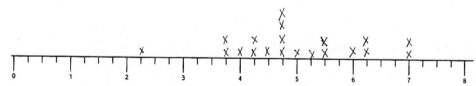

T: Which pencil measurement is the most frequent this time?

Answers will vary by class. The most frequent above is $4\frac{3}{4}$ inches.

T: If the length of our strips didn't change, why is the most frequent measurement different this time?

Lesson 1: Measure and compare pencil lengths to the nearest 1/2, 1/4, and 1/8 of an inch and analyze the data through line plots.

Date: 11/10/13

4.A.6

S: The unit on the ruler we used to measure and record was different. → The smaller units made it possible for me to get closer to the real length of my strip. → I rounded to the nearest quarter inch so I had to move my X to a different mark on the ruler. Other people probably had to do the same thing.

NOTES ON
MULTIPLE MEANS OF
REPRESENTATION:

Write math vocabulary words on sentence strips and display as they are used in context (e.g., *precise, accurate*).

T: Yes, the ruler with smaller units (every quarter inch instead of every half inch) allowed us to be more precise with our measurement. This ruler (point to the $\frac{1}{4}$ plot on the board) has more fractional units in a given length, which allows for a more precise measurement. It's a bit like when we round a number by hundreds or tens. Which rounded number will be closer to the actual? Why? Turn and talk.

S: When we round to the tens place we can be closer to the actual number, because we are using smaller units.

T: That's exactly what's happening here when we measure to the nearest quarter inch versus the nearest half inch. How did your measurements either change or not change?

S: My first was 4 inches but my second was closer to 4 and quarter. → My first measurement was 4 and a half inches. My second was 4 and 2 quarter inches, but that's the same as 4 and a half inches. → When I measured with the half-inch ruler, my first was closer to 4 inches than to 3 and a half inches, but when I measured with the fourth-inch ruler, it was closer to 3 and 3 quarter inches, because it was a little closer to 3 and 3 quarter inches than 4 inches.

T: Our next task is to measure our strips to the nearest eighth of an inch and record our data in a third line plot. Look at the first two line plots. What do you think the shape of the third line plot will look like? Turn and talk.

S: The line plot will be flatter than the first two. → There are more choices for our measurements on the ruler, so I think that there will be more places where there will only be one X than on the other rulers. → The eighth-inch ruler will show the differences between pencil lengths more than the half-inch or fourth-inch rulers.

Follow the sequence above for measuring and recording line plots.

T: Let's find out how accurate our measurements are. Raise your hand if your actual strip length was on or very close to one of the eighth-inch markings on the ruler. (It is likely that many more students will raise their hands than before.)

S: (Raise hands.)

T: Work with your partner to answer Problem 5 on your Problem Set.

You may want to copy down the line plots on the board for later analysis with your class.

Problem Set (10 minutes)

Students should do their personal best to complete the Problem Set within the allotted 10 minutes. Some problems do not specify a method for solving. This is an intentional reduction of scaffolding that invokes MP.5, Use Appropriate Tools Strategically. Students should solve these problems using the RDW approach used for Application Problems.

Lesson 1:	Measure and compare pencil lengths to the nearest 1/2, 1/4, and 1/8 of an inch and analyze the data through line plots.
Date:	11/10/13

4.A.7

For some classes, it may be appropriate to modify the assignment by specifying which problems students should work on first. With this option, let the careful sequencing of the Problem Set guide your selections so that problems continue to be scaffolded. Balance word problems with other problem types to ensure a range of practice. Assign incomplete problems for homework or at another time during the day.

Student Debrief (10 minutes)

Lesson Objective: Measure and compare pencil lengths to the nearest 1/2, 1/4, and 1/8 of an inch and analyze the data through line plots.

The Student Debrief is intended to invite reflection and active processing of the total lesson experience.

Invite students to review their solutions for the Problem Set. They should check work by comparing answers with a partner before going over answers as a class. Look for

misconceptions or misunderstandings that can be addressed in the Debrief. Guide students in a conversation to debrief the Problem Set and process the lesson.

You may choose to use any combination of the questions below to lead the discussion. However, it is recommended that the first bullet be a focus for this lesson's discussion.

- How many of you had a pencil length that didn't fall directly on an inch, half-inch, quarter-inch, or eighth-inch marking?
  - If you wanted a more precise measurement of your pencil's length, what could you do? (Guide student to see that they could choose smaller fractional units.)
  - When someone tells you, "My pencil is 5 and 3 quarters inches long," is it reasonable to assume that his or her pencil is *exactly* that long? (Guide students to see that in practice, all measurements are approximations, even though we assume they are exact for the sake of calculation.)
- How does the most frequent pencil length change with each line plot? How does the number of each pencil length for each data point change with each line plot? Which line plot had the most

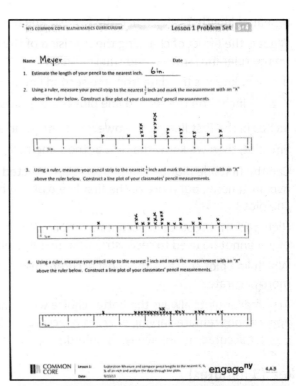

Lesson 1: Measure and compare pencil lengths to the nearest 1/2, 1/4, and 1/8 of an inch and analyze the data through line plots.
Date: 11/10/13

4.A.8

repeated lengths? Which had the fewest repeated lengths?

- What is the effect of changing the precision of the ruler? What happens when you split the wholes on the ruler into smaller and smaller units?

- If all you know is the data from the second line plot, can you reconstruct the first line plot? (No. An X at $3\frac{3}{4}$ inches on the second line plot could represent a pencil as short as $3\frac{1}{2}$ inches or as long as 4 inches in the first line plot. However, if an X is on a half-inch mark—3, $3\frac{1}{2}$, 4, $4\frac{1}{2}$, etc.—on the second line plot, then we know that it is at the same half-inch mark in the first line plot.)

- Can the first line plot be completely reconstructed knowing only the data from the third line plot? (No, in general, but more of the first line plot can be reconstructed from the third than the second line plot.)

- High-performing student accommodation: Which points on the third line plot can be used and which ones cannot be used to reconstruct the first line plot?

- Which line plot contains the most accurate measurements? Why? Why are smaller units generally more accurate?

- Are smaller units always the better choice when measuring? (Lead students to see that different applications require varying degrees of accuracy. Smaller units do allow for greater accuracy, but greater accuracy is not always required.)

Exit Ticket (3 minutes)

After the Student Debrief, instruct students to complete the Exit Ticket. A review of their work will help you assess the students' understanding of the concepts that were presented in the lesson today and plan more effectively for future lessons. You may read the questions aloud to the students.

Lesson 1: Measure and compare pencil lengths to the nearest 1/2, 1/4, and 1/8 of an inch and analyze the data through line plots.

Date: 11/10/13

4.A.9

Name _____   Date _____

1. Estimate the length of your pencil to the nearest inch. _____

2. Using a ruler, measure your pencil strip to the nearest $\frac{1}{2}$ inch and mark the measurement with an X above the ruler below. Construct a line plot of your classmates' pencil measurements.

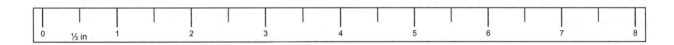

3. Using a ruler, measure your pencil strip to the nearest $\frac{1}{4}$ inch and mark the measurement with an X above the ruler below. Construct a line plot of your classmates' pencil measurements.

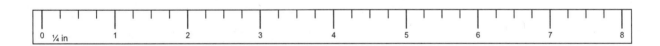

4. Using a ruler, measure your pencil strip to the nearest $\frac{1}{8}$ inch and mark the measurement with an X above the ruler below. Construct a line plot of your classmates' pencil measurements.

COMMON CORE™ | **Lesson 1:**   Measure and compare pencil lengths to the nearest 1/2, 1/4, and 1/8 of an inch and analyze the data through line plots.   **4.A.10**

Date: 11/10/13

5. Use all three of your line plots to answer the following.

    a. Compare the three plots and write one sentence that describes how the plots are alike and one sentence that describes how they are different.

    b. What is the difference between the measurements of the longest and shortest pencils on each of the three line plots?

    c. Write a sentence describing how you could create a more precise ruler to measure your pencil strip.

COMMON CORE™

Lesson 1:   Measure and compare pencil lengths to the nearest 1/2, 1/4, and 1/8 of an inch and analyze the data through line plots.

Date: 11/10/13

4.A.11

Name _____   Date _____

1. Draw a line plot for the following data measured in inches:

$1\frac{1}{2}, 2\frac{3}{4}, 3, 2\frac{3}{4}, 2\frac{1}{2}, 2\frac{3}{4}, 3\frac{3}{4}, 3, 3\frac{1}{2}, 2\frac{1}{2}, 3\frac{1}{2}$

2. Explain how you decided to divide your wholes into fractional parts, and how you decided where your number scale should begin and end.

COMMON CORE™   Lesson 1:   Measure and compare pencil lengths to the nearest 1/2, 1/4, and 1/8
of an inch and analyze the data through line plots.   4.A.12
Date: 11/10/13

Name _____   Date _____

1. A meteorologist set up rain gauges at various locations around a city, and recorded the rainfall amounts in the table below. Use the data in the table to create a line plot using $\frac{1}{8}$ inches.

a. Which location received the most rainfall?

b. Which location received the least rainfall?

c. Which rainfall measurement was the most frequent?

d. What is the total rainfall in inches?

Location	Rainfall Amount (inches)
1	$\frac{1}{8}$
2	$\frac{3}{8}$
3	$\frac{3}{4}$
4	$\frac{3}{4}$
5	$\frac{1}{4}$
6	$1\frac{1}{4}$
7	$\frac{1}{8}$
8	$\frac{1}{4}$
9	1
10	$\frac{1}{8}$

Lesson 1:   Measure and compare pencil lengths to the nearest 1/2, 1/4, and 1/8
of an inch and analyze the data through line plots.

Date: 11/10/13

4.A.13

Topic B

Fractions as Division

5.NF.3

Focus Standard:	5.NF.3	Interpret a fraction as division of the numerator by the denominator ($a/b = a \div b$). Solve word problems involving division of whole numbers leading to answers in the form of fractions or mixed numbers, e.g., by using visual fraction models or equations to represent the problem. *For example, interpret 3/4 as the result of dividing 3 by 4, noting that 3/4 multiplied by 4 equals 3, and that when 3 wholes are shared equally among 4 people each person has a share of size 3/4. If 9 people want to share a 50-pound sack of rice equally by weight, how many pounds of rice should each person get? Between what two whole numbers does your answer lie?*
Instructional Days:	4	
Coherence -Links from:	G4–M5	Fraction Equivalence, Ordering, and Operations
	G4–M6	Decimal Fractions
-Links to:	G6–M2	Arithmetic Operations Including Dividing by a Fraction

Interpreting fractions as division is the focus of Topic B. Equal sharing with area models (both concrete and pictorial) gives students an opportunity to make sense of the division of whole numbers with answers in the form of fractions or mixed numbers (e.g., seven brownies shared by three girls, three pizzas shared by four people). Discussion also includes an interpretation of remainders as a fraction (**5.NF.3**). Tape diagrams provide a linear model of these problems. Moreover, students see that by renaming larger units in terms of smaller units, division resulting in a fraction is just like whole number division.

Topic B continues as students solve real world problems (**5.NF.3**) and generate story contexts for visual models. The topic concludes with students making connections between models and equations while reasoning about their results (e.g., between what two whole numbers does the answer lie?).

A Teaching Sequence Towards Mastery of Fractions as Division

Objective 1: Interpret a fraction as division.
(Lessons 2–3)

Objective 2: Use tape diagrams to model fractions as division.
(Lesson 4)

Objective 3: Solve word problems involving the division of whole numbers with answers in the form of fractions or whole numbers.
(Lesson 5)

Lesson 2

Objective: Interpret a fraction as division.

Suggested Lesson Structure

▪ Application Problem	(8 minutes)	
▪ Fluency Practice	(12 minutes)	
▪ Concept Development	(30 minutes)	
▪ Student Debrief	(10 minutes)	
Total Time	**(60 minutes)**	

Application Problem (8 minutes)

The line plot shows the number of miles run by Noland in his PE class last month, rounded to the nearest quarter mile.

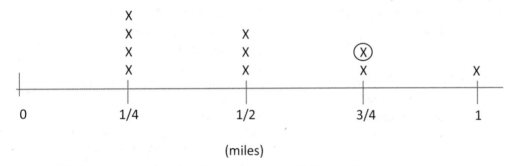

(miles)

a. If Noland ran once a day, how many days did he run?

b. How many miles did Noland run altogether last month?

c. Look at the circled data point. The actual distance Noland ran that day was at least ____mile and less than ____mile.

Note: This Application Problem reinforces the work of yesterday's lesson. Part (c) provides an extension for early finishers.

Fluency Practice (12 minutes)

▪ Factors of 100 **4.NF.5**	(2 minutes)	
▪ Compare Fractions **4.NF.2**	(4 minutes)	
▪ Decompose Fractions **4.NF.3**	(3 minutes)	
▪ Divide with Remainders **5.NF.3**	(3 minutes)	

Lesson 2:	Interpret a fraction as division.
Date:	11/10/13

4.B.3

Factors of 100 (2 minutes)

Note: This fluency prepares students for fractions with denominators of 4, 20, 25, and 50 in G5–M4–Topic G.

    T: (Write 50 × ____ = 100.) Say the equation filling in the missing factor.

    S: 50 × 2 = 100.

Continue with the following possible suggestions: 25 × ____ = 100, 4 × ____ = 100, 20 × ____ = 100, 50 × ____ = 100.

    T: I'm going to say a factor of 100. You say the other factor that will make 100.

    T: 20.

    S: 5.

Continue with the following possible suggestions: 25, 50, 5, 10, and 4.

Compare Fractions (4 minutes)

Materials: (S) Personal white boards

Note: This fluency reviews Grade 4 and Grade 5–Module 3 concepts.

    T: (Project a tape diagram partitioned into 2 equal parts. Shade 1 of the parts.) Say the fraction.

    S: 1 half.

    T: (Write $\frac{1}{2}$ to the right of the tape diagram. Directly below the first tape diagram, project another tape diagram partitioned into 4 equal parts. Shade 3 of the parts.) Say this fraction.

    S: 3 fourths.

    T: What's a common unit that we could use to compare these fractions?

    S: Fourths. → Eighths. → Twelfths.

    T: Let's use fourths. (Below write $\frac{1}{2}$ ____ $\frac{3}{4}$, write $\frac{}{4}$ ____ $\frac{3}{4}$.) On your boards, write in the unknown numerator and a greater than or less than symbol.

    S: (Write $\frac{2}{4} < \frac{3}{4}$.)

Continue with the following possible suggestions, comparing $\frac{1}{2}$ and $\frac{3}{8}$, $\frac{5}{8}$ and $\frac{1}{2}$, $\frac{5}{8}$ and $\frac{3}{4}$, and $\frac{3}{4}$ and $\frac{7}{8}$.

Decompose Fractions (4 minutes)

Materials: (S) Personal white boards

Note: This fluency reviews Grade 4 and Grade 5–Module 3 concepts.

NOTES ON MULTIPLE MEANS OF REPRESENTATION:

For English language learners or students who need to review the relative size of fractional units, folding square paper into various units of halves, thirds, fourths, and eighths can be beneficial. Allow students time to fold, cut, label and compare the units in relation to the whole and each other.

Lesson 2:   Interpret a fraction as division.
Date: 11/10/13

4.B.4

T: (Write a number bond with $\frac{3}{5}$ as the whole and 3 missing parts.) On your boards, break apart 3 fifths into unit fractions.

S: (Write $\frac{1}{5}$ for each missing part.)

T: Say the multiplication equation for this bond.

S: $3 \times \frac{1}{5} = \frac{3}{5}$.

Continue with the following possible suggestions: $\frac{2}{3}$, $\frac{3}{10}$, and $\frac{5}{8}$.

Divide with Remainders (4 minutes)

Materials: (S) Personal white boards

Note: This fluency prepares students for this lesson's Concept Development.

T: (Write $8 \div 2 =$ ___.) Say the quotient.

S: 4.

T: Say the remainder.

S: There isn't one.

T: (Write $9 \div 2 =$ ___.) Quotient?

S: 4.

T: Remainder?

S: 1.

Continue with the following possible suggestions: $25 \div 5$, $27 \div 5$, $9 \div 3$, $10 \div 3$, $16 \div 4$, $19 \div 4$, $12 \div 6$, and $11 \div 6$.

Concept Development (30 minutes)

Materials: (S) Personal white boards, 15 square pieces of paper per pair of students

Problem 1

$2 \div 2$

$1 \div 2$

$1 \div 3$

$2 \div 3$

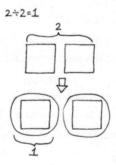

T: Imagine we have 2 crackers. Use two pieces of your paper to represent the crackers. Share the crackers equally between 2 people.

S: (Distribute 1 cracker per person.)

T: How many crackers did each person get?

Lesson 2:   Interpret a fraction as division.
Date: 11/10/13

4.B.5

S: 1 cracker.

T: Say a division sentence that tells what you just did with the cracker.

S: 2 ÷ 2 = 1.

T: I'll record that with a drawing. (Draw the 2 ÷ 2 = 1 image on the board.)

T: Now imagine that there is only 1 cracker to share between 2 people. Use your paper and scissors to show how you would share the cracker.

S: (Cut one paper into halves.)

MP.4 T: How much will each person get?

S: 1 half of a cracker.

T: Work with your partner to write a number sentence that shows how you shared the cracker equally.

S: $1 \div 2 = \frac{1}{2}$. → $\frac{2}{2} \div 2 = \frac{1}{2}$. → 2 halves ÷ 2 = 1 half.

T: I'll record your thinking on the board with another drawing. (Draw the 1 ÷ 2 drawing, and write the number sentence beneath it.)

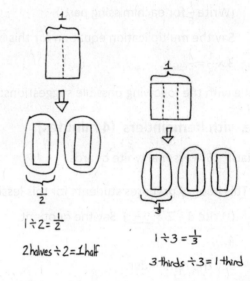

$1 \div 2 = \frac{1}{2}$

2 halves ÷ 2 = 1 half

$1 \div 3 = \frac{1}{3}$

3 thirds ÷ 3 = 1 third

Repeat this sequence with 1 ÷ 3.

T: (Point to both division sentences on the board.) Look at these two number sentences. What do you notice? Turn and talk.

S: Both problems start with 1 whole, but it gets divided into 2 parts in the first problem and 3 parts in the second one. → I noticed that both of the answers are fractions, and the fractions have the same digits in them as the division expressions. → When you share the same size whole with 2 people, you get more than when you share it with 3 people. → The fraction looks a lot like the division expression, but it's the amount that each person gets out of the whole.

T: (Point to the number sentences.) We can write the division expression as a fraction. 1 divided by 2 is the same as 1 half. 1 divided by 3 is the same as 1 third.

T: Let's consider sharing 2 crackers with 3 people. Thinking about 1 divided by 3, how much do you think each person would get? Turn and talk.

S: It's double the amount of crackers shared with the same number of people. Each person should get twice as much as before, so they should get 2 thirds. → The division sentence can be written like a fraction, so 2 divided by 3 would be the same as 2 thirds.

T: Use your materials to show how you would share 2 crackers with 3 people.

S: (Work.)

NOTES ON MULTIPLE MEANS OF EXPRESSION:

Students with fine motor deficits may find the folding and cutting of the concrete materials taxing. Consider allowing them to either serve as reporter for their learning group sharing the findings, or allowing them to use online virtual manipulatives.

Lesson 2:   Interpret a fraction as division.
Date: 11/10/13

4.B.6

Problem 2

$3 \div 2$

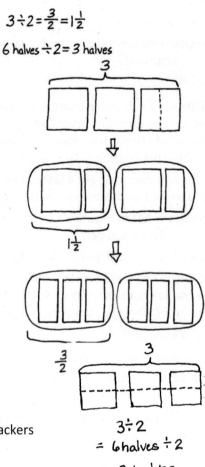

T: Now, let's take 3 crackers and share them equally with 2 people. (Draw 3 squares on the board, underneath the squares, draw 2 circles.) Turn and talk about how you can share these crackers. Use your materials to show your thinking.

S: I have 3 crackers, so I can give 1 whole cracker to both people. Then I'll just have to split the third cracker into halves and share it. → Since there are 2 people, we could cut each cracker into 2 parts and then share them equally that way.

T: Let's record these ideas by drawing. We have 3 crackers. I heard someone say that there is enough for each person to get a whole cracker. Draw a whole cracker in each circle.

S: (Draw.)

T: How many crackers remain?

S: 1 cracker.

T: What must we do with the remaining cracker if we want to keep sharing equally?

S: Divide it in 2 equal parts. → Split it in half.

T: Add that to your drawing. How many halves will each person get?

S: 1 half.

T: Record that by drawing one-half into each circle. How many crackers did each person receive?

S: 1 and $\frac{1}{2}$ crackers.

T: (Write $3 \div 2 = 1\frac{1}{2}$ beneath the drawing.) How many halves are in 1 and 1 half?

S: 3 halves.

T: (Write $\frac{3}{2}$ next to the equation.) I noticed that some of you cut the crackers in 2 equal parts before you began sharing. Let's draw that way of sharing. (Re-draw 3 wholes. Divide them in halves horizontally.) How many halves were in 3 crackers?

S: 6 halves.

T: What's 6 halves divided by 2? Draw it.

S: 3 halves.

Lesson 2:	Interpret a fraction as division.
Date:	11/10/13

4.B.7

Problem 3

$4 \div 2$

$5 \div 2$

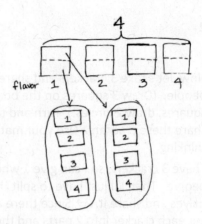

T: Imagine 4 crackers shared with 2 people. How many would each person get?

S: 2 crackers.

T: (Write $4 \div 2 = 2$ on the board.) Let's now imagine that all four crackers are different flavors, and both people would like to taste all of the flavors. How could we share the crackers equally to make that possible? Turn and talk.

S: To be sure everyone got a taste of all 4 crackers, we would need to split all the crackers in half first, and then share.

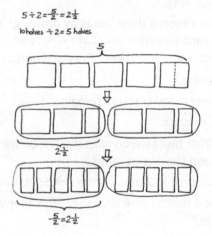

T: How many halves would we have to share in all? How many would each person get?

S: 8 halves in all. Each person would get 4 halves.

T: Let me record that. (Write 8 halves ÷ 2 = 4 halves.) Although the crackers were shared in units of one-half, what is the total amount of crackers each person receives?

S: 2 whole crackers.

Follow the sequence above to discuss $5 \div 2$ using 5 crackers of the same flavor followed by 5 different flavored crackers. Discuss the two ways of sharing.

T: (Point to the division equations that have been recorded.) Look at all the division problems we just solved. Talk to your neighbor about the patterns you see in the quotients.

S: The numbers in the problems are the same as the numbers in the quotients. → The division expressions can be written as fractions with the same digits. → The numerators are the wholes that we shared. The denominators show how many equal parts we made. → The numerators are like the dividends, and the denominators are like the divisors. → Even the division symbol looks like a fraction. The dot on top could be a numerator and the dot on the bottom could be a denominator.

T: Will this always be true? Let's test a few. Since 1 divided by 4 equals 1 fourth, what is 1 divided by 5?

S: 1 fifth.

T: (Write $1 \div 5 = \frac{1}{5}$.) What is $1 \div 7$?

S: 1 seventh.

T: 3 divided by 7?

S: 3 sevenths.

T: Let's try expressing fractions as division. Say a division expression that is equal to 3 eighths.

S: 3 divided by 8.

T: 3 tenths?

S: 3 divided by 10.

T: 3 hundredths?

S: 3 divided by 100.

Problem Set (10 minutes)

Students should do their personal best to complete the Problem Set within the allotted 10 minutes. For some classes, it may be appropriate to modify the assignment by specifying which problems they work on first. Some problems do not specify a method for solving. Students solve these problems using the RDW approach used for Application Problems.

Student Debrief (10 minutes)

Lesson Objective: Interpret a fraction as division.

The Student Debrief is intended to invite reflection and active processing of the total lesson experience.

Invite students to review their solutions for the Problem Set. They should check work by comparing answers with a partner before going over answers as a class. Look for misconceptions or misunderstandings that can be addressed in the Debrief. Guide students in a conversation to debrief the Problem Set and process the lesson.

You may choose to use any combination of the questions below to lead the discussion.

- What did you notice about Problems 4(a) and 4(b)? What were the wholes, or dividends, and what were the divisors?

- What was your strategy to solve Problem 1(c)?

- What pattern did you notice between 1(b) and 1(c)? What was the relationship between the size of the dividends and the quotients?

- Discuss the division sentence for Problem 2. What number is the whole and what number is the divisor? How is the division sentence different from 2 ÷ 3?

- Explain to your partner the two sharing approaches in Problem 3. (The first approach is to give each

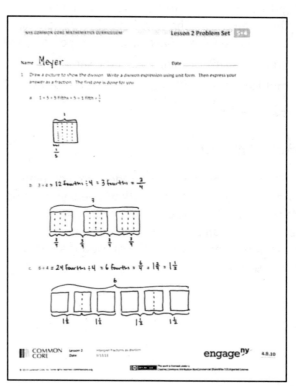

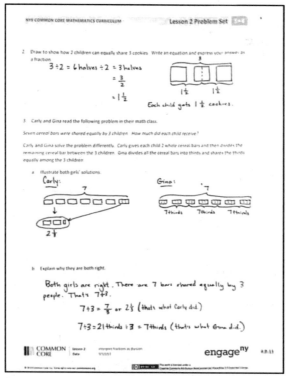

COMMON CORE™

Lesson 2:   Interpret a fraction as division.
Date: 11/10/13

4.B.9

girl 1 whole then partition the remaining bars. The second approach is to partition all 7 bars, 21 thirds, and share the thirds equally.) When might one approach be more appropriate? (If the cereal bars were different flavors, and each person wanted to try each flavor.)

- True or false? Dividing by 2 is the same as multiplying by $\frac{1}{2}$. (If needed, revisit the fact that $3 \div 2 = \frac{3}{2} = 3 \times \frac{1}{2}$.)

Exit Ticket (3 minutes)

After the Student Debrief, instruct students to complete the Exit Ticket. A review of their work will help you assess the students' understanding of the concepts that were presented in the lesson today and plan more effectively for future lessons. You may read the questions aloud to the students.

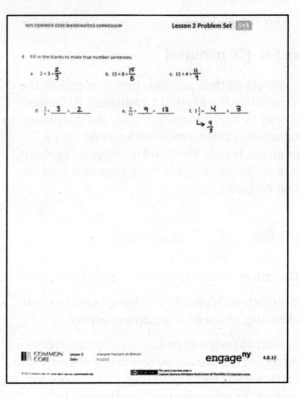

COMMON CORE™

Lesson 2:   Interpret a fraction as division.
Date: 11/10/13

4.B.10

Name _____   Date _____

1. Draw a picture to show the division. Write a division expression using unit form. Then express your
    answer as a fraction. The first one is done for you.

    a. $1 \div 5 = 5$ fifths $\div 5 = 1$ fifth $= \dfrac{1}{5}$

    b. $3 \div 4$

    c. $6 \div 4$

2. Draw to show how 2 children can equally share 3 cookies. Write an equation and express your answer as a fraction.

3. Carly and Gina read the following problem in their math class.

Seven cereal bars were shared equally by 3 children. How much did each child receive?

Carly and Gina solve the problem differently. Carly gives each child 2 whole cereal bars and then divides the remaining cereal bar between the 3 children. Gina divides all the cereal bars into thirds and shares the thirds equally among the 3 children.

a. Illustrate both girls' solutions.

b. Explain why they are both right.

Lesson 2:   Interpret a fraction as division.
Date: 11/10/13

4.B.12

4. Fill in the blanks to make true number sentences.

a. $2 \div 3 = $ ——

b. $15 \div 8 = $ ——

c. $11 \div 4 = $ ——

d. $\frac{3}{2} = $ _____ $\div$ _____

e. $\frac{9}{13} = $ _____ $\div$ _____

f. $1\frac{1}{3} = $ _____ $\div$ _____

Name _____   Date _____

1. Draw a picture that shows the division expression. Then write an equation and solve.

    a. $3 \div 9$ b. $4 \div 3$

2. Fill in the blanks to make true number sentences.

    a. $21 \div 8 = \overline{}$ b. $\frac{7}{4} =$ _____ $\div$ _____   c. $4 \div 9 = \overline{}$ d. $1\frac{2}{7} =$ _____ $\div$ _____

COMMON CORE™   Lesson 2:   Interpret a fraction as division.
Date: 11/10/13

4.B.14

Name _____   Date _____

1. Draw a picture to show the division. Express your answer as a fraction.

   a. $1 \div 4$

   b. $3 \div 5$

   c. $7 \div 4$

2. Using a picture, show how six people could share four sandwiches. Then write an equation and solve.

3. Fill in the blanks to make true number sentences.

a. $2 \div 7 = $ ___

b. $39 \div 5 = $ ___

c. $13 \div 3 = $ ___

d. $\frac{9}{5} = $ _____ $\div$ _____

e. $\frac{19}{28} = $ _____ $\div$ _____

f. $1\frac{3}{5} = $ _____ $\div$ _____

COMMON CORE™

Lesson 2:   Interpret a fraction as division.
Date: 11/10/13

4.B.16

Lesson 3

Objective: Interpret a fraction as division.

Suggested Lesson Structure

■ Fluency Practice   (12 minutes)
■ Application Problem   (5 minutes)
■ Concept Development   (33 minutes)
■ Student Debrief   (10 minutes)

   Total Time   **(60 minutes)**

Fluency Practice (12 minutes)

▪ Convert to Hundredths **4.NF.5**   (3 minutes)
▪ Compare Fractions **4.NF.2**   (4 minutes)
▪ Fractions as Division **5.NF.3**   (3 minutes)
▪ Write Fractions as Decimals **4.NF.5**   (2 minutes)

Convert to Hundredths (3 minutes)

Materials: (S) Personal white boards

Note: This fluency prepares students for decimal fractions later in the module.

   T: I'll say a factor, and then you'll say the factor you need to multiply it by to get 100. 50.
   S: 2.

Continue with the following possible suggestions: 25, 20, and 4.

   T: (Write $\frac{1}{4} = \frac{}{100}$.) How many fours are in 100?
   S: 25.
   T: Write the equivalent fraction.
   S: (Write $\frac{1}{4} = \frac{25}{100}$.)

Continue with the following possible suggestions: $\frac{3}{4} = \frac{}{100}$, $\frac{1}{50} = \frac{}{100}$, $\frac{3}{50} = \frac{}{100}$, $\frac{1}{20} = \frac{}{100}$, $\frac{3}{20} = \frac{}{100}$, $\frac{1}{25} = \frac{}{100}$, and $\frac{2}{25} = \frac{}{100}$.

	Lesson 3:	Interpret a fraction as division.
	Date:	11/10/13

4.B.17

Compare Fractions (4 minutes)

Materials: (S) Personal white boards

Note: This fluency reviews Grade 4 and Grade 5–Module 3 concepts.

T: (Write $\frac{1}{2} - \frac{1}{6}$.) Write a greater than or less than symbol.

S: (Write $\frac{1}{2} > \frac{1}{6}$.)

T: Why is this true?

S: Both have 1 unit, but halves are larger than sixths.

Continue with the following possible suggestions: $\frac{2}{3}$ and $\frac{1}{8}$, $\frac{3}{4}$ and $\frac{3}{8}$, $\frac{2}{5}$ and $\frac{9}{10}$, and $\frac{5}{8}$ and $\frac{5}{7}$.

Students should be able to reason about these comparisons without the need for common units. Reasoning such as *greater* or *less than* half or *the same number* of different sized units should be the focus.

Fractions as Division (3 minutes)

Materials: (S) Personal white boards

Note: This fluency reviews G5–M4–Lesson 2 content.

T: (Write $1 \div 3$.) Write a complete number sentence using the expression.

S: (Write $1 \div 3 = \frac{1}{3}$.)

Continue with the following possible sequence: $1 \div 4$ and $2 \div 3$.

T: (Write $5 \div 2$.) Write a complete number sentence using the expression.

S: (Write $5 \div 2 = \frac{5}{2}$ or $5 \div 2 = 2\frac{1}{2}$.)

Continue with the following possible suggestions: $13 \div 5$, $7 \div 6$, and $17 \div 4$.

T: (Write $\frac{4}{3}$.) Say the fraction.

S: 4 thirds.

T: Write a complete number sentence using the fraction.

S: (Write $4 \div 3 = \frac{4}{3}$ or $4 \div 3 = 1\frac{1}{3}$.)

Continue with the following possible suggestions: $\frac{13}{2}$, $\frac{23}{4}$, and $\frac{32}{5}$.

Write Fractions as Decimals (2 minutes)

Note: This fluency prepares students for fractions with denominators of 4, 20, 25, and 50 in G5–M4–Topic G.

T: (Write $\frac{1}{10}$.) Say the fraction.

S: 1 tenth.

T: Say it as a decimal.

Lesson 3:   Interpret a fraction as division.
Date: 11/10/13

4.B.18

S: 0.1.

Continue with the following possible suggestions: $\frac{2}{10}, \frac{3}{10}, \frac{7}{10}, \frac{5}{10}$, and $\frac{9}{10}$.

T: (Write 0.1 =___.) Write the decimal as a fraction.

S: (Write 0.1 = $\frac{1}{10}$.)

Continue with the following possible suggestions: 0.2, 0.4, 0.8, and 0.6.

Application Problem (5 minutes)

Hudson is choosing a seat in art class. He scans the
room and sees a 4-person table with 1 bucket of art
supplies, a 6-person table with 2 buckets of supplies,
and a 5-person table with 2 buckets of supplies.
Which   table should Hudson choose if he wants the
largest share of art supplies? Support your answer
with pictures.

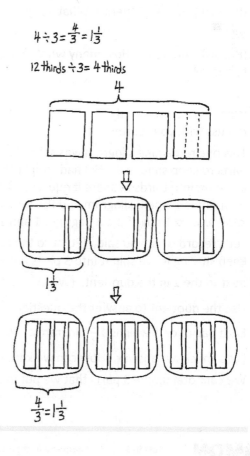

Note: Students must first use division to see which fractional portion of art supplies is available at each table.
Then students compare the fractions and find which represents the largest value.

Concept Development (33 minutes)

Materials: (S) Personal white boards

Problem 1

A baker poured 4 kilograms of oats equally into 3 bags. What is
the weight of each bag of oats?

T: In our story, which operation will be needed to find
how much each bag of oats weighs?

S: Division.

T: Turn and discuss with your partner how you know and
what the division sentence would be.

S: The total is 4 kg of oats being divided into 3 bags, so
the division sentence is 4 divided by 3. → The whole is
4, and the divisor is 3.

T: Say the division expression.

S: 4 ÷ 3.

T: (Write 4 ÷ 3 and draw 4 squares on the board.) Let's
represent the kilograms with squares like we used
yesterday. They are easier to cut into equal shares

than circles.

T: Turn and talk about how you'll share the 4 kg of oats equally in 3 bags. Draw a picture to show your thinking.

S: Every bag will get a whole kilogram of oats, and then we will split the last kilogram equally into 3 thirds to share. So, each bag gets a whole kilogram and one-third of another one. → I can cut all four kilograms into thirds. Then split them into the 3 bags. Each bag will get 4 thirds of kg. → I know the answer is four over three because that is just another way to write 4 ÷ 3.

T: As we saw yesterday, there are two ways of dividing the oats. Let me record your approaches. (Draw the approaches on the board and restate.) Let's say the division sentence with the quotient.

S: 4 ÷ 3 = 4 thirds. → 4 ÷ 3 = 1 and 1 third.

T: (Point to the diagram on board.) When we cut them all into thirds and shared, how many thirds, in all, did we have to share?

S: 12 thirds.

T: Say the division sentence in unit form starting with 12 thirds.

S: 12 thirds ÷ 3 = 4 thirds.

T: (Write 12 thirds ÷ 3 = 4 thirds on the board.) What is 4 thirds as a mixed number?

S: 1 and 1 third.

T: (Write algorithm on board.) Let's show how we divided the oats using the division algorithm.

T: How many groups of 3 can I make with 4 kilograms?

S: 1 group of three.

T: (Record 1 in the quotient.) What's 1 group of three?

S: 3.

T: (Record 3 under 4.) How many whole kilograms are left to share?

S: 1.

T: What did we do with this last kilogram? Turn and discuss with your partner.

S: This one remaining kilogram was split into 3 equal parts to keep sharing it. → I had to split the last kilogram into thirds to share it equally. → The quotient is 1 whole kilogram and the remainder is 1. → The quotient is 1 whole kilogram and 1 third kilogram. → Each of the 3 bags get 1 and 1 third kilogram of oats.

T: Let's record what you said. (Point to the remainder of 1.) This remainder is 1 left over kilogram. To keep sharing it, we split it into 3 parts (point to the divisor), so each bag gets 1 third. I'll write 1 third next to the 1 in the quotient. (Write $\frac{1}{3}$ next to the quotient of 1.)

T: Use the quotient to answer the question.

S: Each bag of oats weighs $1\frac{1}{3}$ kilograms.

T: Let's check our answer. How can we know if we put the right amount of oats in each bag?

S: We can total up the 3 parts that we put in each bag when we divided the kilograms. → The total we

$$3\overline{)4}^{\,1\frac{1}{3}}$$
$$-3$$
$$1$$

Check: $3 \times 1\frac{1}{3}$

$= 1\frac{1}{3} + 1\frac{1}{3} + 1\frac{1}{3}$

$= 3 + \frac{3}{3}$

$= 4$

Each bag of oats weighs $1\frac{1}{3}$ Kilograms.

Lesson 3:   Interpret a fraction as division.
Date: 11/10/13

4.B.20

get should be the same as our whole. → The sum of the equal parts should be the same as our dividend.

T: We have 3 groups of $1\frac{1}{3}$. Say the multiplication sentence.

S: $3 \times 1\frac{1}{3}$.

T: Express 3 copies of $1\frac{1}{3}$ using repeated addition.

S: $1\frac{1}{3} + 1\frac{1}{3} + 1\frac{1}{3}$.

T: Is the total the same number of kilograms we had before we shared?

S: The total is 4 kilograms. → It is the same as our whole before we shared. → 3 ones plus 3 thirds is 3 plus 1. That's 4.

T: We've seen more than one way to write down how to share 4 kilograms in 3 bags. Why is the quotient the same using the algorithm?

S: The same thing is happening to the flour. It is being divided into 3 parts. → We are just using another way to write it.

T: Let's use different strategies in our next problem as well.

Problem 2

If the baker doubles the number of kilograms of oats to be poured equally into 3 bags, what is the weight of each bag of oats?

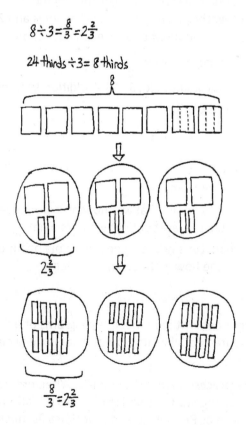

T: What's the whole in this problem? Turn and share with your partner.

S: 4 doubled is 8. → 4 times 2 is 8. → The baker now has 8 kilograms of oats to pour into 3 bags.

T: Say the whole.

S: 8.

T: Say the divisor.

S: 3.

T: Say the division expression for this problem.

S: 8 ÷ 3.

T: Compare this expression with the one we just did. What do you notice?

S: The whole is twice as much as the problem before. → The number of shares is the same.

T: Using that insight, make a prediction about the quotient of this problem.

S: Since the whole is twice as much shared with the same number of bags, then the answer should be twice as much as the answer to the last problem. → Two times 4 thirds is equal to 8 thirds. → The answer should be

double. So it should be $1\frac{1}{3} + 1\frac{1}{3}$ and that is $2\frac{2}{3}$.

T: Work with your partner to solve, and confirm the predictions you made. Each partner should use a different strategy for sharing the kilograms and draw a picture of his or her thinking. Then, work together to solve using the standard algorithm.

Circulate as students work.

T: How many kilograms are in each bag this time? Whisper and tell your partner.

S: Each bag gets 2 whole kilograms and $\frac{2}{3}$ of another one. →
Each bag gets a third of each kilogram which would be 8 thirds. → 8 thirds is the same as $2\frac{2}{3}$ kilograms.

T: If we split all the kilograms into thirds before we share, how many thirds are in all 8 kilograms?

S: 24 thirds.

T: Say the division sentence in unit form.

S: 24 thirds ÷ 3 = 8 thirds.

T: (Set up the standard algorithm on the board and solve it together.) The quotient is 2 wholes and 2 thirds. Use the quotient to answer the question.

S: Each bag of oats weighs $2\frac{2}{3}$ kilograms.

T: Let's now check it. Say the addition sentence for 3 groups of $2\frac{2}{3}$.

S: $2\frac{2}{3} + 2\frac{2}{3} + 2\frac{2}{3} = 8$.

T: So, $8 \div 3 = 2\frac{2}{3}$. How does this quotient compare with our predictions?

S: This answer is what we thought it would be. → It was double the last quotient which is what we predicted.

T: Great. Let's now change our whole one more time and see how it affects the quotient.

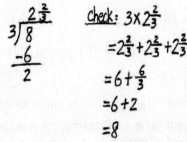

$$\begin{array}{r} 2\frac{2}{3} \\ 3\overline{\smash{)}8} \\ -6 \\ \hline 2 \end{array}$$

check: $3 \times 2\frac{2}{3}$
$= 2\frac{2}{3} + 2\frac{2}{3} + 2\frac{2}{3}$
$= 6 + \frac{6}{3}$
$= 6 + 2$
$= 8$

Each bag of oats weighs $2\frac{2}{3}$ kilograms.

NOTES ON MULTIPLE MEANS OF REPRESENTATION:

For those students who need the support of concrete materials, continue to use square paper and scissors to represent the equal shares along with the pictorial and abstract representations.

Problem 3

If the baker doubles the number of kilograms of oats again and they are poured equally into 3 bags, what is the weight of each bag of oats?

Repeat the process used in Problem 2. When predicting the quotient, be sure students notice that this equation is two times as much as Problem 1, and four times as much as Problem 2. This is important for the scaling interpretation of multiplication.

$16 \div 3 = \frac{16}{3} = 5\frac{1}{3}$

$$\begin{array}{r} 5\frac{1}{3} \\ 3\overline{\smash{)}16} \\ -15 \\ \hline 1 \end{array}$$

check: $3 \times 5\frac{1}{3}$
$= 5\frac{1}{3} + 5\frac{1}{3} + 5\frac{1}{3}$
$= 15 + \frac{3}{3}$
$= 16$

Each bag of oats weighs $5\frac{1}{3}$ kilograms.

The closing extension of the dialogue, in which students realize the efficiency of the algorithm, is detailed below.

T: Say the division expression for this problem.

S: $16 \div 3$.

T: Say the answer as a fraction greater than 1.

S: 16 thirds.

T: What would be an easy strategy to solve this problem? Draw out 16 wholes to split into 3 groups, or use the standard algorithm? Turn and discuss with a partner.

S: (Share.)

T: Solve this problem independently using the standard algorithm. You may also draw if you like.

S: (Work.)

T: Let's solve using the standard algorithm. (Set up standard algorithm and solve on the board.) What is 16 thirds as a mixed number?

S: $5\frac{1}{3}$.

T: Use the quotient to answer the question.

S: Each bag of oats weighs $5\frac{1}{3}$ kilograms.

T: Let's check with repeated addition. Say the entire addition sentence.

S: $5\frac{1}{3} + 5\frac{1}{3} + 5\frac{1}{3} = 16$.

T: So $16 \div 3 = 5\frac{1}{3}$. How does this quotient compare with our predictions?

S: This answer is what we thought it would be. → It was quadruple the first quotient. → We were right; it was double of the last quotient, which is what we predicted.

NOTES ON
MULTIPLE MEANS
OF REPRESENTATION:

Fractions are generally represented in student materials using equation editing software using horizontal line to separate numerator from denominator (e.g., $\frac{3}{5}$). However, it may be wise to expose students to other formats of notating fractions, such as those which use a diagonal to separate numerator from denominator (e.g., $^3/_5$ or $\frac{3}{5}$).

Problem Set (10 minutes)

Students should do their personal best to complete the Problem Set within the allotted 10 minutes. For some classes, it may be appropriate to modify the assignment by specifying which problems they work on first. Some problems do not specify a method for solving. Students solve these problems using the RDW approach used for Application Problems.

Student Debrief (10 minutes)

Lesson Objective: Interpret a fraction as division.

The Student Debrief is intended to invite reflection and active processing of the total lesson experience.

Invite students to review their solutions for the Problem Set. They should check work by comparing answers

Lesson 3:   Interpret a fraction as division.
Date: 11/10/13

with a partner before going over answers as a class. Look for misconceptions or misunderstandings that can be addressed in the Debrief. Guide students in a conversation to debrief the Problem Set and process the lesson.

You may choose to use any combination of the questions below to lead the discussion.

- What pattern did you notice between Problems 1(b) and 1(c)? Look at the whole and the divisor. Is 3 halves greater than, less than, or equal to 6 fourths? What about the answers?

- What's the relationship between the answers for Problems 2(a) and 2(b)? Explain it to your partner. (Students should note that Problem 2(b) is four times as much as Problem 2(a).) Can you generate a problem where the answer is the same as Problem (a), or the same as Problem (b)?

- Explain to your partner how you solved for Problem 3(a)? Why do we need one more warming box than our actual quotient?

- We expressed our remainders today as fractions. Compare this with the way we expressed our remainders as decimals in Module 2. How is it alike? How is it different?

Exit Ticket (3 minutes)

After the Student Debrief, instruct students to complete the Exit Ticket. A review of their work will help you assess the students' understanding of the concepts that were presented in the lesson today and plan more effectively for future lessons. You may read the questions aloud to the students.

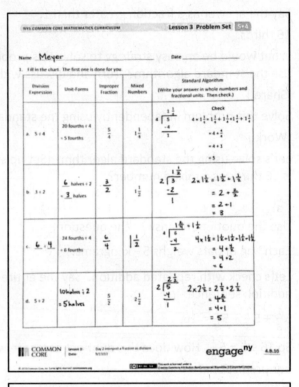

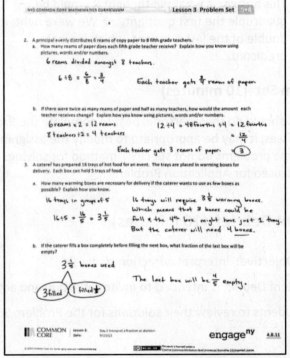

Name _____   Date _____

1. Fill in the chart. The first one is done for you.

Division Expression	Unit Forms	Improper Fraction	Mixed Numbers	Standard Algorithm (Write your answer in whole numbers and fractional units, then check.)
a. $5 \div 4$	20 fourths ÷ 4 = 5 fourths	$\frac{5}{4}$	$1\frac{1}{4}$	$4\overline{)\begin{array}{l}1\frac{1}{4}\\5\\-4\\\hline 1\end{array}}$ Check $4 \times 1\frac{1}{4} = 1\frac{1}{4} + 1\frac{1}{4} + 1\frac{1}{4} + 1\frac{1}{4}$ $= 4 + \frac{4}{4}$ $= 4 + 1$ $= 5$
b. $3 \div 2$	___ halves ÷ 2 = ___ halves		$1\frac{1}{2}$	
c. ___ ÷ ___	24 fourths ÷ 4 = 6 fourths			$4\overline{)6}$
d. $5 \div 2$		$\frac{5}{2}$	$2\frac{1}{2}$	

Lesson 3: Interpret a fraction as division.
Date: 11/10/13

4.B.25

2. A principal evenly distributes 6 reams of copy paper to 8 fifth-grade teachers.
   a. How many reams of paper does each fifth-grade teacher receive? Explain how you know using pictures, words, or numbers.

   b. If there were twice as many reams of paper and half as many teachers, how would the amount each teacher receives change? Explain how you know using pictures, words, or numbers.

3. A caterer has prepared 16 trays of hot food for an event. The trays are placed in warming boxes for delivery. Each box can hold 5 trays of food.

   a. How many warming boxes are necessary for delivery if the caterer wants to use as few boxes as possible? Explain how you know.

   b. If the caterer fills a box completely before filling the next box, what fraction of the last box will be empty?

Lesson 3:   Interpret a fraction as division.
Date: 11/10/13

4.B.26

Name _____   Date _____

1. A baker made 9 cupcakes, each a different type. Four people want to share them equally. How many cupcakes will each person get?

   Fill in the chart to show how to solve the problem.

Division Expression	Unit Forms	Fractions and Mixed numbers	Standard Algorithm

Draw to show your thinking:

Name _____   Date _____

1. Fill in the chart. The first one is done for you.

Division Expression	Unit Forms	Improper Fractions	Mixed Numbers	Standard Algorithm (Write your answer in whole numbers and fractional units, then check.)
a. $4 \div 3$	12 thirds ÷ 3 = 4 thirds	$\frac{4}{3}$	$1\frac{1}{3}$	$\begin{array}{r} 1\frac{1}{3} \\ 3\overline{)\,4} \\ -3 \\ \hline 1 \end{array}$ Check $3 \times 1\frac{1}{3} = 1\frac{1}{3} + 1\frac{1}{3} + 1\frac{1}{3}$ $= 3 + \frac{3}{3}$ $= 3 + 1$ $= 4$
b. ___ ÷ ___	___ fifths ÷ 5 = ___ fifths		$1\frac{2}{5}$	
c. ___ ÷ ___	___ halves ÷ 2 = ___ halves			$2\overline{)\,7}$
d. $7 \div 4$		$\frac{7}{4}$		

COMMON CORE™

Lesson 3: Interpret a fraction as division.
Date: 11/10/13

4.B.28

2. A coffee shop uses 4 liters of milk every day.

    a. If they have 15 liters of milk in the refrigerator, after how many days will they need to purchase more? Explain how you know.

    b. If they only use half as much milk each day, after how many days will they need to purchase more?

3. Polly buys 14 cupcakes for a party. The bakery puts them into boxes that hold 4 cupcakes each.

    a. How many boxes will be needed for Polly to bring all the cupcakes to the party? Explain how you know.

    b. If the bakery completely fills as many boxes as possible, what fraction of the last box is empty? How many more cupcakes are needed to fill this box?

Lesson 4

Objective: Use tape diagrams to model fractions as division.

Suggested Lesson Structure

■ Fluency Practice   (12 minutes)
■ Application Problem   (7 minutes)
■ Concept Development   (31 minutes)
■ Student Debrief   (10 minutes)
   Total Time   **(60 minutes)**

Fluency Practice (12 minutes)

- Write Fractions as Decimals **5.NF.3**   (4 minutes)
- Convert to Hundredths **4.NF.5**   (4 minutes)
- Fractions as Division **5.NF.3**   (4 minutes)

Write Fractions as Decimals (4 minutes)

Note: This fluency prepares students for G5–M4–Topic G.

   T: (Write $\frac{1}{10}$.) Say the fraction.
   S: 1 tenth.
   T: Say it as a decimal.
   S: Zero point one.

Continue with the following possible suggestions: $\frac{2}{10}$, $\frac{3}{10}$, $\frac{8}{10}$, and $\frac{5}{10}$.

   T: (Write $\frac{1}{100}$ = _____.) Say the fraction.
   S: 1 hundredth.
   T: Say it as a decimal.
   S: Zero point zero one.

Continue with the following possible suggestions: $\frac{2}{100}$, $\frac{3}{100}$, $\frac{9}{100}$, and $\frac{13}{100}$.

   T: (Write 0.01 = _____.) Say it as a fraction.
   S: 1 hundredth.
   T: (Write 0.01 = $\frac{1}{100}$.)

Lesson 4:   Use tape diagrams to model fractions as division.
Date: 11/10/13

Continue with the following possible suggestions: 0.02, 0.09, 0.11, and 0.39.

Convert to Hundredths (4 minutes)

Materials: (S) Personal white boards

Note: This fluency prepares students for G5–M4–Topic G.

T: (Write: $\frac{1}{4} = \frac{}{100}$.) Write the equivalent fraction.

S: (Write $\frac{1}{4} = \frac{25}{100}$.)

T: (Write $\frac{1}{4} = \frac{25}{100} = $ ____.) Write 1 fourth as a decimal.

S: (Write $\frac{1}{4} = \frac{25}{100} = 0.25$.)

Continue with the following possible suggestions: $\frac{3}{4}, \frac{1}{50}, \frac{7}{50}, \frac{12}{50}, \frac{1}{20}, \frac{7}{20}, \frac{11}{20}, \frac{1}{25}, \frac{2}{25}, \frac{9}{25}$, and $\frac{11}{25}$.

Fractions as Division (4 minutes)

Materials: (S) Personal white boards

Note: This fluency reviews G5–M6–Lessons 2 and 3 content.

T: (Write 1 ÷ 2.) Solve.

S: (Write $1 \div 2 = \frac{1}{2}$.)

Continue with the following possible sequence: 1 ÷ 5 and 3 ÷ 4.

T: (Write 7 ÷ 2.) Solve.

S: (Write $7 \div 2 = \frac{7}{2}$ or $7 \div 2 = 3\frac{1}{2}$.)

Continue with the following possible suggestions: 12 ÷ 5, 11 ÷ 6, 19 ÷ 4, 31 ÷ 8, and 49 ÷ 9.

T: (Write $\frac{5}{3}$.) Write the fraction as a whole number division expression.

S: (Write 5 ÷ 3.)

Continue with the following possible suggestions: $\frac{11}{2}, \frac{15}{4}$, and $\frac{24}{5}$, 37 ÷ 8, and 40 ÷ 9.

NOTES ON
MULTIPLE MEANS OF
ACTION AND
EXPRESSION:

If students are comfortable with interpreting fractions as division, consider foregoing the written component of this fluency and ask students to visualize the fractions, making this activity more abstract.

Application Problem (7 minutes)

Four grade-levels need equal time for indoor recess, and the gym is available for three hours.

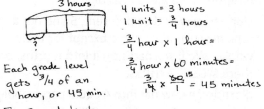

Each grade level gets $^3/_4$ of an hour, or 45 min.

For 2 grade levels at once, the time doubles to 90 min or $1\frac{1}{2}$ hours.

4 units = 3 hours
1 unit = $\frac{3}{4}$ hours

$\frac{3}{4}$ hour × 1 hour =

$\frac{3}{4}$ hour × 60 minutes =

$\frac{3}{4} \times \frac{60}{1}^{15} = 45$ minutes

45 minutes × 2 = 90 minutes

$\frac{90}{60} = \frac{9}{6} = 1\frac{3}{6} = 1\frac{1}{2}$ hours

COMMON CORE™

Lesson 4:   Use tape diagrams to model fractions as division.
Date: 11/10/13

4.B.31

a.   How many hours of recess will each grade level receive? Draw a picture to support your answer.

b.   How many minutes?

c.   If the gym could accommodate two grade-levels at once, how many hours of recess would each grade-level get?

Note: Students practice division with fractional quotients, which leads into the day's lesson. Note that the whole remains constant in (c) while the divisor is cut in half. Lead students to analyze the effect of this halving on the quotient as related to the doubling of the whole from previous problems.

Concept Development (31 minutes)

Materials: (S) Personal white boards

Problem 1

Eight tons of gravel is equally divided between 4 dump trucks. How much gravel is in one dump truck?

T: Say a division sentence to solve the problem.

S: 8 ÷ 4 = 2.

T: Model this problem with a tape diagram. (Pause as students work.)

T: We know that 4 units are equal to 8 tons. (Write 4 units = 8.) We want to find what 1 unit is equal to.

T: (Write 1 unit = 8 ÷ 4.)

T: How many tons of gravel is in one dump truck?

S: 2.

T: Use your quotient to answer the question.

S: Each dump truck held 2 tons of gravel.

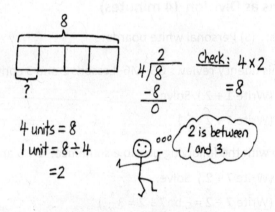

Problem 2

Five tons of gravel is equally divided between 4 dump trucks. How much gravel is in one dump truck?

T: (Change values from previous problem to 5 tons and 4 trucks on board.) How would our drawing be different if we had 5 tons of gravel?

S: Our whole would be different, 5 and not 8. → The tape diagram is the same except for the value of the whole. We'll still partition it into fourths, because there are still 4 trucks.

T: (Partition a new bar into 4 equal parts labeled with 5 as the whole.)

T: We know that these 4 units are equal to 5 tons. (Write 4 units = 5.) We want to find what 1 unit is

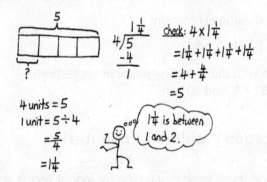

Lesson 4:   Use tape diagrams to model fractions as division.
Date: 11/10/13

4.B.32

equal to. (Write a question mark beneath 1 fourth of the bar.) What is the division expression you'll use to find what 1 unit is?

S: 5 ÷ 4.

T: (Write 1 unit = 5 ÷ 4.) 5 ÷ 4 is?

S: Five-fourths.

T: So each unit is equal to five-fourths tons of gravel. Can we prove this using the standard algorithm?

T: What is 5 ÷ 4?

S: One and one-fourth.

T: (Write $5 ÷ 4 = 1\frac{1}{4}$.) Use your quotient to answer the question.

S: Each dump truck held one and one-fourth tons of gravel.

T: Visualize a number line. Between which two adjacent whole numbers is 1 and one-fourth?

S: 1 and 2.

T: Check our work using repeated addition.

NOTES ON MULTIPLE MEANS OF ACTION AND EXPRESSION:

Provide number lines with fractional markings for the students who still need support to visualize the placement of the fractions.

Problem 3

A 3 meter ribbon is cut into 4 equal pieces to make flowers. What is the length of each piece?

T: (Write 3 ÷ 4 on the board.) Work with a partner and draw a tape diagram to solve.

T: Say the division expression you solved.

S: 3 divided by 4.

T: Say the answer as a fraction.

S: Three-fourths.

T: (Write $\frac{3}{4}$ on the board.) In this case, does it make sense to use the standard algorithm to solve? Turn and talk.

S: No, it's just 3 divided by 4, which is $\frac{3}{4}$. → I don't think so. It's really easy. → We could, but the quotient of zero looks strange to me. It's just easier to say 3 divided by 4 equals 3 fourths.

T: Use your quotient to answer the question.

S: Each piece of ribbon is $\frac{3}{4}$ m long.

T: Let's check the answer. Say the multiplication expression starting with 4.

S: $4 \times \frac{3}{4}$. → $\frac{12}{4}$. → 3.

T: Our answer is correct. If we wanted to place our quotient of $\frac{3}{4}$ on a number line, between what two

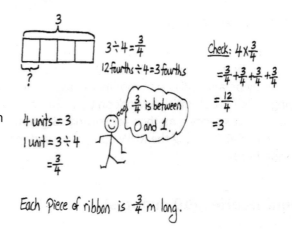

$3 ÷ 4 = \frac{3}{4}$

12 fourths ÷ 4 = 3 fourths

4 units = 3

1 unit = 3 ÷ 4

$= \frac{3}{4}$

$\frac{3}{4}$ is between 0 and 1.

Check: $4 \times \frac{3}{4}$

$= \frac{3}{4} + \frac{3}{4} + \frac{3}{4} + \frac{3}{4}$

$= \frac{12}{4}$

$= 3$

Each piece of ribbon is $\frac{3}{4}$ m long.

adjacent whole numbers would we place it?

    S: 0 and 1.

Problem 4

14 gallons of water is used to completely fill 3 fish tanks. If each tank holds the same amount of water, how many gallons will each tank hold?

    T: Let's read this problem together. (All read.) Work with a partner to solve this problem. Draw a tape diagram and solve using the standard algorithm.

    T: Say the division equation you solved?

    S: $14 \div 3 = \frac{14}{3}$.

    T: Say the quotient as a mixed number?

    S: $4\frac{2}{3}$.

    T: Use your quotient to answer the question.

    S: The volume of each fish tank is $4\frac{2}{3}$ gallons.

    T: So, between which two adjacent whole numbers does our answer lie?

    S: Between 4 and 5.

    T: Check your answer with multiplication.

    S: (Check their answers.)

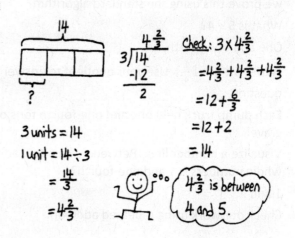

Problem Set (10 minutes)

Students should do their personal best to complete the Problem Set within the allotted 10 minutes. For some classes, it may be appropriate to modify the assignment by specifying which problems they work on first. Some problems do not specify a method for solving. Students solve these problems using the RDW approach used for Application Problems.

Student Debrief (10 minutes)

Lesson Objective: Use tape diagrams to model fractions as division.

The Student Debrief is intended to invite reflection and active processing of the total lesson experience.

Invite students to review their solutions for the Problem Set. They should check work by comparing answers with a

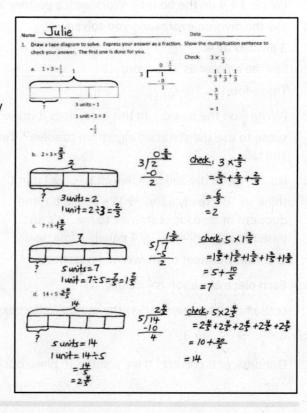

Lesson 4:   Use tape diagrams to model fractions as division.
Date: 11/10/13

4.B.3

partner before going over answers as a class. Look for misconceptions or misunderstandings that can be addressed in the Debrief. Guide students in a conversation to debrief the Problem Set and process the lesson.

You may choose to use any combination of the questions below to lead the discussion.

- What pattern did you notice between Problem 1(a) and Problems 1(b), 1(c), and 1(d)? What did you notice about the wholes or dividends and the divisors?

- In Problem 2(c), can you name the fraction of $\frac{55}{10}$ using a larger fractional unit? In other words, can you simplify it? Is this the same point on the number line?

- Compare Problems 3 and 4. What's the division sentence for both problems? What's the whole and divisor for each problem? (Problem 3's division expression is 4 ÷ 5, and Problem 4's division expression is 5 ÷ 4.)

- Explain to your partner the difference between the questions asked in Problem 4(a) and 4(b). (Problem 4(a) is asking the fraction of the birdseeds, which is one-fourth and 4(b) is asking the number of pounds of birdseeds which is 1 and one-fourth.)

- How was our learning today built on what we learned yesterday? (Students may point out that the models used today were more abstract than the concrete materials of previous days or that they were able to see the fractions as division more easily as equations than in days previous.)

Exit Ticket (3 minutes)

After the Student Debrief, instruct students to complete the Exit Ticket. A review of their work will help you assess the students' understanding of the concepts that were presented in the lesson today and plan more effectively for future lesson. You may read the questions aloud to the students.

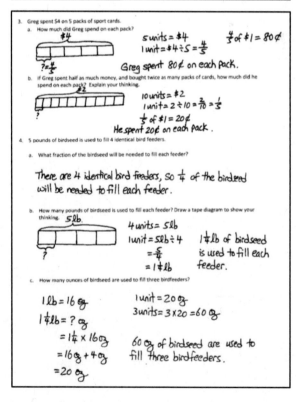

COMMON CORE™

Lesson 4:   Use tape diagrams to model fractions as division.
Date: 11/10/13

4.B.35

Name _____   Date _____

1. Draw a tape diagram to solve. Express your answer as a fraction. Show the multiplication sentence to check your answer. The first one is done for you.

a. $1 \div 3 =$

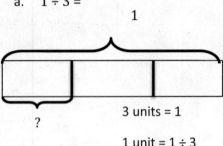

3 units = 1

1 unit = $1 \div 3$

$= \dfrac{1}{3}$

Check: $3 \times \dfrac{1}{3}$

$$3\overline{\smash{\big)}\begin{array}{l} 0 \quad \frac{1}{3} \\ 1 \\ -0 \\ \hline 1 \end{array}}$$

$= \dfrac{1}{3} + \dfrac{1}{3} + \dfrac{1}{3}$

$= \dfrac{3}{3}$

$= 1$

b. $2 \div 3 = \underline{\quad}$

c. $7 \div 5 = \underline{\quad}$

d. $14 \div 5 = \underline{\quad}$

COMMON CORE™

Lesson 4:   Use tape diagrams to model fractions as division.
Date: 11/10/13

4.B.36

2. Fill in the chart. The first one is done for you.

Division Expression	Fraction	Between which two whole numbers is your answer?	Standard Algorithm
a. $13 \div 3$	$\dfrac{13}{3}$	4 and 5	$\begin{array}{r} 4\ \tfrac{1}{3} \\ 3\,\overline{)\,13} \\ \underline{-12} \\ 1 \end{array}$
b. $6 \div 7$		0 and 1	$7\,\overline{)\,6}$
c. ____ $\div$ ____	$\dfrac{55}{10}$		$\overline{}$
d. ____ $\div$ ____	$\dfrac{32}{40}$		$40\,\overline{)\,32}$

Lesson 4:   Use tape diagrams to model fractions as division.
Date: 11/10/13

4.B.37

3. Greg spent $4 on 5 packs of sport cards.
   a. How much did Greg spend on each pack?

   b. If Greg spent half as much money, and bought twice as many packs of cards, how much did he spend on each pack? Explain your thinking.

4. Five pounds of birdseed is used to fill 4 identical bird feeders.
   a. What fraction of the birdseed will be needed to fill each feeder?

   b. How many pounds of birdseed are used to fill each feeder? Draw a tape diagram to show your thinking.

   c. How many ounces of birdseed are used to fill three birdfeeders?

Lesson 4:   Use tape diagrams to model fractions as division.
Date: 11/10/13

4.B.38

Name _____ Date _____

Matthew and his 3 siblings are weeding a flower bed with an area of 9 square yards. If they share the job equally, how many square yards of the flower bed will each child need to weed? Use a tape diagram to show your thinking.

Name _____   Date _____

1. Draw a tape diagram to solve. Express your answer as a fraction. Show the addition sentence to support your answer. The first one is done for you.

a. $1 \div 4 = \frac{1}{4}$

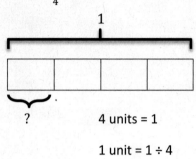

?   4 units = 1

1 unit = 1 ÷ 4

$= \frac{1}{4}$

Check:

$4 \times \frac{1}{4}$

$= \frac{1}{4} + \frac{1}{4} + \frac{1}{4} + \frac{1}{4}$

$= \frac{4}{4}$

$= 1$

b. $4 \div 5 =$ ⎯

c. $8 \div 5 =$ ⎯

d. $14 \div 3 =$ ⎯

2. Fill in the chart. The first one is done for you.

Division Expression	Fraction	Between which two whole numbers is your answer?	Standard Algorithm
a. $16 \div 5$	$\dfrac{16}{5}$	3 and 4	$5 \overline{\smash{\big)}\, \begin{array}{r} 3 \;\; \frac{1}{5} \\ 16 \\ -15 \\ \hline 1 \end{array}}$
b. ____ ÷ ____	$\dfrac{3}{4}$	0 and 1	
c. ____ ÷ ____	$\dfrac{7}{2}$		$2 \overline{\smash{\big)}\, 7}$
d. ____ ÷ ____	$\dfrac{81}{90}$		

3. Jackie cut a 2-yard spool into 5 equal lengths of ribbon.
    a. How long is each piece of ribbon? Draw a tape diagram to show your thinking.

    b. What is the length of each ribbon in feet? Draw a tape diagram to show your thinking.

4. Baa Baa the black sheep had 7 pounds of wool. If he separated the wool into 3 bags, each holding the same amount of wool, how much wool would be in 2 bags?

5. An adult sweater is made from 2 pounds of wool. This is 3 times as much wool as it takes to make a baby sweater. How much wool does it take to make a baby sweater? Use a tape diagram to solve.

Lesson 5

Objective: Solve word problems involving the division of whole numbers with answers in the form of fractions or whole numbers.

Suggested Lesson Structure

■ Fluency Practice   (12 minutes)
  Concept Development   (38 minutes)
■ Student Debrief   (10 minutes)

   Total Time   **(60 minutes)**

Fluency Practice (12 minutes)

▪ Fraction of a Set **4.NF.4**   (4 minutes)
▪ Write Division Sentences as Fractions **5.NF.3**   (3 minutes)
▪ Write Fractions as Mixed Numbers **5.NF.3**   (5 minutes)

Fraction of a Set (4 minutes)

Materials: (S) Personal white boards

Note: This fluency prepares students for G5–M4–Lesson 6.

   T: (Write $10 \times \frac{1}{2}$.) 10 copies of one-half is…?

   S: 5.

   T: (Write $10 \times \frac{1}{5}$.) 10 copies of one-fifth is…?

   S: 2.

Continue with the following possible sequence: $8 \times \frac{1}{2}$, $8 \times \frac{1}{4}$, $6 \times \frac{1}{3}$, $30 \times \frac{1}{6}$, $42 \times \frac{1}{7}$, $42 \times \frac{1}{6}$, $48 \times \frac{1}{8}$, $54 \times \frac{1}{9}$, and $54 \times \frac{1}{6}$.

Write Division Sentences as Fractions (3 minutes)

Materials: (S) Personal white boards

Note: This fluency reviews G5–M4–Lesson 4.

   T: (Write $9 \div 30 =$ ____.) Write the quotient as a fraction.

COMMON CORE™   Lesson 5:   Solve word problems involving the division of whole numbers with
                                       answers in the form of fractions or whole numbers.
                     Date: 11/9/13

4.B.43

S: (Write $9 \div 30 = \frac{9}{30}$.)

T: Write it as a decimal.

S: (Write $9 \div 30 = \frac{3}{10} = 0.3$.)

Continue with the following possible suggestions: $28 \div 40$, $18 \div 60$, $63 \div 70$, $24 \div 80$, and $63 \div 90$.

Write Fractions as Mixed Numbers (5 minutes)

Materials: (S) Personal white boards

Note: This fluency reviews G5–M4–Lesson 4.

T: (Write $\frac{13}{2} = \underline{\quad} \div \underline{\quad} = \underline{\quad}$.) Write the fraction as a division problem and mixed number.

S: (Write $\frac{13}{2} = 13 \div 2 = 6\frac{1}{2}$.)

Continue with the following possible suggestions: $\frac{11}{2}, \frac{17}{2}, \frac{44}{2}, \frac{31}{10}, \frac{23}{10}, \frac{47}{10}, \frac{89}{10}, \frac{8}{3}, \frac{13}{3}, \frac{26}{3}, \frac{9}{4}, \frac{13}{4}, \frac{15}{4}$, and $\frac{35}{4}$.

Concept Development (38 minutes)

Materials: (S) Problem Set

Suggested Delivery of Instruction for Solving Lesson 5's Word Problems

1. Model the problem.

Have two pairs of students who can successfully model the problem work at the board while the others work independently or in pairs at their seats. Review the following questions before beginning the first problem:

- Can you draw something?
- What can you draw?
- What conclusions can you make from your drawing?

As students work, circulate. Reiterate the questions above. After two minutes, have the two pairs of students share only their labeled diagrams. For about one minute, have the demonstrating students receive and respond to feedback and questions from their peers.

2. Calculate to solve and write a statement.

Give everyone two minutes to finish work on that question, sharing their work and thinking with a peer. All should write their equations and statements of the answer.

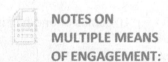

NOTES ON MULTIPLE MEANS OF ENGAGEMENT:

Appropriate scaffolds help all students feel successful. Students may use translators, interpreters, or sentence frames to present their solutions and respond to feedback. Models shared may include concrete manipulatives. If the pace of the lesson is a consideration, allow presenters to prepare beforehand.

Lesson 5: Solve word problems involving the division of whole numbers with answers in the form of fractions or whole numbers.

Date: 11/9/13

4.B.44

3. Assess the solution for reasonableness.

Give students one to two minutes to assess and explain the reasonableness of their solution.

Problem 1

A total of 2 yards of fabric is used to make 5 identical pillows. How much fabric is used for each pillow?

This problem requires understanding of the whole and the divisor. The whole of 2 is divided by 5, which results in a quotient of 2 fifths. Circulate, looking for different visuals (tape diagram and the region models from G5–M4–Lessons 2–3) to facilitate a discussion as to how these different models support the solution of $\frac{2}{5}$.

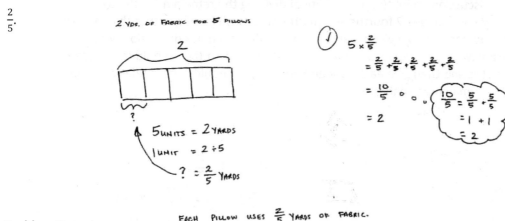

Problem 2

An ice-cream shop uses 4 pints of ice cream to make 6 sundaes. How many pints of ice cream are used for each sundae?

This problem also requires the students' understanding of the whole versus the divisor. The whole is 4, and it is divided equally into 6 units with the solution of 4 sixths. Students should not have to use the standard algorithm to solve, because they should be comfortable interpreting the division expression as a fraction and vice versa. Circulate, looking for alternate modeling strategies that can be quickly mentioned or explored more deeply, if desired. Students might express 4 sixths as 2 thirds. The tape diagram illustrates that larger units of 2 can be made. Quickly model a tape with 6 parts (now representing 1 pint), shade 4, and circle sets of 2.

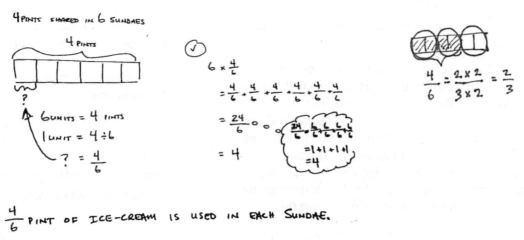

Lesson 5:	Solve word problems involving the division of whole numbers with answers in the form of fractions or whole numbers.	
Date:	11/9/13	4.B.45

Problem 3

An ice-cream shop uses 6 bananas to make 4 identical sundaes. How much banana is used in each sundae? Use a tape diagram to show your work.

This problem has the same two digits (4 and 6) as the previous problem. However, it is important for students to realize that the digits take on a new role, either as whole or divisor, in this context. Six wholes divided by 4 is equal to 6 fourths or 1 and 2 fourths. Although it is not required that students use the standard algorithm, it can be easily employed to find the mixed number value of $1\frac{2}{4}$.

Students may also be engaged in a discussion about the practicality of dividing the remaining of the 2 bananas into fourths and then giving each sundae 2 fourths. Many students may clearly see that the bananas can instead be divided into halves and each sundae given 1 and 1 half. Facilitate a quick discussion with students about which form of the answer makes more sense given our story context (i.e., should the sundae maker divide all the bananas in fourths and then give each sundae 6 fourths, or should each sundae be given a whole banana and then divide the remaining bananas?).

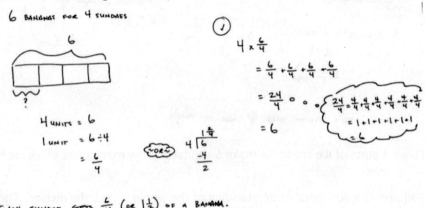

Problem 4

Julian has to read 4 articles for school. He has 8 nights to read them. He decides to read the same number of articles each night.

  a. How many articles will he have to read per night?

  b. What fraction of the reading assignment will he read each night?

In this problem Julian must read 4 articles over the course of 8 nights. The solution of 4 eighths of an article each night might imply that Julian can simply divide each article into eighths and read any 4 articles on any of the 8 nights. Engage in a discussion that allows students to see that 4 eighths must be interpreted as 4 consecutive eighths or 1 half of an article. It would be most practical for Julian to read the first half of an article one night and the remaining half the following night. In this manner, he will finish his reading assignment in the 8 days. Part (b)

NOTES ON
MULTIPLE MEANS FOR
ACTION AND
EXPRESSION:

Support English language learners as they explain their thinking. Provide sentence starters and a word bank. Examples are given below.

Sentence starters:

"I had _____ (unit) in all."

"1 unit equals _____."

Word bank:

fraction of   divided by   remainder

half as much   twice as many

Lesson 5:   Solve word problems involving the division of whole numbers with
Date: answers in the form of fractions or whole numbers.
             11/9/13

4.B.46

provides for deeper thinking about units being considered.

Students must differentiate between the article-as-unit and assignment-as-unit to answer. While 1 half of an article is read each night, the assignment has been split into eight parts. Take the opportunity to discuss with students whether or not the articles are all equal in length. Since we are not told, we make a simplifying assumption in order to solve, finding that each night 1 eighth of the assignment must be read. Discuss how the answer would change if one article were twice the length of the other three.

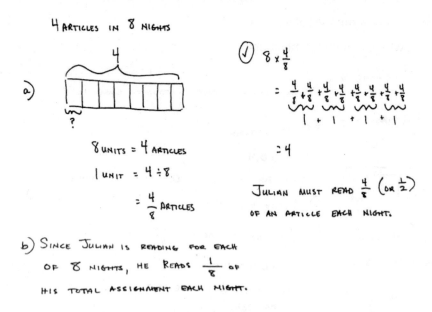

Problem 5

Forty students shared 5 pizzas equally. How much pizza did each student receive? What fraction of the pizza did each student receive?

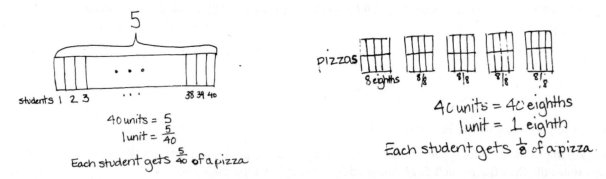

As this is the fifth problem on the page, students may recognize the division expression very quickly and realize that 5 divided by 40 yields 5 fortieths of pizza per student, but in this context it is interesting to discuss with students the practicality of serving the pizzas in fortieths. Here, one might better ask, "How can I make 40 equal parts out of 5 pizzas?" This question leads to thinking about making the least number of cuts to each pizza—eighths. Now the simplified answer of 1 eighth of a pizza per student makes more sense. The follow-up question points to the changing of the unit from *how much pizza per student* (1 eighth of a pizza) to *what fraction of the total* (1 fortieth of the total amount). Because there are so many slices to be made,

COMMON CORE™   Lesson 5: Solve word problems involving the division of whole numbers with answers in the form of fractions or whole numbers.

Date: 11/9/13

4.B.47

students may use the *dot, dot, dot* format to show the smaller units in their tape diagram. Others may opt to simply show their work with an equation.

Problem 6

Lillian had 2 two-liter bottles of soda, which she distributed equally between 10 glasses.

  a. How much soda was in each glass? Express your answer as a fraction of a liter.

  b. Express your answer as a decimal number of liters.

  c. Express your answer as a whole number of milliliters.

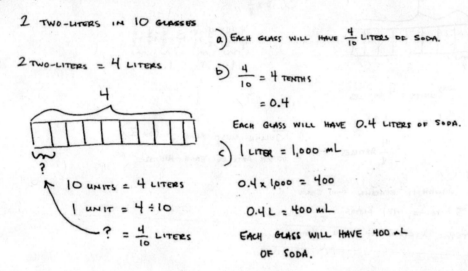

This is a three-part problem that asks students to find the amount of soda in each glass. Carefully guide students when reading the problem so they can interpret that 2 two-liter bottles are equal to 4 liters total. The whole of 4 liters is then divided by 10 glasses to get 4 tenths liters of soda per glass. In order to answer Part (b), students need to remember how to express fractions as decimals (i.e., $\frac{1}{10} = 0.1$, $\frac{1}{100} = 0.01$, and $\frac{1}{1000} = 0.001$). For Part (c), students may need to be reminded about the equivalency between liters and milliliters (1 L = 1,000 mL).

Problem 7

The Calef family likes to paddle along the Susquehanna River.

  a. They paddled the same distance each day over the course of 3 days, traveling a total of 14 miles. How many miles did they travel each day? Show your thinking in a tape diagram.

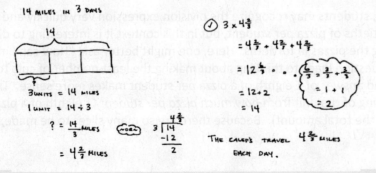

Lesson 5: Solve word problems involving the division of whole numbers with answers in the form of fractions or whole numbers.

Date: 11/9/13

4.B.48

b. If the Calefs went half their daily distance each day, but extended their trip to twice as many days, how far would they travel?

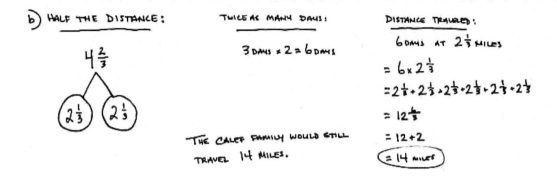

In Part (a), students can easily use the standard algorithm to solve 14 miles divided by 3 days is equal to 4 and 2 thirds miles per day. Part (b) requires some deliberate thinking. Guide the students to read the question carefully before solving it.

Student Debrief (10 minutes)

Lesson Objective: Solve word problems involving the division of whole numbers with answers in the form of fractions or whole numbers.

The Student Debrief is intended to invite reflection and active processing of the total lesson experience.

Invite students to review their solutions for the Problem Set. They should check work by comparing answers with a partner before going over answers as a class. Look for misconceptions or misunderstandings that can be addressed in the Debrief. Guide students in a conversation to debrief the Problem Set and process the lesson.

You may choose to use any combination of the questions below to lead the discussion.

- How are the problems alike? How are they different?
- How was your solution the same as and different from those that were demonstrated?
- Did you see other solutions that surprised you or made you see the problem differently?
- Why should we assess reasonableness after solving?
- Were there problems in which it made more sense to express the answer as a fraction rather than a mixed number and vice versa? Give examples.

Exit Ticket (3 minutes)

After the Student Debrief, instruct students to complete the Exit Ticket. A review of their work will help you assess the students' understanding of the concepts that were presented in the lesson today and plan more effectively for future lessons. You may read the questions aloud to the students.

Lesson 5:	Solve word problems involving the division of whole numbers with answers in the form of fractions or whole numbers.
Date:	11/9/13

4.B.49

Name _____   Date _____

1. A total of 2 yards of fabric is used to make 5 identical pillows. How much fabric is used for each pillow?

2. An ice-cream shop uses 4 pints of ice cream to make 6 sundaes. How many pints of ice cream are used for each sundae?

3. An ice-cream shop uses 6 bananas to make 4 identical sundaes. How much banana is used in each sundae? Use a tape diagram to show your work.

Lesson 5:	Solve word problems involving the division of whole numbers with answers in the form of fractions or whole numbers.	
Date:	11/9/13	4.B.50

© 2013 Common Core, Inc. All rights reserved. commoncore.org

4. Julian has to read 4 articles for school. He has 8 nights to read them. He decides to read the same number of articles each night.

   a. How many articles will he have to read per night?

   b. What fraction of the reading assignment will he read each night?

5. Forty students shared 5 pizzas equally. How much pizza will each student receive? What fraction of the pizza did each student receive?

6. Lillian had 2 two-liter bottles of soda, which she distributed equally between 10 glasses.

   a. How much soda was in each glass? Express your answer as a fraction of a liter.

b.   Express your answer from as a decimal number of liters.

c.   Express your answer as a whole number of milliliters.

7.   The Calef family likes to paddle along the Susquehanna River.

a.   They paddled the same distance each day over the course of 3 days, travelling a total of 14 miles. How many miles did they travel each day? Show your thinking in a tape diagram.

b.   If the Calefs went half their daily distance each day, but extended their trip to twice as many days, how far would they travel?

Lesson 5:   Solve word problems involving the division of whole numbers with answers in the form of fractions or whole numbers.

Date: 11/9/13

4.B.52

Name _____   Date _____

A grasshopper covered a distance of 5 yards in 9 equal hops. How many yards did the grasshopper travel on each hop?

a.   Draw a picture to support your work.

b.   How many yards did the grasshopper travel after hopping twice?

Lesson 5:   Solve word problems involving the division of whole numbers with answers in the form of fractions or whole numbers.
Date: 11/9/13

4.B.53

© 2013 Common Core, Inc. All rights reserved. commoncore.org

Name _____ Date _____

1. When someone donated 14 gallons of paint to Rosendale Elementary School, the fifth grade decided to use it to paint murals. They split the gallons equally among the four classes.
   a. How much paint did each class have to paint their mural?

   b. How much paint will three classes use? Show your thinking using words, numbers, or pictures.

   c. If 4 students share a 30 square foot wall equally, how many square feet of the wall will be painted by each student?

   d. What fraction of the wall will each student paint?

 **Lesson 5:** Solve word problems involving the division of whole numbers with answers in the form of fractions or whole numbers.

Date: 11/9/13

4.B.54

2. Craig bought a 3-foot long baguette, and then made 4 equally sized sandwiches with it.

   a. What portion of the baguette was used for each sandwich? Draw a visual model to help you solve this problem.

   b. How long, in feet, is one of Craig's sandwiches?

   c. How many inches long is one of Craig's sandwiches?

3. Scott has 6 days to save enough money for a $45 concert ticket. If he saves the same amount each day, what is the minimum amount he must save each day in order to reach his goal? Express your answer in dollars.

Lesson 5: Solve word problems involving the division of whole numbers with answers in the form of fractions or whole numbers.

Date: 11/9/13

4.B.55

Topic C

Multiplication of a Whole Number by a Fraction

5.NF.4a

Focus Standard:	5.NF.4a	Apply and extend previous understandings of multiplication to multiply a fraction or whole number by a fraction.
		a. Interpret the product of $(a/b) \times q$ as a parts of a partition of q into b equal parts; equivalently, as the result of a sequence of operations $a \times q \div b$. For example, use a visual fraction model to show $(2/3 \times 4 = 8/3$, and create a story context for this equation. Do the same with $(2/3) \times (4/5) = 8/15$. (In general, $(a/b) \times (c/d) = ac/bd$.)
Instructional Days:	4	
Coherence -Links from:	G4–M5	Fraction Equivalence, Ordering, and Operations
-Links to:	G6–M2	Arithmetic Operations Including Dividing by a Fraction

In Topic C, students interpret finding a fraction of a set (3/4 *of* 24) as multiplication of a whole number by a fraction (3/4 × 24) and use tape diagrams to support their understandings (**5.NF.4a**). This in turn leads students to see division by a whole number as equivalent to multiplication by its reciprocal. That is, division by 2, for example, is the same as multiplication by 1/2.

Students also use the commutative property to relate fraction of a set to the Grade 4 repeated addition interpretation of multiplication by a fraction. This opens the door for students to reason about various strategies for multiplying fractions and whole numbers. Students apply their knowledge of fraction of a set and previous conversion experiences (with scaffolding from a conversion chart, if necessary) to find a fraction of a measurement, thus converting a larger unit to an equivalent smaller unit (e.g., 1/3 min = 20 seconds and 2 1/4 feet = 27 inches).

A Teaching Sequence Towards Mastery of Multiplication of a Whole Number by a Fraction

Objective 1: Relate fractions as division to fraction of a set.
(Lesson 6)

Objective 2: Multiply any whole number by a fraction using tape diagrams.
(Lesson 7)

Objective 3: Relate fraction of a set to the repeated addition interpretation of fraction multiplication.
(Lesson 8)

Objective 4: Find a fraction of a measurement, and solve word problems.
(Lesson 9)

Lesson 6

Objective: Relate fractions as division to fraction of a set.

Suggested Lesson Structure

▮ Application Problem	(6 minutes)	
▮ Fluency Practice	(12 minutes)	
▮ Concept Development	(32 minutes)	
▮ Student Debrief	(10 minutes)	
Total Time	**(60 minutes)**	

Application Problem (6 minutes)

Olivia is half the age of her brother, Adam. Olivia's sister, Ava, is twice as old as Adam. Adam is 4 years old. How old is each sibling? Use tape diagrams to show your thinking.

Note: This Application Problem is intended to activate students' prior knowledge of *half of* in a simple context as a precursor to today's more formalized introduction to fraction of a set.

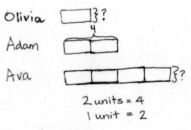

Fluency Practice (12 minutes)

- Sprint: Divide Whole Numbers **5.NF.3**   (8 minutes)
- Fractions as Division **5.NF.3**   (4 minutes)

Sprint: Divide Whole Numbers (8 minutes)

Materials: (S) Divide Whole Numbers Sprint

Note: This Sprint reviews G5–M4–Lessons 2–4.

Fractions as Division (4 minutes)

Materials: (S) Personal white boards

Note: This fluency reviews G5–M4–Lesson 5.

　　T: I'll say a division sentence. You write it as a fraction. 4 ÷ 2.

S: $\frac{4}{2}$.

T: $6 \div 4$.

S: $\frac{6}{4}$.

T: $3 \div 4$.

S: $\frac{3}{4}$.

T: $2 \div 10$.

S: $\frac{2}{10}$.

T: Rename this fraction using fifths.

S: $\frac{1}{5}$.

T: (Write $\frac{56}{2}$.) Write the fraction as a division equation and solve.

S: $56 \div 2 = 28$.

Continue with the following possible suggestions: 6 thirds, 9 thirds, 18 thirds, $\frac{54}{3}$, 8 fourths, 12 fourths, 28 fourths, and $\frac{72}{4}$.

Concept Development (32 minutes)

Materials: (S) Two-sided counters, drinking straws, personal white boards

Problem 1

$\frac{1}{3}$ of 6 = ___

T: Make an array with 6 counters turned to the red side and use your straws to divide your array into 3 equal parts.

T: Write a division sentence for what you just did.

S: $6 \div 3 = 2$.

T: Rewrite your division sentence as a fraction and speak it as you write it.

S: (Write $\frac{6}{3}$.) 6 divided by 3.

T: If I want to show 1 third of this set, how many counters should I turn over to yellow? Turn and talk.

S: Two counters. → Each group is 1 third of all the counters, so we would have to turn over 1 group of 2 counters. → Six divided by 3 tells us there are 2 in each group.

T: 1 third of 6 is equal to?

S: 2.

NOTES ON MULTIPLE MEANS OF ACTION AND EXPRESSION:

If students struggle with the set model of this lesson, consider allowing them to fold a square of paper into the desired fractional parts. Then have them place the counters in the sections created by the folding.

Lesson 6: Relate fractions as division to fraction of a set.
Date: 11/10/13

4.C.4

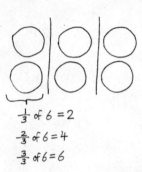

T: (Write $\frac{1}{3}$ of 6 = 2.) How many counters should be turned over to show 2 thirds? Whisper to your partner how you know.

S: I can count from our array. One third is 2 counters, then 2 thirds is 4 counters. → Six divided by 3 once is 2 counters. Double that is 4 counters. → I know 1 group out of 3 groups is 2 counters, so 2 groups out of 3 would be 4 counters. → Since $\frac{1}{3}$ of 6 is equal to 2, then $\frac{2}{3}$ of 6 is double that. Two plus 2 is 4. → 6 ÷ 3 × 2, but I wrote 6 ÷ 3 as a fraction.

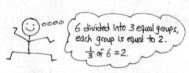

T: (Write $\frac{2}{3}$ of 6 = ___.) What is 2 thirds of 6 counters?

S: 4 counters.

T: (Write $\frac{3}{3}$ of 6 = ___.) What is 3 thirds of 6 counters?

S: 6 counters.

T: How do you know? Turn and discuss with your partner.

S: I counted 2, 4, 6. → $\frac{3}{3}$ is a whole, and our whole set is 6 counters.

T: Following this pattern, what is 4 thirds of 6?

S: It would be more than 6. → It would be more than the whole set. We would have to add 2 more counters. It would be 8. → 6 divided by 3 times 4 is 8.

**NOTES ON
MULTIPLE MEANS OF
REPRESENTATION:**

It is acceptable for students to orient their arrays in either direction. For example, in Problem 2, students may arrange their counters in the 3 × 4 arrangement pictured, or they may show a 4 × 3 array that is divided by the straws horizontally.

Problem 2

$\frac{1}{4}$ of 12 = ___

T: Make an array using 12 counters turned to the red side. Use your straws to divide the array into fourths. (Draw an array on the board.)

T: How many counters did you place in each fourth?

S: 3.

T: Write the division sentence as a fraction on your board.

S: $\frac{12}{4}$ = 3.

T: What is 1 fourth of 12?

S: 3.

T: (Write $\frac{1}{4}$ of 12 = 3.) 1 fourth of 12 is equal to 3. Look at your array. What fraction of 12 is equal to 6 counters? Turn and discuss with your partner.

S: I see 2 groups is equal to 6 so the answer is $\frac{2}{4}$. → Since 1 fourth is equal to 3, and 6 is double that much, I can double 1 fourth to get 2 fourths.

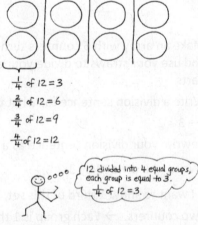

Lesson 6:   Relate fractions as division to fraction of a set.
Date: 11/10/13

4.C.5

T: (Write $\frac{2}{4}$ of 12 = 6.) 2 fourths of 12 is equal to 6. What is another way to say 2 fourths?

S: 1 half.

T: Is 1 half of 12 equal to 6?

S: Yes.

Follow this sequence with $\frac{1}{3}$ of 9, $\frac{1}{6}$ of 12, and $\frac{1}{5}$ of 15, as necessary.

Problem 3

Mrs. Pham has 8 apples. She wants to give $\frac{3}{4}$ of the apples to her students. How many apples will her students get?

T: Use your counters or draw an array to show how many apples Mrs. Pham has.

S: (Represent 8 apples.)

T: (Write $\frac{3}{4}$ of 8 = ___.) How will we find 3 fourths of 8? Turn and talk.

S: I divided my counters to make 4 equal parts. Then I counted the number in 3 of those parts. → I can draw 4 rows of 2 and count 2, 4, 6, so the answer is 6 apples. → I need to make fourths. That's 4 equal parts, but I only want to know about 3 of them. There are 2 in 1 part and 6 in 3 parts. → I know if 1 fourth is equal to 2, then 3 fourths is 3 groups of 2. The answer is 6 apples.

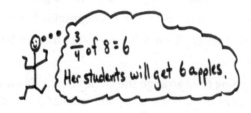

Problem 4

In a class of 24 students, $\frac{5}{6}$ are boys. How many boys are in the class?

T: How many students are in the whole class?

S: 24.

T: What is the question?

S: How many boys are in the class?

T: What fraction of the whole class of 24 are boys?

S: $\frac{5}{6}$.

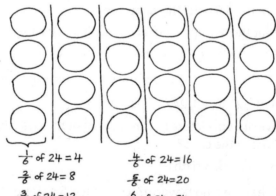

T: Will our answer be more than half of the class or less than half? How do you know? Turn and talk.

S: 5 sixths is more than half, so the answer should be more than 12. → Half of the class would be 12, which would also be 3 sixths. We need more sixths than that so our answer will be more than 12.

T: (Write $\frac{5}{6}$ of 24 = ___ on the board.) Use your counters or draw to solve. Turn and discuss with a partner.

S: We should draw a total of 24 circles, and then split them into 6 equal groups. → We can draw 4 groups of 6 circles. We will have 6 columns representing 6 groups, and each group will have 4

Lesson 6:   Relate fractions as division to fraction of a set.
Date: 11/10/13

4.C.6

circles. → We could draw 6 rows of 4 circles to show 6 equal parts. We only care how many are in 5 of the rows, and 5 × 4 is 20 boys. → We need to find sixths, so we need to divide the set into 6 equal parts, but we only need to know how many are in 5 of the groups. That's 4, 8, 12, 16, 20. There are 20 boys in the class.

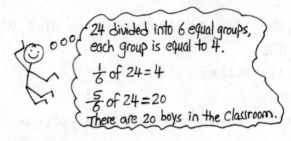

T: (Point to the drawing on the board.) Let's think of this another way. What is $\frac{1}{6}$ of 24?

S: 4.

T: How do we know? Say the division sentence.

S: 24 ÷ 6 = 4.

T: How can we use $\frac{1}{6}$ of 24 to help us solve for $\frac{5}{6}$ of 24? Whisper and tell your partner.

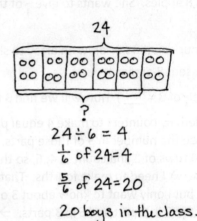

S: $\frac{1}{6}$ of 24 is equal to 4. $\frac{5}{6}$ of 24 is just 5 groups of 4. 4 + 4 + 4 + 4 + 4 = 20. → I know each group is 4. To find 5 groups, I can multiply 5 × 4 = 20. → $\frac{24}{6}$ (24 divided by 6) times 5 is 20.

T: I'm going to rearrange the circles a bit. (Draw a bar directly beneath the array and label 24.) We said we needed to find sixths, so how many units should I cut the whole into?

S: We need 6 units the same size.

T: (Cut the bar into 6 equal parts.) If 6 units are 24, how many circles in one unit? How do you know?

S: Four, because 24 ÷ 6 is 4.

T: (Write $\frac{1}{6}$ of 24 = 4 under the bar.) Let me draw 4 counters into each unit. Count with me as I write.

S: 4, 8, 12, 16, 20, 24.

T: We are only interested in the part of the class that is boys. How many of these units represent the boys in the class?

S: 5 units. → 5 sixths.

T: What are 5 units worth? Or, what is 5 sixths of 24? (Draw a bracket around 5 units and write $\frac{5}{6}$ of 24 = ___.)

S: 20.

T: (Write the answer on the board.)

T: Answer the question with a sentence.

S: There are 20 boys in the class.

Lesson 6:   Relate fractions as division to fraction of a set.
Date: 11/10/13

4.C.7

Problem Set (10 minutes)

Students should do their personal best to complete the Problem Set within the allotted 10 minutes. For some classes, it may be appropriate to modify the assignment by specifying which problems they work on first. Some problems do not specify a method for solving. Students solve these problems using the RDW approach used for Application Problems.

Student Debrief (10 minutes)

Lesson Objective: Relate fractions as division to fraction of a set.

The Student Debrief is intended to invite reflection and active processing of the total lesson experience.

Invite students to review their solutions for the Problem Set. They should check work by comparing answers with a partner before going over answers as a class. Look for misconceptions or misunderstandings that can be addressed in the Debrief. Guide students in a conversation to debrief the Problem Set and process the lesson.

You may choose to use any combination of the questions below to lead the discussion.

- What pattern did you notice in Problem 1(a)? (Students may say it skip-counts by threes or that all the answers are multiples of 3.) Based on this pattern, what do you think the answer for $\frac{4}{3}$ of 9 is? Why is this more than 9? (Because 4 thirds is more than a whole, and 9 is the whole.)

- How did you solve for the last question in 1(c)? Explain to your partner.

- In Problem 1(d), what did you notice about the two fractions $\frac{4}{8}$ and $\frac{6}{8}$? Can you name them using a larger unit (simplify them)? What connections did you make about $\frac{4}{8}$ of 24 and $\frac{1}{2}$ of 24, $\frac{6}{8}$ of 24 and $\frac{3}{4}$ of 24?

- When solving these problems (fraction of a set), how important is it to first find out how many are

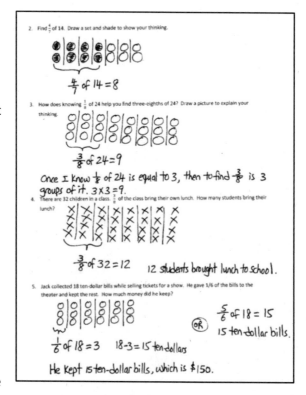

Lesson 6: Relate fractions as division to fraction of a set.
Date: 11/10/13

4.C.8

in each group (unit)? Explain your thinking to a partner.

- Is this a true statement? (Write $\frac{2}{3}$ of 18 = $\frac{18}{3}$ × 2.) Two-thirds of 18 is the same as 18 divided by 3, times 2. Why or why not?

Exit Ticket (3 minutes)

After the Student Debrief, instruct students to complete the Exit Ticket. A review of their work will help you assess the students' understanding of the concepts that were presented in the lesson today and plan more effectively for future lessons. You may read the questions aloud to the students.

Lesson 6:   Relate fractions as division to fraction of a set.
Date: 11/10/13

4.C.9

A

Correct _____

Write the Fraction, Whole Number, or Mixed Number.

1	$1 \div 2 =$		23	$6 \div 2 =$	
2	$1 \div 3 =$		24	$7 \div 2 =$	
3	$1 \div 8 =$		25	$8 \div 8 =$	
4	$2 \div 2 =$		26	$9 \div 8 =$	
5	$2 \div 3 =$		27	$15 \div 8 =$	
6	$3 \div 3 =$		28	$8 \div 4 =$	
7	$3 \div 4 =$		29	$11 \div 4 =$	
8	$3 \div 10 =$		30	$15 \div 2 =$	
9	$3 \div 5 =$		31	$24 \div 5 =$	
10	$5 \div 5 =$		32	$17 \div 4 =$	
11	$6 \div 5 =$		33	$20 \div 3 =$	
12	$7 \div 5 =$		34	$13 \div 6 =$	
13	$9 \div 5 =$		35	$30 \div 7 =$	
14	$2 \div 3 =$		36	$27 \div 8 =$	
15	$4 \div 4 =$		37	$49 \div 9 =$	
16	$5 \div 4 =$		38	$29 \div 6 =$	
17	$7 \div 4 =$		39	$47 \div 7 =$	
18	$4 \div 2 =$		40	$53 \div 8 =$	
19	$5 \div 2 =$		41	$67 \div 9 =$	
20	$10 \div 5 =$		42	$59 \div 6 =$	
21	$11 \div 5 =$		43	$63 \div 8 =$	
22	$13 \div 5 =$		44	$71 \div 9 =$	

COMMON CORE™ | **Lesson 6:** | Relate fractions as division to fraction of a set.
| **Date:** | 11/10/13

4.C.10

B

Improvement _____   # Correct _____

Write the Fraction, Whole Number, or Mixed Number.

1	$1 \div 3 =$		23	$15 \div 5 =$	
2	$1 \div 4 =$		24	$16 \div 5 =$	
3	$1 \div 10 =$		25	$6 \div 6 =$	
4	$5 \div 5 =$		26	$7 \div 6 =$	
5	$5 \div 6 =$		27	$11 \div 6 =$	
6	$3 \div 3 =$		28	$6 \div 3 =$	
7	$3 \div 7 =$		29	$8 \div 3 =$	
8	$3 \div 10 =$		30	$13 \div 2 =$	
9	$3 \div 4 =$		31	$23 \div 5 =$	
10	$4 \div 4 =$		32	$15 \div 4 =$	
11	$5 \div 4 =$		33	$19 \div 4 =$	
12	$2 \div 2 =$		34	$19 \div 6 =$	
13	$3 \div 2 =$		35	$31 \div 7 =$	
14	$4 \div 5 =$		36	$37 \div 8 =$	
15	$10 \div 10 =$		37	$50 \div 9 =$	
16	$11 \div 10 =$		38	$17 \div 6 =$	
17	$13 \div 10 =$		39	$48 \div 7 =$	
18	$10 \div 5 =$		40	$51 \div 8 =$	
19	$11 \div 5 =$		41	$68 \div 9 =$	
20	$13 \div 5 =$		42	$53 \div 6 =$	
21	$4 \div 2 =$		43	$61 \div 8 =$	
22	$5 \div 2 =$		44	$70 \div 9 =$	

COMMON CORE™ **Lesson 6:** Relate fractions as division to fraction of a set.
Date: 11/10/13

4.C.1▶

Name _____ Date _____

1. Find the value of each of the following.

a.

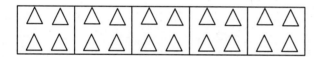

$\frac{1}{3}$ of 9 =

$\frac{2}{3}$ of 9 =

$\frac{3}{3}$ of 9 =

b.

$\frac{1}{3}$ of 15 =

$\frac{2}{3}$ of 15 =

$\frac{3}{3}$ of 15 =

c.

$\frac{1}{5}$ of 20=

$\frac{4}{5}$ of 20 =

$\frac{}{5}$ of 20 = 20

d.

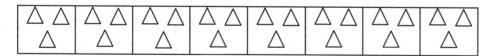

$\frac{1}{8}$ of 24 =

$\frac{3}{8}$ of 24 =

$\frac{4}{8}$ of 24 =

$\frac{6}{8}$ of 24 =

$\frac{7}{8}$ of 24 =

2. Find $\frac{4}{7}$ of 14. Draw a set and shade to show your thinking.

3. How does knowing $\frac{1}{8}$ of 24 help you find three-eighths of 24? Draw a picture to explain your thinking.

4. There are 32 students in a class. Of the class, $\frac{3}{8}$ bring their own lunch. How many students bring their lunch?

5. Jack collected 18 ten dollar bills while selling tickets for a show. He gave $\frac{1}{6}$ of the bills to the theater and kept the rest. How much money did he keep?

Lesson 6:   Relate fractions as division to fraction of a set.
Date: 11/10/13

4.C.13

Name _____   Date _____

1. Find the value of each of the following.

a. $\frac{1}{4}$ of 16 =

b. $\frac{3}{4}$ of 16 =

2. Out of 18 cookies, $\frac{2}{3}$ are chocolate chip. How many of the cookies are chocolate chip?

COMMON CORE™

Lesson 6: Relate fractions as division to fraction of a set.
Date: 11/10/13

4.C.14

Name _____   Date _____

1. Find the value of each of the following.

    a.

    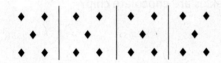

    $\frac{1}{3}$ of 12 =

    $\frac{2}{3}$ of 12 =

    $\frac{3}{3}$ of 12 =

    b.

    $\frac{1}{4}$ of 20 = $\frac{3}{4}$ of 20 =

    $\frac{2}{4}$ of 20 = $\frac{4}{4}$ of 20 =

    c.

    $\frac{1}{5}$ of 35 = $\frac{3}{5}$ of 35 = $\frac{5}{5}$ of 35 =

    $\frac{2}{5}$ of 35 = $\frac{4}{5}$ of 35 = $\frac{6}{5}$ of 35 =

Lesson 6:   Relate fractions as division to fraction of a set.
Date: 11/10/13

4.C.15

2. Find $\frac{2}{3}$ of 18. Draw a set and shade to show your thinking.

3. How does knowing $\frac{1}{5}$ of 10 help you find $\frac{3}{5}$ of 10? Draw a picture to explain your thinking.

4. Sara just turned 18 years old. She spent $\frac{4}{9}$ of her life living in Rochester, NY. For how many years did Sara live in Rochester?

5. A farmer collects 12 dozen eggs from her chickens. She sells $\frac{5}{6}$ of the eggs at the farmers' market and gives the rest to friends and neighbors.

  a. How many eggs does she give away?

  b. If she sells each dozen for $4.50, how much will she earn from the eggs she sells?

Lesson 7

Objective: Multiply any whole number by a fraction using tape diagrams.

Suggested Lesson Structure

■ Fluency Practice   (12 minutes)
■ Application Problem   (5 minutes)
■ Concept Development   (33 minutes)
■ Student Debrief   (10 minutes)
   Total Time   **(60 minutes)**

Fluency Practice (12 minutes)

- Read Tape Diagrams **5.NF.4**   (4 minutes)
- Half of Whole Numbers **5.NF.4**   (4 minutes)
- Fractions as Whole Numbers **5.NF.3** (4 minutes)

Read Tape Diagrams (4 minutes)

Materials: (S) Personal white boards

Note: This fluency prepares students to multiply fractions by whole numbers during the Concept Development.

   T: (Project a tape diagram with 10 partitioned into 2 equal units.) Say the whole.
   S: 10.
   T: On your boards, write the division sentence.
   S: (Write 10 ÷ 2 = 5.)

Continue with the following possible sequence: 6 ÷ 2, 9 ÷ 3, 12 ÷ 3, 8 ÷ 4, 12 ÷ 4, 25 ÷ 5, 40 ÷ 5, 42 ÷ 6, 63 ÷ 7, 64 ÷ 8, and 54 ÷ 9.

Half of Whole Numbers (4 minutes)

Materials: (S) Personal white boards

Note: This fluency reviews G5–M4–Lesson 6 content and prepares students to multiply fractions by whole numbers during the Concept Development using tape diagrams.

   T: Draw 4 counters. What's half of 4?
   S: 2.

T: (Write $\frac{1}{2}$ of 4 = 2.) Say a division sentence that helps you find the answer.

S: 4 ÷ 2 = 2.

Continue with the following possible sequence: half of 10, half of 8, 1 half of 30, 1 half of 54, 1 fourth of 20, 1 fourth of 16, 1 third of 9, and 1 third of 18.

Fractions as Whole Numbers (4 minutes)

Materials: (S) Personal white boards

Note: This fluency reviews G5–M4–Lesson 5 and reviews denominators that are equivalent to hundredths. Direct students to use their personal white boards for calculations that they cannot do mentally.

T: I'll say a fraction. You say it as a division problem. 4 halves.

S: 4 ÷ 2 = 2.

Continue with the following possible suggestions:
$\frac{6}{2}$, $\frac{14}{2}$, $\frac{54}{2}$, $\frac{40}{20}$, $\frac{80}{20}$, $\frac{180}{20}$, $\frac{960}{20}$, $\frac{10}{5}$, $\frac{15}{5}$, $\frac{35}{5}$, $\frac{85}{5}$, $\frac{100}{50}$, $\frac{150}{50}$, $\frac{300}{50}$, $\frac{900}{50}$, $\frac{8}{4}$, $\frac{12}{4}$, $\frac{24}{4}$, $\frac{96}{4}$, $\frac{50}{25}$, $\frac{75}{25}$, and $\frac{800}{25}$.

Application Problem (5 minutes)

Mr. Peterson bought a case (24 boxes) of fruit juice. One-third of the drinks were grape and two-thirds were cranberry. How many boxes of each flavor did Mr. Peterson buy? Show your work using a tape diagram or an array.

Note: This Application Problem requires students to use skills explored in G5–M4–Lesson 6. Students are finding fractions of a set and showing their thinking with models.

Concept Development (33 minutes)

Materials: (S) Personal white boards

Problem 1

What is $\frac{3}{5}$ of 35?

T: (Write $\frac{3}{5}$ of 35 = ___ on the board.) We used two different models (counters and arrays) yesterday to find fractions of sets. We will use tape diagrams to help us today.

T: We have to find 3 fifths of 35. Draw a bar to represent

NOTES ON MULTIPLE MEANS OF REPRESENTATION:

Please note throughout the lesson that division sentences are written as fractions in order to reinforce the interpretation of a fraction as division. When reading the fraction notation, the language of division should be used. For example, in Problem 1,

1 unit = $\frac{35}{5}$ should be read as 1 unit equals 35 divided by 5.

Lesson 7:   Multiply any whole number by a fraction using tape diagrams.
Date: 11/10/13

4.C.18

our whole. What's our whole?

S: 35.

T: (Draw a bar and label 35.) How many units should we cut the whole into?

S: 5.

T: How do you know?

S: The denominator tells us we want fifths. → That is the unit being named by the fraction. → We are asked about fifths so we know we need 5 equal parts.

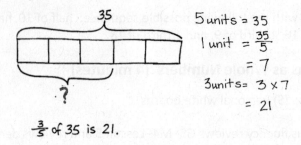

$\frac{3}{5}$ of 35 is 21.

T: (Cut the bar into 5 equal units.) We know 5 units are equal to 35. How do we find the value of 1 unit? Say the division sentence.

S: 35 ÷ 5 = 7.

T: (Write 5 units = 35, 1 unit = 35 ÷ 5 = 7.) Have we answered our question?

S: No, we found 1 unit is equal to 7, but the question is to find 3 units. → We need 3 fifths. When we divide by 5, that's just 1 fifth of 35.

T: How will we find 3 units?

S: Multiply 3 and 7 to get 21. → We could add 7 + 7 + 7. → We could put 3 of the 1 fifths together. That would be 21.

T: What is $\frac{3}{5}$ of 35?

S: 21.

NOTES ON MULTIPLE MEANS OF ACTION AND EXPRESSION:

Students with fine motor deficits may find drawing tape diagrams difficult. Graph paper may provide some support, or online sources like the Thinking Blocks website may also be helpful.

Problem 2

Aurelia buys 2 dozen roses. Of these roses, $\frac{3}{4}$ are red and the rest are white. How many white roses did she buy?

T: What do you know about this problem? Turn and share with your partner.

S: I know the whole is 2 dozen, which is 24. → $\frac{3}{4}$ are red roses, and $\frac{1}{4}$ are white roses. The total is 24 roses. → The information in the problem is about red roses, but the question is about the other part, the white roses.

T: Discuss with your partner how you'll solve this problem.

S: We can first find the total red roses, then subtract from 24 to get the white roses. →

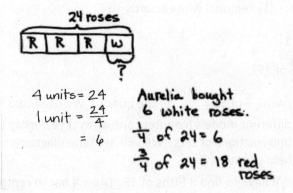

4 units = 24
1 unit = $\frac{24}{4}$
= 6

Aurelia bought 6 white roses.
$\frac{1}{4}$ of 24 = 6
$\frac{3}{4}$ of 24 = 18 red roses

| Lesson 7: | Multiply any whole number by a fraction using tape diagrams. |
| Date: | 11/10/13 |

4.C.19

Since I know $\frac{1}{4}$ of the whole is white roses, I can find $\frac{1}{4}$ of 24 to find the white roses. And that's faster.

T: Work with a partner to draw a tape diagram and solve.

T: Answer the question for this problem.

S: She bought 6 white roses.

Problem 3

Rosie had 17 yards of fabric. She used one-third of it to make a quilt. How many yards of fabric did Rosie use for the quilt?

T: What can you draw? Turn and share with your partner.

T: Compare this problem with the others we've done today.

S: The answer is not a whole number. → The quotient is not a whole number. → We were still looking for fractional parts, but the answer isn't a whole number.

T: We can draw a bar that shows 17 and divide it into thirds. How do we find the value of one unit?

S: Divide 17 by 3.

T: How much fabric is one-third of 17 yards?

S: $\frac{17}{3}$ yards. → $5\frac{2}{3}$ yards.

T How would you find 2 thirds of 17?

S: Double $5\frac{2}{3}$. → Multiply $5\frac{2}{3}$ times 2. → Subtract $5\frac{2}{3}$ from 17.

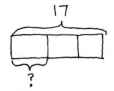

Repeat this sequence with $\frac{2}{5}$ of 11, if necessary.

NOTES ON MULTIPLE MEANS OF REPRESENTATION:

The added complexity of finding a fraction of a quantity that is not a multiple of the denominator may require a return to concrete materials for some students. Allow them access to materials that can be folded and cut to model Problem 3 physically. Five whole squares can be distributed into each unit of 1 third. Then the remaining whole squares can be cut into thirds and distributed among the units of thirds. Be sure to make the connection to the fraction form of the division sentence and the written recording of the division algorithm.

Problem 4

$\frac{2}{3}$ of a number is 8. What is the number?

T: How is this problem different from the ones we just solved?

S: In the first problem, we knew the total and wanted to find a part of it. In this one, we know how much 2 thirds is, but not the whole. → They told us the whole and asked us about a part last time. This time they told us about a part and asked us to find the whole.

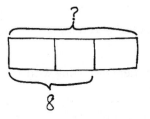

T: Draw a bar to represent the whole. What kind of units will we need to divide the whole into?

Lesson 7:   Multiply any whole number by a fraction using tape diagrams.
Date: 11/10/13

4.C.20

S: Thirds.

T: What else do we know? Turn and tell your partner.

S: We know that 2 thirds is the same as 8 so it means we can label 2 of the units with a bracket and 8. → The units are thirds. We know about 2 of them. They are equal to 8 together. We don't know what the whole bar is worth so we have to put a question mark there.

T: How can knowing what 2 units are worth help us find the whole?

S: Since we know that 2 units = 8, then we can divide to find 1 unit is equal to 4.

T: (Write 2 units = 8 ÷ 2 = 4.) Let's record 4 inside each unit. Can we find the whole now?

S: Yes. We can add 4 + 4 + 4 =12. → We can multiply 3 times 4, which is equal to 12.

T: (Write 3 units = 3 × 4 = 12.) Answer the question for this problem.

S: The number is 12.

T: Let's think about it and check to see if it makes sense. (Write $\frac{2}{3}$ of 12 = 8.) Work independently on your personal board and solve to find what 2 thirds of 12 is.

Problem 5

Tiffany spent $\frac{4}{7}$ of her money on a teddy bear. If the teddy bear cost $24, how much money did she have at first?

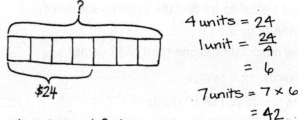

T: Which problem that we've worked today is most like this one?

S: This one is just like Problem 4. We have information about a part, and we have to find the whole.

T: What can you draw? Turn and share with your partner.

S: We can draw a bar for all the money. We can show what the teddy bear costs. It costs $24, and it's $\frac{4}{7}$ of her total money. We can put a question mark over the whole bar.

T: Do we have enough information to find the value of 1 unit?

S: Yes.

T: How much is one unit? How do you know?

S: 4 units = $24, so 1 unit = $6.

T: How will we find the amount of money she had at first?

S: Multiply $6 by 7.

T: Say the multiplication sentence starting with 7.

S: 7 × $6 = $42.

T: Answer the question in this problem.

S: Tiffany had $42 at first.

Lesson 7:   Multiply any whole number by a fraction using tape diagrams.
Date: 11/10/13

4.C.21

Problem Set (10 minutes)

Students should do their personal best to complete the Problem Set within the allotted 10 minutes. For some classes, it may be appropriate to modify the assignment by specifying which problems they work on first. Some problems do not specify a method for solving. Students solve these problems using the RDW approach used for Application Problems.

Student Debrief (10 minutes)

Lesson Objective: Multiply any whole number by a fraction using tape diagrams.

The Student Debrief is intended to invite reflection and active processing of the total lesson experience.

Invite students to review their solutions for the Problem Set. They should check work by comparing answers with a partner before going over answers as a class. Look for misconceptions or misunderstandings that can be addressed in the Debrief. Guide students in a conversation to debrief the Problem Set and process the lesson.

You may choose to use any combination of the questions below to lead the discussion.

- What pattern relationships did you notice between Problems 1(a) and 1(b)? (The whole of 36 is double of 18. That's why the answer is 12, which is also double of 6.)

- What pattern did you notice between Problems 1(c) and 1(d)? (The fraction of 3 eighths is half of 3 fourths. That is why the answer is 9, which is also half of 18.)

- Look at Problems 1(e) and 1(f). We know that 4 fifths and 1 seventh aren't equal, so how did we get the same answer?

- Compare Problems 1(c) and 1(k). How are they similar, and how are they different? (The questions involve the same numbers, but in Problem 1(c), 3 fourths is the unknown quantity, and in Problem 1(k) it is the known quantity. In Problem 1(c) the whole is known, but in Problem

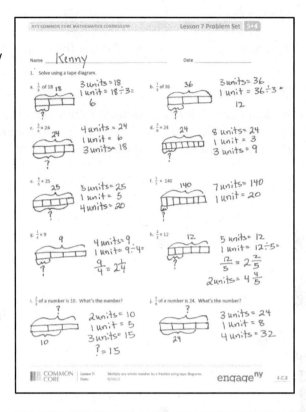

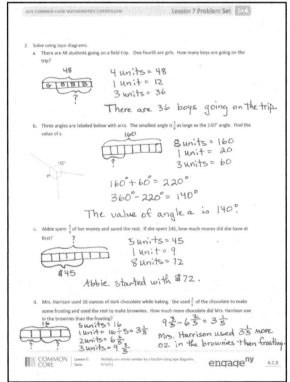

1(k) the whole is unknown.)

- How did you solve for Problem 2(b)? Explain your strategy or solution to a partner.

- There are a couple of different methods to solve Problem 2(c). Find someone who used a different approach from yours and explain your thinking.

Exit Ticket (3 minutes)

After the Student Debrief, instruct students to complete the Exit Ticket. A review of their work will help you assess the students' understanding of the concepts that were presented in the lesson today and plan more effectively for future lessons. You may read the questions aloud to the students.

Lesson 7:   Multiply any whole number by a fraction using tape diagrams.
Date: 11/10/13

4.C.23

Name _____   Date _____

1. Solve using a tape diagram.

   a. $\frac{1}{3}$ of 18

   b. $\frac{1}{3}$ of 36

   c. $\frac{3}{4} \times 24$

   d. $\frac{3}{8} \times 24$

   e. $\frac{4}{5} \times 25$

   f. $\frac{1}{7} \times 140$

   g. $\frac{1}{4} \times 9$

   h. $\frac{2}{5} \times 12$

   i. $\frac{2}{3}$ of a number is 10. What's the number?

   j. $\frac{3}{4}$ of a number is 24. What's the number?

COMMON CORE™

Lesson 7:   Multiply any whole number by a fraction using tape diagrams.
Date: 11/10/13

4.C.24

2. Solve using tape diagrams.

   a. There are 48 students going on a field trip. One-fourth are girls. How many boys are going on the trip?

   b. Three angles are labeled below with arcs. The smallest angle is $\frac{3}{8}$ as large as the 160° angle. Find the value of angle a.

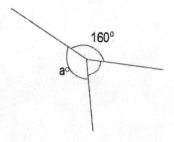

   c. Abbie spent $\frac{5}{8}$ of her money and saved the rest. If she spent $45, how much money did she have at first?

   d. Mrs. Harrison used 16 ounces of dark chocolate while baking. She used $\frac{2}{5}$ of the chocolate to make some frosting and used the rest to make brownies. How much more chocolate did Mrs. Harrison use in the brownies than in the frosting?

COMMON CORE™ Lesson 7: Multiply any whole number by a fraction using tape diagrams.
Date: 11/10/13

4.C.2

Name _____   Date _____

Solve using a tape diagram.

a. $\frac{3}{5}$ of 30

b. $\frac{3}{5}$ of a number is 30. What's the number?

c. Mrs. Johnson baked 2 dozen cookies. Two-thirds of them were oatmeal. How many oatmeal cookies did Mrs. Johnson bake?

Name _____   Date _____

1. Solve using a tape diagram.

    a. $\frac{1}{4}$ of 24   b. $\frac{1}{4}$ of 48

    c. $\frac{2}{3} \times 18$ d. $\frac{2}{6} \times 18$

    e. $\frac{3}{7} \times 49$ f. $\frac{3}{10} \times 120$

    g. $\frac{1}{3} \times 31$ h. $\frac{2}{5} \times 20$

    i. $\frac{1}{4} \times 25$ j. $\frac{3}{4} \times 25$

    k. $\frac{3}{4}$ of a number is 27. What's the number?   l. $\frac{2}{5}$ of a number is 14. What's the number?

COMMON CORE™

Lesson 7:   Multiply any whole number by a fraction using tape diagrams.
Date: 11/10/13

4.C.2

2. Solve using tape diagrams.

   a. A skating rink sold 66 tickets. Of these, $\frac{2}{3}$ were children's tickets, and the rest were adult tickets. How many adult tickets were sold?

   b. A straight angle is split into two smaller angles as shown. The smaller angle's measure is $\frac{1}{6}$ that of a straight angle. What is the value of angle a?

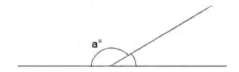

   c. Annabel and Eric made 17 ounces of pizza dough. They used $\frac{5}{8}$ of the dough to make a pizza and used the rest to make calzones. What is the difference between the amount of dough they used to make pizza and the amount of dough they used to make calzones?

   d. The New York Rangers hockey team won $\frac{3}{4}$ of their games last season. If they lost 21 games, how many games did they play in the entire season?

Lesson 8

Objective: Relate fraction of a set to the repeated addition interpretation of fraction multiplication.

Suggested Lesson Structure

■ Fluency Practice   (12 minutes)
■ Application Problem   (8 minutes)
■ Concept Development   (30 minutes)
■ Student Debrief   (10 minutes)

Total Time   **(60 minutes)**

Fluency Practice (12 minutes)

- Convert Measures **4.MD.1**   (5 minutes)
- Fractions as Whole Numbers **5.NF.3**   (3 minutes)
- Multiply a Fraction Times a Whole Number **5.NF.4**   (4 minutes)

Convert Measures (5 minutes)

Materials: (S) Personal white boards, Grade 5 Mathematics Reference Sheet

Note: This fluency prepares students for G5–M4–Lessons 9–12 content. Allow students to use the Grade 5 Mathematics Reference Sheet if they are confused, but encourage them to answer questions without looking at it.

T: (Write 1 ft = _____ in.) How many inches are in 1 foot?
S: 12 inches.
T: (Write 1 ft = 12 in. Below it, write 2 ft = _____ in.) 2 feet?
S: 24 inches.
T: (Write 2 ft = 12 in. Below it, write 3 ft = _____ in.) 3 feet?
S: 36 inches.
T: (Write 3 ft = 36 in. Below it, write 4 ft = _____ in.) 4 feet?
S: 48 inches.
T: (Write 4 ft = 48 in. Below it, write 10 ft = _____ in.) On your boards, write the equation.
S: (Write 10 ft = 120 in.)
T: (Write 10 ft × _____ = _____ in.) Write the multiplication equation you used to solve it.
S: (Write 10 ft × 12 = 120 in.)

Lesson 8:	Relate fraction of a set to the repeated addition interpretation of fraction multiplication.
Date:	11/10/13

4.C.29

Continue with the following possible sequence: 1 pint = 2 cups, 2 pints = 4 cups, 3 pints = 6 cups, 9 pints = 18 cups, 1 yd = 3 ft, 2 yd = 6 ft, 3 yd = 9 ft, 7 yd = 21 ft, 1 gal = 4 qt, 2 gal = 8 qt, 3 gal = 12 qt, and 8 gal = 32 qt.

Fractions as Whole Numbers (3 minutes)

Materials: (S) Personal white boards

Note: This fluency reviews G5–M4–Lesson 5 and reviews denominators that are equivalent to hundredths. Direct students to use their personal boards for calculations that they cannot do mentally.

T: I'll say a fraction. You say it as a division problem. 4 halves.

S: $4 \div 2 = 2$.

Continue with the following possible suggestions:

 $\frac{6}{2}, \frac{12}{2}, \frac{52}{2}, \frac{40}{20}, \frac{60}{20}, \frac{120}{20}, \frac{740}{20}, \frac{10}{5}, \frac{15}{5}, \frac{45}{5}, \frac{75}{5}, \frac{100}{50}, \frac{150}{50}, \frac{400}{50}, \frac{700}{50}, \frac{8}{4}, \frac{12}{4}, \frac{20}{4}, \frac{72}{4}, \frac{50}{25}, \frac{75}{25}$, and $\frac{400}{25}$.

Multiply a Fraction Times a Whole Number (4 minutes)

Materials: (S) Personal white boards

Note: This fluency reviews G5–M4–Lesson 7 content.

T: (Project a tape diagram of 12 partitioned into 3 equal units. Shade in 1 unit.) What fraction of 12 is shaded?

S: 1 third.

T: Read the tape diagram as a division equation.

S: $12 \div 3 = 4$.

T: (Write $12 \times \underline{\hphantom{xxx}} = 4$.) On your boards, write the equation, filling in the missing fraction.

S: (Write $12 \times \frac{1}{3} = 4$.)

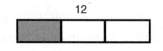

$$\frac{12}{3} = 4$$

$$12 \times \frac{1}{3} = 4$$

Continue with the following possible suggestions: $28 \times \frac{1}{7}$, $\frac{1}{4} \times 24$, $\frac{3}{4} \times 24$, $\frac{1}{8} \times 56$, and $\frac{3}{8} \times 56$.

Application Problem (8 minutes)

Sasha organizes the art gallery in her town's community center. This month she has 24 new pieces to add to the gallery.

Of the new pieces, $\frac{1}{6}$ of them are photographs and $\frac{2}{3}$ of them are paintings. How many more paintings are there than photos?

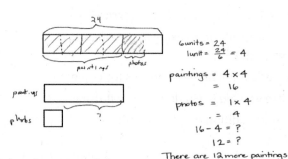

Note: This Application Problem requires students to find two fractions of the same set—a recall of the concepts from G5–M4–Lessons 6–7 in preparation for today's lesson.

Lesson 8:   Relate fraction of a set to the repeated addition interpretation of fraction multiplication.

Date: 11/10/13

4.C.30

Concept Development (30 minutes)

Materials: (S) Personal white boards

Problem 1

$\frac{2}{3} \times 6 =$ _____

T: (Write 2 × 6 on the board.) Read this expression out loud.

S: 2 times 6.

T: In what different ways can we interpret the meaning of this expression? Discuss with your partner.

S: We can think of it as 6 times as much as 2. → 6 + 6. → We could think of 6 copies of 2. → 2 + 2 + 2 + 2 + 2 + 2.

T: True, we can find 2 copies of 6, but we could also think about 2 added 6 times. What is the property that allows us to multiply the factors in any order?

S: Commutative property.

T: (Write $\frac{2}{3} \times 6$ on the board.) How can we interpret this expression? Turn and talk.

S: 2 thirds of 6. → 6 copies of 2 thirds. → 2 thirds added together 6 times.

T: This expression can be interpreted in different ways, just as the whole number expression. We can say it's $\frac{2}{3}$ of 6 or 6 groups of $\frac{2}{3}$. (Write $\frac{2}{3} \times 6$ and $6 \times \frac{2}{3}$ on the board as shown below.)

T: Use a tape diagram to find 2 thirds of 6. (Point to $\frac{2}{3} \times 6$.)

S: (Solve.)

$$\frac{2}{3} \times 6 = \frac{2}{3} \text{ of } 6 \qquad\qquad 6 \times \frac{2}{3}$$

T: Let me record our thinking. We see in the diagram that 3 units is 6. (Write 3 units = 6.) We divide 6 by 3 find 1 unit. (Write $\frac{6}{3}$.) So, 2 units is 2 times 6 divided by 3. (Write $2 \times \frac{6}{3}$ and the rest of the thinking in the table as shown above.)

T: Now, let's think of it as 6 groups (or copies) of $\frac{2}{3}$ like you did in Grade 4. Solve it using repeated addition on your board.

S: (Solve.)

T: (Write $\frac{2}{3} + \frac{2}{3} + \frac{2}{3} + \frac{2}{3} + \frac{2}{3} + \frac{2}{3}$ on the board.)

T: What multiplication expression gave us 12?

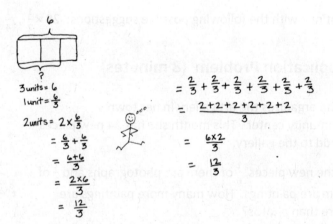

Lesson 8:	Relate fraction of a set to the repeated addition interpretation of fraction multiplication.
Date:	11/10/13

4.C.31

S: 6×2.

T: (Write on board.) What unit are we counting?

S: Thirds.

T: Let me write what I hear you saying. (Write (6×2) thirds on the board.) Now let me write it another way. (Write $= \frac{6 \times 2}{3}$.) 6 times 2 thirds.

NOTES ON MULTIPLE MEANS OF REPRESENTATION:

If students have difficulty remembering that dividing by a common factor allows a fraction to be renamed, consider a return to the Grade 4 notation for finding equivalent fractions as follows:

$$\frac{2}{3} \times 9 = \frac{2 \times 9}{3} = \frac{2 \times 3 \times 3}{3}$$

The decomposition in the numerator makes the common factor of 3 apparent. Students may also be reminded that multiplying by $\frac{3}{3}$ is the same as multiplying by 1.

T: In both ways of thinking what is the product? Why is it the same?

S: It's 12 thirds because 2×6 thirds is the same as 6×2 thirds. → It's the commutative property again. It doesn't matter what order we multiply, it's the same product.

T: How many wholes is 12 thirds? How much is 12 divided by 3?

S: 4.

T: Let's use something else we learned in Grade 4 to rename this fraction using larger units before we multiply. (Point to $\frac{2 \times 6}{3}$.) Look for a factor that is shared by the numerator and the denominator. Turn and talk.

S: Two and 3 only have a common factor of 1, but 3 and 6 have a common factor of 3. → I know the numerator of 6 can be divided by 3 to get 2, and the denominator of 3 can be divided by 3 to get 1.

T: We can rename this fraction just like in Grade 4 by dividing both the numerator and the denominator by 3. Watch me. 6 divided by 3 is 2. (Cross out 6, write 2 above 6.) 3 divided by 3 is 1. (Cross out 3, write 1 below 3.)

T: What does the numerator show now?

S: 2×2.

T: What's the denominator?

S: 1.

T: (Write $\frac{2 \times 2}{1} = \frac{4}{1}$.) This fraction was 12 thirds, now it is 4 wholes. Did we change the amount of the fraction by naming it using larger units? How do you know?

S: It is the same amount. Thirds are smaller than wholes, so it takes 12 thirds to show the same amount as 4 wholes. → It is the same. The unit got larger, so the number we needed to show the amount got smaller. → There are 3 thirds in 1 whole so 12 thirds makes 4 wholes. It is the same. → When we divide the numerator and the denominator by the same the number, it's like dividing by 1 and dividing by 1 doesn't change the value of the number.

COMMON CORE™   **Lesson 8:**   Relate fraction of a set to the repeated addition interpretation of fraction multiplication.   **4.C.32**

                Date: 11/10/13

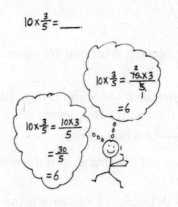

$$10 \times \frac{3}{5} = \underline{\quad}$$

Problem 2

$$\frac{3}{5} \times 10 = \underline{\quad}$$

T: Finding $\frac{3}{5}$ of 10 is the same as finding the product of 10 copies of $\frac{3}{5}$. I can rewrite this expression in unit form as (10 × 3) fifths or as a fraction. (Write $\frac{10 \times 3}{5}$.) 10 times 3 fifths. Multiply in your head and say the product.

S: 30 fifths.

T: $\frac{30}{5}$ is equivalent to how many wholes?

S: 6 wholes.

T: So, if $10 \times \frac{3}{5}$ is equal to 6, is it also true that 3 fifths of 10 is 6? How do you know?

S: Yes, it is true. 1 fifth of 10 is 2, so 3 fifths would be 6. → The commutative property says we can multiply in any order. This is true of fractional numbers too, so the product would be the same. → 3 fifths is a little more than half, so 3 fifths of 10 should be a little more than 5. 6 is a little more than 5.

T: Now, let's work this problem again, but this time let's find a common factor and rename before we multiply. (Follow the sequence from Problem 1.)

S: (Work.)

T: Did dividing the numerator and the denominator by the same common factor change the quantity? Why or why not?

S: (Share.)

NOTES ON MULTIPLE MEANS OF ACTION AND EXPRESSION:

While the focus of today's lesson is the transition to a more abstract understanding of fraction of a set, do not be too quick to drop pictorial representations. Tape diagrams are powerful tools in helping students make connections to the abstract. Throughout the lesson, continue to ask, "Can you draw something?" These drawings also provide formative assessment opportunities for teachers, and allow a glimpse into the thinking of

Problem 3

$$\frac{7}{6} \times 24 = \underline{\quad}$$

$$\frac{7}{6} \times 27 = \underline{\quad}$$

T: Before we solve, what do you notice that is different this time?

S: The fraction of the set that we are finding is more than a whole this time. All the others were fractions less than 1.

T: Let's estimate the size of our product. Turn and talk.

S: This is like the one from the Problem Set yesterday. We need more than a whole set, so the answer will be more than 24. → We need 1 sixth more than a whole set of 24, so the answer will be a little more than 24.

Lesson 8: Relate fraction of a set to the repeated addition interpretation of fraction multiplication.

Date: 11/10/13

4.C.33

T: (Write $\frac{24 \times 7}{6}$ on the board.) 24 times 7 sixths. Can you multiply 24 times 7 in your head?

S: You could, but it's a lot to think about to do it mentally.

T: Because this one is harder to calculate mentally, let's use the renaming strategies we've seen to solve this problem. Turn and share how we can get started.

S: We can divide the numerator and denominator by the same common factor.

Continue with the sequence from Problem 2 having students name the common factor and rename as shown above. Then proceed to $\frac{7}{6} \times 27 =$ _____.

T: Compare this problem to the last one.

S: The whole is a little more than last time. → The fraction we are looking for is the same, but the whole is bigger. → We probably need to rename this one before we multiply like the last one because 7 × 27 is harder to do mentally.

T: Let's rename first. Name a factor that 27 and 6 share.

S: 3.

T: Let's divide the numerator and denominator by this common factor. 27 divided by 3 is 9. (Cross out 27, and write 9 above 27.) 6 divided by 3 is 2. (Cross out 6, and write 2 below 6.) We've renamed this fraction. What's the new name?

S: $\frac{9 \times 7}{2}$. (9 times 7 divided by 2.)

T: Has this made it easier for us to solve this mentally? Why?

S: Yes, the numbers are easier to multiply now. → The numerator is a basic fact now and I know 9 × 7!

T: Have we changed the amount that is represented by this fraction? Turn and talk.

S: No, it's the same amount. We just renamed it using a bigger unit. → We renamed it just like any other fraction by looking for a common factor. This doesn't change the amount.

T: Say the product as a fraction greater than one.

S: 63 halves. (Write $= \frac{63}{2}$.)

T: We could express $\frac{63}{2}$ as a mixed number, but we don't have to.

T: (Point to $\frac{27 \times 7}{6}$.) To compare, let's multiply without renaming and see if we get the same product.

T: What's the fraction?

S: $\frac{189}{6}$.

T: (Write $= \frac{189}{6}$.) Rewrite that as a fraction greater than 1, using the largest units that you can. What do you notice?

Lesson 8:   Relate fraction of a set to the repeated addition interpretation of
             fraction multiplication.

Date: 11/10/13

4.C.34

© 2013 Common Core, Inc. All rights reserved. commoncore.org

S: (Work to find $\frac{63}{2}$.) We get the same answer, but it was harder to get to it. → 189 is a large number, so it's harder for me to find the common factor with 6. → I can't do it in my head. I needed to use paper and pencil to simplify.

T: So, sometimes, it makes our work easier and more efficient to rename with larger units, or simplify, first and then multiply.

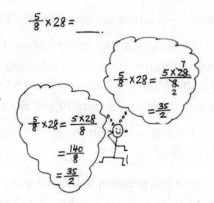

Repeat this sequence with $\frac{5}{8} \times 28 =$ ____.

Problem 4

$\frac{2}{3}$ hour = ____ minutes

T: We are looking for part of an hour. Which part?

S: 2 thirds of an hour.

T: Will 2 thirds of an hour be more than 60 minutes or less? Why?

S: It should be less because it isn't a whole hour. → A whole hour, 60 minutes, would be 3 thirds, we only want 2 thirds so it should be less than 60 minutes.

T: Turn and talk with your partner about how you might find 2 thirds of an hour.

S: I know the whole is 60 minutes, and the fraction I want is $\frac{2}{3}$. → We have to find what's $\frac{2}{3}$ of 60.

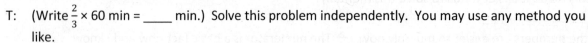

T: (Write $\frac{2}{3} \times 60$ min = ____ min.) Solve this problem independently. You may use any method you like.

S: (Solve.)

T: (Select students to share their solutions with the class.)

Repeat this sequence with $\frac{3}{4}$ of a foot.

Problem Set (10 minutes)

Students should do their personal best to complete the Problem Set within the allotted 10 minutes. For some classes, it may be appropriate to modify the assignment by specifying which problems they work on first. Some problems do not specify a method for solving. Students solve these problems using the RDW approach used for Application Problems.

Today's Problem Set is lengthy. Students may benefit from additional guidance. Consider working one problem from each section as a class before directing students to solve the remainder of the problems independently.

Lesson 8:   Relate fraction of a set to the repeated addition interpretation of
fraction multiplication.
Date: 11/10/13

4.C.35

Student Debrief (10 minutes)

Lesson Objective: Relate fraction of a set to the repeated addition interpretation of fraction multiplication.

The Student Debrief is intended to invite reflection and active processing of the total lesson experience.

Invite students to review their solutions for the Problem Set. They should check work by comparing answers with a partner before going over answers as a class. Look for misconceptions or misunderstandings that can be addressed in the Debrief. Guide students in a conversation to debrief the Problem Set and process the lesson.

You may choose to use any combination of the questions below to lead the discussion.

- Share and explain your solution for Problem 1 with a partner.

- What do you notice about Problems 2(a) and 2(c)? (Problem 2(a) is 3 groups of $\frac{7}{4}$, which is equal to $3 \times \frac{7}{4} = \frac{21}{4}$, and 2(c) is 3 groups of $\frac{4}{7}$, which is equal to $3 \times \frac{4}{7} = \frac{12}{7}$.)

- What do you notice about the solutions in Problems 3 and 4? (All the products are whole numbers.)

- We learned to solve fraction of a set problems using the repeated addition strategy and multiplication and simplifying strategies today. Which one do you think is the most efficient way to solve a problem? Does it depend on the problems?

- Why is it important to learn more than one strategy to solve a problem?

Exit Ticket (3 minutes)

After the Student Debrief, instruct students to complete the Exit Ticket. A review of their work will help you assess the students' understanding of the concepts that were presented in the lesson today and plan more effectively for future lessons. You may read the questions aloud to the students.

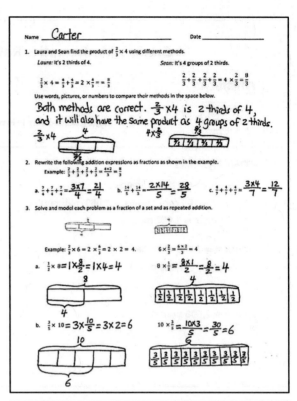

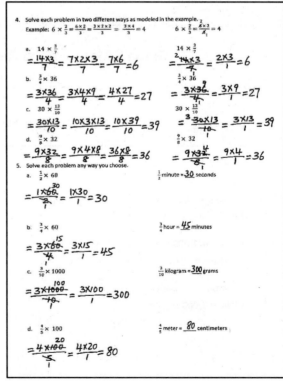

Lesson 8: Relate fraction of a set to the repeated addition interpretation of fraction multiplication.

Date: 11/10/13

4.C.36

Grade 5 Mathematics Reference Sheet

FORMULAS

Right Rectangular Prism

Volume = lwh
Volume = Bh

CONVERSIONS

1 centimeter = 10 millimeters
1 meter = 100 centimeters = 1,000 millimeters
1 kilometer = 1,000 meters

1 gram = 1,000 milligrams
1 kilogram = 1,000 grams

1 pound = 16 ounces
1 ton = 2,000 pounds

1 cup = 8 fluid ounces
1 pint = 2 cups
1 quart = 2 pints
1 gallon = 4 quarts

1 liter = 1,000 milliliters
1 kiloliter = 1,000 liters

1 mile = 5,280 feet
1 mile = 1,760 yards

Grade 5 Mathematics Reference Sheet

FORMULAS

Right Rectangular Prism

Volume = lwh
Volume = Bh

CONVERSIONS

1 centimeter = 10 millimeters
1 meter = 100 centimeters = 1,000 millimeters
1 kilometer = 1,000 meters

1 gram = 1,000 milligrams
1 kilogram = 1,000 grams

1 pound = 16 ounces
1 ton = 2,000 pounds

1 cup = 8 fluid ounces
1 pint = 2 cups
1 quart = 2 pints
1 gallon = 4 quarts

1 liter = 1,000 milliliters
1 kiloliter = 1,000 liters

1 mile = 5,280 feet
1 mile = 1,760 yards

COMMON CORE™

Lesson 8: Relate fraction of a set to the repeated addition interpretation of fraction multiplication.
Date: 11/10/13

4.C.37

Name _____   Date _____

1. Laura and Sean find the product of $\frac{2}{3} \times 4$ using different methods.

    Laura: It's 2 thirds of 4.   *Sean:* It's 4 groups of 2 thirds.

    $\frac{2}{3} \times 4 = \frac{4}{3} + \frac{4}{3} = 2 \times \frac{4}{3} = = \frac{8}{3}$ $\frac{2}{3} + \frac{2}{3} + \frac{2}{3} + \frac{2}{3} = 4 \times \frac{2}{3} = \frac{8}{3}$

    Use words, pictures, or numbers to compare their methods in the space below.

2. Rewrite the following addition expressions as fractions as shown in the example.

    Example: $\frac{2}{3} + \frac{2}{3} + \frac{2}{3} + \frac{2}{3} = \frac{4 \times 2}{3} = \frac{8}{3}$

    a. $\frac{7}{4} + \frac{7}{4} + \frac{7}{4} =$ b. $\frac{14}{5} + \frac{14}{5} =$ c. $\frac{4}{7} + \frac{4}{7} + \frac{4}{7} =$

3. Solve and model each problem as a fraction of a set and as repeated addition.

    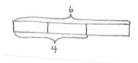

    Example: $\frac{2}{3} \times 6 = 2 \times \frac{6}{3} = 2 \times 2 = 4.$ $6 \times \frac{2}{3} = \frac{6 \times 2}{3} = 4$

    a. $\frac{1}{2} \times 8$ $8 \times \frac{1}{2}$

    b. $\frac{3}{5} \times 10$ $10 \times \frac{3}{5}$

COMMON CORE™   Lesson 8:   Relate fraction of a set to the repeated addition interpretation of
                          fraction multiplication.   **4.C.38**
                 Date: 11/10/13

© 2013 Common Core, Inc. All rights reserved. **commoncore.org**

4. Solve each problem in two different ways as modeled in the example.

   Example: $6 \times \frac{2}{3} = \frac{6 \times 2}{3} = \frac{3 \times 2 \times 2}{3} = \frac{3 \times 4}{3} = 4$ $6 \times \frac{2}{3} = \frac{\overset{2}{\cancel{6} \times 2}}{\underset{1}{\cancel{3}}} = 4$

   a. $14 \times \frac{3}{7}$ $14 \times \frac{3}{7}$

   b. $\frac{3}{4} \times 36$ $\frac{3}{4} \times 36$

   c. $30 \times \frac{13}{10}$ $30 \times \frac{13}{10}$

   d. $\frac{9}{8} \times 32$ $\frac{9}{8} \times 32$

5. Solve each problem any way you choose.

   a. $\frac{1}{2} \times 60$ $\frac{1}{2}$ minute = _____ seconds

   b. $\frac{3}{4} \times 60$ $\frac{3}{4}$ hour = _____ minutes

   c. $\frac{3}{10} \times 1000$ $\frac{3}{10}$ kilogram = _____ grams

   d. $\frac{4}{5} \times 100$ $\frac{4}{5}$ meter = _____ centimeters

COMMON CORE™ | Lesson 8: Relate fraction of a set to the repeated addition interpretation of fraction multiplication.
Date: 11/10/13

4.C.39

Name _____   Date _____

1. Solve each problem in two different ways as modeled in the example.

a.   Example: $\frac{2}{3} \times 6 = \frac{2 \times 6}{3} = \frac{12}{3} = 4$ b. $\frac{2}{3} \times 6 = \frac{2 \times \cancel{6}^{2}}{\cancel{3}_{1}} = 4$

a. $\frac{2}{3} \times 15$ $\frac{2}{3} \times 15$

b. $\frac{5}{4} \times 12$ $\frac{5}{4} \times 12$

COMMON CORE™ | Lesson 8: | Relate fraction of a set to the repeated addition interpretation of
fraction multiplication.

Date: 11/10/13

4.C.40

Name _____   Date _____

1. Rewrite the following expressions as shown in the example.

   Example: $\frac{2}{3} + \frac{2}{3} + \frac{2}{3} + \frac{2}{3} = \frac{4 \times 2}{3} = \frac{8}{3}$

   a. $\frac{5}{3} + \frac{5}{3} + \frac{5}{3}$
   b. $\frac{13}{5} + \frac{13}{5}$
   c. $\frac{9}{4} + \frac{9}{4} + \frac{9}{4}$

2. Solve each problem in two different ways as modeled in the example.

   Example: $\frac{2}{3} \times 6 = \frac{2 \times 6}{3} = \frac{12}{3} = 4$ b. $\frac{2}{3} \times 6 = \frac{2 \times \cancel{6}^{2}}{\cancel{3}_{1}} = 4$

   a. $\frac{3}{4} \times 16$ $\frac{3}{4} \times 16$

   b. $\frac{4}{3} \times 12$ $\frac{4}{3} \times 12$

   c. $40 \times \frac{11}{10}$ $40 \times \frac{11}{10}$

   d. $\frac{7}{6} \times 36$ $\frac{7}{6} \times 36$

   e. $24 \times \frac{5}{8}$ $24 \times \frac{5}{8}$

COMMON CORE™

Lesson 8:   Relate fraction of a set to the repeated addition interpretation of fraction multiplication.

Date: 11/10/13

4.C.41

f. $18 \times \frac{5}{12}$

$18 \times \frac{5}{12}$

g. $\frac{10}{9} \times 21$

$\frac{10}{9} \times 21$

3. Solve each problem any way you choose.

a. $\frac{1}{3} \times 60$

$\frac{1}{3}$ minute = _____ seconds

b. $\frac{4}{5} \times 60$

$\frac{4}{5}$ hour = _____ minutes

c. $\frac{7}{10} \times 1000$

$\frac{7}{10}$ kilogram = _____ grams

d. $\frac{3}{5} \times 100$

$\frac{3}{5}$ meter = _____ centimeters

COMMON CORE™ | Lesson 8: Relate fraction of a set to the repeated addition interpretation of fraction multiplication.
Date: 11/10/13

4.C.42

Lesson 9

Objective: Find a fraction of a measurement, and solve word problems.

Suggested Lesson Structure

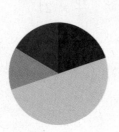

■ Fluency Practice   (12 minutes)
■ Application Problem   (8 minutes)
▢ Concept Development (30 minutes)
■ Student Debrief   (10 minutes)
  Total Time   **(60 minutes)**

Fluency Practice (12 minutes)

▪ Multiply Whole Numbers by Fractions with Tape Diagrams **5.NF.4**   (4 minutes)
▪ Convert Measures **4.MD.1**   (4 minutes)
▪ Multiply a Fraction and a Whole Number **5.NF.4**   (4 minutes)

Multiply Whole Numbers by Fractions with Tape Diagrams (4 minutes)

Materials: (S) Personal white boards

Note: This fluency reviews G5–M4–Lesson 7 content.

  T: (Project a tape diagram of 8 partitioned into 2 equal units. Shade in 1 unit.) What fraction of 8 is shaded?

  S: 1 half.

  T: Read the tape diagram as a division equation.

  S: $8 \div 2 = 4$.

  T: (Write $8 \times \underline{} = 4$.) On your boards, write the equation, filling in the missing fraction.

  S: (Write $8 \times \frac{1}{2} = 4$.)

Continue with the following possible suggestions: $35 \times \frac{1}{7}, \frac{1}{4} \times 16, \frac{3}{4} \times 16, \frac{1}{8} \times 48,$ and $\frac{5}{8} \times 48$.

Convert Measures (4 minutes)

Materials: (S) Personal white boards, Grade 5 Mathematics Reference Sheet (G5–M4–Lesson 8)

Note: This fluency prepares students for G5–M4–Lessons 9–12. Allow students to use the conversion reference sheet if they are confused, but encourage them to answer questions without looking at it.

COMMON CORE | Lesson 9:   Find a fraction of a measurement, and solve word problems.
                | Date: 11/9/13

T: (Write 1 pt = __ c.) How many cups are in one pint?

S: 2 cups.

T: (Write 1 pt = 2 c. Below it, write 2 pt = __ c.) 2 pints?

S: 4 cups.

T: (Write 2 pt = 4 c. Below it, write 3 pt = __ c.) 3 pints?

S: 6 cups.

T: (Write 3 pt = 6 c. Below it, write 7 pt = __ c.) On your boards, write the equation.

S: (Write 7 pt = 14 c.)

T: Write the multiplication equation you used to solve it.

S: (Write 7 pt × 2 = 14 c.)

Continue with the following possible sequence: 1 ft = 12 in, 2 ft = 24 in, 4 ft = 48 in, 1 yd = 3 ft, 2 yd = 6 ft, 3 yd = 9 ft, 9 yd = 27 ft, 1 gal = 4 qt, 2 gal = 8 qt, 3 gal = 12 qt, and 6 gal = 24 qt.

Multiply a Fraction and a Whole Number (4 minutes)

Materials: (S) Personal white boards

Note: This fluency reviews G5–M4–Lesson 8 content.

T: (Write $\frac{1}{2} \times 4 = $ ____.) On your boards, write the equation as a repeated addition sentence and solve.

S: (Write $\frac{1}{2} + \frac{1}{2} + \frac{1}{2} + \frac{1}{2} = \frac{4}{2} = 2$.)

T: (Write $\frac{1}{2} \times 4 = \frac{\underline{\quad} \times \underline{\quad}}{2}$.) On your boards, fill in the multiplication expression for the numerator.

S: (Write $\frac{1}{2} \times 4 = \frac{1 \times 4}{2}$.)

T: (Write $\frac{1}{2} \times 4 = \frac{1 \times 4}{2} = \frac{\quad}{\quad} = $ ____.) Fill in the missing numbers.

S: (Write $\frac{1}{2} \times 4 = \frac{1 \times 4}{2} = \frac{4}{2} = 2$.)

T: (Write $\frac{1}{2} \times 4 = \frac{1 \times 4}{2} = $ ____.) Find a common factor to simplify, then multiply.

S: (Write $\frac{1}{2} \times 4 = \frac{1 \times \overset{2}{\cancel{4}}}{\underset{1}{\cancel{2}}} = \frac{2}{1} = 2$.)

Continue with the following possible suggestions: $6 \times \frac{1}{3}$, $6 \times \frac{2}{3}$, $\frac{3}{4} \times 8$, and $9 \times \frac{2}{3}$.

Application Problem (8 minutes)

There are 42 people at a museum. Two-thirds of them are children. How many children are at the museum?

Extension: If 13 of the children are girls, how many more boys than girls are at the museum?

Note: Today's Application Problem is a multi-step problem. Students must find a fraction of a set and then use that information to answer the question. The numbers are large enough to encourage simplifying strategies as taught in G5–M4–Lesson 8 without being overly burdensome for students who prefer to multiply and then simplify or still prefer to draw their solution using a tape diagram.

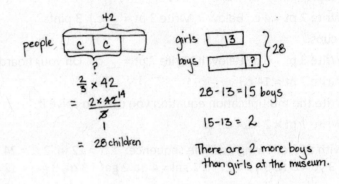

Concept Development (30 minutes)

Materials: (T) Grade 5 Mathematics Reference Sheet (posted) (S) Personal white board, Grade 5 Mathematics Reference Sheet (G5–M4–Lesson 8)

Problem 1

$\frac{1}{4}$ lb = _____ oz

T:　(Post Problem 1 on the board.) Which is a larger unit, pounds or ounces?

S:　Pounds.

T:　So, we are expressing a fraction of a larger unit as the smaller unit. We want to find $\frac{1}{4}$ of 1 pound. (Write $\frac{1}{4}$ × 1 lb.) We know that 1 pound is the same as how many ounces?

S:　16 ounces.

T:　Let's rename the pound in our expression as ounces. Write it on your personal board.

S:　(Write $\frac{1}{4}$ × 16 ounces.)

T:　(Write $\frac{1}{4}$ × 1 lb = $\frac{1}{4}$ × 16 ounces.) How do you know this is true?

S:　It's true because we just renamed the pound as the same amount in ounces. → One pound is the same amount as 16 ounces.

T:　How will we find how many ounces are in a fourth of a pound? Turn and talk.

S: We can find $\frac{1}{4}$ of 16. → We can multiply $\frac{1}{4} \times 16$. → It's a fraction of a set. We'll just multiply 16 by a fourth. → We can draw a tape diagram and find one-fourth of 16.

T: Choose one with your partner and solve.

S: (Work.)

T: How many ounces are equal to one-fourth of a pound?

S: 4 ounces. (Write $\frac{1}{4}$ lb = 4 oz.)

T: So, each fourth of a pound in our tape diagram is equal to 4 ounces. How many ounces in two-fourths of a pound?

S: 8 ounces.

T: Three-fourths of a pound?

S: 12 ounces.

Problem 2

$\frac{3}{4}$ ft = _____ in

T: Compare this problem to the first one. Turn and talk.

S: We're still renaming a fraction of a larger unit as a smaller unit. → This time we're changing feet to inches, so we need to think about 12 instead of 16. → We were only finding 1 unit last time; this time we have to find 3 units.

T: (Write $\frac{3}{4} \times 1$ foot.) We know that 1 foot is the same as how many inches?

S: 12 inches.

T: Let's rename the foot in our expression as inches. Write it on your white board.

S: (Write $\frac{3}{4} \times 12$ inches.)

T: (Write $\frac{3}{4} \times 1$ ft $= \frac{3}{4} \times 12$ inches.) Is this true? How do you know?

S: This is just like last time. We didn't change the amount that we have in the expression. We just renamed the 1 foot using 12 inches. → Twelve inches and one foot are exactly the same length.

T: Before we solve this, let's estimate our answer. We are finding part of 1 foot. Will our answer be more than 6 inches or less than 6 inches? How do you know? Turn and talk.

S: Six inches is half a foot. We are looking for 3 fourths of a foot. Three-fourths is greater than one-half so our answer will be more than 6. → It will be more than 6 inches. Six is only half and 3 fourths is almost a whole foot.

Lesson 9:   Find a fraction of a measurement, and solve word problems.
Date: 11/9/13

4.C.46

T: Work with a neighbor to solve this problem. One of you can use multiplication to solve and the other can use a tape diagram to solve. Check your neighbor's work when you're finished.

S: (Work and share.)

T: Reread the problem and fill in the blank.

S: $\frac{3}{4}$ feet = 9 inches.

T: How can 3 fourths be equal to 9? Turn and talk.

S: Because the units are different, the numbers will be different, but show the same amount. → Feet are larger than inches, so it takes more inches than feet to show the same amount. → If you measured 3 fourths of a foot with a ruler and then measured 9 inches with a ruler, they would be exactly the same length. → If you measure the same length using feet and then using inches, you will always have more inches than feet because inches are smaller.

Problem 3

Mr. Corsetti spends $\frac{2}{3}$ of every year in Florida. How many months does he spend in Florida each year?

T: Work independently. You may use either a tape diagram or a multiplication sentence to solve.

T: Use your work to answer the question.

S: Mr. Corsetti spends 8 months in Florida each year.

Repeat this sequence with $\frac{2}{3}$ yard = _____ft and $\frac{2}{5}$ hour = _____minutes.

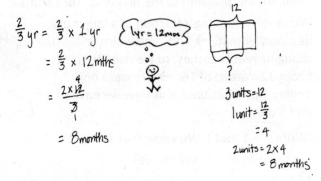

Problem Set (10 minutes)

Students should do their personal best to complete the Problem Set within the allotted 10 minutes. For some classes, it may be appropriate to modify the assignment by specifying which problems they work on first. Some problems do not specify a method for solving. Students solve these problems using the RDW approach used for Application Problems.

Student Debrief (10 minutes)

Lesson Objective: Find a fraction of a measurement, and solve word problems.

The Student Debrief is intended to invite reflection and active processing of the total lesson experience.

Invite students to review their solutions for the Problem Set. They should check work by comparing answers with a partner before going over answers as a class. Look for misconceptions or misunderstandings that can be addressed in the Debrief. Guide students in a conversation to debrief the Problem Set and process the lesson.

Lesson 9:   Find a fraction of a measurement, and solve word problems.
Date: 11/9/13

> **NOTES ON MULTIPLE MEANS OF ENGAGEMENT:**
>
> Challenge students to make conversions between fractions of gallons to pints or cups, or fractions of a day to minutes or even seconds.

You may choose to use any combination of the questions below to lead the discussion.

- Share and explain your solution for Problem 3 with your partner.

- In Problem 3, could you tell, without calculating, whether Mr. Paul bought more cashews or walnuts? How did you know?

- How did you solve Problem 3(c)? Is there more than one way to solve this problem? (Yes, there is more than one way to solve this problem, i.e., finding $\frac{7}{8}$ of 16 and $\frac{3}{4}$ of 16, and then subtracting, versus subtracting $\frac{7}{8} - \frac{3}{4}$, and then finding the fraction of 16.) Share your strategy with a partner.

- How did you solve Problem 3(d)? Share and explain your strategy with a partner.

Exit Ticket (3 minutes)

After the Student Debrief, instruct students to complete the Exit Ticket. A review of their work will help you assess the students' understanding of the concepts that were presented in the lesson today and plan more effectively for future lessons. You may read the questions aloud to the students.

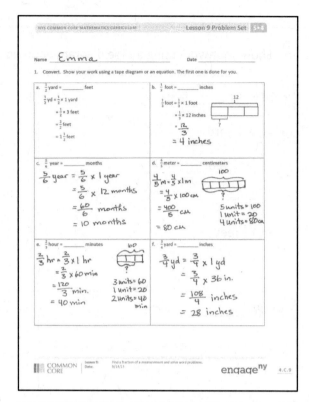

COMMON CORE™

Lesson 9:   Find a fraction of a measurement, and solve word problems.
Date: 11/9/13

4.C.48

Name _____   Date _____

1. Convert. Show your work using a tape diagram or an equation. The first one is done for you.

a. $\frac{1}{2}$ yard = _____ feet $\frac{1}{2}$ yd $= \frac{1}{2} \times 1$ yard $\quad = \frac{1}{2} \times 3$ feet $\quad = \frac{3}{2}$ feet $\quad = 1\frac{1}{2}$ feet	b. $\frac{1}{3}$ foot = _____ inches $\frac{1}{3}$ foot $= \frac{1}{3} \times 1$ foot $\quad = \frac{1}{3} \times 12$ inches $\quad =$ 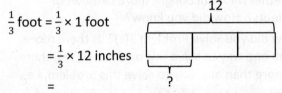
c. $\frac{5}{6}$ year = _____ months	d. $\frac{4}{5}$ meter = _____ centimeters
e. $\frac{2}{3}$ hour = _____ minutes	f. $\frac{3}{4}$ yard = _____ inches

2. Mrs. Lang told her class that the class's pet hamster is $\frac{1}{4}$ ft in length. How long is the hamster in inches?

3. At the market, Mr. Paul bought $\frac{7}{8}$ lb of cashews and $\frac{3}{4}$ lb of walnuts.
   a. How many ounces of cashews did Mr. Paul buy?

   b. How many ounces of walnuts did Mr. Paul buy?

   c. How many more ounces of cashews than walnuts did Mr. Paul buy?

   d. If Mrs. Toombs bought $1\frac{1}{2}$ pounds of pistachios, who bought more nuts, Mr. Paul or Mrs. Toombs? How many ounces more?

4. A jewelry maker purchased 20 inches of gold chain. She used $\frac{3}{8}$ of the chain for a bracelet. How many inches of gold chain did she have left?

COMMON
CORE™ | Lesson 9: | Find a fraction of a measurement, and solve word problems.
Date: | 11/9/13

4.C.50

© 2013 Common Core, Inc. All rights reserved. **commoncore.org**

Name _____ Date _____

1. Express 36 minutes as a fraction of an hour: 36 minutes = _____hour

2. Solve.

a. $\frac{2}{3}$ ft = _____inches   b. $\frac{2}{5}$ meter = _____ cm   c. $\frac{5}{6}$ year = _____ months

COMMON CORE™

Lesson 9:   Find a fraction of a measurement, and solve word problems.
Date: 11/9/13

4.C.51

4.C.52

Name _____ Date _____

1. Convert. Show your work using a tape diagram or an equation. The first one is done for you.

a. $\frac{1}{4}$ yard = _____ inches	b. $\frac{1}{6}$ foot = _____ inches
$\frac{1}{4}$ yd = $\frac{1}{4}$ × 1 yard $\quad = \frac{1}{4}$ × 36 inches $\quad = \frac{36}{4}$ inches $\quad = 9$ inches	$\frac{1}{6}$ foot = $\frac{1}{6}$ × 1 foot $\quad = \frac{1}{6}$ × 12 inches $\quad =$ 12 ?
c. $\frac{3}{4}$ year = _____ months	d. $\frac{3}{5}$ meter = _____ centimeters
e. $\frac{5}{12}$ hour = _____ minutes	f. $\frac{2}{3}$ yard = _____ inches

2. Michelle measured the length of her forearm. It was $\frac{3}{4}$ of a foot. How long is her forearm in inches?

COMMON CORE™ | Lesson 9: | Find a fraction of a measurement, and solve word problems.
Date: | 11/9/13

4.C.52

3. At the market, Ms. Winn bought $\frac{3}{4}$ lb of grapes and $\frac{5}{8}$ lb of cherries.

   a. How many ounces of grapes did Ms. Winn buy?

   b. How many ounces of cherries did Ms. Winn buy?

   c. How many more ounces of grapes than cherries did Ms. Winn buy?

   d. If Mr. Phillips bought $1\frac{3}{4}$ pounds of raspberries, who bought more fruit, Ms. Winn or Mr. Phillips? How many ounces more?

4. A gardener has 10 pounds of soil. He used $\frac{5}{8}$ of the soil for his garden. How many pounds of soil did he use in the garden? How many pounds did he have left?

Lesson 9: Find a fraction of a measurement, and solve word problems.
Date: 11/9/13

4.C.53

Topic D

Fraction Expressions and Word Problems

5.OA.1, 5.OA.2, 5.NF.4a, 5.NF.6

Focus Standard:	5.OA.1	Use parentheses, brackets, or braces in numerical expressions, and evaluate expressions with these symbols.
	5.OA.2	Write simple expressions that record calculations with numbers, and interpret numerical expressions without evaluating them. *For example, express the calculation "add 8 and 7, then multiply by 2" as 2 × (8 +7). Recognize that 3 × (18932 + 921) is three times as large as 18932 + 921, without having to calculate the indicated sum or product.*
	5.NF.4a	Apply and extend previous understandings of multiplication to multiply a fraction or whole number by a fraction.
		a. Interpret the product of *(a/b) × q* as *a* parts of a partition of *q* into *b* equal parts; equivalently, as the result of a sequence of operations *a × q ÷ b*. *For example, use a visual fraction model to show (2/3 × 4 = 8/3, and create a story context for this equation. Do the same with (2/3) × (4/5) = 8/15. (In general, (a/b) × (c/d) = ac/bd.)*
	5.NF.6	Solve real world problems involving multiplication of fractions and mixed numbers, e.g., by using visual fraction models or equations to represent the problem.
Instructional Days:	3	
Coherence -Links from:	G4–M2	Unit Conversions and Problem Solving with Metric Measurement
-Links to:	G6–M2	Arithmetic Operations Including Dividing by a Fraction

Interpreting numerical expressions opens Topic D as students learn to evaluate expressions with parentheses, such as 3 × (2/3 – 1/5) or 2/3 × (7 +9) (**5.OA.1**). They then learn to interpret numerical expressions such as *3 times the difference between 2/3 and 1/5* or *two thirds the sum of 7 and 9* (**5.OA.2**). Students generate word problems that lead to the same calculation (**5.NF.4a**), such as, "Kelly combined 7 ounces of carrot juice and 5 ounces of orange juice in a glass. Jack drank 2/3 of the mixture. How much did Jack drink?" Solving word problems (**5.NF.6**) allows students to apply new knowledge of fraction multiplication in context, and tape diagrams are used to model multi-step problems requiring the use of addition, subtraction, and multiplication of fractions.

A Teaching Sequence Towards Mastery of Fraction Expressions and Word Problems

Objective 1: Compare and evaluate expressions with parentheses.
(Lesson 10)

Objective 2: Solve and create fraction word problems involving addition, subtraction, and multiplication.
(Lessons 11–12)

Lesson 10

Objective: Compare and evaluate expressions with parentheses.

Suggested Lesson Structure

■ Fluency Practice   (12 minutes)
■ Application Problem   (5 minutes)
□ Concept Development   (33 minutes)
■ Student Debrief   (10 minutes)

   Total Time   **(60 minutes)**

Fluency Practice (12 minutes)

- Convert Measures from Small to Large Units **4.MD.1**   (5 minutes)
- Multiply a Fraction and a Whole Number **5.NF.4**   (3 minutes)
- Find the Unit Conversion **5.MD.2**   (4 minutes)

Convert Measures from Small to Large Units (5 minutes)

Materials: (S) Personal white boards, Grade 5 Mathematics Reference Sheet

Note: This fluency reviews G5–M4–Lesson 9 and prepares students for G5–M4–Lessons 10–12 content. Allow students to use the conversion reference sheet if they are confused, but encourage them to answer questions without looking at it.

   T: (Write 12 in = __ ft.) How many feet are in 12 inches?
   S: 1 foot.
   T: (Write 12 in = 1 ft. Below it, write 24 in = __ ft.) 24 inches?
   S: 2 feet.
   T: (Write 24 in = 2 ft. Below it, write 36 in = __ ft.) 36 inches?
   S: 3 feet.
   T: (Write 36 in = 3 ft. Below it, write 48 in = __ ft.) 48 inches?
   S: 4 feet.
   T: (Write 48 in = 4 ft. Below it, 120 in = __ ft.) On your boards, write the equation.
   S: (Write 120 in = 10 ft.)
   T: (Write 120 in ÷ __ = __ ft.) Write the division equation you used to solve it.
   S: (Write 120 in ÷ 12 = 10 ft.)

Continue with the following possible sequence: 2 c = 1 pt, 4 c = 2 pt, 6 c = 3 pt, 16 c = 8 pt, 3 ft = 1 yd,

COMMON CORE™	Lesson 10:	Compare and evaluate expressions with parentheses.	
	Date:	11/10/13	**4.D.3**

6 ft = 2 yd, 9 ft = 3 yd, 27 ft = 9 yd, 4 qt = 1 gal, 8 qt = 2 gal, 12 qt = 3 gal, and 24 qt = 6 gal.

Multiply a Fraction and a Whole Number (3 minutes)

Materials: (S) Personal white boards

Note: This fluency reviews G5–M4–Lesson 8.

T: ($\frac{1}{2} \times 6 = \frac{\underline{\quad} \times \underline{\quad}}{2}$.) On your boards, fill in the multiplication expression for the numerator.

S: (Write $\frac{1}{2} \times 6 = \frac{1 \times 6}{2}$.)

T: (Write $\frac{1}{2} \times 6 = \frac{1 \times 6}{2} = \underline{\quad} = \underline{\quad}$.) Fill in the missing numbers.

S: (Write $\frac{1}{2} \times 6 = \frac{1 \times 6}{2} = \frac{6}{2} = 3$.)

T: (Write $\frac{1}{2} \times 6 = \frac{1 \times 6}{2} = \underline{\quad}$.) Find a common factor to simplify. Then multiply.

S: (Write $\frac{1}{2} \times 6 = \frac{1 \times \overset{3}{\cancel{6}}}{\underset{1}{\cancel{2}}} = \frac{3}{1} = 3$.)

Continue with the following possible suggestions: $6 \times \frac{1}{3}$, $9 \times \frac{2}{3}$, $\frac{3}{4} \times 12$, and $12 \times \frac{5}{6}$.

Find the Unit Conversion (4 minutes)

Materials: (S) Personal white boards

Note: This fluency reviews G5–M4–Lesson 9.

T: 1 foot is equal to how many inches?

S: 12 inches.

T: (Write 1 ft = 12 inches to label the tape diagram.
Below it, write $\frac{2}{3}$ ft = $\frac{2}{3} \times 1$ ft.) Rewrite the
expression on the right of the equation on your
board substituting 12 inches for 1 foot.

S: (Write $\frac{2}{3} \times 12$ inches.)

T: How many inches in each third? Represent the
division using a fraction.

S: $\frac{12}{3}$.

T: How many inches in 2 thirds of a foot? Keep the division as a fraction.

S: (Write $\frac{12}{3} \times 2 = 8$ inches.)

T: Let's read it. 12 divided by 3 times 2.

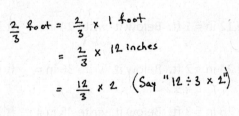

Lesson 10:   Compare and evaluate expressions with parentheses.
Date: 11/10/13

4.D.4

T: How many inches are equal to $\frac{2}{3}$ foot?

S: 8 inches.

Continue with the following possible sequence: $\frac{1}{4}$ lb = __ oz, $\frac{5}{6}$ yr = __ months, $\frac{7}{8}$ lb = __ oz, and $\frac{3}{4}$ hr = __ min.

Application Problem (5 minutes)

Bridget has \$240. She spent $\frac{3}{5}$ of her money and saved the rest. How much more money did she spend than save?

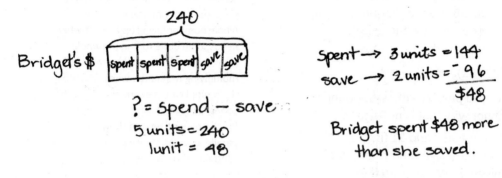

Note: This Application Problem provides a quick review of fraction of a set, which students have been working on in Topic C, and provides a bridge to the return to this work in G5–M4–Lesson 11. It is also a multi-step problem.

Concept Development (33 minutes)

Materials: (S) Personal white boards

Problem 1: Write an expression to match a tape diagram. Then evaluate.

a.

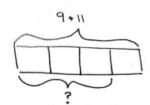

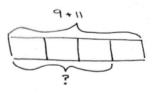

T: (Post the first tape diagram.) Read the expression that names the whole.

S: 9 + 11.

T: What do we call the answer to an addition sentence?

S: A sum.

T: So our whole is the sum of 9 and 11. (Write *the sum of 9 and 11* next to tape diagram.) How many units is the sum being divided into?

S: Four.

T: What is the name of that fractional unit?

S: Fourths.

T: How many fourths are we trying to find?

S: 3 fourths.

T: So, this tape diagram is showing 3 fourths of the sum of 9 and 11. (Write *3 fourths* next to *the sum of 9 and 11*.) Work with a partner to write a numerical expression to match these words.

S: $(9 + 11) \times \frac{3}{4}$. $\rightarrow \frac{3}{4} \times (9 + 11)$. $\rightarrow \frac{9 + 11}{4} \times 3$.

T: I noticed that many of you put parentheses around 9 + 11. Explain to a neighbor why that is necessary.

S: The parentheses tell us to add 9 and 11 first, and then multiply. $\rightarrow$ If the parentheses weren't there, we would have to multiply first. We want to find the sum first and then multiply. $\rightarrow$ We can find the sum of 9 and 11 first, and then divide the sum by 4.

T: Work with a partner to evaluate or simplify this expression.

S: (Work to find 15.)

NOTES ON MULTIPLE MEANS OF REPRESENTATION:

If students have difficulty understanding the value of a unit as a subtraction sentence, write a whole number on one side of a small piece of construction paper and the equivalent subtraction expression on the other. Place the paper on the model with the whole number facing up and ask what needs to be done to find the whole. (Most will understand the process of multiplying to find the whole.) Write the multiplication expression using the paper, whole number side up. Then flip the paper over and show the parallel expression using the subtraction sentence.

b.

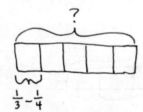

T: (Post the second tape diagram.) Look at this model. How is it different from the previous example?

S: This time we don't know the whole. $\rightarrow$ In this diagram, the whole is being divided into fifths, not fourths. $\rightarrow$ Here we know what 1 fifth is. We know it is the difference of $\frac{1}{3}$ and $\frac{1}{4}$ $\rightarrow$ We have to multiply the difference of $\frac{1}{3}$ and $\frac{1}{4}$ by 5 to find the whole.

T: Read the subtraction expression that tells the value of one unit (or 1 fifth) in the model. (Point to $\frac{1}{3} - \frac{1}{4}$.)

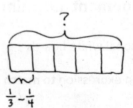

"5 times the difference of $\frac{1}{3}$ and $\frac{1}{4}$"

$$5 \times \left(\frac{1}{3} - \frac{1}{4} \right)$$
$$= 5 \times \left(\frac{4}{12} - \frac{3}{12} \right)$$
$$= 5 \times \frac{1}{12}$$
$$= \frac{5 \times 1}{12}$$
$$= \frac{5}{12}$$

S: One-third minus one-fourth.

T: What is the name for the answer to a subtraction problem?

S: A difference.

T: This unit is the difference of one-third and one-fourth. (Write *the difference of* $\frac{1}{3}$ *and* $\frac{1}{4}$ next to the tape diagram.) How many of these $\left(\frac{1}{3} - \frac{1}{4}\right)$ units does our model show?

S: 5 units of $\frac{1}{3} - \frac{1}{4}$.

T: Work with a partner to write a numerical expression to match these words.

S: $5 \times \left(\frac{1}{3} - \frac{1}{4}\right)$ or $\left(\frac{1}{3} - \frac{1}{4}\right) \times 5$.

T: Do we need parentheses for this expression?

S: Yes, we need to subtract first before multiplying.

T: Evaluate this expression independently. Then compare your work with a neighbor.

Problem 2: Write and evaluate an expression from word form.

T: (Write *the product of 4 and 2, divided by 3* on the board.) Read the expression.

S: The product of 4 and 2, divided by 3.

T: Work with a partner to write a matching numerical expression.

S: $(4 \times 2) \div 3$. $\rightarrow \frac{4 \times 2}{3}$. $\rightarrow 4 \times 2 \div 3$.

T: Were the parentheses necessary here? Why or why not?

S: No. Because the product came first and we can do multiplication and division left to right. We didn't need them. $\rightarrow$ I wrote it as a fraction. I didn't use parentheses because I knew before I could divide by 3. I needed to find the product in the numerator.

T: Work independently to evaluate your expression. Express your answer as both a fraction greater than one and as a mixed number. Check your work with a neighbor when you're finished.

S: (Work to find $\frac{8}{3}$ and $2\frac{2}{3}$. Then check.)

NOTES ON
MULTIPLE MEANS OF
REPRESENTATION:

It may be necessary to prompt students to use fraction notation for the division portion of the expression. Pointing out the format of the division sign—*dot over dot*—may serve as a good reminder. Reminding students of problems from the beginning of G5–Module 4 may also be helpful, (e.g.,

$2 \div 3 = \frac{2}{3}$).

Problem 3: Evaluate and compare equivalent expressions.

a. $2 \div 3 \times 4$

b. 4 thirds doubled

c. $2 \div (3 \times 4)$

d. $\frac{2}{3} \times 4$

e. 4 copies of the sum of one-third and one-third

f. $(2 \div 3) \times 4$

T: Evaluate these expressions with your partner. Keep working until I call time. Be prepared to share.

COMMON CORE™

Lesson 10: Compare and evaluate expressions with parentheses.
Date: 11/10/13

4.D.7

S: (Work.)

T: Share your work with someone else's partner. What do you notice?

S: The answer is 8 thirds every time except in (c). → All of the expressions are equivalent except (c). These are just different ways of expressing $\frac{8}{3}$.

T: What was different about (c)?

S: Since the expression had parentheses, we had to multiply first, then divide. It was equal to 2 twelfths. → It's tricky because all of the digits and operations are the same as all the others, but the order of them and the parentheses resulted in a different value.

T: Work with a partner to find another way to express $\frac{3}{5} \times 6$.

S: (Work. Possible expressions include: $3 \times (6 \div 5)$. → $3 \times 6 \div 5$. → $3 \times \frac{6}{5}$. → Six times the value of 3 divided by 5, etc.)

Invite students to share their expressions on the board and to discuss.

Problem 5: Compare expressions in word form and numerical form.

a. $\frac{1}{8}$ the sum of 6 and 14 ◯ $(6 + 14) \div 8$

b. $4 \times \frac{8}{3}$ ◯ 4 times the quotient of 3 and 8

c. Subtract 2 from $\frac{1}{2}$ of 9 ◯ $(11 \div 2) - 2$

T: Let's use <, >, or = to compare expressions. (Write $\frac{1}{8}$ *the sum of 6 and 14* and *(6 + 14) ÷ 8* on the board.) Draw a tape diagram for each expression and compare them.

S: (Write $\frac{1}{8}$ *the sum of 6 and 14 = (6 + 14) ÷ 8*.)

T: What do you notice about the diagrams?

S: They are drawn exactly the same way. → We don't even need to evaluate the expressions in order to compare them. You can see that they will simplify to the same quantity. → I knew it would be the same before I drew it because finding 1 eighth of something and dividing by 8 are the same thing.

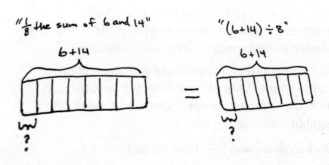

T: Look at the next pair of expressions. Work with your partner to compare them without calculating.

S: (Work and write $4 \times \frac{8}{3}$ > 4 times the quotient of 3 and 8.)

T: How did you compare these expressions without calculating?

Lesson 10:   Compare and evaluate expressions with parentheses.
Date: 11/10/13

4.D.8

S: They both multiply something by 4. Since 8 thirds is greater than 3 eighths, the expression on the left is larger. → Since both expressions multiply with a factor of 4, the fraction that shows the smaller amount results in a product that is also less.

T: Compare the final pair of expressions independently without calculating. Be prepared to share your thoughts.

S: (Work and write *subtract 2 from* $\frac{1}{2}$ *of 9 < (11 ÷ 2) – 2.*)

T: How did you know which expression was greater? Turn and talk.

S: Eleven divided by 2 is 11 halves and 11 halves is greater than 9 halves. → Half of 9 is less than half of 11, and since we're subtracting 2 from both of them, the expression on the right is greater.

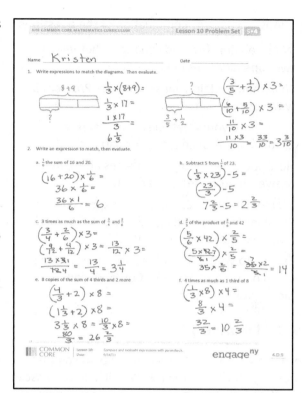

Problem Set (10 minutes)

Students should do their personal best to complete the Problem Set within the allotted 10 minutes. For some classes, it may be appropriate to modify the assignment by specifying which problems they work on first. Some problems do not specify a method for solving. Students solve these problems using the RDW approach used for Application Problems.

Student Debrief (10 minutes)

Lesson Objective: Compare and evaluate expressions with parentheses.

The Student Debrief is intended to invite reflection and active processing of the total lesson experience.

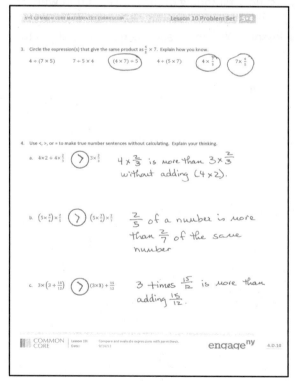

Invite students to review their solutions for the Problem Set. They should check work by comparing answers with a partner before going over answers as a class. Look for misconceptions or misunderstandings that can be addressed in the Debrief. Guide students in a conversation to debrief the Problem Set and process the lesson.

COMMON CORE ™

Lesson 10:   Compare and evaluate expressions with parentheses.
Date: 11/10/13

4.D.9

You may choose to use any combination of the questions below to lead the discussion.

- What relationships did you notice between the two tape diagrams in Problem 1?
- Share and explain your solution for Problem 3 with your partner.
- What were your strategies of comparing Problem 4? Explain it to your partner.
- How does the use of parentheses affect the answer in Problems 4(b) and 4(c)?
- Were you able to compare the expressions in Problem 4(c) without calculating? What made it more difficult than (a) and (b)?
- Explain to your partner how you created the line plot in Problem 5(d)? Compare your line plot to your partner's.

Exit Ticket (3 minutes)

After the Student Debrief, instruct students to complete the Exit Ticket. A review of their work will help you assess the students' understanding of the concepts that were presented in the lesson today and plan more effectively for future lessons. You may read the questions aloud to the students.

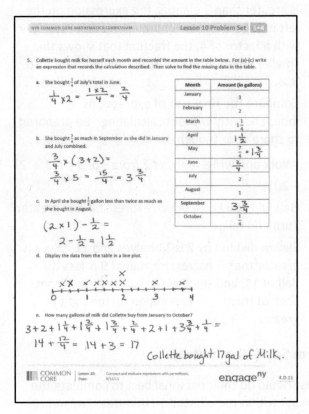

COMMON CORE™

Lesson 10:   Compare and evaluate expressions with parentheses.
Date: 11/10/13

4.D.10

Name _____   Date _____

1. Write expressions to match the diagrams. Then evaluate.

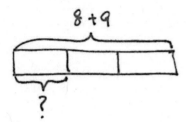

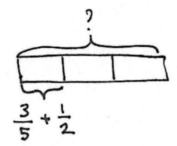

2. Write an expression to match, then evaluate.

a. $\frac{1}{6}$ the sum of 16 and 20.

b. Subtract 5 from $\frac{1}{3}$ of 23.

c. 3 times as much as the sum of $\frac{3}{4}$ and $\frac{2}{6}$.

d. $\frac{2}{5}$ of the product of $\frac{5}{6}$ and 42.

e. 8 copies of the sum of 4 thirds and 2 more.

f. 4 times as much as 1 third of 8.

3. Circle the expression(s) that give the same product as $\frac{4}{5} \times 7$. Explain how you know.

$4 \div (7 \times 5)$ $7 \div 5 \times 4$ $(4 \times 7) \div 5$ $4 \div (5 \times 7)$ $4 \times \frac{7}{5}$ $7 \times \frac{4}{5}$

4. Use <, >, or = to make true number sentences without calculating. Explain your thinking.

  a. $4 \times 2 + 4 \times \frac{2}{3}$ $\bigcirc$ $3 \times \frac{2}{3}$

  b. $\left(5 \times \frac{3}{4}\right) \times \frac{2}{5}$ $\bigcirc$ $\left(5 \times \frac{3}{4}\right) \times \frac{2}{7}$

  c. $3 \times \left(3 + \frac{15}{12}\right)$ $\bigcirc$ $(3 \times 3) + \frac{15}{12}$

5. Collette bought milk for herself each month and recorded the amount in the table below. For (a–c) write an expression that records the calculation described. Then solve to find the missing data in the table.

a. She bought $\frac{1}{4}$ of July's total in June.

b. She bought $\frac{3}{4}$ as much in September as she did in January and July combined.

c. In April she bought $\frac{1}{2}$ gallon less than twice as much as she bought in August.

Month	Amount (in gallons)
January	3
February	2
March	$1\frac{1}{4}$
April	
May	$\frac{7}{4}$
June	
July	2
August	1
September	
October	$\frac{1}{4}$

d. Display the data from the table in a line plot.

e. How many gallons of milk did Collette buy from January to October?

Name _____   Date _____

1. Rewrite these expressions using words.

   a. $\frac{3}{4} \times \left(2\frac{2}{5} - \frac{5}{6}\right)$ b. $2\frac{1}{4} + \frac{8}{3}$

2. Write an equation, then solve.

   a. Three less than one-fourth of the product of eight thirds and nine.

Name _____   Date _____

1. Write expressions to match the diagrams. Then evaluate.

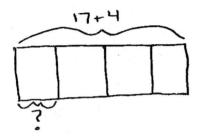

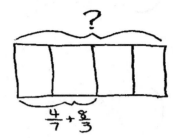

2. Circle the expression(s) that give the same product as $6 \times 1\frac{3}{8}$. Explain how you know.

$8 \div (3 \times 6)$ $3 \div 8 \times 6$ $(6 \times 3) \div 8$ $(8 \div 6) \times 3$ $6 \times \frac{8}{3}$ $\frac{3}{8} \times 6$

3. Write an expression to match, then evaluate.

   a. $\frac{1}{8}$ the sum of 23 and 17.

   b. Subtract 4 from $\frac{1}{6}$ of 42.

   c. 7 times as much as the sum of $\frac{1}{3}$ and $\frac{4}{5}$.

   d. $\frac{2}{3}$ of the product of $\frac{3}{8}$ and 16.

   e. 7 copies of the sum of 8 fifths and 4.

   f. 15 times as much as 1 fifth of 12.

4. Use <, >, or = to make true number sentences without calculating. Explain your thinking.

a. $\frac{2}{3} \times (9 + 12)$ ◯ $15 \times \frac{2}{3}$

b. $\left(3 \times \frac{5}{4}\right) \times \frac{3}{5}$ ◯ $\left(3 \times \frac{5}{4}\right) \times \frac{3}{8}$

c. $6 \times \left(2 + \frac{32}{16}\right)$ ◯ $(6 \times 2) + \frac{32}{16}$

5. Fantine bought flour for her bakery each month and recorded the amount in the table to the right. For (a–c) write an expression that records the calculation described. Then solve to find the missing data in the table.

a. She bought $\frac{4}{5}$ of January's total in August.

b. She bought $\frac{7}{8}$ as much in April as she did in October and July combined.

Month	Amount (in pounds)
January	3
February	2
March	$1\frac{1}{4}$
April	
May	$\frac{7}{6}$
June	
July	$2\frac{1}{4}$
August	
September	$\frac{14}{5}$
October	$\frac{3}{4}$

c.　In June she bought $\frac{3}{5}$ pound less than six times as much as she bought in May.

d.　Display the data from the table in a line plot.

e.　How many pounds of flour did Fantine buy from January to October?

Lesson 10:　　Compare and evaluate expressions with parentheses.
Date:　　　　11/10/13

4.D.17

Lesson 11

Objective: Solve and create fraction word problems involving addition, subtraction, and multiplication.

Suggested Lesson Structure

■ Fluency Practice   (12 minutes)
▨ Concept Development   (38 minutes)
■ Student Debrief   (10 minutes)
   Total Time   **(60 minutes)**

Fluency Practice (12 minutes)

- Convert Measures **4.MD.1**   (5 minutes)
- Multiply Whole Numbers by Fractions Using Two Methods **5.NF.4**   (3 minutes)
- Write the Expression to Match the Diagram **5.NF.4**   (4 minutes)

Convert Measures (5 minutes)

Materials: (S) Personal white boards, Grade 5 Mathematics Reference Sheet

Note: This fluency reviews G5–M4–Lessons 9–10 and prepares students for G5–M4–Lessons 11–12 content. Allow students to use the conversion reference sheet if they are confused, but encourage them to answer questions without looking at it.

  T: (Write 2 c = __ pt.) How many pints are in 2 cups?
  S: 1 pint.
  T: (Write 2 c = 1 pt. Below it, write 4 c = __ pt.) 4 cups?
  S: 2 pints.
  T: (Write 4 c = 2 pt. Below it, write 6 c = __ pt.) 6 cups?
  S: 3 pints.
  T: (Write 6 c = 3 pt. Below it, write 20 c = __ pt.) On your boards, write the equation.
  S: (Write 20 c = 10 pt.)
  T: (Write 20 c ÷ __ = __ pt.) Write the division equation you used to solve it.
  S: (Write 20 c ÷ 2 = 10 pt.)

Continue with the following possible sequence: 12 in = 1 ft, 24 in = 2 ft, 48 in = 4 ft, 3 ft = 1 yd, 6 ft = 2 yd, 9 ft = 3 yd, 24 ft = 8 yd, 4 qt = 1 gal, 8 qt = 2 gal, 12 qt = 3 gal, and 36 qt = 9 gal.

Lesson 11:	Solve and create fraction word problems involving addition, subtraction, and multiplication.
Date:	11/10/13

4.D.18

Multiply Whole Numbers by Fractions Using Two Methods (3 minutes)

Materials: (S) Personal white boards

Note: This fluency reviews G5–M4–Lesson 8.

T: (Write $\frac{1}{2} \times 8 = \frac{\underline{\quad} \times \underline{\quad}}{2}$.) On your boards, write the equation and fill in the multiplication expression for the numerator.

S: (Write $\frac{1}{2} \times 8 = \frac{1 \times 8}{2}$.)

T: (Write $\frac{1}{2} \times 8 = \frac{1 \times 8}{2} = \underline{\quad} = \underline{\quad}$.) Fill in the missing numbers.

S: (Write $\frac{1}{2} \times 8 = \frac{1 \times 8}{2} = \frac{8}{2} = 4$.)

T: (Write $\frac{1}{2} \times 8 = \frac{1 \times 8}{2}$.) Divide by a common factor and solve.

S: (Write $\frac{1}{2} \times 8 = \frac{1 \times \cancel{8}^{4}}{\cancel{2}_{1}} = 4$.)

T: Did you get the same answer using both methods?

S: Yes.

Continue with the following possible suggestions: $12 \times \frac{1}{4}$, $12 \times \frac{3}{4}$, $\frac{2}{3} \times 15$, and $18 \times \frac{5}{6}$.

Write the Expression to Match the Diagram (4 minutes)

Materials: (S) Personal white boards

Note: This fluency reviews G5–M4–Lesson 10.

T: (Project a tape diagram partitioned into 3 equal parts with 8 + 3 as the whole.) Say the value of the whole.

S: 11.

T: On your boards, write an expression to match the diagram.

S: (Write (8 + 3) ÷ 3.)

T: Solve the expression.

S: (Beneath (8 + 3) ÷ 3, write $\frac{11}{3}$. Beneath $\frac{11}{3}$, write $3\frac{1}{3}$.)

Repeat this sequence for the following suggestion: (5 + 6) ÷ 3.

T: (Project a tape diagram partitioned into 3 equal parts. Beneath one of the units, write $\frac{1}{2} + \frac{1}{4}$.) On your boards, write an expression to match the diagram.

S: (Write $\left(\frac{1}{2} + \frac{1}{4}\right) \times 3$.)

T: Solve the expression.

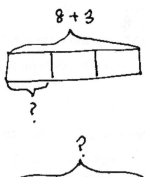

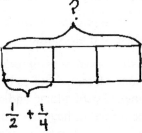

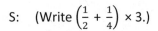

Lesson 11:   Solve and create fraction word problems involving addition,
              subtraction, and multiplication.
Date: 11/10/13

4.D.19

S: (Beneath $\frac{1}{2}$ + $\frac{1}{4}$ × 3, write $\frac{3}{4}$ × 3. Beneath it, write $\frac{9}{4}$. And, beneath that, write $2\frac{1}{4}$.)

Continue with the following possible suggestion: $\left(\frac{1}{2} + \frac{2}{3}\right)$ × 5.

Concept Development (38 minutes)

Materials: (S) Problem Set

Note: Because today's lesson involves solving word problems, time allocated to the Application Problem has been allotted to the Concept Development.

Suggested Delivery of Instruction for Solving Lesson 11's Word Problems

1. Model the problem.

Have two pairs of student who can successfully model the problem work at the board while the others work independently or in pairs at their seats. Review the following questions before beginning the first problem:

- Can you draw something?
- What can you draw?
- What conclusions can you make from your drawing?

As students work, circulate. Reiterate the questions above. After two minutes, have the two pairs of students share only their labeled diagrams. For about one minute, have the demonstrating students receive and respond to feedback and questions from their peers.

2. Calculate to solve and write a statement.

Give everyone two minutes to finish work on that question, sharing their work and thinking with a peer. All should then write their equations and statements of the answer.

3. Assess the solution for reasonableness.

Give students one to two minutes to assess and explain the reasonableness of their solution.

A general instructional note on today's problems: The problem solving in today's lesson requires that students combine their previous knowledge of adding and subtracting fractions with new knowledge of multiplying to find fractions of a set. The problems have been designed to encourage flexibility in thinking by offering many avenues for solving each one. Be sure to conclude the work with plenty of time for students to present and compare approaches.

NOTES ON
MULTIPLE MEANS OF
ENGAGEMENT:

When a task offers varied approaches for solving, an efficient way to have all students' work shared is to hold a "museum walk."

This method for sharing works best when a purpose for the looking is given. For example, students might be asked to note similarities and differences in the drawing of a model or approach to calculation. Students can indicate the similarities or differences by using sticky-notes to color code the displays, or they may write about what they notice in a journal.

Lesson 11:	Solve and create fraction word problems involving addition, subtraction, and multiplication.
Date:	11/10/13

4.D.20

Problem 1

Kim and Courtney share a 16-ounce box of cereal. By the end of the week, Kim has eaten $\frac{3}{8}$ of the box, and Courtney has eaten $\frac{1}{4}$ of the box of cereal. What fraction of the box is left?

Method 1: Kim: $\frac{3}{8}$ of $16 = \frac{3 \times \overset{2}{\cancel{16}}}{\cancel{8}} = 6$

Courtney: $\frac{1}{4}$ of $16 = \frac{1 \times \overset{4}{\cancel{16}}}{\cancel{4}} = 4$

$6 + 4 = \boxed{10 \text{ oz.}}$

16 oz.

ate 10 oz.   left = ?

$16 - 10 = 6 \text{ oz.}$

$\frac{6}{16} = \boxed{\frac{3}{8}}$

$\frac{3}{8}$ of the box is left.

Method 2: $\frac{3}{8} + \frac{1}{4}$

$= \frac{3}{8} + \frac{2}{8}$

$= \frac{5}{8}$

$\frac{5}{8}$ of $16 = \frac{5 \times \overset{2}{\cancel{16}}}{\cancel{8}} = \boxed{10 \text{ oz.}}$

$1 - \frac{5}{8} = \frac{8}{8} - \frac{5}{8} = \boxed{\frac{3}{8}}$

$\frac{3}{8}$ of the box is left.

To complete Problem 1, students must find fractions of a set and use skills learned in Module 3 to add or subtract fractions.

As exemplified, students may solve this multi-step word problem using different methods. Consider demonstrating these two methods of solving Problem 1 if both methods are not mentioned by students. Point out that the rest of today's Problem Set can be solved using multiple strategies as well.

If desired, this problem's complexity may be increased by changing the amount of the cereal in the box to 20 ounces and Courtney's fraction to $\frac{1}{3}$. This will produce a mixed number for both girls. Kim's portion becomes $7\frac{1}{2}$ ounces and Courtney's becomes $6\frac{2}{3}$.

Problem 2

Mathilde has 20 pints of green paint. She uses $\frac{2}{5}$ of it to paint a landscape and $\frac{3}{10}$ of it while painting a clover. She decides that for her next painting she will need 14 pints of green paint. How much more paint will she need to buy?

2).
<u>Method 1:</u>   Landscape: $\frac{2}{5}$ of 20 = $\frac{2 \times \overset{4}{20}}{5}$ = 8   <u>Method 2:</u>

Clover: $\frac{3}{10}$ of 20 = $\frac{3 \times \overset{2}{20}}{10}$ = 6 $\frac{2}{5} + \frac{3}{10}$ $\frac{7}{10}$ of 20 = $\frac{7 \times \overset{2}{20}}{10}$ = 14 pt.

used: 8+6 = 14 pt.   = $\frac{4}{10} + \frac{3}{10}$ 20 - 14 = 6 pt.
left over: 20 - 14 = 6 pt.   = $\frac{7}{10}$ 14 - 6 = $\boxed{8 pt.}$
need for next job: 14 - 6 = $\boxed{8 pt.}$

She will need to buy 8 more pints of paint.

<u>Method 3</u>

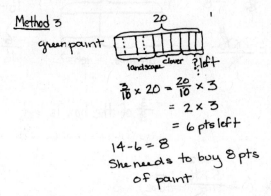

$\frac{3}{10} \times 20 = \frac{20}{10} \times 3$
$= 2 \times 3$
$= 6$ pts left

14 - 6 = 8
She needs to buy 8 pts
of paint

Complexity is increased here as students are called on to maintain a high level of organization as they keep track of the attribute of paint *used* and *not used*. Multiple approaches should be encouraged. For Methods 1 and 2, the *used* paint is the focus of the solution. Students may choose to find the fractions of the whole (fraction of a set) Mathilde has used on each painting or may first add the separate fractions before finding the fraction of the whole. Subtracting that portion from the 14 pints she'll need for her next project yields the answer to the question. Method 3 finds the left over paint and simply subtracts it from the 14 pints needed for the next painting.

Problem 3

Jack, Jill, and Bill each carried a 48-ounce bucket full of water down the hill. By the time they reached the bottom, Jack's bucket was only $\frac{3}{4}$ full, Jill's was $\frac{2}{3}$ full, and Bill's was $\frac{1}{6}$ full. How much water did they spill altogether on their way down the hill?

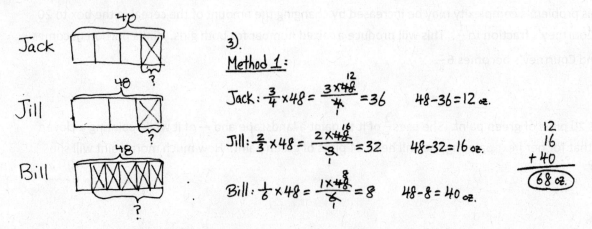

3).
<u>Method 1:</u>

Jack: $\frac{3}{4} \times 48 = \frac{3 \times \overset{12}{48}}{4} = 36$ 48 - 36 = 12 oz.

Jill: $\frac{2}{3} \times 48 = \frac{2 \times \overset{16}{48}}{3} = 32$ 48 - 32 = 16 oz.

Bill: $\frac{1}{6} \times 48 = \frac{1 \times \overset{8}{48}}{6} = 8$ 48 - 8 = 40 oz.

$\begin{array}{r} 12 \\ 16 \\ + 40 \\ \hline \boxed{68 \text{ oz.}} \end{array}$

Lesson 11:   Solve and create fraction word problems involving addition,
               subtraction, and multiplication.
Date: 11/10/13

4.D.22

Method 2:

Jack: $\frac{3}{4}$ full $\Rightarrow \frac{1}{4} \times 48 = \frac{1 \times \overset{12}{\cancel{48}}}{\cancel{4}} = 12$ oz.

Jill: $\frac{2}{3}$ full $\Rightarrow \frac{1}{3} \times 48 = \frac{1 \times \overset{16}{\cancel{48}}}{\cancel{3}} = 16$ oz.

Bill: $\frac{1}{6}$ full $\Rightarrow \frac{5}{6} \times 48 = \frac{5 \times \overset{8}{\cancel{48}}}{\cancel{6}} = 40$ oz.

$$\begin{array}{r} 12 \\ 16 \\ + \ 40 \\ \hline \boxed{68 \text{ oz.}} \end{array}$$

They spilled 68 ounces of water on their way down the hill.

This problem is much like Problem 2 in that students keep track of one attribute—*spilled water* or *un-spilled water*. However, the inclusion of a third person, Bill, requires that students keep track of even more information. In Method 1, a student may opt to find the fraction of water still remaining in each bucket. This process requires the students to then subtract those portions from the 48 ounces that each bucket held originally. In Method 2 students may decide to find what fraction of the water has been spilled by *counting on* to a whole (e.g., if 3 fourths remain in Jack's bucket, then only 1 fourth has been spilled.) This is a more direct approach to the solution as subtraction from 48 is not necessary.

Problem 4

Mrs. Diaz makes 5 dozen cookies for her class. One-ninth of her 27 students are absent the day she brings the cookies. If she shares the cookies equally among the students who are present, how many cookies will each student get?

9 units = 27

1 unit = $\frac{27}{9}$

     = 3

27 − 3 = 24 present

5 × 12 = 60 cookies

$\frac{60^{\div 12}}{24_{\div 12}} = \frac{5}{2} = 2\frac{1}{2}$ cookies

Each student gets $2\frac{1}{2}$ cookies.

4).

Method 1:   5 dozens = 5 × 12 = 60 cookies

$\frac{1}{9} \times 27 = \frac{1 \times \overset{3}{\cancel{27}}}{\cancel{9}} = 3$ absent

27 − 3 = 24 present

$60 \div 24 = \boxed{2\frac{1}{2} \text{ cookies}}$

$$\begin{array}{r} 2\frac{12}{24} = 2\frac{1}{2} \\ 24\overline{)60} \\ -48 \\ \hline 12 \end{array}$$

Method 2:   5 dozens = 5 × 12 = 60 cookies

$\frac{1}{9}$ absent $\Rightarrow \frac{8}{9}$ present

$\frac{8}{9} \times 27 = \frac{8 \times \overset{3}{\cancel{27}}}{\cancel{9}} = 24$ present

$60 \div 24 = 2\frac{12}{24} = \boxed{2\frac{1}{2} \text{ cookies}}$

Each student will get $2\frac{1}{2}$ cookies.

COMMON CORE™   Lesson 11:   Solve and create fraction word problems involving addition, subtraction, and multiplication.   **4.D.23**

Date: 11/10/13

This problem is straightforward, yet the division of the cookies at the end provides an opportunity to call out the division interpretation of a fraction. With quantities like 60 and 24, students will likely lean toward the long division algorithm, so using fraction notation to show the division may need to be discussed as an alternative. Using the fraction and renaming using larger units may be the more efficient approach given the quantities. The similarities and differences of these approaches certainly bear a moment's discussion. In addition, the practicality of sharing cookies in twenty-fourths can lead to a discussion of renaming $2\frac{12}{24}$ as $2\frac{1}{2}$.

Problem 5

Create a story problem about a fish tank for the tape diagram below. Your story must include a fraction.

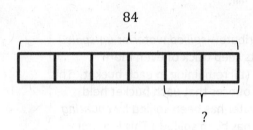

5)
There are 84 fish in the fish tank. $\frac{4}{6}$ of the fish are goldfish, and the rest are guppies. How many guppies are in the fish tank?

5) There are 84 organisms in a freshwater aquarium. One half of the organisms are top-feeding fish. One sixth are crustaceans. The remaining organisms are apple snails. How many snails are in the tank?

In this problem, students are shown a tape diagram marking 84 as the whole and partitioned into 6 equal units (or sixths). The question mark should signal students to find $\frac{2}{6}$ of the whole.

Students are asked to create a word problem about a fish tank. Students should be encouraged to use their creativity while generating a word problem, but remain mathematically sound. Two sample stories are included here, but this is a good opportunity to have students share aloud their own word problems.

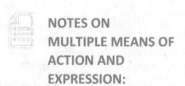

NOTES ON MULTIPLE MEANS OF ACTION AND EXPRESSION:

In general, early finishers for this lesson will be students who use an abstract, more procedural approach to solving. These students might be asked to work the problems again using a well-drawn tape diagram using color that would explain why their calculation is valid. These models could be displayed in hallways or placed in a class book.

Lesson 11:   Solve and create fraction word problems involving addition, subtraction, and multiplication.
Date: 11/10/13

4.D.24

Student Debrief (10 minutes)

Lesson Objective: Solve and create fraction word problems involving addition, subtraction, and multiplication.

The Student Debrief is intended to invite reflection and active processing of the total lesson experience.

Invite students to review their solutions for the Problem Set. They should check work by comparing answers with a partner before going over answers as a class. Look for misconceptions or misunderstandings that can be addressed in the Debrief. Guide students in a conversation to debrief the Problem Set and process the lesson.

You may choose to use any combination of the questions below to lead the discussion.

- How are the problems alike? How are they different?

- How many strategies can you use to solve the problems?

- How was your solution the same and different from those that were demonstrated?

- Did you see other solutions that surprised you or made you see the problem differently?

- How many different story problems can you create for Problem 5?

Exit Ticket (3 minutes)

After the Student Debrief, instruct students to complete the Exit Ticket. A review of their work will help you assess the students' understanding of the concepts that were presented in the lesson today and plan more effectively for future lessons. You may read the questions aloud to the students.

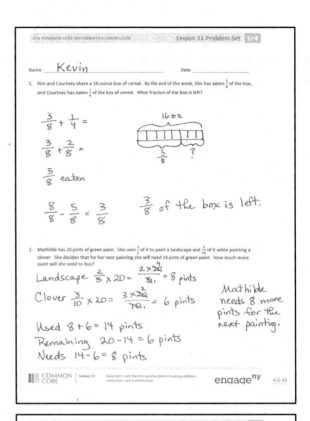

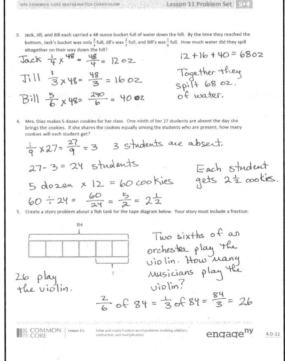

COMMON CORE ™

Lesson 11: Solve and create fraction word problems involving addition,
subtraction, and multiplication.

Date: 11/10/13

4.D.25

Name _____ Date _____

1. Kim and Courtney share a 16-ounce box of cereal. By the end of the week, Kim has eaten $\frac{3}{8}$ of the box, and Courtney has eaten $\frac{1}{4}$ of the box of cereal. What fraction of the box is left?

2. Mathilde has 20 pints of green paint. She uses $\frac{2}{5}$ of it to paint a landscape and $\frac{3}{10}$ of it while painting a clover. She decides that for her next painting she will need 14 pints of green paint. How much more paint will she need to buy?

COMMON CORE™

Lesson 11:   Solve and create fraction word problems involving addition, subtraction, and multiplication.

Date: 11/10/13

4.D.26

3. Jack, Jill, and Bill each carried a 48-ounce bucket full of water down the hill. By the time they reached the bottom, Jack's bucket was only $\frac{3}{4}$ full, Jill's was $\frac{2}{3}$ full, and Bill's was $\frac{1}{6}$ full. How much water did they spill altogether on their way down the hill?

4. Mrs. Diaz makes 5 dozen cookies for her class. One-ninth of her 27 students are absent the day she brings the cookies. If she shares the cookies equally among the students who are present, how many cookies will each student get?

5. Create a story problem about a fish tank for the tape diagram below. Your story must include a fraction.

84

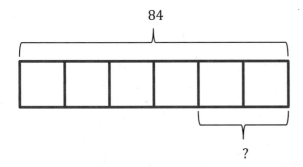

?

COMMON CORE Lesson 11: Solve and create fraction word problems involving addition, subtraction, and multiplication.

Date: 11/10/13

4.D.27

© 2013 Common Core, Inc. All rights reserved. commoncore.org

Name _____ Date _____

1. Use a tape diagram to solve.

   a. $\frac{2}{3}$ of 5

Lesson 11:	Solve and create fraction word problems involving addition, subtraction, and multiplication.
Date:	11/10/13

4.D.28

Name _____   Date _____

1. Jenny's mom says she has an hour before it's bedtime. Jenny spends $\frac{3}{5}$ of the hour texting a friend and $\frac{3}{8}$ of the remaining time brushing her teeth and putting on her pajamas. She spends the rest of the time reading her book. How long did Jenny read?

2. A-Plus Auto Body is painting flames on a customer's car. They need $2\frac{1}{2}$ pints of red, 3 pints of orange, $\frac{3}{4}$ pint of yellow, and 7 pints of blue paint. They use $\frac{3}{4}$ of the blue paint to make the flames. They need $7\frac{3}{4}$ pints to paint the next car blue. How much more blue paint will they need to buy?

3. Giovanna, Frances, and their dad each carried a 10-pound bag of soil into the backyard. After putting soil in the first flower bed, Giovanna's bag was $\frac{5}{8}$ full, Frances' bag was $\frac{2}{5}$ full, and their dad's was $\frac{3}{4}$ full. How many ounces of soil did they put in the first flower bed altogether?

4. Mr. Chan made 252 cookies for the Annual Fifth Grade Class Bake Sale. They sold $\frac{3}{4}$ of them and $\frac{3}{9}$ of the remaining cookies were given to P.T.A. members. Mr. Chan allowed the 12 student-helpers to divide the cookies that were left equally. How many cookies will each student get?

5. Create a story problem about a farm for the tape diagram below. Your story must include a fraction.

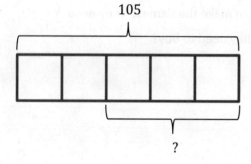

COMMON CORE™ | Lesson 11:   Solve and create fraction word problems involving addition, subtraction, and multiplication.
Date: 11/10/13

4.D.30

Lesson 12

Objective: Solve and create fraction word problems involving addition, subtraction, and multiplication.

Suggested Lesson Structure

■ Fluency Practice   (12 minutes)
■ Application Problem   (6 minutes)
☐ Concept Development   (32 minutes)
■ Student Debrief   (10 minutes)

   Total Time   **(60 minutes)**

Fluency Practice (12 minutes)

- Convert Measures **4.MD.1**   (4 minutes)
- Multiply a Fraction and a Whole Number **5.NF.3**   (4 minutes)
- Write the Expression to Match the Diagram **5.NF.4**   (4 minutes)

Convert Measures (4 minutes)

Materials: (S) Personal white boards, Grade 5 Mathematics Reference Sheet

Note: This fluency reviews G5–M4–Lessons 9–11 and prepares students for G5–M4–Lesson 12 content. Allow students to use the conversion reference sheet if they are confused, but encourage them to answer questions without looking at it.

    T: (Write 1 ft = ___ in.) How many inches are in 1 foot?
    S: 12 inches.
    T: (Write 1 ft = 12 in. Below it, write 2 ft = ___ in.) 2 feet?
    S: 24 inches.
    T: (Write 2 ft = 24 in. Below it, write 4 ft = ___ in.) 4 feet?
    S: 48 inches.
    T: Write the multiplication equation you used to solve it.
    S: (Write 4 ft × 12 = 48 in.)

Continue with the following possible sequence: 1 pint = 2 cups, 2 pints = 4 cups, 7 pints = 14 cups, 1 yard = 3 ft, 2 yards = 6 ft, 6 yards = 18 ft, 1 gal = 4 qt, 2 gal = 8 qt, 9 gal = 36 qt.

    T: (Write 2 c = ___ pt.) How many pints are in 2 cups?

Lesson 12:	Solve and create fraction word problems involving addition, subtraction, and multiplication.
Date:	11/10/13

4.D.31

S: 1 pint.

T: (Write 2 c = 1 pt. Below it, write 4 c = __ pt.) 4 cups?

S: 2 pints.

T: (Write 4 c = 2 pt. Below it, write 10 c = __ pt.) 10 cups?

S: 5 pints

T: Write the division equation you used to solve it.

S: (Write 10 c ÷ 2 = 5 pt.)

Continue with the following possible sequence: 12 in = 1 ft, 36 in = 3 ft, 3 ft = 1 yd, 12 ft = 4 yd, 4 qt = 1 gal, and 28 qt = 7 gal.

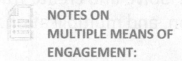

NOTES ON MULTIPLE MEANS OF ENGAGEMENT:

For English language learners and struggling students, provide the conversion reference sheet included in G5–M4–Lesson 9.

Multiply a Fraction and a Whole Number (4 minutes)

Materials: (S) Personal white boards

Note: This fluency reviews G5–M4–Lessons 9–11.

T: (Write 9 ÷ 3 = __.) Say the division sentence.

S: 9 ÷ 3 = 3.

T: (Write $\frac{1}{3}$ × 9 = __.) Say the multiplication sentence.

S: $\frac{1}{3}$ × 9 = 3.

T: (Write $\frac{2}{3}$ × 9 = __.) On your boards, write the multiplication sentence.

S: (Write $\frac{2}{3}$ × 9 = 6.)

T: (Write 9 × $\frac{2}{3}$ = __.) On your boards, write the multiplication sentence.

S: (Write 9 × $\frac{2}{3}$ = 6.)

Continue with the following possible sequence: 12 ÷ 6, $\frac{1}{6}$ × 12, $\frac{5}{6}$ × 12, 12 × $\frac{5}{6}$, $\frac{1}{8}$ × 24, 24 × $\frac{1}{8}$, 24 × $\frac{3}{8}$, $\frac{2}{3}$ × 12, and 12 × $\frac{3}{4}$.

Write the Expression to Match the Diagram (4 minutes)

Materials: (S) Personal white boards

Note: This fluency reviews G5–M4–Lessons 10–11.

T: (Project a tape diagram partitioned into 3 equal units with 15 as the whole and 2 units shaded.) Say the value of the whole.

S: 15.

T: On your boards, write an expression to match the diagram using a fraction.

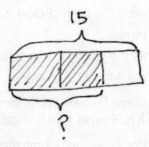

Lesson 12:   Solve and create fraction word problems involving addition, subtraction, and multiplication.
Date: 11/10/13

4.D.32

S: (Write $\frac{2}{3}$ × 15 or 15 × $\frac{2}{3}$.)

T: To solve we can write 15 divided by 3 to find the value of one unit, times 2. (Write $\frac{15}{3}$ × 2 as you say the words.)

T: Find the value of the expression.

S: (Write $\frac{15}{3}$ × 2 = 10.)

Continue this process for the following possible suggestion: $\frac{3}{5}$ × 45, $\frac{3}{4}$ × 32, $\frac{5}{6}$ × 54, and $\frac{7}{8}$ × 64.

Application Problem (6 minutes)

Complete the table.

$\frac{2}{3}$ yds	_____ feet
4 pounds	_____ ounces
8 tons	_____ pounds
$\frac{3}{4}$ gallon	_____ quarts
$\frac{5}{12}$ year	_____ months
$\frac{4}{5}$ hour	_____ minutes

Note: The chart requires students to work within many customary systems reviewing the work of G5–M4–Lesson 9. Students may need a conversion chart (see G5–M4–Lesson 9) to scaffold this problem.

Concept Development (32 minutes)

Materials: (S) Problem Set

Suggested Delivery of Instruction for Solving Lesson 12's Word Problems

1. Model the problem.

Have two pairs of student who can successfully model the problem work at the board while the others work independently or in pairs at their seats. Review the following questions before beginning the first problem:

- Can you draw something?
- What can you draw?
- What conclusions can you make from your drawing?

As students work, circulate. Reiterate the questions above. After two minutes, have the two pairs of students share only their labeled diagrams. For about one minute, have the demonstrating students receive and respond to feedback and questions from their peers.

2. Calculate to solve and write a statement.

Give everyone two minutes to finish work on that question, sharing their work and thinking with a peer. All should then write their equations and statements of the answer.

3. Assess the solution for reasonableness.

Give students one to two minutes to assess and explain the reasonableness of their solution.

A general instructional note on today's problems: Today's problems are more complex than those found in G5–M4–Lesson 11. All are multi-step. Students should be strongly encouraged to draw before attempting to solve. As in G5–M4–Lesson 11, multiple approaches to solving all the problems are possible. Students should be given time to share and compare thinking during the Debrief.

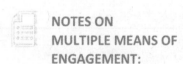

NOTES ON MULTIPLE MEANS OF ENGAGEMENT:

The complexity of the language involved in today's problems may pose significant challenges to English language learners or those students with learning differences that affect language processing. Consider pairing these students with those in the class who are adept at drawing clear models. These visuals and the peer interaction they generate can be invaluable bridges to making sense of the written word.

Lesson 12:	Solve and create fraction word problems involving addition, subtraction, and multiplication.
Date:	11/10/13

4.D.34

Problem 1

A baseball team played 32 games and lost 8. Katy was the catcher in $\frac{5}{8}$ of the winning games and $\frac{1}{4}$ of the losing games.

   a. What fraction of the games did the team win?

   b. In how many games did Katy play catcher?

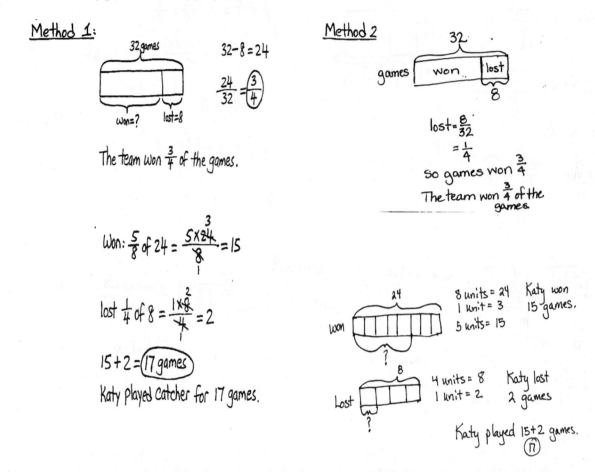

While Part A is relatively straightforward, there are still varied approaches for solving. Students may find the difference between the number of games played and lost to find the number of games won (24) expressing this difference as a fraction ($\frac{24}{32}$). Alternately they may conclude that the losing games are $\frac{1}{4}$ of the total and deduce that winning games must constitute $\frac{3}{4}$. Watch for students distracted by the fractions $\frac{5}{8}$ and $\frac{1}{4}$ written in the stem and somehow try to involve them in the solution to Part (a). Complexity increases as students must employ the fraction of a set strategy twice, carefully matching each fraction with the appropriate number of games and finally combining the number of games that Katy played to find the total.

Lesson 12:   Solve and create fraction word problems involving addition, subtraction, and multiplication.

Date: 11/10/13

4.D.35

Problem 2

In Mrs. Elliott's garden, $\frac{1}{8}$ of the flowers are red, $\frac{1}{4}$ of them are purple, and $\frac{1}{5}$ of the remaining flowers are pink. If there are 128 flowers, how many flowers are pink?

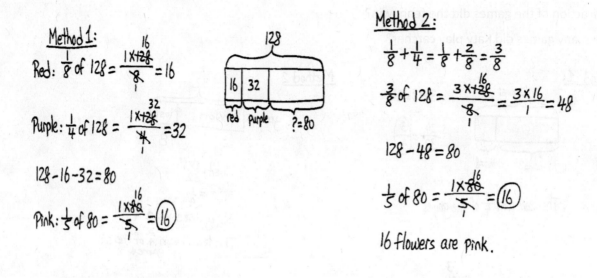

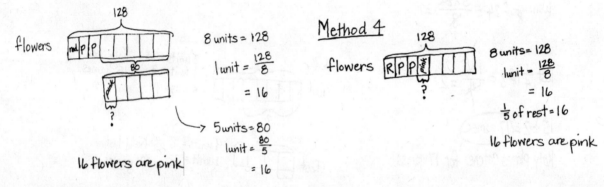

The increase in complexity for this problem comes as students are asked to find the number of pink flowers in the garden. This portion of the flowers refers to 1 fifth of the *remaining* flowers (i.e., 1 fifth of those that are not red or purple), *not* 1 fifth of the total. Some students may realize (as in Method 4) that 1 fifth of the remainder is simply equal to 1 unit or 16 flowers. Multiple methods of drawing and solving are possible. Some of the possibilities are pictured above.

COMMON CORE™

Lesson 12: Solve and create fraction word problems involving addition, subtraction, and multiplication.
Date: 11/10/13

4.D.36

Problem 3

Lillian and Darlene plan to get their homework finished within one hour. Darlene completes her math homework in $\frac{3}{5}$ hour. Lillian completes her math homework with $\frac{5}{6}$ hour remaining. Who completes her homework faster and by how many minutes?

Bonus: Give the answer as a fraction of an hour.

<u>Method 1:</u>   <u>Method 2:</u>

4) Darlene: $\frac{3}{5}$ of an hour $= \frac{3}{5} \times 60 = \frac{3 \times 60^{12}}{5_1} = 36$ min

Lillian: $\frac{5}{6}$ of an hour <u>remaining</u> $\rightarrow \frac{1}{6}$ of an hour

$\frac{1}{6} \times 60 = \frac{1 \times 60^{10}}{6_1} = 10$ min

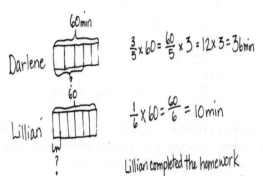

$\frac{3}{5} \times 60 = \frac{60}{5} \times 3 = 12 \times 3 = 36$ min

$\frac{1}{6} \times 60 = \frac{60}{6} = 10$ min

Lillian completed the homework 26 minutes faster than Darlene.

36 min - 10 min = 26 min

Lillian completed the homework faster. She did it 26 minutes faster.

Bonus: 26 min as a fraction of an hour

$\rightarrow \frac{26}{60} = \frac{13}{30}$ of an hour faster

The way in which Lillian's time is expressed makes for a bit of complexity in this problem. Students must recognize that she only took $\frac{1}{6}$ hour to complete the assignment. Many students may quickly recognize that Lillian worked faster as $\frac{1}{6} < \frac{3}{5}$. However, students must go further to find exactly how many minutes faster. The bonus requires them to give the fraction of an hour. Simplification of this fraction should not be required but may be discussed.

Problem 4

Create and solve a story problem about a baker and some flour whose solution is given by the expression $\frac{1}{4} \times (3 + 5)$.

The pastry chef mixes $\frac{1}{4}$ cup of sugar into each cup of flour. He uses 3 cups of wheat flour and 5 cups of rice flour. How many cups of sugar does he use in all?

$$\frac{1}{4} \times (3 + 5)$$
$$= \frac{3+5}{4}$$
$$= \frac{8}{4}$$
$$= 2 \qquad \text{He uses 2 cups of sugar.}$$

A baker combined 3 cups of sugar with 5 cups of flour together in a bowl. He used $\frac{1}{4}$ of the mixture to bake cookies. How many cups of the mixture did he use?

$$\frac{1}{4} \times (3+5)$$
$$= \frac{1}{4} \times 8$$
$$= \frac{1 \times 8}{4}$$
$$= \textcircled{2} \qquad \text{He used 2 cups of the mixture.}$$

Working backwards from expression to story may be challenging for some students. Since the expression given contains parentheses, the story created must first involve the addition or combining of 3 and 5. For students in need of assistance, drawing a tape diagram first may be of help. Then, asking the simple prompt, "What would a baker add together or combine?" may be enough to get the students started. Evaluating $\frac{1}{4} \times (3 + 5)$ should pose no significant challenge to students. Note that the story of the chef interprets the expression as repeated addition of a fourth where the story of the baker interprets the expression as a fraction of a set.

Problem 5

Create and solve a story problem about a baker and 36 kilograms of an ingredient that is modeled by the following tape diagram. Include at least one fraction in your story.

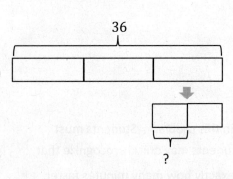

6).
A baker poured a bag of 36 kg of flour equally into 3 containers. He then used $\frac{1}{2}$ of one container of flour to make pretzels. How many kilograms of flour did he use to make the pretzels?

3 units = 36 kg
1 unit = 36 ÷ 3 = 12 kg
$\frac{1}{2}$ of 12 = $\frac{1 \times \overset{6}{\cancel{12}}}{\underset{1}{\cancel{2}}}$ = 6 kg

He used 6 kg of flour to make pretzels.

Again, students are asked to both create and then solve a story problem, this time using a given tape diagram. The challenge here is that this tape diagram implies a two-step word problem. The whole, 36, is first partitioned into thirds, and then one of those thirds is divided in half. The story students create should reflect this two-part drawing. Students should be encouraged to share aloud and discuss their stories and thought process for solving.

Lesson 12: Solve and create fraction word problems involving addition, subtraction, and multiplication.

Date: 11/10/13

4.D.38

Problem 6

Of the students in Mr. Smith's fifth grade class, $\frac{1}{3}$ were absent on Monday. Of the students in Mrs. Jacobs' class, $\frac{2}{5}$ were absent on Monday. If there were 4 students absent in each class on Monday, how many students are in each class?

For this problem, students need to find the whole. An interesting aspect of this problem is that fractional amounts of different wholes can be the same amount. In this case, two-fifths of 10 is the same as one-third of 12. This should be discussed with students.

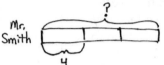

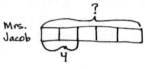

1 unit = 4
3 units = 12
There are 12 students
in Mr. Smith's class.

2 units = 4
1 unit = 2
5 units = 10
There are 10 students
in Mrs. Jacob's class.

Student Debrief (10 minutes)

Lesson Objective: Solve and create fraction word problems involving addition, subtraction, and multiplication.

The Student Debrief is intended to invite reflection and active processing of the total lesson experience.

Invite students to review their solutions for the Problem Set. They should check work by comparing answers with a partner before going over answers as a class. Look for misconceptions or misunderstandings that can be addressed in the Debrief. Guide students in a conversation to debrief the Problem Set and process the lesson.

You may choose to use any combination of the questions below to lead the discussion.

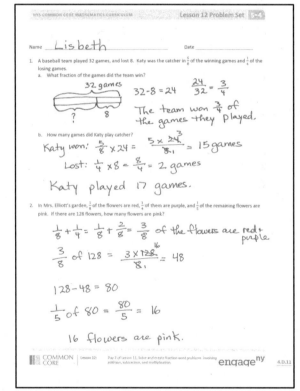

- How are the problems alike? How are they different?

- How many strategies can you use to solve the problems?

- How was your solution the same and different from those that were demonstrated?

- Did you see other solutions that surprised you or made you see the problem differently?

- How many different story problems can you create for Problem 5 and Problem 6?

COMMON CORE™ | Lesson 12: Solve and create fraction word problems involving addition, subtraction, and multiplication.
Date: 11/10/13

4.D.39

Exit Ticket (3 minutes)

After the Student Debrief, instruct students to complete the Exit Ticket. A review of their work will help you assess the students' understanding of the concepts that were presented in the lesson today and plan more effectively for future lessons. You may read the questions aloud to the students.

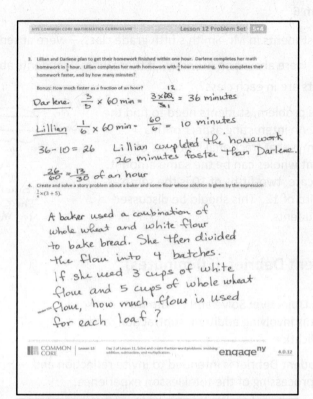

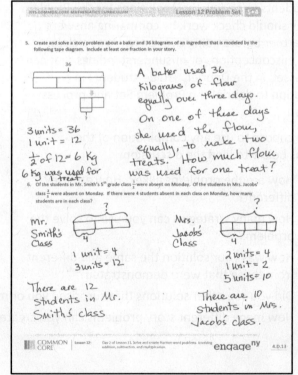

| Lesson 12: | Solve and create fraction word problems involving addition, subtraction, and multiplication. | 4.D.40 |
| Date: | 11/10/13 | |

Name _____   Date _____

1. A baseball team played 32 games, and lost 8. Katy was the catcher in $\frac{5}{8}$ of the winning games and $\frac{1}{4}$ of the losing games.
    a. What fraction of the games did the team win?

    b. In how many games did Katy play catcher?

2. In Mrs. Elliott's garden, $\frac{1}{8}$ of the flowers are red, $\frac{1}{4}$ of them are purple, and $\frac{1}{5}$ of the remaining flowers are pink. If there are 128 flowers, how many flowers are pink?

COMMON CORE™ | Lesson 12:   Solve and create fraction word problems involving addition,
                     subtraction, and multiplication.   4.D.41
                     | Date: 11/10/13

© 2013 Common Core, Inc. All rights reserved. commoncore.org

3. Lillian and Darlene plan to get their homework finished within one hour. Darlene completes her math homework in $\frac{3}{5}$ hour. Lillian completes her math homework with $\frac{5}{6}$ hour remaining. Who completes her homework faster and by how many minutes?

   Bonus: Give the answer as a fraction of an hour.

4. Create and solve a story problem about a baker and some flour whose solution is given by the expression $\frac{1}{4} \times (3 + 5)$.

Lesson 12:   Solve and create fraction word problems involving addition,
                 subtraction, and multiplication.

Date: 11/10/13

4.D.42

5. Create and solve a story problem about a baker and 36 kilograms of an ingredient that is modeled by the following tape diagram. Include at least one fraction in your story.

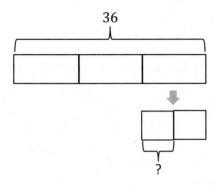

6. Of the students in Mr. Smith's fifth grade class, $\frac{1}{3}$ were absent on Monday. Of the students in Mrs. Jacobs' class, $\frac{2}{5}$ were absent on Monday. If there were 4 students absent in each class on Monday, how many students are in each class?

COMMON CORE™ | Lesson 12:   Solve and create fraction word problems involving addition,
          subtraction, and multiplication.
          Date: 11/10/13   4.D.43

Name _____ Date _____

In a classroom, $\frac{1}{6}$ of the students are wearing blue shirts and $\frac{2}{3}$ are wearing white shirts. There are 36 students in the class. How many students are wearing a shirt other than blue or white?

Name _____ Date _____

1. Terrence finished a word search in $\frac{3}{4}$ the time it took Frank. Charlotte finished the word search in $\frac{2}{3}$ the time it took Terrence. Frank finished the word search in 32 minutes. How long did it take Charlotte to finish the word search?

2. Ms. Phillips ordered 56 pizzas for a school fundraiser. Of the pizzas ordered, $\frac{2}{7}$ of them were pepperoni, 19 were cheese, and the rest were veggie pizzas. What fraction of the pizzas was veggie?

 | Lesson 12: | Solve and create fraction word problems involving addition, subtraction, and multiplication.

Date: | 11/10/13

4.D.45

3. In an auditorium, $\frac{1}{6}$ of the students are fifth graders, $\frac{1}{3}$ are fourth graders, and $\frac{1}{4}$ of the remaining students are second graders. If there are 96 students in the auditorium, how many second graders are there?

4. At a track meet, Jacob and Daniel compete in the 220 m hurdles. Daniel finishes in $\frac{3}{4}$ of a minute. Jacob finishes with $\frac{5}{12}$ of a minute remaining. Who ran the race in the faster time?

Bonus: Give the answer as a fraction of a minute.

COMMON CORE™

Lesson 12: Solve and create fraction word problems involving addition, subtraction, and multiplication.

Date: 11/10/13

4.D.4

5. Create and solve a story problem about a runner who is training for a race. Include at least one fraction in your story.

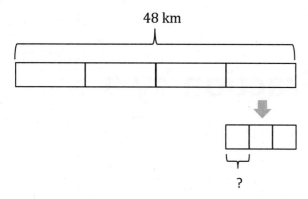

6. Create and solve a story problem about a two friends and their weekly allowance whose solution is given by the expression $\frac{1}{5} \times (12 + 8)$.

COMMON CORE™

Lesson 12:   Solve and create fraction word problems involving addition, subtraction, and multiplication.

Date: 11/10/13

4.D.47

Topic E
Multiplication of a Fraction by a Fraction

5.NBT.7, 5.NF.4a, 5.NF.6, 5.MD.1, 5.NF.4b

Focus Standard:	5.NBT.7	Add, subtract, multiply, and divide decimals to hundredths, using concrete models or drawings and strategies based on place value, properties of operations, and/or the relationship between addition and subtraction; relate the strategy to a written method and explain the reasoning used.
	5.NF.4a	Apply and extend previous understandings of multiplication to multiply a fraction or whole number by a fraction.
		a. Interpret the product of $(a/b) \times q$ as a parts of a partition of q into b equal parts; equivalently, as the result of a sequence of operations $a \times q \div b$. *For example, use a visual fraction model to show (2/3 × 4 = 8/3, and create a story context for this equation. Do the same with (2/3) × (4/5) = 8/15. (In general, (a/b) × (c/d) = ac/bd.)*
	5.NF.6	Solve real world problems involving multiplication of fractions and mixed numbers, e.g., by using visual fraction models or equations to represent the problem.
	5.MD.1	Convert among different-sized standard measurement units within a given measurement system (e.g., convert 5 cm to 0.05 m), and use these conversions in solving multi-step, real world problems.
Instructional Days:	8	
Coherence -Links from:	G4–M6	Decimal Fractions
	G5–M2	Multi-Digit Whole Number and Decimal Fraction Operations
-Links to:	G6–M2	Arithmetic Operations Including Division by a Fraction
	G6–M4	Expressions and Equations

Topic E introduces students to multiplication of fractions by fractions—both in fraction and decimal form (**5.NF.4a**, **5.NBT.7**). The topic starts with multiplying a unit fraction by a unit fraction, and progresses to multiplying two non-unit fractions. Students use area models, rectangular arrays, and tape diagrams to model the multiplication. These familiar models help students draw parallels between whole number and fraction multiplication and solve word problems. This intensive work with fractions positions students to extend their previous work with decimal-by-whole number multiplication to decimal-by-decimal multiplication. Just as students used unit form to multiply fractional units by wholes in Module 2 (e.g., 3.5 × 2 = 35 tenths × 2 ones = 70 tenths), they will connect fraction-by-fraction multiplication to multiply fractional units-by-fractional units. (3.5 × 0.2 = 35 tenths × 2 tenths = 70 hundredths).

$\frac{3}{4}$ of a foot $= \frac{3}{4} \times 12$ inches

1 foot = 12 inches

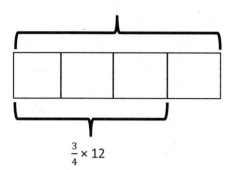

$\frac{3}{4} \times 12$

Express $5\frac{3}{4}$ ft as inches.

$5\frac{3}{4}$ ft $= (5 \times 12)$ inches $+ (\frac{3}{4} \times 12)$ inches

$= 60 + 9$ inches

$= 69$ inches

Reasoning about decimal placement is an integral part of these lessons. Finding fractional parts of customary measurements and measurement conversion (**5.MD.1**) concludes Topic E. Students convert smaller units to fractions of a larger unit (e.g., 6 inches = 1/2 ft). The inclusion of customary units provides a meaningful context for many common fractions (1/2 pint = 1 cup, 1/3 yard = 1 foot, 1/4 gallon = 1 quart, etc.). This topic, together with the fraction concepts and skills learned in Module 3, opens the door to a wide variety of application word problems (**5.NF.6**).

A Teaching Sequence Towards Mastery of Multiplication of a Fraction by a Fraction

Objective 1: Multiply unit fractions by unit fractions.
          (Lesson 13)

Objective 2: Multiply unit fractions by non-unit fractions.
          (Lesson 14)

Objective 3: Multiply non-unit fractions by non-unit fractions.
          (Lesson 15)

Objective 4: Solve word problems using tape diagrams and fraction-by-fraction multiplication.
          (Lesson 16)

Objective 5: Relate decimal and fraction multiplication.
          (Lessons 17–18)

Objective 6: Convert measures involving whole numbers, and solve multi-step word problems.
          (Lesson 19)

Objective 7: Convert mixed unit measurements, and solve multi-step word problems.
          (Lesson 20)

Lesson 13

Objective: Multiply unit fractions by unit fractions.

Suggested Lesson Structure

- ■ Fluency Practice   (8 minutes)
- ■ Concept Development   (42 minutes)
- ■ Student Debrief   (10 minutes)
- **Total Time**   **(60 minutes)**

Fluency Practice (8 minutes)

- Multiply a Fraction and a Whole Number **5.NF.3**   (4 minutes)
- Convert Measures **4.MD.1**   (4 minutes)

Multiply a Fraction and a Whole Number (4 minutes)

Materials: (S) Personal white boards

Note: This fluency reviews G5–M4–Lessons 9–11.

> T: (Write $\frac{8}{4}$.) Say the division sentence.
>
> S: 8 ÷ 4 = 2.
>
> T: (Write $\frac{1}{4} \times 8 =$ ___.) Say the multiplication sentence.
>
> S: $\frac{1}{4} \times 8 = 2$.
>
> T: (Write $\frac{3}{4} \times 8 =$ ___.) On your boards, write the multiplication sentence.
>
> S: (Write $\frac{3}{4} \times 8 = 6$.)
>
> T: (Write $8 \times \frac{3}{4} =$ ___.) On your boards, write the multiplication sentence.
>
> S: (Write $8 \times \frac{3}{4} = 6$.)

Continue with the following possible sequence: $\frac{18}{6}$, $\frac{1}{6} \times 18$, $\frac{5}{6} \times 18$, $18 \times \frac{5}{6}$, $\frac{1}{8} \times 16$, $16 \times \frac{1}{8}$, $16 \times \frac{5}{8}$, $\frac{2}{3} \times 15$, and $20 \times \frac{3}{4}$.

	Lesson 13:	Multiply unit fractions by unit fractions.	
	Date:	11/10/13	**4.E.3**

Convert Measures (4 minutes)

Materials: (S) Personal white boards, Grade 5 Mathematics Reference Sheet (G5–M4–Lesson 8)

Note: This fluency reviews G5–M4–Lesson 12 and prepares students for this lesson. Allow students to use the conversion reference sheet if they are confused, but encourage them to answer questions without looking at it.

Convert the following. Draw a tape diagram if it helps you.

a. $\frac{1}{3}$ yd = _____ft = _____inches

b. $\frac{2}{3}$ yd = _____ft = _____inches

c. $\frac{1}{3}$ hour = _____minutes

d. $\frac{2}{3}$ hour = _____minutes

e. $\frac{1}{4}$ year = _____months

f. $\frac{3}{4}$ year = _____months

Concept Development (42 minutes)

NOTES ON MULTIPLE MEANS OF ENGAGEMENT:

While the lesson moves to the pictorial level of representation fairly quickly, be aware that many students may need the scaffold of the concrete model (paper folding and shading) to fully comprehend the concepts. Make these materials available and model their use throughout the remainder of the module.

Materials: (S) Personal white boards, 4" × 2" rectangular paper (several pieces per student), scissors

Note: Today's lesson is lengthy, so the time normally allotted for an Application Problem has been allocated to the Concept Development. The last problem in the sequence can be considered the Application Problem for today.

Problem 1

Jan has 4 pans of crispy rice treats. She sends $\frac{1}{2}$ of the pans to school with her children. How many pans of crispy rice treats does Jan send to school?

Note: To progress from finding a fraction of a whole number to a fraction of a fraction, the following sequence is then used: 2 pans, 1 pan, $\frac{1}{2}$ pan.

T: (Post Problem 1 on the board and read it aloud with the students.) Work with your partner to write a multiplication sentence that explains your thinking. Be prepared to share. (Allow students time to work.)

T: What fraction of the pans does Jan send to school?

S: One-half of them.

Lesson 13: Multiply unit fractions by unit fractions.
Date: 11/10/13

4.E.4

T: How many pans did Jan have?

S: 4 pans.

T: What is one-half of 4 pans?

S: 2 pans.

T: Show the multiplication sentence that you wrote to explain your thinking.

S: (Show $\frac{1}{2} \times 4$ pans = 2 pans or $4 \times \frac{1}{2} = 2$ pans.)

T: Say the answer in a complete sentence.

S: Jan sent 2 pans of crispy rice treats to school.

T: (Erase the 4 in the text of the problem and replace it with a 2.) Imagine that Jan has 2 pans of treats. If she still sends half of the pans to school, how many pans will she send? Write a multiplication sentence to show how you know.

S: (Write $\frac{1}{2} \times 2$ pans = 1 pan.)

T: (Replace the 2 in the problem with a 1.) Now, imagine that she only has 1 pan. If she still sends half to school, how many pans will she send? Write the multiplication sentence.

S: (Write $\frac{1}{2} \times 1$ pan = $\frac{1}{2}$ pan.)

T: (Erase the 1 in problem and replace it with $\frac{1}{2}$. Read the problem aloud with students.) What if Jan only has half a pan and wants to send half of it to school? What is different about this problem?

S: There's only $\frac{1}{2}$ of a pan instead of a whole pan. → Jan is still sending half the treats to school but now we'll find half of a half, not half of 1. → The amount we have is less than a whole.

T: Let's say that your piece of paper represents the pan of treats. Turn and talk to your partner about how you can use your rectangular paper to find out what fraction of the whole pan of treats Jan sent to school.

S: (May fold or shade the paper to show the problem.)

T: Many of you shaded half of your paper, then partitioned that half into 2 equal parts and shaded one of them, like this. (Model as seen at right.)

 T: We now have two different size units shaded in our model. I can see the part that Jan sent to school, but I need to name this unit. In order to name the part she sent (point to the double shaded unit), all of the units in the whole must be the same size as this one. Turn and talk to your partner about how we can split the rest of the pan so that all the units are the same as our double-shaded one. Use your paper to show your thinking.

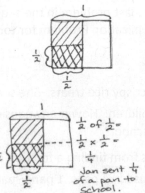

S: We could cut the other half in half too. That would make 4 units the same size. → We could keep cutting across the rest of the whole. That would make the whole pan cut into 4 equal parts. → Half of a half is a fourth.

T: Let me record that. (Partition the un-shaded half using a dotted line.) Look at our model. What's

---

Lesson 13: Multiply unit fractions by unit fractions.
Date: 11/10/13

4.E.5

the name for the smallest units we have drawn now?

S: Fourths.

T: She sent half of the treats she had, but what fraction *of the whole pan* of treats did Jan send to school?

S: One-fourth of the whole pan.

T: Write a multiplication sentence that shows your thinking.

S: (Write $\frac{1}{2} \times \frac{1}{2} = \frac{1}{4}$.)

Problem 2

Jan has $\frac{1}{3}$ pan of crispy rice treats. She sends $\frac{1}{2}$ of the treats to school with her children. How many pans of crispy rice treats does Jan send to school?

T: (Erase $\frac{1}{2}$ in the text of Problem 1 and replace it with $\frac{1}{3}$.) Imagine that Jan only has a third of a pan, and she still wants to send half of the treats to school. Will she be sending a greater amount or a smaller amount of treats to school than she sent in our last problem? How do you know? Turn and discuss with your partner.

S: It will be a smaller part of a whole pan because she had half a pan before. Now she only has 1 third of a pan. → 1 third is less than 1 half, so half of a third is less than half of a half. → 1 half is larger than 1 third, so she sent more in the last problem than this one.

T: We need to find $\frac{1}{2}$ of $\frac{1}{3}$ pan. (Write $\frac{1}{2}$ of $\frac{1}{3} = \frac{1}{2} \times \frac{1}{3}$ on the board.) I'll draw a model to represent this problem while you use your paper to model it. (Draw a rectangle on the board.) This rectangle shows 1 whole pan. (Label 1 above the rectangle.) Fold your paper then shade it to show how much of this one pan Jan has at first.

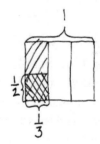

S: (Fold in thirds and shade 1 third of the whole.)

T: (On the board, partition the rectangle vertically into 3 parts, shade in 1 of them, and label $\frac{1}{3}$ below it.) What fraction of the treats did Jan send to school?

S: One-half.

T: Jan sends $\frac{1}{2}$ of this part to school. (Point to 1 shaded portion.) How can I show $\frac{1}{2}$ of this part? Turn and talk to your partner, and show your thinking with your paper.

S: We can draw a line to cut it in half. → We need to split it into 2 equal parts and shade only 1 of them.

T: I hear you saying that I should partition the one-third into 2 equal parts and then shade only 1. (Draw a horizontal line through the shaded third and shade the bottom half. Label the double shaded area as $\frac{1}{2}$.)

NOTES ON MULTIPLE MEANS OF REPRESENTATION:

There will be students who notice the patterns within the algorithm quickly and want to use it to find the product. Be sure those students are questioned deeply and can articulate the reasoning and meaning of the product in relationship to the whole.

COMMON CORE™   Lesson 13:   Multiply unit fractions by unit fractions.
Date: 11/10/13

4.E.6

Again, now I have two different size shaded units. What do I need to do with this horizontal line in order to be able to name the units? Turn and talk.

S: We could cut the other thirds in half too. That would make 6 units the same size. → We could keep cutting across the rest of the whole. That would make the whole pan cut into 6 equal parts. → 1 third is the same as 2 sixths. Half of 2 sixths is 1 sixth.

T: Let me record that. (Partition the un-shaded thirds using a dotted line.) What's the name for the units we have drawn now?

S: Sixths.

T: What fraction of the pan of treats did Jan send to school?

S: One-sixth of the whole pan.

T: One-half of one-third is one-sixth. (Write $\frac{1}{2} \times \frac{1}{3} = \frac{1}{6}$.)

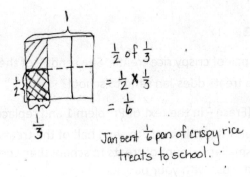

Repeat a similar sequence with Problem 3, but have students draw a matchbook-size model on their paper rather than folding their paper. Be sure that students articulate clearly the finding of a common unit in order to name the product.

Problem 3

Jan has $\frac{1}{3}$ a pan of crispy rice treats. She sends $\frac{1}{4}$ of the treats to school with her children. How many pans of crispy rice treats does Jan send to school?

T: (Write $\frac{1}{4}$ of $\frac{1}{3}$ and $\frac{1}{3}$ of $\frac{1}{4}$ on the board.) Let's compare finding 1 fourth of 1 third with finding 1 third of 1 fourth. What do you notice about these problems? Turn and talk.

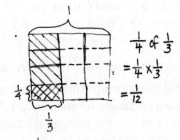

S: They both have 1 fourth and 1 third in them, but they're flip-flopped. → They have the same factors, but they are in a different order.

T: Will the order of the factors affect the size of the product? Talk to your partner.

S: It doesn't when we multiply whole numbers. → But is that true for fractions too? → That means 1 fourth of 1 third is the same as a third of a fourth.

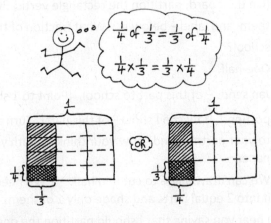

T: We just drew the model for $\frac{1}{4}$ of $\frac{1}{3}$. Let's draw an area model for $\frac{1}{3}$ of $\frac{1}{4}$ to find out if we will have the same answer. In $\frac{1}{3}$ of $\frac{1}{4}$, the amount we start with is 1 fourth pan. Draw a whole, shade $\frac{1}{4}$, and label it.

(Draw a rectangular box and cut it vertically into 4 equal parts and label $\frac{1}{4}$. Point to the 1 shaded part.) How do I take a third of this fourth?

S: Cut the fourth into 3 parts.

Lesson 13: Multiply unit fractions by unit fractions.
Date: 11/10/13

4.E.7

T: How will we name this new unit?

S: Cut the other fourths into 3 equal parts, too.

T: (Partition each unit into thirds and label $\frac{1}{3}$.) How many of these units make our whole?

S: Twelve.

T: What is their name?

S: Twelfths.

T: What's $\frac{1}{3}$ of $\frac{1}{4}$?

S: 1 twelfth.

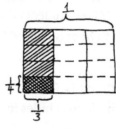

T: (Write $\frac{1}{3} \times \frac{1}{4} = \frac{1}{12}$.) These multiplication sentences have the same answer. But the shape of the twelfth is different. How do you know that 12 equal parts can be different shapes but the same fraction?

S: What matters is that they are 12 equal parts of the same whole. → It's like if we have a square, there are lots of ways to show a half, or 2 equal parts. The area has to be the same, not the shape.

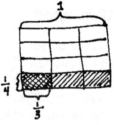

T: True. What matters is the parts have the same area. We can prove $\frac{1}{3} \times \frac{1}{4} = \frac{1}{4} \times \frac{1}{3}$ with another drawing. Start with the same brownie pan. Draw fourths horizontally, and shade 1 fourth. Now let's double shade 1 third of that fourth (extend the units with dotted lines). Is the exact same amount shaded in the two pans?

S: Yes!

T: So, we see in another way that $\frac{1}{4}$ of $\frac{1}{3} = \frac{1}{3}$ of $\frac{1}{4}$. Review how to prove that with our rectangles. Turn and talk.

S: We shade a fourth of a third, drawing the thirds vertically first, then we shaded a third of a fourth, drawing the fourths horizontally first. They were exactly the same part of the whole. → I can shade a fourth and then take a third of it, or I can shade a third and then take a fourth of it, and I get the same answer either way.

T: What do we know about multiplication that supports the truth of the number sentence $\frac{1}{3} \times \frac{1}{4} = \frac{1}{4} \times \frac{1}{3}$?

S: The commutative property works with fractions the same as whole numbers. The order of the factors doesn't change the product. → Taking a fourth of a third is like taking a smaller part of a bigger unit, while taking a third of a fourth is like taking a bigger part of a smaller unit. Either way, you're getting the same size share.

T: We can express $\frac{1}{4}$ of $\frac{1}{3}$ as $\frac{1}{4} \times \frac{1}{3}$ or $\frac{1}{3} \times \frac{1}{4}$. (Write $\frac{1}{4} \times \frac{1}{3} = \frac{1}{3} \times \frac{1}{4}$.) They are equivalent expressions.

Problem 4

A sales lot is filled with vehicles for sale. $\frac{1}{3}$ of the vehicles are pickup trucks. $\frac{1}{3}$ of the trucks are white. What fraction of all the vehicles are white pickup trucks?

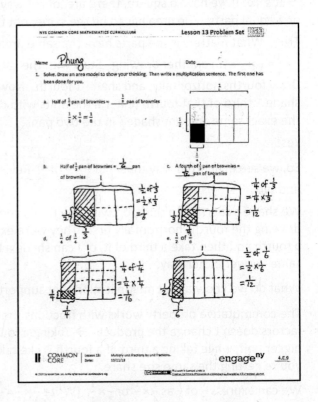

T: (Post Problem 4 on the board and read it aloud with students.) Work with your partner to draw an area model and solve. Write a multiplication sentence to show your thinking. (Allow students time to work.)

T: What is a third of one-third?

S: $\frac{1}{9}$.

T: Say the answer to the question in a complete sentence.

S: One-ninth of the vehicles in the lot are white pickup trucks.

Problem Set (10 minutes)

Students should do their personal best to complete the Problem Set within the allotted 10 minutes. For some classes, it may be appropriate to modify the assignment by specifying which problems they work on first. Some problems do not specify a method for solving. Students solve these problems using the RDW approach used for Application Problems.

Student Debrief (10 minutes)

Lesson Objective: Multiply unit fractions by unit fractions.

The Student Debrief is intended to invite reflection and active processing of the total lesson experience.

Invite students to review their solutions for the Problem Set. They should check work by comparing answers with a partner before going over answers as a class. Look for misconceptions or misunderstandings that can be addressed in the Debrief. Guide students in a conversation to debrief the Problem Set and process the lesson.

You may choose to use any combination of the questions below to lead the discussion.

■   In Problem 1, what is the relationship between Parts (a) and (d)? (Part (a) is double Part (d)). Between Parts (b) and (c)? (Part (b) is double (c).) Between Parts (b) and (e)? (Part (b) is double (e).)

Lesson 13:   Multiply unit fractions by unit fractions.
Date: 11/10/13

4.E.9

- Why is the product for Problem 1(d) smaller than 1(c)? Explain your reasoning to your partner.

- Share and compare your solution with a partner for Problem 2.

- Compare and contrast Problem 3 and Problem 1(b). Discuss with your partner.

- How is solving for the product of fraction and a whole number the same as or different from solving fraction of a fraction? Can you use some of the similar strategies? Explain your thinking to a partner.

Exit Ticket (3 minutes)

After the Student Debrief, instruct students to complete the Exit Ticket. A review of their work will help you assess the students' understanding of the concepts that were presented in the lesson today and plan more effectively for future lessons. You may read the questions aloud to the students.

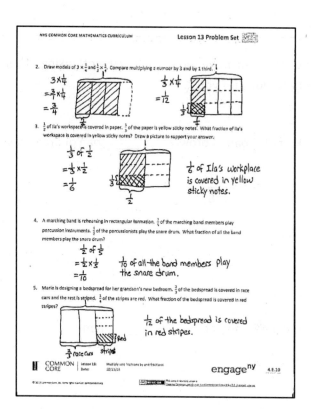

COMMON CORE

Lesson 13:   Multiply unit fractions by unit fractions.
Date: 11/10/13

4.E.10

Name _____   Date _____

1. Solve. Draw an area model to show your thinking. Then write a multiplication sentence. The first one has been done for you.

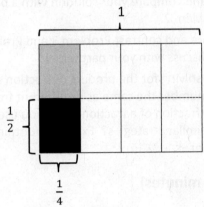

a.   Half of $\frac{1}{4}$ pan of brownies = ___$\frac{1}{8}$___ pan of brownies

$$\frac{1}{2} \times \frac{1}{4} = \frac{1}{8}$$

b.   Half of $\frac{1}{3}$ pan of brownies = _____ pan of brownies

c.   A fourth of $\frac{1}{3}$ pan of brownies = _____ pan of brownies

d. $\frac{1}{4}$ of $\frac{1}{4}$

e. $\frac{1}{2}$ of $\frac{1}{6}$

2. Draw models of $3 \times \frac{1}{4}$ and $\frac{1}{3} \times \frac{1}{4}$. Compare multiplying a number by 3 and by 1 third.

3. $\frac{1}{2}$ of Ila's workspace is covered in paper. $\frac{1}{3}$ of the paper is yellow sticky notes. What fraction of Ila's workspace is covered in yellow sticky notes? Draw a picture to support your answer.

4. A marching band is rehearsing in rectangular formation. $\frac{1}{5}$ of the marching band members play percussion instruments. $\frac{1}{2}$ of the percussionists play the snare drum. What fraction of all the band members play the snare drum?

5. Marie is designing a bedspread for her grandson's new bedroom. $\frac{2}{3}$ of the bedspread is covered in race cars and the rest is striped. $\frac{1}{4}$ of the stripes are red. What fraction of the bedspread is covered in red stripes?

COMMON CORE™

Lesson 13: Multiply unit fractions by unit fractions.
Date: 11/10/13

4.E.12

Name _____ Date _____

1. Solve. Draw an area model and write a number sentence to show your thinking.

   a. $\frac{1}{3} \times \frac{1}{3} =$

2. Ms. Sheppard cuts $\frac{1}{2}$ of a piece of construction paper. She uses $\frac{1}{6}$ of the piece to make a flower. What fraction of the sheet of paper does she use to make the flower?

Name _____ Date _____

1. Solve. Draw an area model to show your thinking.

   a. Half of $\frac{1}{2}$ cake = _____ cake

   b. One-third of $\frac{1}{2}$ cake = _____ cake

   c. $\frac{1}{4}$ of $\frac{1}{2}$

   d. $\frac{1}{2} \times \frac{1}{5}$

   e. $\frac{1}{3} \times \frac{1}{3}$

   f. $\frac{1}{4} \times \frac{1}{3}$

2. Noah mows $\frac{1}{2}$ of his property and leaves the rest wild. He decides to use $\frac{1}{5}$ of the wild area for a vegetable garden. What fraction of the property is used for the garden? Draw a picture to support your answer.

Lesson 13: Multiply unit fractions by unit fractions.
Date: 11/10/13

4.E.14

3. Fawn plants $\frac{2}{3}$ of the garden with vegetables. Her son plants the remainder of the garden. He decides to use $\frac{1}{2}$ of his space to plant flowers, and in the rest he plants herbs. What fraction of the entire garden is planted in flowers? Draw a picture to support your answer.

4. Diego eats $\frac{1}{5}$ of a loaf of bread each day. On Tuesday, Diego eats $\frac{1}{4}$ of the day's portion before lunch. What fraction of the whole loaf does Diego eat before lunch on Tuesday? Draw a model to support your thinking.

Lesson 14

Objective: Multiply unit fractions by non-unit fractions.

Suggested Lesson Structure

■ Fluency Practice   (12 minutes)
■ Application Problem   (6 minutes)
■ Concept Development   (32 minutes)
■ Student Debrief   (10 minutes)
  Total Time   **(60 minutes)**

Fluency Practice (12 minutes)

- Sprint: Multiply a Fraction and a Whole Number **5.NF.3**   (8 minutes)
- Fractions as Whole Numbers **5.NF.4**   (4 minutes)

Sprint: Multiply a Fraction and Whole Number (8 minutes)

Materials: (S) Multiply a Fraction and Whole Number Sprint

Note: This Sprint reviews G5–M4–Lessons 9–12 content.

Fractions as Whole Numbers (4 minutes)

Materials: (S) Personal white boards

Note: This fluency reviews G5–M4–Lesson 5 and reviews denominators that are easily converted to hundredths. Direct students to use their personal boards for calculations that they cannot do mentally.

    T: I'll say a fraction. You say it as a division problem, and give the quotient. 4 halves.

    S: $4 \div 2 = 2$.

Continue with the following possible suggestions:

$\frac{6}{2}, \frac{14}{2}, \frac{54}{2}, \frac{40}{20}, \frac{80}{20}, \frac{180}{20}, \frac{960}{20}, \frac{10}{5}, \frac{15}{5}, \frac{35}{5}, \frac{85}{5}, \frac{100}{50}, \frac{150}{50}, \frac{300}{50}, \frac{900}{50}, \frac{8}{4}, \frac{12}{4}, \frac{24}{4}, \frac{96}{4}, \frac{50}{25}, \frac{75}{25},$ and $\frac{800}{25}$.

Application Problem (6 minutes)

Solve by drawing an area model and writing a multiplication sentence.

Beth had $\frac{1}{4}$ box of candy. She ate $\frac{1}{2}$ of the candy. What fraction of the whole box does she have left?

Extension: If Beth decides to refill the box, what fraction of the box would need to be refilled?

Note: This Application Problem activates prior knowledge of the multiplication of unit fractions by unit fractions in preparation for today's lesson.

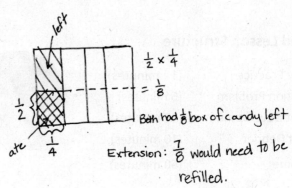

$\frac{1}{2} \times \frac{1}{4}$

$= \frac{1}{8}$

Beth had $\frac{1}{8}$ box of candy left

Extension: $\frac{7}{8}$ would need to be refilled.

Concept Development (32 minutes)

Materials: (S) Personal white boards

Problem 1

Jan had $\frac{3}{5}$ pan of crispy rice treats. She sent $\frac{1}{3}$ of the treats to school. What fraction of the whole pan did she send to school?

> T: (Write Problem 1 on the board.) How is this problem different than the ones we solved yesterday? Turn and talk.
>
> S: Yesterday, Jan always had 1 fraction unit of treats. She had 1 half or 1 third or 1 fourth. Today she has 3 fifths. This one has a 3 in one of the numerators. → We only multiplied unit fractions yesterday.
>
> T: In this problem, what are we finding $\frac{1}{3}$ of?
>
> S: 3 fifths of a pan of treats.
>
> T: Before we find $\frac{1}{3}$ of Jan's $\frac{3}{5}$, visualize this. If there are 3 bananas, how many would $\frac{1}{3}$ of the bananas be? Turn and talk.
>
> S: Well, if you have 3 bananas, one-third of that is just 1 banana. → One-third of 3 of any unit is just one of those units. → 1 third of 3 is always 1. It doesn't matter what the unit is.
>
> T: What is $\frac{1}{3}$ of 3 *pens*?
>
> S: 1 pen.

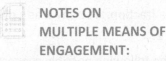

$\frac{1}{3} \times \frac{3}{5}$

$= \frac{1}{3}$ of 3 fifths

$= 1$ fifth

NOTES ON MULTIPLE MEANS OF ENGAGEMENT:

Consider allowing learners who grasp these multiplication concepts quickly to draw models and create story problems to accompany them. If there are technology resources available, allow these students to produce screencasts explaining fraction by fraction multiplication for absent or struggling classmates.

Lesson 14: Multiply unit fractions by non-unit fractions.
Date: 11/10/13

4.E.17

T: What is $\frac{1}{3}$ of 3 *books*?

S: 1 book.

T: (Write $= \frac{1}{3}$ of 3 fifths.) So, then, what is $\frac{1}{3}$ of 3 *fifths*?

S: 1 fifth.

T: (Write = 1 fifth.) $\frac{1}{3}$ of 3 fifths equals 1 fifth. Let's draw a model to prove your thinking. Draw an area model showing $\frac{3}{5}$.

S/T: (Draw, shade, and label the area model.)

T: If we want to show $\frac{1}{3}$ of $\frac{3}{5}$, what must we do to each of these 3 units? (Point to each of the shaded fifths.)

S: Split each one into thirds.

T: Yes, partition each of these units, these fifths, into 3 equal parts.

S/T: (Partition, shade, and label the area model.)

T: In order to name these parts, what must we do to the rest of the whole?

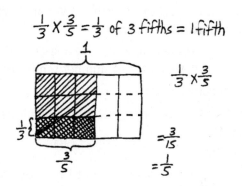

S: Partition the other fifths into 3 equal parts also.

T: Show that using dotted lines. What new unit have we created?

S: Fifteenths.

T: How many fifteenths are in the whole?

S: 15.

T: How many fifteenths are double-shaded?

S: 3.

T: (Write $\frac{1}{3} \times \frac{3}{5} = \frac{3}{15}$ next to the area model.) I thought we said that our answer was 1 fifth. So, how is it that our model shows 3 fifteenths? Turn and talk.

S: 3 fifteenths is another way to show 1 fifth. → I can see 5 equal groups in this model. They each have 3 fifteenths in them. Only 1 of those 5 is double shaded, so it's really only 1 fifth shaded here too. → The answer is 1 fifth. It's just chopped into fifteenths in the model.

T: Let's explore that a bit. Looking at your model, how many groups of 3 fifteenths do you see? Turn and talk.

MP.2

S: There are 5 groups of 3 fifteenths in the whole. → I see 1 group that's double-shaded. I see 2 more groups that are single-shaded, and then there are 2 groups that aren't shaded at all. That makes 5 groups of 3 fifteenths.

T: Out of the 5 groups that we see, how many are double-shaded?

S: 1 group.

T: 1 out of 5 groups is what fraction?

S: 1 fifth.

Lesson 14:   Multiply unit fractions by non-unit fractions.
Date: 11/10/13

4.E.18

T: Does our area model support our thinking from before?

S: Yes, $\frac{1}{3}$ of 3 fifths equals 1 fifth.

Problem 2

Jan had $\frac{3}{4}$ pan of crispy rice treats. She sent $\frac{1}{3}$ of the treats to school. What fraction of the whole pan did she send to school?

T: What are we finding $\frac{1}{3}$ of this time?

S: $\frac{1}{3}$ of 3 fourths.

T: (Write $= \frac{1}{3}$ of 3 fourths.) Based on what we learned in the previous problem, what do you think the answer will be for $\frac{1}{3}$ of 3 fourths? Whisper and tell a partner.

S: Just like $\frac{1}{3}$ of 3 apples is equal to 1 apple, and $\frac{1}{3}$ of 3 fifths is equal to 1 fifth. We know that $\frac{1}{3}$ of 3 fourths is equal to 1 fourth. → We are taking 1 third of 3 units again. The units are fourths this time, so the answer is 1 fourth.

T: Work with a neighbor to solve one-third of 3 fourths. One of you can draw the area model while the other writes a matching number sentence.

S: (Work and share.)

T: In your model, when you partitioned each of the fourths into 3 equal parts, what new unit did you create?

S: Twelfths.

T: How many twelfths represent 1 third of 3 fourths?

S: 3 twelfths.

T: Say 3 twelfths in its simplest form.

S: 1 fourth.

T: So, $\frac{1}{3}$ of 3 fourths is equal to what?

S: 1 fourth.

T: Look back at the two problems we just solved. If $\frac{1}{3}$ of 3 fifths is 1 fifth and $\frac{1}{3}$ of 3 fourths is 1 fourth, what then is $\frac{1}{3}$ of 3 eighths?

S: 1 eighth.

T: $\frac{1}{3}$ of 3 tenths?

S: 1 tenth.

T: $\frac{1}{3}$ of 3 hundredths?

S: 1 hundredth.

T: Based on what you've just learned, what is $\frac{1}{4}$ of 4 fifths?

S: 1 fifth.

$$\frac{1}{3} \times \frac{3}{4} = \frac{1}{3} \text{ of } 3 \text{ fourths} = 1 \text{ fourth}$$

$$\frac{1}{3} \times \frac{3}{4}$$

$$= \frac{3}{12}$$

$$= \frac{1}{4}$$

Lesson 14:   Multiply unit fractions by non-unit fractions.
Date: 11/10/13

4.E.19

T: $\frac{1}{2}$ of 2 fifths?

S: 1 fifth.

T: $\frac{1}{4}$ of 4 sevenths?

S: 1 seventh.

Problem 3

$\frac{1}{2} \times \frac{4}{5}$

T: We need to find 1 half of 4 fifths. If this were 1 half of 4 bananas, how many bananas would we have?

S: 2 bananas.

T: How can you use this thinking to help you find 1 half of 4 fifths? Turn and talk.

S: It's half of 4, so it must be 2. This time it's 4 fifths, so half would be 2 fifths. → Half of 4 is always 2. It doesn't matter that it is fifths. The answer is 2 fifths.

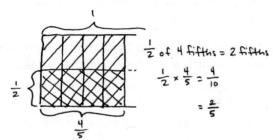

T: It sounds like we agree that 1 half of 4 fifths is 2 fifths. Let's draw a model to confirm our thinking. Work with your partner and draw an area model.

S: (Draw.)

T: I notice that our model shows that the product is 4 tenths, but we said a moment ago that our product was 2 fifths. Did we make a mistake? Why or why not?

S: No, 4 tenths is just another name for 2 fifths. → I can see 5 groups of 4 tenths, but only 2 of them are double-shaded. Two out of 5 groups is another way to say 2 fifths.

Repeat this sequence with $\frac{1}{3} \times \frac{6}{7}$.

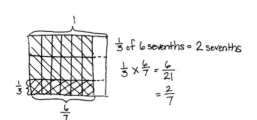

T: What patterns do you notice in our multiplication sentences? Turn and talk.

S: I notice that the denominator in the product is the product of the two denominators in the factors until we simplified. → I notice that you can just multiply the numerators and then multiply the denominators to get the numerator and denominator in the final answer. → When you split the amount in the second factor into thirds, it's like tripling the units, so it's just like multiplying the first unit by 3. But the units get smaller so you have the same amount that you started with.

T: As we are modeling the rest of our problems, let's notice if this pattern continues.

COMMON CORE™ | Lesson 14:   Multiply unit fractions by non-unit fractions.
                    | Date: 11/10/13

4.E.20

Problem 4

$\frac{3}{4}$ of Benjamin's garden is planted in vegetables. Carrots are planted in $\frac{1}{2}$ of his vegetable section of the garden. How much of Benjamin's garden is planted in carrots?

T: Write a multiplication expression to represent the amount of his garden planted in carrots.

S: $\frac{1}{2} \times \frac{3}{4}$. → $\frac{1}{2}$ of $\frac{3}{4}$.

T: I'll write this in unit form. (Write $\frac{1}{2}$ of 3 fourths on the board.) Compare this problem with the last ones. Turn and talk.

S: This one seems trickier because all the others were easy to halve. They were all even numbers of units. → This is half of 3. I know that's 1 and 1 half, but the unit is fourths and I don't know how to say $1\frac{1}{2}$ fourths.

T: Could we name 3 fourths of Benjamin's garden using another unit that makes it easier to halve? Turn and talk with your partner, and then write the amount in unit form.

S: We need a unit that lets us name 3 fourths with an even number of units. We could use 6 eighths. → 6 eighths is the same amount as 3 fourths and 6 is a multiple of 2.

T: What is 1 half of 6?

S: 3.

T: So, what is 1 half of 6 eighths?

S: 3 eighths.

T: Let's draw our model to confirm our thinking. (Allow students time to draw.)

T: Looking at our model, what was the new unit that we used to name the parts of the garden?

S: Eighths.

T: How much of Benjamin's garden is planted in carrots?

S: 3 eighths.

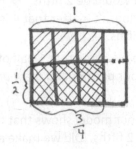

$\frac{1}{2}$ of 3 fourths = ? fourths

$\frac{1}{2} \times \frac{3}{4} = \frac{3}{8}$

Problem 5

$\frac{3}{4}$ of $\frac{1}{2}$

T: (Post Problem 5 on the board.) Solve this by drawing a model and writing a multiplication sentence. (Allow students time to work.)

T: Compare this model to the one we drew for Benjamin's garden. Turn and talk.

S: It's similar. The fractions are the same, but when you draw this one you have to start with 1 half and then chop that into fourths. → The model for this problem looks like what we drew

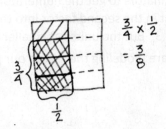

$\frac{3}{4} \times \frac{1}{2}$

$= \frac{3}{8}$

Lesson 14:   Multiply unit fractions by non-unit fractions.
Date: 11/10/13

4.E.2

for Benjamin's garden, except it's been turned on its side. → When we wrote the multiplication sentence, the factors are switched around. → This time we're finding 3 fourths of a half, not a half of 3 fourths. → If this were another garden, less of the garden is planted in vegetables overall. Last time it was 3 fourths of the garden, this time it would be only half. The fraction of the whole garden that is carrots is the same, but now there is only 1 eighth of the garden planted in other vegetables. Last time, 3 eighths of the garden would have had other vegetables.

T: I hear you saying that $\frac{1}{2}$ of $\frac{3}{4}$ and $\frac{3}{4}$ of $\frac{1}{2}$ are equivalent expressions. (Write $\frac{1}{2} \times \frac{3}{4} = \frac{3}{4} \times \frac{1}{2}$.) Can you give an equivalent expression for $\frac{1}{2} \times \frac{3}{5}$?

S: $\frac{1}{2}$ of $\frac{3}{5}$. → $\frac{3}{5}$ of $\frac{1}{2}$. → $\frac{3}{5} \times \frac{1}{2}$.

T: Show me another pair of equivalent expressions that involve fraction multiplication.

S: (Work and share.)

Problem 6

Mr. Becker, the gym teacher, uses $\frac{3}{5}$ of his kickballs in class. Half of the remaining balls are given to students for recess. What fraction of all the kickballs is given to students for recess?

T: (Post Problem 6 and read it aloud with students.) This time, let's solve using a tape diagram.

S/T: (Draw a tape diagram.)

T: What fraction of the balls does Mr. Becker use in class?

S: 3 fifths. (Partition the diagram into fifths and label $\frac{3}{5}$ *used in class*.)

T: What fraction of the balls is remaining?

S: 2 fifths.

T: How many of those are given to students for recess?

S: One half of them.

T: What is one-half of 2?

S: 1.

T: What's one half of 2 fifths?

S: 1 fifth.

T: Write a number sentence and make a statement to answer the question.

S: $\frac{1}{2}$ of 2 fifths = 1 fifth. One-fifth of Mr. Becker's kickballs are given to students to use at recess.

Repeat this sequence using $\frac{1}{3} \times \frac{3}{5}$.

Problem Set (10 minutes)

Students should do their personal best to complete the Problem Set within the allotted 10 minutes. For some classes, it may be appropriate to modify the assignment by specifying which problems they work on first. Some problems do not specify a method for solving. Students solve these problems using the RDW approach used for Application Problems.

Student Debrief (10 minutes)

Lesson Objective: Multiply unit fractions by non-unit fractions.

The Student Debrief is intended to invite reflection and active processing of the total lesson experience.

Invite students to review their solutions for the Problem Set. They should check work by comparing answers with a partner before going over answers as a class. Look for misconceptions or misunderstandings that can be addressed in the Debrief. Guide students in a conversation to debrief the Problem Set and process the lesson.

You may choose to use any combination of the questions below to lead the discussion.

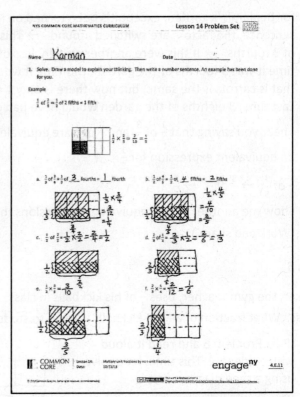

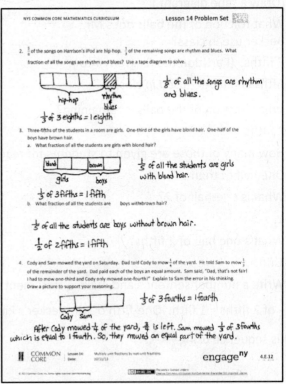

- In Problem 1, what is the relationship between Parts (a) and (b)? (Part (b) is double (a).)

- Share and explain your solution for Problem 1(c) to your partner. Why is taking 1 half of 2 halves equal to 1 half? Is it true for all numbers? 1 half of $\frac{6}{6}$? 1 half of $\frac{8}{8}$? 1 half of 8 wholes?

- How did you solve Problem 3? Explain your strategy to a partner.

- What kind of picture did you draw to solve Problem 4? Share and explain your solution to a partner.

- We noticed some patterns when we wrote our multiplication sentences. Did you notice the same patterns in your Problem Set? (Students should note the multiplication of the numerators and denominators to produce the product.)

Lesson 14:   Multiply unit fractions by non-unit fractions.
Date: 11/10/13

4.E.23

- Explore with students the commutative property in real life situations. While the numeric product (fraction of the whole) is the same, are the situations also the same? (For example, $\frac{1}{3} \times \frac{1}{2} = \frac{1}{2} \times \frac{1}{3}$.) Is a class of fifth-graders in which half are girls (a third of which wear glasses) the same as a class of fifth-graders in which 1 third are girls (half of which wear glasses)?

Exit Ticket (3 minutes)

After the Student Debrief, instruct students to complete the Exit Ticket. A review of their work will help you assess the students' understanding of the concepts that were presented in the lesson today and plan more effectively for future lessons. You may read the questions aloud to the students.

A

Correct _____

Solve.

1	$\frac{1}{5} \times 2 =$		23	$\frac{5}{6} \times 12 =$	
2	$\frac{1}{5} \times 3 =$		24	$\frac{1}{3} \times 15 =$	
3	$\frac{1}{5} \times 4 =$		25	$\frac{2}{3} \times 15 =$	
4	$4 \times \frac{1}{5} =$		26	$15 \times \frac{2}{3} =$	
5	$\frac{1}{8} \times 3 =$		27	$\frac{1}{5} \times 15 =$	
6	$\frac{1}{8} \times 5 =$		28	$\frac{2}{5} \times 15 =$	
7	$\frac{1}{8} \times 7 =$		29	$\frac{4}{5} \times 15 =$	
8	$7 \times \frac{1}{8} =$		30	$\frac{3}{5} \times 15 =$	
9	$3 \times \frac{1}{10} =$		31	$15 \times \frac{3}{5} =$	
10	$7 \times \frac{1}{10} =$		32	$18 \times \frac{1}{6} =$	
11	$\frac{1}{10} \times 7 =$		33	$18 \times \frac{5}{6} =$	
12	$4 \div 2 =$		34	$\frac{5}{6} \times 18 =$	
13	$4 \times \frac{1}{2} =$		35	$24 \times \frac{1}{4} =$	
14	$6 \div 3 =$		36	$\frac{3}{4} \times 24 =$	
15	$\frac{1}{3} \times 6 =$		37	$32 \times \frac{1}{8} =$	
16	$10 \div 5 =$		38	$32 \times \frac{3}{8} =$	
17	$10 \times \frac{1}{5} =$		39	$\frac{5}{8} \times 32 =$	
18	$\frac{1}{3} \times 9 =$		40	$32 \times \frac{7}{8} =$	
19	$\frac{2}{3} \times 9 =$		41	$\frac{5}{9} \times 54 =$	
20	$\frac{1}{4} \times 8 =$		42	$63 \times \frac{7}{9} =$	
21	$\frac{3}{4} \times 8 =$		43	$56 \times \frac{3}{7} =$	
22	$\frac{1}{6} \times 12 =$		44	$\frac{6}{7} \times 49 =$	

COMMON CORE™ | **Lesson 14:** Multiply unit fractions by non-unit fractions.
| **Date:** 11/10/13

4.E.25

B   Improvement _____   # Correct _____

Solve.

1	$\frac{1}{7} \times 2 =$		23	$\frac{3}{4} \times 8 =$	
2	$\frac{1}{7} \times 3 =$		24	$\frac{1}{5} \times 15 =$	
3	$\frac{1}{7} \times 4 =$		25	$\frac{2}{5} \times 15 =$	
4	$4 \times \frac{1}{7} =$		26	$\frac{4}{5} \times 15 =$	
5	$\frac{1}{10} \times 3 =$		27	$\frac{3}{5} \times 15 =$	
6	$\frac{1}{10} \times 7 =$		28	$15 \times \frac{3}{5} =$	
7	$\frac{1}{10} \times 9 =$		29	$\frac{1}{3} \times 15 =$	
8	$9 \times \frac{1}{10} =$		30	$\frac{2}{3} \times 15 =$	
9	$3 \times \frac{1}{8} =$		31	$15 \times \frac{2}{3} =$	
10	$5 \times \frac{1}{8} =$		32	$24 \times \frac{1}{6} =$	
11	$\frac{1}{8} \times 5 =$		33	$24 \times \frac{5}{6} =$	
12	$10 \div 5 =$		34	$\frac{5}{6} \times 24 =$	
13	$10 \times \frac{1}{5} =$		35	$20 \times \frac{1}{4} =$	
14	$9 \div 3 =$		36	$\frac{3}{4} \times 20 =$	
15	$\frac{1}{3} \times 9 =$		37	$24 \times \frac{1}{8} =$	
16	$10 \div 2 =$		38	$24 \times \frac{3}{8} =$	
17	$10 \times \frac{1}{2} =$		39	$\frac{5}{8} \times 24 =$	
18	$\frac{1}{3} \times 6 =$		40	$24 \times \frac{7}{8} =$	
19	$\frac{2}{3} \times 6 =$		41	$\frac{5}{9} \times 63 =$	
20	$\frac{1}{6} \times 12 =$		42	$54 \times \frac{7}{9} =$	
21	$\frac{5}{6} \times 12 =$		43	$49 \times \frac{3}{7} =$	
22	$\frac{1}{4} \times 8 =$		44	$\frac{6}{7} \times 56 =$	

COMMON CORE™   **Lesson 14:**   Multiply unit fractions by non-unit fractions.
           Date: 11/10/13   **4.E.26**

Name _____   Date _____

1. Solve. Draw a model to explain your thinking. Then write a number sentence. An example has been done for you.

Example:

$\frac{1}{2}$ of $\frac{2}{5}$ = $\frac{1}{2}$ of 2 fifths = 1 fifth

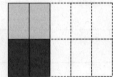 $\frac{1}{2} \times \frac{2}{5} = \frac{2}{10} = \frac{1}{5}$

a. $\frac{1}{3}$ of $\frac{3}{4}$ = $\frac{1}{3}$ of ____ fourths = ____ fourth   b. $\frac{1}{2}$ of $\frac{4}{5}$ = $\frac{1}{2}$ of ____ fifths = ____fifths

c. $\frac{1}{2}$ of $\frac{2}{2}$ =   d. $\frac{2}{3}$ of $\frac{1}{2}$ =

e. $\frac{1}{2} \times \frac{3}{5}$ =   f. $\frac{2}{3} \times \frac{1}{4}$ =

2. $\frac{5}{8}$ of the songs on Harrison's iPod are hip-hop. $\frac{1}{3}$ of the remaining songs are rhythm and blues. What fraction of all the songs are rhythm and blues? Use a tape diagram to solve.

3. Three-fifths of the students in a room are girls. One-third of the girls have blond hair. One-half of the boys have brown hair.
    a. What fraction of all the students are girls with blond hair?

    b. What fraction of all the students are boys without brown hair?

4. Cody and Sam mowed the yard on Saturday. Dad told Cody to mow $\frac{1}{4}$ of the yard. He told Sam to mow $\frac{1}{3}$ of the remainder of the yard. Dad paid each of the boys an equal amount. Sam said, "Dad, that's not fair! I had to mow one-third and Cody only mowed one-fourth!" Explain to Sam the error in his thinking. Draw a picture to support your reasoning.

	Lesson 14:	Multiply unit fractions by non-unit fractions.	
	Date:	11/10/13	4.E.28

Name _____ Date _____

1. Solve. Draw a model to explain your thinking. Then write a number sentence.

   a. $\frac{1}{3}$ of $\frac{3}{7}$ =

2. In a cookie jar, $\frac{1}{4}$ of the cookies are chocolate chip, and $\frac{1}{2}$ of the rest are peanut butter. What fraction of all the cookies are peanut butter?

COMMON CORE

Lesson 14: Multiply unit fractions by non-unit fractions.
Date: 11/10/13

4.E.29

Name _____   Date _____

1. Solve. Draw a model to explain your thinking.

a. $\frac{1}{2}$ of $\frac{2}{3} = \frac{1}{2}$ of ____ thirds = ____ thirds

b. $\frac{1}{2}$ of $\frac{4}{3} = \frac{1}{2}$ of ____ thirds = ____ thirds

c. $\frac{1}{3}$ of $\frac{3}{5} =$

d. $\frac{1}{2} \times \frac{6}{8} =$

e. $\frac{1}{3} \times \frac{4}{5} =$

f. $\frac{4}{5} \times \frac{1}{3} =$

2. Sarah has a photography blog. $\frac{3}{7}$ of her photos are of nature. $\frac{1}{4}$ of the rest are of her friends. What fraction of all Sarah's photos is of her friends? Support your answer with a model.

3. At Laurita's Bakery, $\frac{3}{5}$ of the baked goods are pies, and the rest are cakes. $\frac{1}{3}$ of the pies are coconut. $\frac{1}{6}$ of the cakes are angel-food.

    a. What fraction of all of the baked goods at Laurita's Bakery are coconut pies?

    b. What fraction of all of the baked goods at Laurita's Bakery are angel-food cakes?

4. Grandpa Mick opened a pint of ice cream. He gave his youngest grandchild $\frac{1}{5}$ of the ice cream and his middle grandchild $\frac{1}{4}$ of the remaining ice cream. Then he gave his oldest grandchild $\frac{1}{3}$ of the ice cream that was left after serving the others.

    a. Who got the most ice cream? How do you know? Draw a picture to support your reasoning.

    b. What fraction of the pint of ice cream will be left if Grandpa Mick serves himself the same amount as the second grandchild?

Lesson 14: Multiply unit fractions by non-unit fractions.
Date: 11/10/13

4.E.31

Lesson 15

Objective: Multiply non-unit fractions by non-unit fractions.

Suggested Lesson Structure

■ Fluency Practice   (12 minutes)

■ Application Problem   (7 minutes)

□ Concept Development   (31 minutes)

■ Student Debrief   (10 minutes)

Total Time   **(60 minutes)**

Fluency Practice (12 minutes)

- Multiply Fractions **5.NF.4**   (4 minutes)
- Write Fractions as Decimals **5.NF.3**   (4 minutes)
- Convert to Hundredths **4.NF.5**   (4 minutes)

Multiply Fractions (4 minutes)

Materials: (S) Personal white boards

Note: This fluency reviews G5–M4–Lesson 13.

T: (Write $\frac{1}{2}$ of $\frac{1}{3}$.) Say the fraction of a set as a multiplication sentence.

S: $\frac{1}{2} \times \frac{1}{3}$.

T: Draw a rectangle and shade in 1 third.

S: (Draw a rectangle, partition it into 3 equal units, and shade 1 of the units.)

T: To show $\frac{1}{2}$ of $\frac{1}{3}$, how many parts do you need to break the 1 third into?

S: 2.

T: Shade 1 half of 1 third.

S: (Shade 1 of the 2 parts.)

T: How can we name this new unit?

S: Partition the other 2 thirds in half.

T: Show the new units.

S: (Partition the other thirds into 2 equal parts.)

T: How many new units do you have?

COMMON CORE™ | Lesson 15:   Multiply non-unit fractions by non-unit fractions.

              | Date: 11/10/13

4.E.32

S: 6 units.

T: Write the multiplication sentence.

S: (Write $\frac{1}{2} \times \frac{1}{3} = \frac{1}{6}$.)

Continue the process with the following possible sequence: $\frac{1}{3}$ of $\frac{3}{4}$, $\frac{1}{2}$ of $\frac{6}{5}$, and $\frac{3}{5}$ of $\frac{1}{2}$.

Write Fractions as Decimals   (4 minutes)

Note: This fluency prepares students for G5–M4–Lessons 17–18.

T: (Write $\frac{1}{10}$.)   Say the fraction.

S: 1 tenth.

T: Say it as a decimal.

S: Zero point one.

Continue with the following possible suggestions: $\frac{2}{10}$, $\frac{3}{10}$, $\frac{9}{10}$, and $\frac{6}{10}$.

T: (Write $\frac{1}{100}$ = _____.)   Say the fraction.

S: 1 hundredth.

T: Say it as a decimal.

S: Zero point zero one.

Continue with the following possible suggestions: $\frac{2}{100}$, $\frac{8}{100}$, $\frac{9}{100}$, $\frac{11}{100}$, $\frac{17}{100}$, and $\frac{53}{100}$.

T: (Write 0.01 = _____.)   Say it as a fraction.

S: 1 hundredth.

T: (Write 0.01 = $\frac{1}{100}$.)

Continue with the following possible suggestions: 0.02, 0.09, 0.13, and 0.37.

Convert to Hundredths   (4 minutes)

Materials: (S) Personal white boards

Note: This fluency prepares students for G5–M4–Lessons 17–18.

T: (Write $\frac{1}{5} = \frac{}{100}$.)   Write the equivalent fraction.

S: (Write $\frac{1}{5} = \frac{20}{100}$.)

T: (Write $\frac{1}{5} = \frac{20}{100}$ = _____.)   Write 1 fifth as a decimal.

S: (Write $\frac{1}{5} = \frac{20}{100}$ = 0.2.)

Continue with the following possible suggestions: $\frac{2}{5}$, $\frac{4}{5}$, $\frac{1}{50}$, $\frac{9}{50}$, $\frac{11}{50}$, $\frac{1}{4}$, $\frac{3}{4}$, $\frac{1}{25}$, $\frac{2}{25}$, $\frac{7}{25}$, and $\frac{12}{25}$.

Lesson 15:   Multiply non-unit fractions by non-unit fractions.
Date: 11/10/13

4.E.33

Application Problem (7 minutes)

Kendra spent $\frac{1}{3}$ of her allowance on a book and $\frac{2}{5}$ on a snack. If she had four dollars remaining after purchasing a book and snack, what was the total amount of her allowance?

Note: This problem reaches back to addition and subtraction of fractions as well as fraction of a set. Keeping these skills fresh is an important goal of Application Problems.

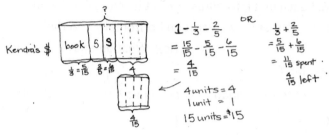

Concept Development (31 minutes)

Materials: (S) Personal white boards

Problem 1

$\frac{2}{3}$ of $\frac{3}{4}$

T: (Post Problem 1 on the board.) How is this problem different from the problems we did yesterday? Turn and talk.

S: In every problem we did yesterday, one factor had a numerator of 1. There are no numerators that are ones today. → Every problem multiplied a unit fraction by a non-unit fraction, or a non-unit fraction by a unit fraction. This is two non-unit fractions.

T: (Write $\frac{1}{3}$ of 3 fourths.) What is 1 third of 3 fourths?

S: 1 fourth.

T: If 1 third of 3 fourths is 1 fourth, what is 2 thirds of 3 fourths? Discuss with your partner.

S: 2 thirds would just be double 1 third, so it would be 2 fourths. → 3 fourths is 3 equal parts so $\frac{1}{3}$ of that would be 1 part or 1 fourth. We want $\frac{2}{3}$ this time, so that is 2 parts, or 2 fourths.

T: Name 2 fourths using halves.

S: 1 half.

T: So, 2 thirds of 3 fourths is 1 half. Let's draw an area model to show the product and check our thinking.

T: I'll draw it on the board, and you'll draw it on your personal board. Let's draw 3 fourths and label it on the bottom. (Draw a rectangle and cut it vertically into 4 units, and shade in 3 units.)

NOTES ON MULTIPLE MEANS OF REPRESENTATION:

Notice the dotted lines in the area model shown below.

If this were an actual pan partially full of brownies, the empty part of the pan would obviously not be cut! However, to name the unit represented by the double-shaded parts, the whole pan must show the same size or type of unit. Therefore, the empty part of the pan must also be partitioned as illustrated by the dotted lines.

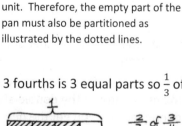

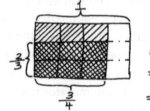

COMMON CORE™   Lesson 15:   Multiply non-unit fractions by non-unit fractions.
Date: 11/10/13

4.E.34

T: (Point to the 3 shaded units.) We now have to take 2 thirds of these 3 shaded units. What do I have to do? Turn and talk.

S: Cut each unit into thirds. → Cut it across into 3 equal parts, and shade in 2 parts.

T: Let's do that now. (Partition horizontally into thirds, shade in 2 thirds and label.)

T: (Point to the whole rectangle.) What unit have we used to rename our whole?

S: Twelfths.

T: (Point to the 6 double-shaded units.) How many twelfths are double-shaded when we took $\frac{2}{3}$ of $\frac{3}{4}$?

S: 6 twelfths.

T: Compare our model to the product we thought about. Do they represent the same product or have we made a mistake? Turn and talk.

S: The units are different, but the answer is the same. 2 fourths and 6 twelfths are both names for 1 half. → When we thought about it, we knew it would be 2 fourths. In the area model, there are 12 parts and we shaded 6 of them. That's half.

T: Both of our approaches show that 2 thirds of 3 fourths is what simplified fraction?

S: $\frac{1}{2}$.

T: Let's write this problem as a multiplication sentence. (Write $\frac{2}{3} \times \frac{3}{4} = \frac{6}{12}$ on the board.) Turn and talk to your partner about the patterns you notice.

S: If you multiply the numerators you get 6 and the denominators you get 12. That's 6 twelfths just like the area model. → It's easy to get a fraction of a fraction, just multiply the top numbers to get the numerator and the bottom to get the denominator. Sometimes you can simplify.

T: So, the product of the denominators tells us the total number of units, 12 (point to the model). The product of the numerators tells us the total number of units selected, 6.

Problem 2

$\frac{2}{3} \times \frac{2}{3}$

T: (Post Problem 2 on the board.) We need 2 thirds of 2 thirds this time. Draw an area model to solve and then write a multiplication sentence. Talk to your partner about whether the patterns are the same as before.

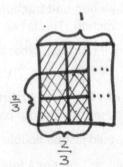

S: It's the same as before. When you multiply the numerators, you get the numerator of the double-shaded part. When you multiply the denominators, you get the denominator of the double-shaded part. → It's pretty cool! The denominator of the product gives the area of the whole rectangle (3 by 3) and the numerator of the product gives the area of the double-shaded part (2 by 2)!

T: Yes, we see from the model that the product of the denominators tells us the total number of units, 9. The product of the numerator tells us the total number of units selected, 4.

Lesson 15:   Multiply non-unit fractions by non-unit fractions.
Date: 11/10/13

Problem 3

a. $\frac{7}{9}$ of $\frac{3}{7}$

b. $\frac{3}{10} \times \frac{5}{9}$

c. $\frac{5}{8} \times \frac{4}{15}$

T: (Post Problem 3(a) on the board.) How would this problem look if we drew an area model for it? Discuss with your partner.

S: We'd have to draw 3 sevenths first, and then split each seventh into ninths. → We'd end up with a model showing sixty-thirds. It would be really hard to draw.

T: You are right. It's not really practical to draw an area model for a problem like this because the units are so small. Could the pattern that we've noticed in the multiplication sentences help us? Turn and talk.

S: $\frac{7}{9}$ of $\frac{3}{7}$ is the same as $\frac{7}{9} \times \frac{3}{7}$. → Our pattern lets us just multiply the numerators and the denominators. → We can multiply and get 21 as the numerator and 63 as the denominator. Then we can simplify and get 1 third.

T: Let me write what I hear you saying. (Write $\frac{7}{9} \times \frac{3}{7} = \frac{7 \times 3}{9 \times 7} = \frac{21}{63}$ on the board.)

T: What's the simplest form for $\frac{21}{63}$? Solve it on your board.

S: $\frac{1}{3}$.

T: Let's use another strategy we learned recently and rename this fraction using larger units before we multiply. (Point to $\frac{7 \times 3}{9 \times 7}$.) Look for factors that are shared by the numerator and the denominator. Turn and talk.

S: There's a 7 in both the numerator and the denominator. → The numerator and denominator have a common factor of 7. → I know the 3 in the numerator can be divided by 3 to get 1 and the 9 in the denominator can be divided by 3 to get 3. → Seven divided by 7 is 1, so both sevens change to ones. The factors of 3 and 9 can both be divided by 3 and changed to 1 and 3.

T: We can rename this fraction by dividing both the numerators and denominators by common factors. Seven divided by 7 is 1, in both the numerator and denominator. (Cross out both sevens and write ones next to them.) Three divided by 3 is 1 in the numerator, and 9 divided by 3 is 3 in the denominator. (Cross out the 3 and 9 and write 1 and 3 respectively, next to them.)

T: What does the numerator show now?

S: 1 × 1.

T: What's the denominator?

S: 3 × 1.

Lesson 15: Multiply non-unit fractions by non-unit fractions.
Date: 11/10/13

4.E.36

T: Now multiply. What is $\frac{7}{9}$ of $\frac{3}{7}$ equal to?

S: $\frac{1}{3}$.

T: Look at the two strategies, which one do you think is the easier and more efficient to use? Turn and talk.

S: The first strategy of simplifying $\frac{21}{63}$ after I multiply is a little bit harder because I have to find the common factors between 21 and 63. → Simplifying first is a little easier. Before I multiply, the numbers are a little smaller so it's easier to see common factors. Also, when I simplify first, the numbers I have to multiply are smaller, and my product is already expressed using the largest unit.

T: (Post Problem 3(b) on the board.) Let's practice using the strategy of simplifying first before we multiply. Work with a partner and solve. Remember, we are looking for common factors before we multiply. (Allow students time to work and share their answers.)

T: What is $\frac{3}{10}$ of $\frac{5}{9}$?

S: $\frac{1}{6}$.

T: Let's confirm that by multiplying first and then simplifying.

S: (Rework the problem to find $\frac{3}{10} \times \frac{5}{9} = \frac{15}{90} = \frac{1}{6}$.)

T: (Post Problem 3(c) on the board.) Solve independently. (Allow students time to solve the problem.)

T: What is $\frac{5}{8}$ of $\frac{4}{15}$?

S: $\frac{1}{6}$.

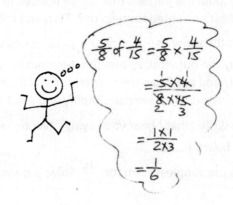

Problem 4

Nigel completes $\frac{3}{7}$ of his homework immediately after school and $\frac{1}{4}$ of the remaining homework before supper. He finishes the rest after dessert. What fraction of his work did he finish after dessert?

T: (Post the problem on the board, and read it aloud with students.) Let's solve using a tape diagram.

S/T: (Draw diagram.)

T: What fraction of his homework does Nigel finish immediately after school?

S: $\frac{3}{7}$.

T: (Partition diagram into sevenths and label 3 of them *after school*.) What fraction of the homework does Nigel have remaining?

S: $\frac{4}{7}$.

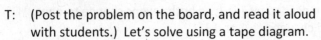

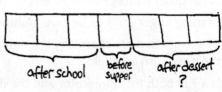

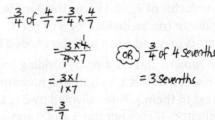

Nigel completes $\frac{3}{7}$ of his homework after dessert.

Lesson 15: Multiply non-unit fractions by non-unit fractions.
Date: 11/10/13

4.E.37

T: What fraction of the remaining homework does Nigel finish before supper?

S: One-fourth of the remaining homework.

T: Nigel completes $\frac{1}{4}$ of 4 sevenths before supper. (Point to the remaining 4 units on the tape diagram.) What's $\frac{1}{4}$ of these 4 units?

S: 1 unit.

T: Then what's $\frac{1}{4}$ of 4 sevenths? (Write $\frac{1}{4}$ of 4 sevenths = _____ sevenths on the board.)

S: 1 seventh. (Label 1 seventh of the diagram *before supper*.)

T: When does Nigel finish the rest? (Point to the remaining units.)

S: After dessert. (Label the remaining $\frac{3}{7}$ *after dessert*.)

T: Answer the question with a complete sentence.

S: Nigel completes $\frac{3}{7}$ of his homework after dessert.

T: Let's imagine that Nigel spent 70 minutes to complete all of his homework. Where would I place that information in the model?

S: Put 70 minutes above the diagram. → We just found out the whole, so we can label it above the tape diagram.

T: How could I find the number of minutes he worked on homework after dessert? Discuss with your partner, then solve.

S: He finished $\frac{4}{7}$ already, so we can find $\frac{4}{7}$ of 70 minutes and then just subtract that from 70 to find how long he spent after dessert. → It's fraction of a set. He does $\frac{3}{7}$ of his homework after dessert. We can multiply to find $\frac{3}{7}$ of 70. That'll be how long he worked after dessert. → We can first find the total minutes he spent after school by solving $\frac{3}{7}$ of 70. Then we know each unit is 10 minutes. → We find what one unit is equal to, which is 10 minutes. Then we know the time he spent after dessert is 3 units. 10 times 3 = 30 minutes.

T: Use your work to answer the question.

S: Nigel spends 30 minutes working after dessert.

NOTES ON MULTIPLE MEANS OF REPRESENTATION:

In these examples, students are simplifying the fractional factors before they multiply. This step may eliminate the need to simplify the product, or make simplifying the product easier.

In order to help struggling students understand this procedure, it may help to use the Commutative Property to reverse the order of the factors. For example:

$$\frac{3 \times 4}{4 \times 7} = \frac{4 \times 3}{4 \times 7}$$

In this example, students may now more readily see that $\frac{4}{4}$ is equivalent to $\frac{1}{1}$, and can be simplified before multiplying.

Problem Set (10 minutes)

Students should do their personal best to complete the Problem Set within the allotted 10 minutes. For some classes, it may be appropriate to modify the assignment by specifying which problems they work on first. Some problems do not specify a method for solving. Students solve these problems using the RDW approach used for Application Problems.

Lesson 15:   Multiply non-unit fractions by non-unit fractions.
Date: 11/10/13

Student Debrief (10 minutes)

Lesson Objective: Multiply non-unit fractions by non-unit fractions.

The Student Debrief is intended to invite reflection and active processing of the total lesson experience.

Invite students to review their solutions for the Problem Set. They should check work by comparing answers with a partner before going over answers as a class. Look for misconceptions or misunderstandings that can be addressed in the Debrief. Guide students in a conversation to debrief the Problem Set and process the lesson.

You may choose to use any combination of the questions below to lead the discussion.

- What is the relationship between Parts (c) and (d) of Problem 1? (Part(d) is double (c).)

- In Problem 2, how are Parts (b) and (d) different from Parts (a) and (c)? (Parts (b) and (d) have two common factors each.)

- Compare the picture you drew for Problem 3 with a partner. Explain your solution.

- In Problem 5, how is the information in the answer to Part (a) different from the information in the answer to Part (b)? What are the different approaches to solving, and is there one strategy that is more efficient than the others? (Using fraction of a set might be more efficient than subtraction.) Explain your strategy to a partner.

Exit Ticket (3 minutes)

After the Student Debrief, instruct students to complete the Exit Ticket. A review of their work will help you assess the students' understanding of the concepts that were presented in the lesson today and plan more effectively for future lessons. You may read the questions aloud to the students.

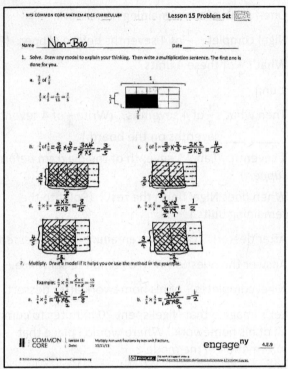

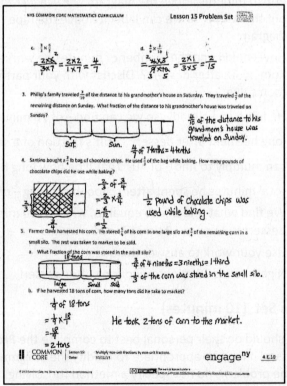

Lesson 15:   Multiply non-unit fractions by non-unit fractions.
Date: 11/10/13

4.E.39

Name _____   Date _____

1. Solve. Draw any model to explain your thinking. Then write a multiplication sentence. The first one is done for you.

    a. $\frac{2}{3}$ of $\frac{3}{5}$

    $$\frac{2}{3} \times \frac{3}{5} = \frac{6}{15} = \frac{2}{5}$$

    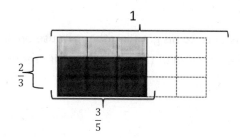

    b. $\frac{3}{4}$ of $\frac{4}{5}$ c. $\frac{2}{5}$ of $\frac{2}{3} =$

    d. $\frac{4}{5} \times \frac{2}{3} =$ e. $\frac{3}{4} \times \frac{2}{3} =$

2. Multiply. Draw a model if it helps you, or use the method in the example.

    Example: $\frac{6}{7} \times \frac{5}{8} = \frac{\overset{3}{\cancel{6}} \times 5}{7 \times \underset{4}{\cancel{8}}} = \frac{15}{28}$

    a. $\frac{3}{4} \times \frac{5}{6}$ b. $\frac{4}{5} \times \frac{5}{8}$

c. $\dfrac{2}{3} \times \dfrac{6}{7}$ _____   d. $\dfrac{4}{9} \times \dfrac{3}{10}$ _____

3. Phillip's family traveled $\dfrac{3}{10}$ of the distance to his grandmother's house on Saturday. They traveled $\dfrac{4}{7}$ of the remaining distance on Sunday. What fraction of the distance to his grandmother's house was traveled on Sunday?

4. Santino bought a $\dfrac{3}{4}$ lb bag of chocolate chips. He used $\dfrac{2}{3}$ of the bag while baking. How many pounds of chocolate chips did he use while baking?

5. Farmer Dave harvested his corn. He stored $\dfrac{5}{9}$ of his corn in one large silo and $\dfrac{3}{4}$ of the remaining corn in a small silo. The rest was taken to market to be sold.
   a. What fraction of the corn was stored in the small silo?

   b. If he harvested 18 tons of corn, how many tons did he take to market?

Lesson 15:   Multiply non-unit fractions by non-unit fractions.
Date: 11/10/13

4.E.41

Name _____   Date _____

1. Solve.

   a. $\frac{2}{3}$ of $\frac{3}{5}$

   b. $\frac{4}{9} \times \frac{3}{8}$

2. A newspaper's cover page is $\frac{3}{8}$ text, and photographs fill the rest. If $\frac{2}{5}$ of the text is an article about endangered species, what fraction of the cover page is the article about endangered species?

COMMON CORE™

Lesson 15:   Multiply non-unit fractions by non-unit fractions.
Date: 11/10/13

4.E.42

Name _____   Date _____

1. Solve. Draw a model to explain your thinking. Then write a multiplication sentence.

   a. $\frac{2}{3}$ of $\frac{3}{4}$

   b. $\frac{2}{5}$ of $\frac{3}{4}$

   c. $\frac{2}{5}$ of $\frac{4}{5}$

   d. $\frac{4}{5}$ of $\frac{3}{4}$

2. Multiply. Draw a model if it helps you.

   a. $\frac{5}{6} \times \frac{3}{10}$

   b. $\frac{3}{4} \times \frac{4}{5}$

   c. $\frac{5}{6} \times \frac{5}{8}$

   d. $\frac{3}{4} \times \frac{5}{12}$

   e. $\frac{8}{9} \times \frac{3}{2}$

   f. $\frac{3}{7} \times \frac{2}{9}$

COMMON CORE™   Lesson 15:   Multiply non-unit fractions by non-unit fractions.
Date: 11/10/13

4.E.43

3. Every morning, Halle goes to school with a 1 liter bottle of water. She drinks $\frac{1}{4}$ of the bottle before school starts and $\frac{2}{3}$ of the rest before lunch.
   a. What fraction of the bottle does Halle drink before lunch?

   b. How many milliliters are left in the bottle at lunch?

4. Moussa delivered $\frac{3}{8}$ of the newspapers on his route in the first hour and $\frac{4}{5}$ of the rest in the second hour. What fraction of the newspapers did Moussa deliver in the second hour?

5. Rose bought some spinach. She used $\frac{3}{5}$ of the spinach on a pan of spinach pie for a party, and $\frac{3}{4}$ of the remaining spinach for a pan for her family. She used the rest of the spinach to make a salad.
   a. What fraction of the spinach did she use to make the salad?

   b. If Rose used 3 pounds of spinach to make the pan of spinach pie for the party, how many pounds of spinach did Rose use to make the salad?

Lesson 16

Objective: Solve word problems using tape diagrams and fraction-by-fraction multiplication.

Suggested Lesson Structure

- ■ Fluency Practice   (8 minutes)
- ■ Concept Development   (42 minutes)
- ■ Student Debrief   (10 minutes)
- **Total Time**   **(60 minutes)**

Fluency Practice (8 minutes)

- Multiply Fractions **5.NF.4**   (3 minutes)
- Multiply Whole Numbers by Decimals **5.NBT.7**   (5 minutes)

Multiply Fractions (3 minutes)

Materials: (S) Personal white boards

Note: This fluency reviews G5–M4–Lessons 14–15.

T: (Write $\frac{1}{3}$ of $\frac{2}{5}$ is _____.) Write the fraction of a set as a multiplication sentence.

S: $\frac{1}{3} \times \frac{2}{5}$.

T: Draw a rectangle and shade in $\frac{2}{5}$.

S: (Draw a rectangle, partition it into 5 equal units, and shade 2 of the units.)

T: To show $\frac{1}{3}$ of $\frac{2}{5}$, how many equal parts to we need?

S: 3.

T: Show 1 third of 2 fifths.

S: (Partition the 2 fifths into thirds, and shade 1 third.)

T: Make the other units the same size as the double shaded ones.

S: (Extend the horizontal thirds across the remaining units using dotted lines.)

T: What unit do we have now?

S: Fifteenths.

**NOTES ON
MULTIPLE MEANS OF
ENGAGEMENT:**

Sixty minutes is allotted for all lessons in Grade 5. All 60 minutes, however, do not need to be consecutive. For example, fluencies can be completed as students wait in line, or when they are transitioning between subjects.

| | Lesson 16: | Solve word problems using tape diagrams and fraction-by-fraction multiplication. |
| | **Date:** | 11/10/13 |

4.E.45

T: How many fifteenths are double-shaded?

S: Two.

T: Write the product and say the sentence.

S: (Write $\frac{1}{3} \times \frac{2}{5} = \frac{2}{15}$.) $\frac{1}{3}$ of $\frac{2}{5}$ is 2 fifteenths.

Continue this process with the following possible sequence: $\frac{2}{3} \times \frac{2}{5}$, $\frac{3}{5} \times \frac{2}{3}$, and $\frac{3}{5} \times \frac{3}{4}$.

Multiply Whole Numbers by Decimals (5 minutes)

Materials: (S) Personal white boards

Note: This fluency prepares students for G5–M4–Lessons 17–18.

T: (Write $\frac{1}{10} + \frac{1}{10} + \frac{1}{10}$). Say the repeated addition sentence.

S: $\frac{1}{10} + \frac{1}{10} + \frac{1}{10} = \frac{3}{10}$.

T: (Write $3 \times \_\_ = \frac{3}{10}$.) On your boards, write the number sentence, filling in the missing number.

S: (Write $3 \times \frac{1}{10} = \frac{3}{10}$.)

T: (Write $3 \times \frac{1}{10} = 3 \times 0.\_\_$.) On your boards, fill in the missing digit.

S: (Write $3 \times \frac{1}{10} = 3 \times 0.1$.)

T: (Write $3 \times 0.1 = 0.\_\_$.) Say the missing digit.

S: 3.

Continue with the following expression: $\frac{1}{10} + \frac{1}{10} + \frac{1}{10} + \frac{1}{10} + \frac{1}{10}$.

T: (Write $7 \times 0.1 = \_\_\_\_$.) On your boards, write the number sentence.

S: (Write $7 \times 0.1 = 0.7$.)

T: (Write $7 \times 0.01 = \_\_\_\_$.) On your boards, write the number sentence.

S: (Write $7 \times 0.01 = 0.07$.)

Continue this process with the following possible sequence: 9×0.1 and 9×0.01.

T: (Write $20 \times \frac{1}{10} = \_\_\_\_$.) On your boards, write the number sentence.

S: (Write $20 \times \frac{1}{10} = \frac{20}{10} = 2$.)

T: (Write $20 \times 0.1 = \_\_\_\_$.) Write the number sentence on your boards.

S: (Write $20 \times 0.1 = 2$.)

T: (Write $20 \times 0.01 = \_\_\_\_$.) Write the number sentence on your boards.

S: (Write $20 \times 0.01 = 0.2$.)

Continue this process with the following possible sequence: 80×0.1 and 80×0.01.

T: (Write $15 \times \frac{1}{10} = \_\_\_\_$.) On your boards, write the number sentence.

S: (Write $15 \times \frac{1}{10} = \frac{15}{10}$.)

T: (Write $15 \times 0.1 =$ ____.) On your boards, write the number sentence and answer as a decimal.

S: (Write $15 \times 0.1 = 1.5$.)

T: (Write $15 \times 0.01 =$ ____.) On your boards, write the number sentence and answer as a decimal.

S: (Write $15 \times 0.01 = 0.15$.)

Continue with the following possible sequence: 37×0.1 and 37×0.01.

Concept Development (42 minutes)

Materials: (S) Problem Set, personal white boards

Note: Because today's lesson involves students in learning a new type of tape diagram, the time normally allotted to the Application Problem has been used in the Concept Development to allow students ample time to draw and solve the story problems.

Note: There are multiple approaches to solving these problems. Modeling for a few strategies is included here, but teachers should not discourage students from using other mathematically sound procedures for solving. The dialogues for the modeled problems are detailed as a scaffold for teachers unfamiliar with fraction tape diagrams.

Problem 2 from the Problem Set opens the lesson and is worked using two different fractions (first 1 fifth, then 2 fifths) so that diagramming of two different whole–part situations may be modeled.

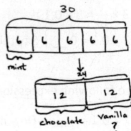

Problem 2

Joakim is icing 30 cupcakes. He spreads mint icing on $\frac{1}{5}$ of the cupcakes and chocolate on $\frac{1}{2}$ of the remaining cupcakes. The rest will get vanilla frosting. How many cupcakes have vanilla frosting?

T: (Display Problem 2, and read it aloud with students.)
     Let's use a tape diagram to model this problem.

T: This problem is about Joakim's cupcakes. What does the first sentence tell us?

S: Joakim has 30 cupcakes.

T: (Draw a diagram and label with a bracket and 30.) Joakim is icing the cupcakes. What fraction of the cupcakes get mint icing?

S: $\frac{1}{5}$ of the cupcakes.

T: How can I show fifths in my diagram?

S: Partition the whole into 5 equal units.

T: How many of those units have mint icing?

S: 1.

Lesson 16:   Solve word problems using tape diagrams and fraction-by-fraction multiplication.

Date: 11/10/13

4.E.4

T: Let's show that now. (Partition the diagram into fifths and label 1 unit mint.)

T: Read the next sentence.

S: (Read.)

T: Where are the remaining cupcakes in our tape?

S: The unlabeled units.

T: Let's drop that part down and draw a new tape to represent the remaining cupcakes. (Draw a new diagram underneath the original whole.)

T: What do we know about these remaining cupcakes?

S: Half of them get chocolate icing.

T: How can we represent that in our new diagram?

S: Cut it into 2 equal parts and label 1 of them chocolate.

T: Let's do that now. (Partition the lower diagram into 2 units and label 1 unit *chocolate*.) What about the rest of the remaining cupcakes?

S: They are vanilla.

T: Let's label the other half *vanilla*. (Model.) What is the question asking us?

S: How many are vanilla?

T: Place a question mark below the portion showing vanilla. (Put a question mark beneath *vanilla*.)

T: Let's look at our diagram to see if we can find how many cupcakes get vanilla icing. How many units does the model show? (Point to original tape.)

S: 5 units.

T: (Write 5 units.) How many cupcakes does Joakim have in all?

S: 30 cupcakes.

T: (Write = 30 cupcakes.) If 5 units equals 30 cupcakes, how can we find the value of 1 unit? Turn and talk.

S: It's like 5 times what equals 30. $5 \times 6 = 30$, so 1 unit equals 6 cupcakes. → We can divide. 30 cupcakes ÷ 5 = 6 cupcakes.

T: What is 1 unit equal to? (Write 1 unit = ____.)

S: 6 cupcakes.

T: Let's write 6 in each unit to show its value. (Write 6 in each unit of original diagram.) That means that 6 cupcakes get mint icing. How many cupcakes remain? (Point to 4 remaining units.) Turn and talk.

S: $30 - 6 = 24$. → $6 + 6 + 6 + 6 = 24$. → 4 units of 6 is 24. $4 \times 6 = 24$.

T: Let's label that on the diagram showing the remaining cupcakes. (Label 24 above the second diagram.) How can we find the number of cupcakes that get vanilla icing? Turn and talk.

S: Half of the 24 cupcakes get chocolate and half get vanilla. Half of 24 is 12. → $24 \div 2 = 12$.

T: What is half of 24?

S: 12.

T: (Write $\frac{24}{2} = 12$ and label 12 in each half of the second diagram.) Write a statement to answer the question.

S: 12 cupcakes have vanilla icing.

T: Let's think of this another way. When we labeled the 1 fifth for the mint icing, what fraction of the cupcakes were remaining?

S: $\frac{4}{5}$.

S: What does Joakim do with the remaining cupcakes?

S: $\frac{1}{2}$ of the remaining cupcakes get chocolate icing.

T: (Write $\frac{1}{2}$ of.) $\frac{1}{2}$ of what fraction?

S: 1 half of 4 fifths.

T: (Write 4 fifths.) What is $\frac{1}{2}$ of 4 fifths?

S: $\frac{2}{5}$.

T: So, 2 fifths of all the cupcakes got chocolate, and 2 fifths of all the cupcakes got vanilla. The question asked us how many cupcakes got vanilla icing. Let's find 2 fifths of all the cupcakes—2 fifths of 30. Work with your partner to solve.

S: 1 fifth of 30 is 6, so 2 fifths of 30 is 12. → $\frac{2}{5} \times 30 = \frac{2 \times 30}{5} = \frac{60}{5} = 12$ → $\frac{2}{5} \times 30 = 2 \times \frac{30}{5} = 2 \times 6 = 12$.

T: So, using fraction multiplication, we got the same answer, 12 cupcakes.

T: This time, let's imagine that Joakim put mint icing on 2 fifths of the cupcakes. Draw another diagram to show that situation.

S: (Draw.)

T: What fraction of the cupcakes are remaining this time?

S: 3 fifths.

T: Let's draw a second tape that is the same length as the remaining part of our whole. (Draw the second tape below the first.) Has the value of one unit changed in our model? Why or why not?

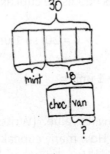

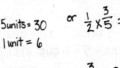

S: The unit is still 6 because the whole is still 30 and we still have fifths. → Each unit is still 6 because we still divided 30 into 5 equal parts.

T: So, how many remaining cupcakes are there this time?

S: 18.

T: Imagine that Joakim still put chocolate icing on half the remaining cupcakes, and the rest were still vanilla. How many cupcakes got vanilla icing this time? Work with a partner to model it in your tape diagram and answer the question with a complete sentence.

S: (Work.)

T: Let's confirm that there were 9 cupcakes that got vanilla icing by using fraction multiplication. How might we do this? Turn and talk.

MP.4

Lesson 16:   Solve word problems using tape diagrams and fraction-by-fraction
             multiplication.
Date: 11/10/13

4.E.4

S: We could just multiply $\frac{1}{2} \times \frac{3}{5}$ and get $\frac{3}{10}$. Then we can find 3 tenths of 30. That's 9! → We can find 1 half of 3 fifths. That gives us the fraction of all the cupcakes that got vanilla icing. We need the number of cupcakes, not just the fraction, so we need to multiply 3 tenths and 30 to get 9 cupcakes. → Nine cupcakes got vanilla frosting.

MP.4

T: Complete Problem 1 and Problem 3 on the Problem Set. Check your work with a neighbor when you're finished. You may use either method to solve.

Solutions for Problems 1 and Problem 3

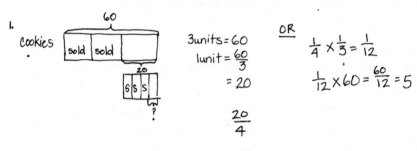

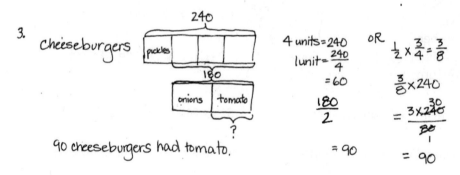

Problem 5

Milan puts $\frac{1}{4}$ of her lawn-mowing money in savings and uses $\frac{1}{2}$ of the remaining money to pay back her sister. If she has $15 left, how much did she have at first?

T: (Post Problem 5 on board, and read it aloud with students.) How is this problem different from the ones we've just solved? Turn and discuss with your partner.

S: In the others, we knew what the whole was, this time we don't. → We know how much money she has left, but we have to figure out what she had at the beginning. It seems like we might have to work backwards. → The other problems were whole-to-part problems. This one is part-to-whole.

T: Let's draw a tape diagram. (Draw a blank tape diagram.) What is the whole in this problem?

S: We don't know yet; we have to find it.

T: I'll put a question mark above our diagram to show that this is unknown. (Label diagram with a question mark.) What fraction of her money does Milan put in savings?

Lesson 16:	Solve word problems using tape diagrams and fraction-by-fraction multiplication.
Date:	11/10/13

4.E.50

S: $\frac{1}{4}$.

T: How can we show that on our diagram?

S: Cut the whole into 4 equal parts and bracket one of them. → Cut it into fourths and label 1 unit savings.

T: (Record on diagram.) What part of our diagram shows the remaining money?

S: The other parts.

T: Let's draw another diagram to represent the remaining money. Notice that I will draw it exactly the same length as those last 3 parts. (Model.) What do we know about this remaining part?

S: Milan gives half of it to her sister.

T: How can we model that?

S: Cut the bar into two parts and label one of them. (Partition the second diagram in halves, and label one of them *sister*.)

T: What about the other half of the remaining money?

S: That's how much she has left. It's $15.

T: Let's label that. (Write $15 in the second equal part.) If this half is $15, (point to labeled half) what do we know about the amount she gave her sister, and what does that tell us about how much was remaining in all? Turn and talk.

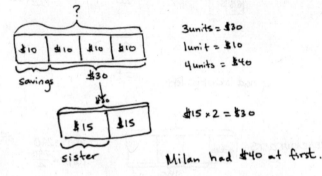

S: If one half is $15, then the other half is $15 too. That makes $30. → $15 + $15 = $30. → $15 × 2 = $30.

T: If the lower tape is worth $30, what do we know about these 3 units in the whole? (Point to original diagram.) Turn and discuss.

S: The remaining money is the same as 3 units, so 3 units is equal to $30. → They represent the same money in two different parts of the diagram. 3 units is equal to $30.

T: (Label 3 units $30.) If 3 units = $30, what is the value of 1 unit?

S: (Work and show 1 unit = $10.)

T: Label $10 inside each of the 3 units. (Model on diagram.) If these 3 units are equal to $10 each, what is the value of this last unit? (Point to savings unit.)

S: $10.

T: (Label $10 inside savings unit.) Look at our diagram. We have 4 units of $10 each. What is the value of the whole?

S: (Work and show 4 units = $40.)

T: Make a statement to answer the question.

S: Milan had $40 at first.

T: Let's check our work using a fraction of a set. What multiplication sentence tells us what fraction of

Lesson 16: Solve word problems using tape diagrams and fraction-by-fraction multiplication.

Date: 11/10/13

4.E.5

all her money Milan gave to her sister? What fraction did she give to her sister?

S: $\frac{1}{2} \times \frac{3}{4} = \frac{3}{8}$.

T: So, $15 should be 3 eighths of $40. Is that true? Let's see. Find $\frac{3}{8}$ of $40 with your partner.

S: (Work and show $\frac{3}{8}$ of $40 = $15.)

T: Does this confirm our answer of $40 as Milan's money at first?

S: Yes!

T: Complete Problem 4 and Problem 6 on the Problem Set. Check your work with a neighbor when you're finished. You may use either method to solve.

Solutions for Problem 4 and Problem 6

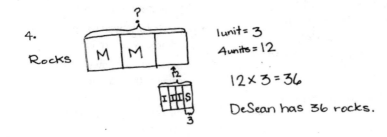

Note: Problem 7 may be used as an extension for early finishers.

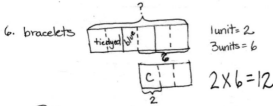

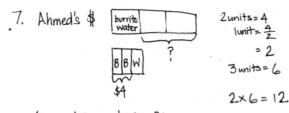

COMMON CORE™

Lesson 16: Solve word problems using tape diagrams and fraction-by-fraction multiplication.

Date: 11/10/13

4.E.52

Problem Set (10 minutes)

The Problem Set forms the basis for today's lesson. Please see the Concept Development for modeling suggestions.

Student Debrief (10 minutes)

Lesson Objective: Multiply non-unit fractions by non-unit fractions.

The Student Debrief is intended to invite reflection and active processing of the total lesson experience.

Invite students to review their solutions for the Problem Set. They should check work by comparing answers with a partner before going over answers as a class. Look for misconceptions or misunderstandings that can be addressed in the Debrief. Guide students in a conversation to debrief the Problem Set and process the lesson.

You may choose to use any combination of the questions below to lead the discussion.

- Did you use the same method for solving Problem 1 and Problem 3? Why or why not? Did you use the same method for solving Problem 4 and Problem 6? Why or why not?

- Were any alternate methods used? If so, explain what you did.

- How was setting up Problem 1 and Problem 3 different from the process for solving Problem 4 and Problem 6? What were your thoughts as you worked?

- Talk about how your tape diagrams helped you to find the solutions today. Give some examples of questions that you could have been able to answer, using the information in your tape diagram.

- Questions for further analysis of tape diagrams:
    - Problem 1: Half of the cookies sold were oatmeal raisin. How many oatmeal raisin cookies were sold?
    - Problem 3: What fraction of the burgers had onions? How many burgers had onions?

NOTES ON MULTIPLE MEANS OF ENGAGEMENT:

If it is anticipated that the student may struggle with a homework assignment, there are several ways to provide support.

- Complete one of the problems or a portion of a problem as an example before the pages are duplicated for students.
- Staple the Problem Set to the homework as a reference.
- Provide a copy of completed homework as a reference.
- Differentiate homework by using some of these strategies for specific students or specifying that only certain problems be completed.

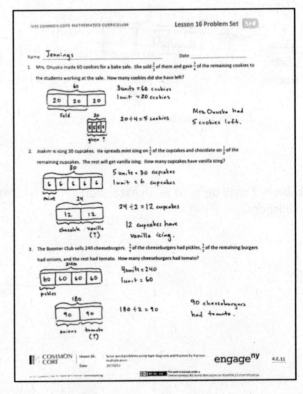

Lesson 16: Solve word problems using tape diagrams and fraction-by-fraction multiplication.
Date: 11/10/13

4.E.5

© 2013 Common Core, Inc. All rights reserved. commoncore.org

- ▪ Problem 4: How many more metamorphic rocks does DeSean have than igneous rocks?
- ▪ Problem 6: If Parks takes off 2 tie-dye bracelets, and puts on 2 more camouflage bracelets, what fraction of all the bracelets would be camouflage?

Exit Ticket (3 minutes)

After the Student Debrief, instruct students to complete the Exit Ticket. A review of their work will help you assess the students' understanding of the concepts that were presented in the lesson today and plan more effectively for future lessons. You may read the questions aloud to the students.

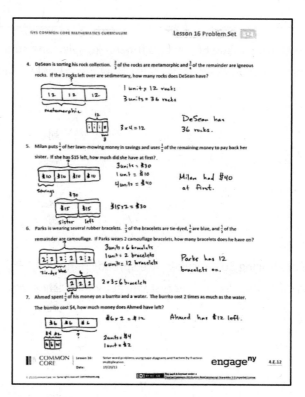

Lesson 16:   Solve word problems using tape diagrams and fraction-by-fraction
                multiplication.
Date: 11/10/13

4.E.54

4.E.5

Name _____   Date _____

1. Mrs. Onusko made 60 cookies for a bake sale. She sold $\frac{2}{3}$ of them and gave $\frac{3}{4}$ of the remaining cookies to the students working at the sale. How many cookies did she have left?

2. Joakim is icing 30 cupcakes. He spreads mint icing on $\frac{1}{5}$ of the cupcakes and chocolate on $\frac{1}{2}$ of the remaining cupcakes. The rest will get vanilla icing. How many cupcakes have vanilla icing?

3. The Booster Club sells 240 cheeseburgers. $\frac{1}{4}$ of the cheeseburgers had pickles, $\frac{1}{2}$ of the remaining burgers had onions, and the rest had tomato. How many cheeseburgers had tomato?

Lesson 16:   Solve word problems using tape diagrams and fraction-by-fraction multiplication.

Date: 11/10/13

4.E.5

4. DeSean is sorting his rock collection. $\frac{2}{3}$ of the rocks are metamorphic and $\frac{3}{4}$ of the remainder are igneous rocks. If the 3 rocks left over are sedimentary, how many rocks does DeSean have?

5. Milan puts $\frac{1}{4}$ of her lawn-mowing money in savings and uses $\frac{1}{2}$ of the remaining money to pay back her sister. If she has $15 left, how much did she have at first?

6. Parks is wearing several rubber bracelets. $\frac{1}{3}$ of the bracelets are tie-dye, $\frac{1}{6}$ are blue, and $\frac{1}{3}$ of the remainder are camouflage. If Parks wears 2 camouflage bracelets, how many bracelets does he have on?

7. Ahmed spent $\frac{1}{3}$ of his money on a burrito and a water. The burrito cost 2 times as much as the water. The burrito cost $4, how much money does Ahmed have left?

COMMON CORE™

Lesson 16:   Solve word problems using tape diagrams and fraction-by-fraction multiplication.

Date: 11/10/13

4.E.56

Name _____ Date _____

1. Three-quarters of the boats in the marina are white, $\frac{4}{7}$ of the remaining boats are blue, and the rest are red. If there are 9 red boats, how many boats are in the marina?

COMMON CORE™

Lesson 16: Solve word problems using tape diagrams and fraction-by-fraction multiplication.

Date: 11/10/13

4.E.5

© 2013 Common Core, Inc. All rights reserved. **commoncore.org**

Name _____   Date _____

Solve using tape diagrams.

1. Anthony bought an 8-foot board. He cut off $\frac{3}{4}$ of the board to build a shelf, and gave $\frac{1}{3}$ of the rest to his brother for an art project. How many inches long was the piece Anthony gave to his brother?

2. Riverside Elementary School is holding a school-wide election to choose a school color. Five-eighths of the votes were for blue, $\frac{5}{9}$ of the remaining votes were for green, and the remaining 48 votes were for red.

    a. How many votes were for blue?

    b. How many votes were for green?

| | Lesson 16: | Solve word problems using tape diagrams and fraction-by-fraction multiplication. | | 4.E.58 |
| Date: | 11/10/13 |

© 2013 Common Core, Inc. All rights reserved. **commoncore.org**

c. If every student got one vote, but there were 25 students absent on the day of the vote, how many students are there at Riverside Elementary School?

d. Seven-tenths of the votes for blue were made by girls. Did girls who voted for blue make up more than or less than half of all votes? Support your reasoning with a picture.

e. How many girls voted for blue?

Lesson 16: Solve word problems using tape diagrams and fraction-by-fraction
multiplication.

Date: 11/10/13

4.E.59

Lesson 17

Objective: Relate decimal and fraction multiplication.

Suggested Lesson Structure

■ Fluency Practice   (12 minutes)
■ Application Problem   (7 minutes)
■ Concept Development   (31 minutes)
■ Student Debrief   (10 minutes)

   Total Time   **(60 minutes)**

Fluency Practice (12 minutes)

- Multiply Fractions **5.NF.4**   (4 minutes)
- Write Fractions as Decimals **5.NF.3**   (4 minutes)
- Multiply Whole Numbers by Decimals **5.NBT.7**   (4 minutes)

Multiply Fractions (4 minutes)

Materials: (S) Personal white boards

Note: This fluency reviews G5–M4–Lessons 13–16.

   T: (Write $\frac{1}{2} \times \frac{1}{3}$.) Say the number sentence.

   S: $\frac{1}{2} \times \frac{1}{3} = \frac{1}{6}$.

Continue the process with $\frac{1}{2} \times \frac{1}{4}$ and $\frac{1}{2} \times \frac{1}{5}$.

   T: (Write $\frac{3}{4} \times \frac{1}{2} =$ _____ .) On your boards, write the number sentence.

   S: (Write $\frac{3}{4} \times \frac{1}{2} = \frac{3}{8}$.)

   T: (Write $\frac{3}{4} \times \frac{1}{3} =$ _____.) Say the number sentence.

   S: $\frac{3}{4} \times \frac{1}{3} = \frac{3}{12}$.

Repeat the process with $\frac{1}{2} \times \frac{2}{2}$, $\frac{1}{3} \times \frac{4}{5}$, and $\frac{2}{3} \times \frac{1}{3}$.

   T: (Write $\frac{2}{5} \times \frac{2}{3} =$ _____.) Say the number sentence.

   S: $\frac{2}{5} \times \frac{2}{3} = \frac{4}{15}$.

Continue the process with $\frac{3}{5} \times \frac{3}{4}$.

T: (Write $\frac{1}{5} \times \frac{2}{3} =$ ____.) On your boards, write the equation.

S: (Write $\frac{1}{5} \times \frac{2}{3} = \frac{2}{15}$.)

T: (Write $\frac{2}{3} \times \frac{3}{2} =$ ____.) On your boards write the equation.

S: (Write $\frac{2}{3} \times \frac{3}{2} = \frac{6}{6} = 1$.)

Continue the process with the following possible suggestions: $\frac{3}{4} \times \frac{2}{3}$, $\frac{3}{8} \times \frac{2}{3}$, and $\frac{2}{5} \times \frac{5}{8}$.

Write Fractions as Decimals (4 minutes)

Materials: (S) Personal white boards

Note: This fluency prepares students for G5–M4–Lessons 17–18.

T: (Write $\frac{1}{10}$.) Say the fraction.

S: 1 tenth.

T: Write it as a decimal.

S: 0.1.

Continue with the following possible suggestions: $\frac{2}{10}$, $\frac{8}{10}$, $\frac{3}{10}$, and $\frac{7}{10}$.

T: (Write $\frac{1}{100}$.) Say the fraction.

S: 1 hundredth.

T: Write it as a decimal.

S: 0.01.

Continue with the following possible suggestions: $\frac{2}{100}$, $\frac{7}{100}$, $\frac{9}{100}$, $\frac{12}{100}$, $\frac{15}{100}$, $\frac{45}{100}$, and $\frac{93}{100}$.

T: (Write 0.01.) Say it as a fraction.

S: 1 hundredth.

T: Write it as a fraction.

S: $\frac{1}{100}$.

Continue with the following possible suggestions: 0.03, 0.09, 0.11, and 0.87.

Multiply Whole Numbers by Decimals (4 minutes)

Materials: (S) Personal white boards

Note: This fluency prepares students for G5–M4–Lessons 17–18. In the following dialogue, several possible student responses are represented.

Lesson 17:	Relate decimal and fraction multiplication.
Date:	11/10/13

4.E.61

T: (Write 2 × 0.1 = ____.) What is 2 copies of 1 tenth?

S: 2 tenths.

T: (Write 0.2 in the number sentence above.)

T: (Erase the product and replace the 2 with a 3.) What is 3 copies of 1 tenth?

S: 3 tenths.

T: Write it as a decimal on your board.

S: 0.3.

T: 4 copies of 1 tenth? Write it as a decimal on your board.

S: 0.4.

T: 7 × 0.1?

S: 0.7.

T: (Write 7 × 0.01 = ____.) What is 7 copies of 1 hundredth?

S: 7 hundredths.

T: Write it as a decimal.

T: What is 5 copies of 1 hundredth? Write it as a decimal.

T: 5 × 0.01?

T: (Write 9 × 0.01 = ____.) On your boards, write the number sentence.

T: (Write 2 × 0.1 = ____.) Say the answer.

T: (Write 20 × 0.1 = ____.) What is 20 copies of 1 tenth?

S: 20 tenths.

T: Rename it using ones.

S: 2 ones.

T: (Write 20 × 0.01 = ____.) On your boards, write the number sentence. What are 20 copies of 1 hundredth?

S: (Write 20 × 0.01 = 0.20.) 20 hundredths.

T: Rename the product using tenths.

S: 2 tenths.

Continue this process with the following possible suggestions, shifting between choral and board responses: 30 × 0.1, 30 × 0.01, 80 × 0.01, and 80 × 0.1. If students are successful with the sequence above, continue with the following: 83 × 0.1, 83 × 0.01, 53 × 0.01, 53 × 0.1, 64 × 0.01, and 37 × 0.1.

Application Problem (7 minutes)

Ms. Casey grades 4 tests during her lunch. She grades $\frac{1}{3}$ of the remainder after school. If she still has 16 tests to grade after school, how many tests are there?

Note: Today's Application Problem recalls the previous lesson's work with tape diagrams. This is a challenging

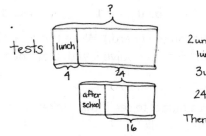

COMMON CORE™ | **Lesson 17:**   Relate decimal and fraction multiplication.
                     Date: 11/10/13

problem in that the value of a part is given and then the value of 2 thirds of the remainder. Possibly remind students to draw without concern initially for proportionality. They have erasers for a reason and can rework the model if they so choose.

Concept Development (31 minutes)

Materials: (S) Personal white boards

Problem 1: a. 0.1 × 4   b. 0.1 × 2   c. 0.01 × 6

T: (Post Problem 1(a) on the board.) Read this multiplication expression using unit form and the word *of*.

S: 1 tenth of 4.

T: Write this expression as a multiplication sentence using a fraction and solve. Do not simplify your product.

S: (Write $\frac{1}{10} \times 4 = \frac{4}{10}$.)

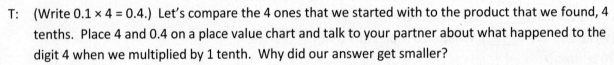

T: Write this as a decimal on your board.

S: (Write 0.4.)

T: (Write 0.1 × 4 = 0.4.) Let's compare the 4 ones that we started with to the product that we found, 4 tenths. Place 4 and 0.4 on a place value chart and talk to your partner about what happened to the digit 4 when we multiplied by 1 tenth. Why did our answer get smaller?

S: The answer is 4 tenths because we were taking a part of 4 so the answer got smaller. → The digit 4 will shift one space to the right because the answer is only part of 4. The answer is 4 tenths. → This is like 4 copies of 1 tenth. → There are 40 tenths in 4 wholes. 1 tenth of 40 is 4. The unit is tenths, so the answer is 4 tenths. → The digit stays the same because we are multiplying by 1 of something, but the unit is smaller, so the decimal point is moving one place to the left.

T: What about $\frac{1}{100}$ of 4? Multiply, then show your thinking on the place value chart.

S: (Work to show 4 hundredths. → 0.04.)

T: What about $\frac{1}{1000}$ of 4?

S: 4 thousandths. → 0.004.

Repeat the sequence with 0.1 × 2 and 0.1 × 6. Ask students to verbalize the patterns they notice.

Problem 2: a. 0.1 × 0.1   b. 0.2 × 0.1   c. 1.2 × 0.1

T: (Post Problem 2(a) on the board.) Write this as a fraction multiplication sentence and solve it with a partner.

MP.4

S: (Write $\frac{1}{10} \times \frac{1}{10} = \frac{1}{100}$.)

T: Let's draw an area model to see if this makes sense. What should I draw first? Turn and talk.

S: Draw a rectangle and cut it vertically into 10 units and shade one of them. (Draw and label $\frac{1}{10}$.)

T: What do I do next?

S: Cut each unit horizontally into 10 equal parts, and shade in 1 of those units.

T: (Cut and label $\frac{1}{10}$.) What units does our model show now?

S: Hundredths.

T: Look at the double-shaded parts, what is $\frac{1}{10}$ of $\frac{1}{10}$? (Save this model for use again in Problem 3(a).)

S: 1 hundredth. → $\frac{1}{100}$.

T: Write the answer as a decimal.

S: 0.01.

T: Let's show this multiplication on the place value chart. When writing 1 tenth, where do we put the digit 1?

S: In the tenths place.

T: Turn and talk to your partner about what happened to the digit 1 that started in the tenths place, when we took 1 tenth of it.

S: The digit shifted 1 place to the right. → We were taking only part of 1 tenth, so the answer is smaller than 1 tenth. It makes sense that the digit shifted to the right one place again because the answer got smaller and we are taking 1 tenth again like in the first problems.

T: (Post Problem 2(b) on the board.) Show me 2 tenths on your place value chart.

S: (Show the digit 2 in the tenths place.)

T: Explain to a partner what will happen to the digit 2 when you multiply it by 1 tenth.

S: Again, it will shift one place to the right. → Every time you multiply by a tenth, no matter what the digit, the value of the digit gets smaller. The 2 shifts one place over to the hundredths place.

T: Show this problem using fraction multiplication and solve.

S: (Work and show $\frac{2}{10} \times \frac{1}{10} = \frac{2}{100}$.)

T: (Post Problem 2(c) on the board.) If we were to show this multiplication on the place value chart, visualize what would happen. Tell your partner what you see.

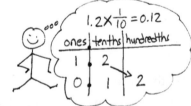

S: The 1 is in the ones place and the 2 is in the tenths place. Both digits would shift one place to the right, so the 1 would be in the tenths place and the 2 would be in the hundredths place. The answer would be 0.12. → Each digit shifts one place each. The answer is 12 hundredths.

T: How can we express 1.2 as a fraction greater than 1? Turn and talk.

S: 1 and 2 tenths is the same as 12 tenths. 12 tenths as a fraction is just 12 over 10.

T: Show the solution to this problem using fraction multiplication.

S: (Work and show $\frac{12}{10} \times \frac{1}{10} = \frac{12}{100}$.)

Lesson 17:	Relate decimal and fraction multiplication.
Date:	11/10/13

4.E.64

Problem 3: a. 0.1×0.01 **b.** 0.5×0.01 **c.** 1.5×0.01

T: (Post Problem 3(a) on the board.) Work with a partner to show this as fraction multiplication.

S: (Work and show $\frac{1}{10} \times \frac{1}{100}$.)

T: What is $\frac{1}{10} \times \frac{1}{100}$?

S: $\frac{1}{1000}$.

T: (Retrieve the model drawn in Problem 2(a).) Remember this model showed 1 tenth of 1 tenth, which is 1 hundredth. We just solved 1 tenth of 1 hundredth, which is 1 thousandth. Turn and talk with your partner about how that would look as a model.

S: If I had to draw it, I'd have to cut the whole into 100 equal parts and just shade 1. Then I'd have to cut just one of those tiny parts into 10 equal parts. If I did that to the rest of the parts, I'd end up with 1,000 equal parts and only 1 of them would be double shaded! → It would be like taking that 1 tiny hundredth and dividing it into 10 parts to make thousandths. I'd need a really fine pencil point!

T: (Point to the tenths on place value chart.) Put 1 tenth on the place value chart. I'm here in the tenths place, and I have to find 1 *hundredth* of this number. The digit 1 will shift in which direction and why?

S: It will shift right, because the product is smaller than what we started with.

T: How many places will it shift?

S: Two places.

T: Why two places? Turn and talk.

S: We shifted one place when multiplying by a tenth, so it should be two places when multiplying by a hundredth. Like when we multiply by 10, that shifts one place to the left, and two places to the left when we multiply by 100. → Our model showed us that finding a hundredth of something is like finding a tenth of a tenth, so we have to shift one place two times.

T: Yes. (Move finger two places to the right to the thousandths place.) So, $\frac{1}{10} \times \frac{1}{100}$ is equal to $\frac{1}{1000}$.

T: (Post Problem 3(b) on the board.) Visualize a place value chart. When writing 0.5, where will the digit 5 be?

S: In the tenths place.

T: What will happen as we multiply by 1 hundredth?

S: The 5 will shift two places to the right to the thousandths place.

T: Say the answer.

S: 5 thousandths.

T: Show the solution to this problem using fraction multiplication.

S: (Write and solve $\frac{5}{10} \times \frac{1}{100} = \frac{5}{1000}$.)

T: Show the answer as a decimal.

S: 0.005.

T: (Post Problem 3(c) on the board.) Express 1.5 as a fraction greater than 1.

S: $\frac{15}{10}$.

T: Show the solution to this problem using fraction multiplication.

S: (Write and show $\frac{15}{10} \times \frac{1}{100} = \frac{15}{1000}$.)

T: Write the answer as a decimal.

S: 0.015.

NOTES ON MULTIPLE MEANS OF REPRESENTATION:

It may be too taxing to ask some students to visualize a place value chart. As in previous problems, a place value chart can be displayed or provided. To provide further support for specific students, teachers can also provide place value disks.

Problem 4: a. 7 × 0.2   b. 0.7 × 0.2   c. 0.07 × 0.2

T: (Post Problem 4(a) on the board.) I'm going to rewrite this problem expressing the decimal as a fraction. (Write $7 \times \frac{2}{10}$.) Are these equivalent expressions? Turn and talk.

S: Yes, $0.2 = \frac{2}{10}$. So they show the same thing. → This is like multiplying fractions like we've been doing.

T: When we multiply, what will the numerator show?

S: 7 × 2.

T: The denominator?

S: 10.

T: (Write $\frac{7 \times 2}{10}$.) Write the answer as a fraction.

S: (Write $\frac{14}{10}$.)

T: Write 14 tenths as a decimal.

S: (Write 1.4.)

T: Think about what we know about the place value chart and multiplying by tenths. Does our product make sense? Turn and talk.

S: Sure! 7 times 2 is 14. So, 7 times 2 tenths is like 7 times 2 times 1 tenth. The answer should be one-tenth the size of 14. → It does make sense. It's like 7 times 2 equals 14, and then the digits in 14 both shift one place to the right because we took only 1 tenth of it. → I know it's like 2 tenths copied 7 times. Five copies of 2 tenths is 1 and then 2 more tenths.

T: (Post Problem 4(b) on the board.) Work with a partner and show the solution using fraction multiplication.

S: (Write and solve $\frac{7}{10} \times \frac{2}{10} = \frac{14}{100}$.)

T: What's 14 hundredths as a decimal?

S: 0.14.

T: (Post Problem 4(c) on the board.) Solve this problem independently. Compare your answer with a partner when you're done. (Allow students time to work and compare answers.)

Lesson 17:	Relate decimal and fraction multiplication.
Date:	11/10/13

4.E.66

T: Say the problem using fractions.

S: $\frac{7}{100} \times \frac{2}{10} = \frac{14}{1000}$.

T: What's 14 thousandths as a decimal?

S: 0.014.

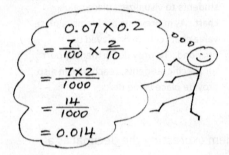

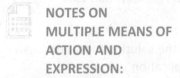

NOTES ON MULTIPLE MEANS OF ACTION AND EXPRESSION:

Teachers and parents alike may want to express multiplying by one-tenth as moving the decimal point one place to the left. Notice the instruction focuses on the movement of the digits in a number. Just like the ones place, the tens place, and all places on the place value chart, the decimal point does not move. It is in a fixed location separating the ones from the tenths.

Problem Set (10 minutes)

Students should do their personal best to complete the Problem Set within the allotted 10 minutes. For some classes, it may be appropriate to modify the assignment by specifying which problems they work on first. Some problems do not specify a method for solving. Students solve these problems using the RDW approach used for Application Problems.

Student Debrief (10 minutes)

Lesson Objective: Relate decimal and fraction multiplication.

The Student Debrief is intended to invite reflection and active processing of the total lesson experience.

Invite students to review their solutions for the Problem Set. They should check work by comparing answers with a partner before going over answers as a class. Look for misconceptions or misunderstandings that can be addressed in the Debrief. Guide students in a conversation to debrief the Problem Set and process the lesson.

You may choose to use any combination of the questions below to lead the discussion.

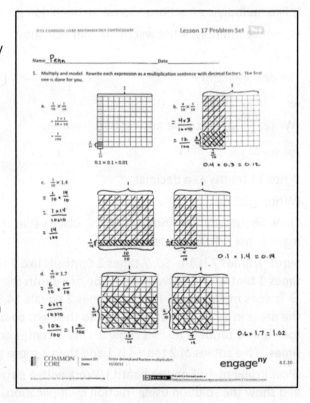

Lesson 17:   Relate decimal and fraction multiplication.
Date: 11/10/13

4.E.67

- In Problem 2, what pattern did you notice between (a), (b), and (c); (d), (e), and (f); and (g), (h), and (i)? (The product is to the tenths, hundredths, and thousandths.)

- Share and explain your solution to Problem 3 with a partner.

- Share your strategy for solving Problem 4 with a partner.

- Explain to your partner why $\frac{1}{10} \times \frac{1}{10} = \frac{1}{100}$ and $\frac{1}{10} \times \frac{1}{100} = \frac{1}{1000}$.

- We know that when we take one-tenth of 3, this shifts the digit 3 one place to the right on the place value chart, because 3 tenths is 1 tenth of 3. When we compare the standard form of 3 to 0.3, it appears that the decimal point has moved. How could thinking of it this way help us? How does the decimal point move when we multiply by 1 tenth? By 1 hundredth?

Exit Ticket (3 minutes)

After the Student Debrief, instruct students to complete the Exit Ticket. A review of their work will help you assess the students' understanding of the concepts that were presented in the lesson today and plan more effectively for future lessons. You may read the questions aloud to the students

COMMON CORE™   Lesson 17:   Relate decimal and fraction multiplication.
Date: 11/10/13   **4.E.68**

© 2013 Common Core, Inc. All rights reserved. commoncore.org

Name _____ Date _____

1. Multiply and model. Rewrite each expression as a multiplication sentence with decimal factors. The first one is done for you.

a. $\frac{1}{10} \times \frac{1}{10}$

$= \frac{1 \times 1}{10 \times 10}$

$= \frac{1}{100}$

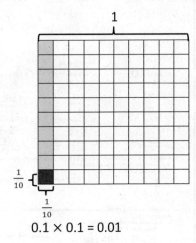

$0.1 \times 0.1 = 0.01$

b. $\frac{4}{10} \times \frac{3}{10}$

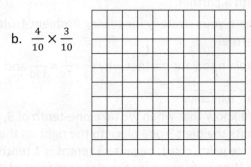

c. $\frac{1}{10} \times 1.4$

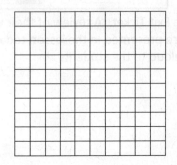 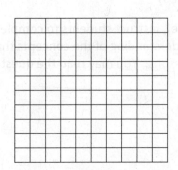

d. $\frac{6}{10} \times 1.7$

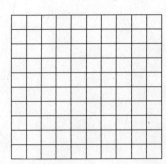 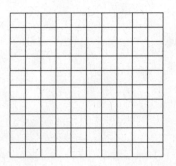

2. Multiply. The first few are started for you.

a. $5 \times 0.7 =$ _____

$= 5 \times \dfrac{7}{10}$

$= \dfrac{5 \times 7}{10}$

$= \dfrac{35}{10}$

$= 3.5$

b. $0.5 \times 0.7 =$ _____

$= \dfrac{5}{10} \times \dfrac{7}{10}$

$= \dfrac{5 \times 7}{10 \times 10}$

$=$

c. $0.05 \times 0.7 =$ _____

$= \dfrac{5}{100} \times \dfrac{7}{10}$

$= \dfrac{\_\_ \times \_\_}{100 \times 10}$

$=$

d. $6 \times 0.3 =$ _____

e. $0.6 \times 0.3 =$ _____

f. $0.06 \times 0.3 =$ _____

g. $1.2 \times 4 =$ _____

h. $1.2 \times 0.4 =$ _____

i. $0.12 \times 0.4 =$ _____

3. A boy scout has a length of rope measuring 0.7 meter. He uses 2 tenths of the rope to tie a knot at one end. How many meters of rope are in the knot?

4. After just 4 tenths of a 2.5 mile race was completed, Lenox took the lead and remained there until the end of the race.
   a. How many miles did Lenox lead the race?

   b. Reid, the second place finisher, developed a cramp with three-tenths of the race remaining. How many miles did Reid run without a cramp?

Name _____   Date _____

1. Multiply and model. Rewrite each expression as a number sentence with decimal factors.

   a. $\frac{1}{10} \times 1.2$

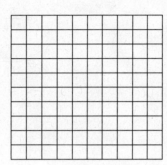   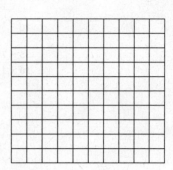

2. Multiply.

   a.   1.5 × 3 = _____   b.   1.5 × 0.3 = _____   c.   0.15 × 0.3 = _____

Name _____ Date _____

1. Multiply and model. Rewrite each expression as a number sentence with decimal factors. The first one is done for you.

a. $\frac{1}{10} \times \frac{1}{10}$

$= \frac{1 \times 1}{10 \times 10}$

$= \frac{1}{100}$

0.1 × 0.1 = 0.01

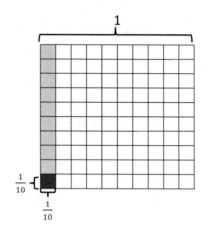

b. $\frac{6}{10} \times \frac{2}{10}$

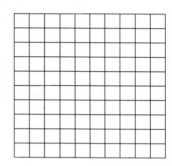

c. $\frac{1}{10} \times 1.6$

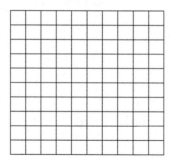   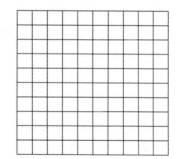

d. $\frac{6}{10} \times 1.9$

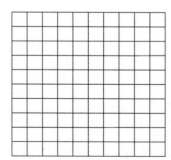   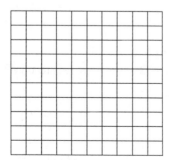

2. Multiply. The first few are started for you.

   a. $4 \times 0.6 = $ _____

   $$= 4 \times \frac{6}{10}$$

   $$= \frac{4 \times 6}{10}$$

   $$= \frac{24}{10}$$

   $$= 2.4$$

   b. $0.4 \times 0.6 = $ _____

   $$= \frac{4}{10} \times \frac{6}{10}$$

   $$= \frac{4 \times 6}{10 \times 10}$$

   $$=$$

   c. $0.04 \times 0.6 = $ _____

   $$= \frac{4}{100} \times \frac{6}{10}$$

   $$= \frac{\_\_ \times \_\_}{100 \times 10}$$

   $$=$$

   d. $7 \times 0.3 = $ _____

   e. $0.7 \times 0.3 = $ _____

   f. $0.07 \times 0.3 = $ _____

   g. $1.3 \times 5 = $ _____

   h. $1.3 \times 0.5 = $ _____

   i. $0.13 \times 0.5 = $ _____

3. Jennifer makes 1.7 liters of lemonade. If she pours 3 tenths of the lemonade in the glass, how many liters of lemonade are in the glass?

4. Cassius walked 6 tenths of a 3.6 mile trail.
   a. How many miles did Cassius have left to hike?

   b. Cameron was 1.3 miles ahead of Cassius. How many miles did Cameron hike already?

Lesson 18

Objective: Relate decimal and fraction multiplication.

Suggested Lesson Structure

■ Fluency Practice   (12 minutes)
■ Application Problem   (8 minutes)
□ Concept Development   (30 minutes)
■ Student Debrief   (10 minutes)

Total Time   **(60 minutes)**

Fluency Practice (12 minutes)

- Sprint: Multiply Fractions **5.NF.4**   (9 minutes)
- Multiply Whole Numbers and Decimals **5.NBT.7**   (3 minutes)

Sprint: Multiply Fractions (9 minutes)

Materials: (S) Multiply Fractions Sprint

Note: This fluency reviews G5–M4–Lesson 13.

Multiply Whole Numbers and Decimals (3 minutes)

Materials: (S) Personal white boards

Note: This fluency reviews G5–M4–Lesson 17.

T: (Write 3 × 2.) Say the number
sentence.

S: 3 × 2 = 6.

T: (Write 3 × 0.2.) On your boards,
write the number sentence and
solve.

S: (Write 3 × 0.2 = 0.6.)

T: (Write 0.3 × 0.2.) On your boards, write the number sentence.

S: (Write 0.3 × 0.2 = 0.06.)

T: (Write 0.03 × 0.2.) On your boards, write the number sentence.

S: (Write 0.03 × 0.2 = 0.006.)

3 × 2 = 6	3 × 0.2 = 0.6	3 × 0.02 = 0.06	0.3 × 0.2 = 0.06
2 × 7 = 14	2 × 0.7 = 1.4	2 × 0.7 = 1.4	0.02 × 0.7 = 0.014
5 × 3 = 15	0.5 × 3 = 1.5	0.5 × 0.3 = 0.15	0.5 × 0.03 = 0.015

COMMON CORE™   Lesson 18:   Relate decimal and fraction multiplication.
Date: 11/10/13

4.E.74

Continue this process with the following possible suggestions: 2×7, 2×0.7, 0.2×0.7, 0.02×0.7, 5×3, 0.5×3, 0.5×0.3, and 0.5×0.03.

Application Problem (8 minutes)

An adult female gorilla is 1.4 meters tall when standing upright. Her daughter is 3 tenths as tall. How much more will the young female gorilla need to grow before she is as tall as her mother?

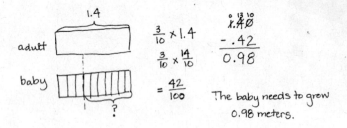

Note: This Application Problem reinforces that multiplying a decimal number by tenths can be interpreted in fraction or decimal form (as practiced in G5–M4–Lesson 17). Students who solve this problem by converting to smaller units (centimeters or millimeters) should be encouraged to compare their process to solving the problem using 1.4 meters.

NOTES ON MULTIPLE MEANS OF ENGAGEMENT:

With reference to Table 2 of the Common Core Learning Standards, this Application Problem is considered a *compare with unknown product* situation. Table 2 is a matrix that organizes story problems or situations into specific categories. Consider presenting this table in a student-friendly format as a tool to help students identify specific types of story problems.

Concept Development (30 minutes)

Materials: (S) Personal white boards

Problem 1: a. 3.2×2.1   **b. 3.2×0.44**   **c. 3.2×4.21**

T: (Post Problem 1(a) on board.) Rewrite this problem as a fraction multiplication expression.

S: (Write $\frac{32}{10} \times \frac{21}{10}$.)

T: Before we multiply these two decimals, let's estimate what our product will be. Turn and talk.

S: 3.2 is pretty close to 3 and 2.1 is pretty close to 2. I'd say our answer will be around 6. → The product will be a little more than 6 because 3.1 is a little more than 3 and 2.1 is a little more than 2. → It's about twice as much as 3.

T: Now that we've estimated, let's solve. (Write $= \frac{32}{10} \times \frac{21}{10}$ on board.) What do we get when we multiply tenths by tenths?

a) $3.2 \times 2.1 = \dfrac{32}{10} \times \dfrac{21}{10}$

$= \dfrac{32 \times 21}{10 \times 10}$

$= \dfrac{672}{100}$

$= 6.72$

$$\begin{array}{r} 32 \text{ tenths} \\ \times\ 21 \text{ tenths} \\ \hline 32 \\ +\ 640 \\ \hline 672 \text{ hundredths} \end{array}$$

$= 6.72$

Lesson 18:   Relate decimal and fraction multiplication.
Date: 11/10/13

4.E.75

S: Hundredths.

T: Let's use unit form to multiply 32 tenths and 21 tenths vertically. Solve with your partner. (Allow students time to work and solve.)

T: (Write $= \frac{32 \times 21}{100}$.) What is 32 tenths times 21 tenths?

S: 672 hundredths.

T: (Write $= \frac{672}{100}$ on the board.) Write this as a decimal.

S: (Write 6.72.)

T: Does this answer make sense given what we estimated the product to be?

S: Yes.

T: (Post Problem 1(b) on the board.) Before we solve this one, turn and talk with your partner to estimate the product.

S: We are still multiplying by 3.2, but this time we want about 3 of almost 1 half. That's like 3 halves, so our answer will be around 1 and a half. → This is about 3 times more than 4 tenths, so the answer will be around 12 tenths. It will be a little more because it's a little more than 3 times as much.

T: Work with a partner and rewrite this problem as a fraction multiplication expression.

S: (Share and show $\frac{32}{10} \times \frac{44}{100}$.)

T: What is 1 tenth of a hundredth?

S: 1 thousandth.

T: (Write $= \frac{32 \times 44}{1000}$.) Work with a partner to multiply. Express your answer as a fraction and as a decimal.

S: (Work and show $\frac{1408}{1000} = 1.408$.)

T: Does this product make sense given our estimates?

S: Yes! It's a little more than 1.2 and a little less than 1.5.

T: (Post Problem 1(c) on the board.) Estimate this product with your partner.

S: Three times as much as 4 is 12. This will be a little more than that because it's a little more than 3 and a little more than 4. → It's still multiplying by something close to 3. This time it's close to 4. 3 fours is 12.

T: Rewrite this problem as a fraction multiplication expression.

S: (Write $\frac{32}{10} \times \frac{421}{100}$.)

T: (Write $= \frac{32}{10} \times \frac{421}{100}$.) Solve independently. Express your answer as a fraction and as a decimal.

S: (Write and solve $\frac{13472}{1000} = 13.472$.)

T: Does our answer make sense? Turn and talk. (Allow students time to discuss with their partners.)

Problem 2: 2.6 × 0.4

T: (Post Problem 2 on the board.) This time, let's rewrite this problem vertically in unit form first. 2.6 is equal to how many tenths?

S: 26 tenths.

T: (Write = 26 tenths.) 0.4 is equal to how many tenths?

S: 4 tenths.

T: (Write × 4 tenths.) Think, what does tenths times tenths result in?

S: Hundredths.

T: Our product will be named in hundredths. I'll name those units right now. (Write hundredths at bottom of algorithm.) Solve 26 times 4.

S: (Work and solve to find 104.)

T: I'll record 104 as the product. (Write 104 in the algorithm.) 104 what? What is our unit?

S: 104 hundredths.

T: Write it in standard form.

S: (Write = 1.04.)

MP.2

T: Work with your partner to solve this using fraction multiplication to confirm our product. (Allow students time to work.)

T: Look back at the original problem. What do you notice about the number of decimal places in the factors and the number of decimal places in our product? Turn and talk.

S: There is one decimal place in each factor and two in the answer. → I see two total decimal places in the factors and two decimal places in the product. They match.

T: Keep this observation in mind as we continue our work. Let's see if it's always true.

Problem 3: a. 3.1 × 1.4   b. 0.31 × 1.4

T: (Post Problem 3(a) on the board.) Please estimate the product with your partner.

S: It should be something close to 3, because 3 times 1 is 3. → Something between 3 and 6, because 1.4 is close to the midpoint of 1 and 2. → It's close to 3 times 1 and a half. That's 4 and a half.

T: Let's use unit form again to solve this, but I will record it slightly differently. Let's think of 3.1 as 31 tenths. (Record 3.1, and use the arrow to show the movement of the decimal and record 31 to the right). If we rename 1.4 as tenths what will we record?

S: 14 tenths.

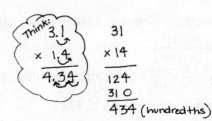

T: Let me record that. (Record as above showing movement with an arrow and writing 14 to the right.) Now multiply 31 and 14. What is the product?

S: 434.

T: 434 what?

Lesson 18:	Relate decimal and fraction multiplication.
Date:	11/10/13

4.E.77

S: 434 hundredths.

T: Name it as a decimal.

S: 4 and 34 hundredths.

T: Let me record that using our new method. (Rewrite 434 beneath the decimal multiplication. Show movement of the decimal two places to the left using two arrows.)

T: What do you notice about the decimal places in the factors and the product this time?

S: This is like before. We have two decimal places in the factors and two decimal places in the answer. → We had tenths times tenths. That's one decimal place times one decimal place. We got hundredths in our answer that's two decimal places. It's just like last time.

T: Keep observing. Let's see if this pattern holds true in our next problems.

T: (Post Problem 3(b) on the board.) Let's think of 0.31 and 1.4 as whole numbers of units. 0.31 is the same as 31 what? 1.4 is the same as 14 what?

S: 31 hundredths and 14 tenths.

T: If we were using fractions to multiply these two numbers, what part of the fraction would 31 x 14 give us?

S: The numerator.

T: What does the numerator of a fraction tell us?

S: The number of units we have.

T: This whole number multiplication problem is the same as our last one. What is 31 times 14?

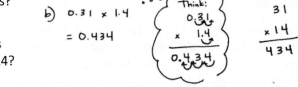

S: 434.

T: While these digits are the same as last time, will our product be the same? Why or why not? Turn and talk.

S: It won't be the same as last time. We are multiplying hundredths and tenths this time so our unit in the answer has to be thousandths. The answer is 434 thousandths. → Last time, we had two decimal places in our factors, so we had two decimal places in our product. This time, there are three decimal places in the factors, so we should have thousandths in the answer. → Last time, we were multiplying by about 3 times as much as 1 and a half. This time, we want around 3 tenths of 1 and a half. That's going to be a lot smaller answer because we only want part of it, so the product couldn't be the same.

T: What is our product?

S: 434 thousandths.

T: Yes, since we remember that 1 hundredth times 1 tenth gives us our unit, the denominator of our fraction. Let's use arrows to show that product. (Write the product and draw corresponding arrows.) Did the pattern that we saw earlier concerning the decimal places of factors and product hold true here as well? Turn and talk. (Allow students time to discuss with their partners.)

Problem 4: 4.2 × 0.12

T: (Post Problem 4 on the board.) Work independently to solve this problem. You may rename the factors as fractions and then multiply, rename the factors in unit form, or show the unit form using arrows. When you're finished, compare your work with a neighbor and explain your thinking.

Lesson 18:   Relate decimal and fraction multiplication.
Date: 11/10/13

4.E.78

S: (Work and share.)

T: What is the product of 4.2 × 0.12?

S: 0.504.

Problem Set (10 minutes)

Students should do their personal best to complete the Problem Set within the allotted 10 minutes. For some classes, it may be appropriate to modify the assignment by specifying which problems they work on first. Some problems do not specify a method for solving. Students solve these problems using the RDW approach used for Application Problems.

Student Debrief (10 minutes)

Lesson Objective: Relate decimal and fraction multiplication.

The Student Debrief is intended to invite reflection and active processing of the total lesson experience.

Invite students to review their solutions for the Problem Set. They should check work by comparing answers with a partner before going over answers as a class. Look for misconceptions or misunderstandings that can be addressed in the Debrief. Guide students in a conversation to debrief the Problem Set and process the lesson.

You may choose to use any combination of the questions below to lead the discussion.

- In Problem 1, what is the relationship between the answers for Parts (a) and (b) and the answers for Parts (c) and (d)? What pattern did you notice between 1(a) and 1(b)? (Part (a) is double (b). Part (c) is 4 times as large as (d).) Explain why that is.

- Compare Problems 1(c) and 2(c). Why are the products not so different? Use estimation, and explain it to your partner.

- Compare Problems 1(d) and 2(d). Why do they have the same digits but a different product? Explain it to your partner.

- What do you notice about the relationship between 3(a) and 3(b)? (Part (a) is half of (b).)

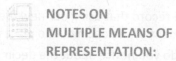

NOTES ON MULTIPLE MEANS OF REPRESENTATION:

Double, *twice*, and *half* are words that can be confusing to all students, but especially English language learners.

- Pre-teach this vocabulary in ways that connect to students' prior knowledge.

- Display posters with graphic representations of these words.

- Ask questions that specifically require students to use this vocabulary.

- Solicit support from physical education, art, and music teachers. Ask them to carefully embed these words into their lessons.

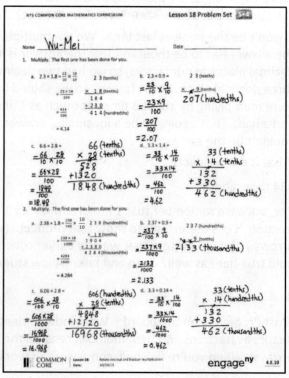

Lesson 18:   Relate decimal and fraction multiplication.
Date: 11/10/13

4.E.79

- For Problem 5, compare and share your solutions with a partner. Explain how you solved.
- In one sentence, explain to your partner the pattern that we discovered today in the number of decimal places in our factors compared to the number of decimal places in our products.

Exit Ticket (3 minutes)

After the Student Debrief, instruct students to complete the Exit Ticket. A review of their work will help you assess the students' understanding of the concepts that were presented in the lesson today and plan more effectively for future lessons. You may read the questions aloud to the students.

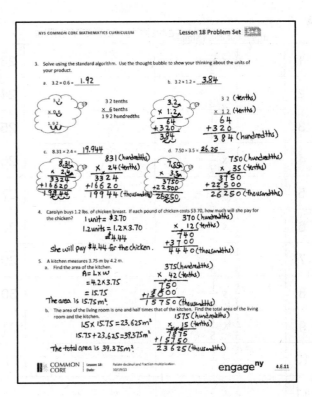

COMMON CORE™

Lesson 18:   Relate decimal and fraction multiplication.
Date: 11/10/13

4.E.80

A

Correct _____

Multiply, but don't simplify.

1	$\frac{1}{2} \times \frac{1}{2} =$		23	$\frac{2}{5} \times \frac{5}{3} =$	
2	$\frac{1}{2} \times \frac{1}{3} =$		24	$\frac{3}{5} \times \frac{5}{2} =$	
3	$\frac{1}{2} \times \frac{1}{4} =$		25	$\frac{1}{3} \times \frac{1}{3} =$	
4	$\frac{1}{2} \times \frac{1}{7} =$		26	$\frac{1}{3} \times \frac{2}{3} =$	
5	$\frac{1}{7} \times \frac{1}{2} =$		27	$\frac{2}{3} \times \frac{2}{3} =$	
6	$\frac{1}{3} \times \frac{1}{2} =$		28	$\frac{2}{3} \times \frac{3}{2} =$	
7	$\frac{1}{3} \times \frac{1}{3} =$		29	$\frac{2}{3} \times \frac{4}{3} =$	
8	$\frac{1}{3} \times \frac{1}{6} =$		30	$\frac{2}{3} \times \frac{5}{3} =$	
9	$\frac{1}{3} \times \frac{1}{5} =$		31	$\frac{3}{2} \times \frac{3}{5} =$	
10	$\frac{1}{5} \times \frac{1}{3} =$		32	$\frac{3}{4} \times \frac{1}{5} =$	
11	$\frac{1}{5} \times \frac{2}{3} =$		33	$\frac{3}{4} \times \frac{4}{5} =$	
12	$\frac{2}{5} \times \frac{2}{3} =$		34	$\frac{3}{4} \times \frac{5}{5} =$	
13	$\frac{1}{4} \times \frac{1}{3} =$		35	$\frac{3}{4} \times \frac{6}{5} =$	
14	$\frac{1}{4} \times \frac{2}{3} =$		36	$\frac{1}{4} \times \frac{6}{5} =$	
15	$\frac{3}{4} \times \frac{2}{3} =$		37	$\frac{1}{7} \times \frac{1}{7} =$	
16	$\frac{1}{6} \times \frac{1}{3} =$		38	$\frac{1}{8} \times \frac{3}{5} =$	
17	$\frac{5}{6} \times \frac{1}{3} =$		39	$\frac{5}{6} \times \frac{1}{4} =$	
18	$\frac{5}{6} \times \frac{2}{3} =$		40	$\frac{3}{4} \times \frac{3}{4} =$	
19	$\frac{5}{4} \times \frac{2}{3} =$		41	$\frac{2}{3} \times \frac{6}{6} =$	
20	$\frac{1}{5} \times \frac{1}{5} =$		42	$\frac{3}{4} \times \frac{6}{2} =$	
21	$\frac{2}{5} \times \frac{2}{5} =$		43	$\frac{7}{8} \times \frac{7}{9} =$	
22	$\frac{2}{5} \times \frac{3}{5} =$		44	$\frac{7}{12} \times \frac{9}{8} =$	

COMMON CORE™

Lesson 18: Relate decimal and fraction multiplication.
Date: 11/10/13

4.E.81

B   Improvement _____   # Correct _____

Multiply, but don't simplify.

1	$\frac{1}{2} \times \frac{1}{3} =$		23	$\frac{3}{5} \times \frac{5}{4} =$	
2	$\frac{1}{2} \times \frac{1}{4} =$		24	$\frac{4}{5} \times \frac{5}{3} =$	
3	$\frac{1}{2} \times \frac{1}{5} =$		25	$\frac{1}{4} \times \frac{1}{4} =$	
4	$\frac{1}{2} \times \frac{1}{9} =$		26	$\frac{1}{4} \times \frac{3}{4} =$	
5	$\frac{1}{9} \times \frac{1}{2} =$		27	$\frac{3}{4} \times \frac{3}{4} =$	
6	$\frac{1}{5} \times \frac{1}{2} =$		28	$\frac{3}{4} \times \frac{4}{3} =$	
7	$\frac{1}{5} \times \frac{1}{3} =$		29	$\frac{3}{4} \times \frac{5}{4} =$	
8	$\frac{1}{5} \times \frac{1}{7} =$		30	$\frac{3}{4} \times \frac{6}{4} =$	
9	$\frac{1}{5} \times \frac{1}{3} =$		31	$\frac{4}{3} \times \frac{4}{6} =$	
10	$\frac{1}{3} \times \frac{1}{5} =$		32	$\frac{2}{3} \times \frac{1}{5} =$	
11	$\frac{1}{3} \times \frac{2}{5} =$		33	$\frac{2}{3} \times \frac{4}{5} =$	
12	$\frac{2}{3} \times \frac{2}{5} =$		34	$\frac{2}{3} \times \frac{5}{5} =$	
13	$\frac{1}{3} \times \frac{1}{4} =$		35	$\frac{2}{3} \times \frac{6}{5} =$	
14	$\frac{1}{3} \times \frac{3}{4} =$		36	$\frac{1}{3} \times \frac{6}{5} =$	
15	$\frac{2}{3} \times \frac{3}{4} =$		37	$\frac{1}{9} \times \frac{1}{9} =$	
16	$\frac{1}{3} \times \frac{1}{6} =$		38	$\frac{1}{5} \times \frac{3}{8} =$	
17	$\frac{2}{3} \times \frac{1}{6} =$		39	$\frac{3}{4} \times \frac{1}{6} =$	
18	$\frac{2}{3} \times \frac{5}{6} =$		40	$\frac{2}{3} \times \frac{2}{3} =$	
19	$\frac{3}{2} \times \frac{3}{4} =$		41	$\frac{3}{4} \times \frac{8}{8} =$	
20	$\frac{1}{5} \times \frac{1}{5} =$		42	$\frac{2}{3} \times \frac{6}{3} =$	
21	$\frac{3}{5} \times \frac{3}{5} =$		43	$\frac{6}{7} \times \frac{8}{9} =$	
22	$\frac{3}{5} \times \frac{4}{5} =$		44	$\frac{7}{12} \times \frac{8}{7} =$	

Name _____   Date _____

1. Multiply. The first one has been done for you.

    a. $2.3 \times 1.8 = \frac{23}{10} \times \frac{18}{10}$

        $= \frac{23 \times 18}{100}$

        $= \frac{414}{100}$

        $= 4.14$

        ```
              2 3 (tenths)
          ×   1 8 (tenths)
          -----------
            1 8 4
          + 2 3 0
          -----------
            4 1 4 (hundredths)
        ```

    b. $2.3 \times 0.9 =$

        ```
              2 3 (tenths)
          ×       9 (tenths)
          -----------
        ```

    c. $6.6 \times 2.8 =$

    d. $3.3 \times 1.4 =$

2. Multiply. The first one has been done for you.

    a. $2.38 \times 1.8 = \frac{238}{100} \times \frac{18}{10}$

        $= \frac{238 \times 18}{1000}$

        $= \frac{4284}{1000}$

        $= 4.284$

        ```
              2 3 8 (hundredths)
          ×     1 8 (tenths)
          -----------
            1 9 0 4
          + 2 3 8 0
          -----------
            4 2 8 4 (thousandths)
        ```

    b. $2.37 \times 0.9 =$

        ```
              2 3 7 (hundredths)
          ×         9 (tenths)
          -----------
        ```

    c. $6.06 \times 2.8 =$

    d. $3.3 \times 0.14 =$

COMMON CORE   Lesson 18:   Relate decimal and fraction multiplication.
Date: 11/10/13

4.E.83

3. Solve using the standard algorithm. Use the thought bubble to show your thinking about the units of your product.

   a. $3.2 \times 0.6 =$ _____

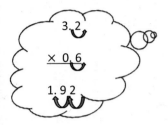

$$
\begin{array}{r}
3\ 2 \text{ tenths} \\
\times\ \ 6 \text{ tenths} \\
\hline
1\ 9\ 2 \text{ hundredths}
\end{array}
$$

   b. $3.2 \times 1.2 =$ _____

$$
\begin{array}{r}
3\ 2 \\
\times\ 1\ 2 \\
\hline
\end{array}
$$

   c. $8.31 \times 2.4 =$ _____

   d. $7.50 \times 3.5 =$ _____

4. Carolyn buys 1.2 lb of chicken breast. If each pound of chicken costs $3.70, how much will she pay for the chicken?

5. A kitchen measures 3.75 m by 4.2 m.
   a. Find the area of the kitchen.

   b. The area of the living room is one and a half times that of the kitchen. Find the total area of the living room and the kitchen.

Name _____ Date _____

1. Multiply.

   a. 3.2 × 1.4 =

   b. 1.6 × 0.7 =

   c. 2.02 × 4.2 =

   d. 2.2 × 0.42 =

Name _____   Date _____

1. Multiply. The first one has been done for you.

a. $3.3 \times 1.6 = \frac{33}{10} \times \frac{16}{10}$

     $= \frac{33 \times 16}{100}$

     $= \frac{528}{100}$

     $= 5.28$

```
      3 3
   ×  1 6
      1 9 8
   + 3 3 0
      5 2 8
```

b. $3.3 \times 0.8 =$

```
      3 3
   ×    8
```

c. $4.4 \times 3.2 =$

d. $2.2 \times 1.6 =$

2. Multiply. The first one has been done for you.

a. $3.36 \times 1.4 = \frac{336}{100} \times \frac{14}{10}$

     $= \frac{336 \times 14}{1000}$

     $= \frac{4,704}{1000}$

     $= 4.704$

```
      3 3 6
   ×    1 4
```

b. $3.35 \times 0.7 =$

```
      3 3 5
   ×      7
```

c. $4.04 \times 3.2 =$

d. $4.4 \times 0.16 =$

3. Solve using the standard algorithm. Use the thought bubble to show your thinking about the units of your product.

a. $3.2 \times 0.6 =$ _____

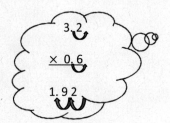

3 2 tenths
$\times\ \ 6$ tenths
1 9 2 hundredths

b. $3.2 \times 1.2 =$ _____

3 2
$\times\ 1\ 2$

c. $7.41 \times 3.4 =$ _____

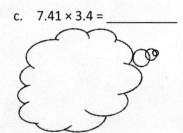

d. $6.50 \times 4.5 =$ _____

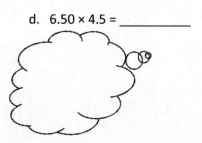

4. Erik buys 2.5 lb of cashews. If each pound of cashews costs $7.70, how much will he pay for the cashews?

5. A swimming pool at a park measures 9.75 m by 7.2 m.
   a. Find the area of the swimming pool.

   b. The area of the playground is one and a half times that of the swimming pool. Find the total area of the swimming pool and the playground.

COMMON CORE™

Lesson 18: Relate decimal and fraction multiplication.
Date: 11/10/13

4.E.87

© 2013 Common Core, Inc. All rights reserved. commoncore.org

Lesson 19

Objective: Convert measures involving whole numbers, and solve multi-step word problems.

Suggested Lesson Structure

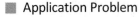

▦ Application Problem	(8 minutes)
■ Fluency Practice	(8 minutes)
▨ Concept Development	(34 minutes)
■ Student Debrief	(10 minutes)
Total Time	**(60 minutes)**

Application Problem (8 minutes)

Angle A of a triangle is $\frac{1}{2}$ the size of angle C. Angle B is $\frac{3}{4}$ the size of angle C. If angle C measures 80 degrees, what are the measures of angle A and angle B?

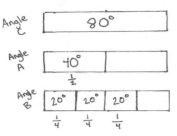

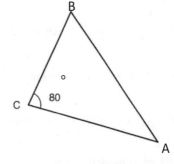

Note: Because today's fluency activity asks students to recall the content of yesterday's lesson, this problem asks students to recall previous learning to find fraction of a set. The presence of a third angle increases complexity.

Fluency Practice (8 minutes)

- Multiply Decimals **5.NBT.7**   (4 minutes)
- Convert Measures **4.MD.1**   (4 minutes)

	Lesson 19:	Convert measures involving whole numbers, and solve multi-step word problems.	4.E.88
	Date:	11/10/13	

Multiply Decimals (4 minutes)

Materials: (S) Personal white boards

Note: This fluency reviews G5–M4–Lessons 17–18.

T: (Write 4 × 2 =____.) Say the number sentence.

S: 4 × 2 = 8.

T: (Write 4 × 0.2 =____.) On your boards, write number sentence.

S: (Write 4 × 0.2 = 0.8.)

T: (Write 0.4 × 0.2 =____.) On your boards, write number sentence.

S: (Write 0.4 × 0.2 = 0.08.)

4 × 2 = 8	4 × 0.2 = 0.8	0.4 × 0.2 = 0.08	0.04 × 0.2 = 0.008
2 × 9 = 18	2 × 0.9 = 1.8	0.2 × 0.9 = 0.18	0.02 × 0.9 = 0.018
4 × 3 = 12	0.4 × 3 = 1.2	0.4 × 0.3 = 0.12	0.4 × 0.03 = 0.012

Continue this process with the following possible suggestions: 2 × 9, 2 × 0.9, 0.2 × 0.9, 0.02 × 0.9, 4 × 3, 0.4 × 3, 0.4 × 0.3, and 0.4 × 0.03.

Convert Measures (4 minutes)

Materials: (S) Personal white boards, Grade 5 Mathematics Reference Sheet (G5–M4–Lesson 8)

Note: This lesson prepares students for G5–M4–Lesson 19. Allow students to use the conversion reference sheet if they are confused, but encourage them to answer questions without looking at it.

T: (Write 1 yd = ____ ft.) How many feet are equal to 1 yard?

S: 3 feet.

T: (Write 1 yd = 3 ft. Below it, write 10 yd = ____ ft.) 10 yards?

S: 30 feet.

Continue with the following possible sequence: 1 pint = 2 cups, 8 pints = 16 cups, 1 ft = 12 in, 4 ft = 48 in, 1 gal = 4 qt, and 8 gal = 32 qt.

T: (Write 2 c = ____ pt.) How many pints are equal to 2 cups?

S: 1 pint.

T: (Write 2 c = 1 pt. Below it, write 16 c = __ pt.) 16 cups?

S: 8 pints.

Continue with the following possible sequence: 12 in = 1 ft, 48 in = 4 ft, 3 ft = 1 yd, 24 ft = 8 yd, 4 qt = 1 gal, and 24 qt = 6 gal.

Concept Development (34 minutes)

Materials: (S) Personal white boards

Problem 1: 30 centimeters = _____ meters

Lesson 19: Convert measures involving whole numbers, and solve multi-step word problems.

Date: 11/10/13

4.E.89

T: (Post Problem 1 on the board.) Which is a larger unit, centimeters or meters?

S: Meters.

T: So, we are expressing a smaller unit in terms of a larger unit. Is 30 cm more or less than 1 meter?

S: Less than 1 meter.

T: Is it more than or less than half a meter? Talk to your partner about how you know.

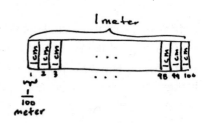

S: It's less than half, because 50 cm is half a meter and this is only 30 cm. → It's less than half, because 30 out of a hundred is less than half.

T: Let's keep that in mind as we work. We want to rename these centimeters using meters.

T: (Write 30 cm = 30 × 1 cm.) We know that 30 cm is the same as 30 copies of 1 cm. Let's rename 1 cm as a fraction of a meter. What fraction of a meter is 1 cm? Turn and talk.

S: It takes 100 cm to make a meter, so 1 cm would be 1 hundredth of a meter. → 100 cm = 1 meter so 1 cm = $\frac{1}{100}$ meter. → 100 out of 100 cm makes 1 whole meter. We're looking at 1 out of 100 cm, so that is 1 hundredth of a meter.

T: (Write 30 cm = 30 × 1 cm = 30 × $\frac{1}{100}$ meter.) How do you know this is true?

S: It's true because we just renamed the centimeter as the same amount in meters. → One centimeter is the same thing as 1 hundredth of a meter.

T: Now we have 30 copies of $\frac{1}{100}$ meter. How many hundredths of a meter is that in all?

S: 30 hundredths of a meter.

T: Write it as a fraction on your board, and then work with a neighbor to express it in simplest form.

S: (Work.)

T: Answer the question in simplest form.

S: 30 cm = $\frac{3}{10}$ m.

T: (Write = $\frac{3}{10}$ m.) Think about our estimate. Does this answer make sense?

S: Yes, we thought it would be less than a half meter, and $\frac{3}{10}$ meter is less than half a meter.

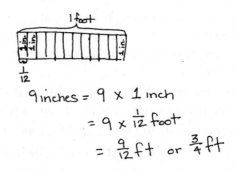

Lesson 19:	Convert measures involving whole numbers, and solve multi-step word problems.
Date:	11/10/13

4.E.90

Problem 2: 9 inches = _____ foot

T: (Write 9 inches = 9 × 1 inch on board.) 9 inches is 9 copies of 1 inch. What fraction of a foot is 1 inch? Draw a tape diagram if it helps you.

S: 1 twelfth foot.

T: Before we rename 1 inch, let's estimate. Will 9 inches be more than half a foot or less than half a foot? Turn and tell your partner how you know.

S: Half a foot is 6 inches. Nine is more than that so it will be more than half. → Half of 12 inches is 6 inches. Nine inches is more than that.

T: (Write $= 9 \times \frac{1}{12}$ foot.) Let's rename 1 inch as a fraction of a foot. Now we have written 9 copies of $\frac{1}{12}$ foot. Are these expressions equivalent?

S: Yes.

T: Multiply. How many feet is the same amount as 9 inches?

S: 9 twelfths of a foot → 3 fourths of a foot.

T: Does this answer make sense? Turn and talk.

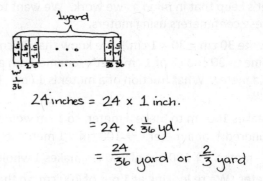

$$24 \text{ inches} = 24 \times 1 \text{ inch.}$$
$$= 24 \times \frac{1}{36} \text{ yd.}$$
$$= \frac{24}{36} \text{ yard or } \frac{2}{3} \text{ yard}$$

Repeat sequence for 24 inches = _____ yard.

Problem 3: Koalas will often sleep for 20 hours a day. For what fraction of a day does a Koala often sleep?

T: (Post Problem 3 on the board.) What will we need to do to solve this problem? Turn and talk.

S: We'll need to express hours in days. → We'll need to convert 20 hours into a fraction of a day.

T: Work with a partner to solve. Express your answer in its simplest form.

S: (Work and share and show 20 hours = $\frac{5}{6}$ day.)

$$20 \text{ hours} = 20 \times 1 \text{ hour}$$
$$= 20 \times \frac{1}{24} \text{ day}$$
$$= \frac{\overset{5}{\cancel{20}} \times 1}{\underset{6}{\cancel{24}}} \text{ day}$$
$$= \frac{5}{6} \text{ day}$$

Problem 4: 15 inches = _____ feet

T: (Post Problem 4 on the board.) Compare this conversion to the others we've done. Turn and talk.

S: We're still converting from a small unit to a larger one. → The last one converted something smaller than a whole day. This is converting something more than a whole foot. Fifteen inches is more than a foot, so our answer will be greater than 1. → We still have to think about what fraction of a foot is 1 inch.

T: Yes, the process of converting will be the same, but our answer will be greater than 1. Let's keep that in mind as we work. Write an equation showing how many copies of 1 inch we have.

S: (Work and show 15 inches = 15 × 1 inch.)

T: What fraction of a foot is 1 inch? Turn and talk.

Lesson 19:	Convert measures involving whole numbers, and solve multi-step word problems.
Date:	11/10/13

4.E.9

S: It takes 12 inches to make a foot, so 1 inch would be 1 twelfth of a foot. → 12 inches = 1 foot so 1 inch = $\frac{1}{12}$ foot.

T: Now we have 15 copies of $\frac{1}{12}$ foot. How many twelfths of a foot is that in all?

S: $\frac{15}{12}$ feet.

T: Work with a neighbor to express $\frac{15}{12}$ in its simplest form.

S: (Work and show 15 inches = $1\frac{1}{4}$ feet.)

Problem 5: 24 ounces = _____ pound

T: (Post Problem 5 on the board.) Work independently to solve this conversion.

S: (Work.)

T: Show the conversion in its simplest form.

S: (Show 24 ounces = $1\frac{1}{2}$ pounds.)

Problem Set (10 minutes)

Students should do their personal best to complete the Problem Set within the allotted 10 minutes. For some classes, it may be appropriate to modify the assignment by specifying which problems they work on first. Some problems do not specify a method for solving. Students solve these problems using the RDW approach used for Application Problems.

Student Debrief (10 minutes)

Lesson Objective: Convert measures involving whole numbers, and solve multi-step word problems.

The Student Debrief is intended to invite reflection and active processing of the total lesson experience.

Invite students to review their solutions for the Problem Set. They should check work by comparing answers with a partner before going over answers as a class. Look for misconceptions or misunderstandings that can be addressed in the Debrief. Guide students in a conversation to debrief the Problem Set and process the lesson.

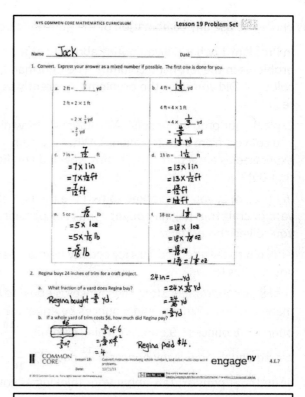

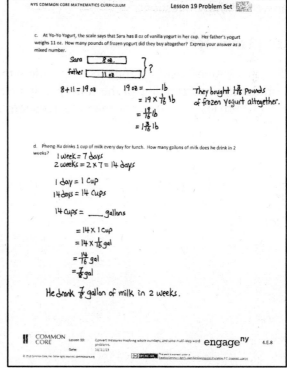

COMMON CORE™

Lesson 19:   Convert measures involving whole numbers, and solve multi-step word problems.
Date: 11/10/13

4.E.92

You may choose to use any combination of the questions below to lead the discussion.

- In Problem 1, what did you notice about all of the problems in the left-hand column? The right-hand column? Did you solve the problems differently as a result?

- Explain your process for solving Problem 4. How did you convert from cups to gallons? What is a cup expressed as a fraction of a gallon? How did you figure that out?

- In Problem 2, you were asked to find the fraction of a yard of craft trim Regina bought. Tell your partner how you solved this problem.

- How did today's second fluency activity help prepare you for this lesson?

- Look back at Problem 1(e). Five ounces is equal to how many pounds? What would 6 ounces be equal to? 7 ounces? 8 ounces? 9 ounces? Think carefully. $\frac{10}{16}$ pound equals how many ounces? $\frac{11}{16}$ pound? $\frac{12}{16}$ pound? $\frac{13}{16}$ pound? Talk about your thinking as you answered those questions.

NOTES ON MULTIPLE MEANS OF ACTION AND EXPRESSION:

Some students may struggle as they try to articulate their ideas. Some strategies that may be used to support these students are given below.

- Ask students to repeat in their own words the teacher's thinking.

- Ask students to add on to either the teacher's thinking or another student's thoughts.

- Give students time to practice with their partners before answering in a larger group.

- Pose a question and ask students to use specific vocabulary in their answers.

Exit Ticket (3 minutes)

After the Student Debrief, instruct students to complete the Exit Ticket. A review of their work will help you assess the students' understanding of the concepts that were presented in the lesson today and plan more effectively for future lessons. You may read the questions aloud to the students.

Lesson 19:   Convert measures involving whole numbers, and solve multi-step word problems.

Date: 11/10/13

4.E.9

Name _____   Date _____

1. Convert. Express your answer as a mixed number if possible. The first one is done for you.

a. 2 ft = ___$\frac{2}{3}$___ yd 2 ft = 2 × 1 ft = 2 × $\frac{1}{3}$ yd = $\frac{2}{3}$ yd	b. 4 ft = _____ yd 4 ft = 4 × 1 ft = 4 × _____ yd = _____ yd
c. 7 in = _____ ft	d. 13 in = _____ ft
e. 5 oz = _____ lb	f. 18 oz = _____ lb

2. Regina buys 24 inches of trim for a craft project.
    a. What fraction of a yard does Regina buy?

    b. If a whole yard of trim costs \$6, how much did Regina pay?

3. At Yo-Yo Yogurt, the scale says that Sara has 8 oz of vanilla yogurt in her cup. Her father's yogurt weighs 11 oz. How many pounds of frozen yogurt did they buy altogether? Express your answer as a mixed number.

4. Pheng-Xu drinks 1 cup of milk every day for lunch. How many gallons of milk does he drink in 2 weeks?

COMMON CORE™   Lesson 19:   Convert measures involving whole numbers, and solve multi-step word problems.

Date: 11/10/13   4.E.9

4.E.96

Name _____ Date _____

1. Convert. Express your answer as a mixed number if possible.

   a. 5 in = _____ ft

   b. 13 in = _____ ft

   c. 9 oz = _____ lb

   d. 18 oz = _____ lb

Name _____   Date _____

1.   Convert. Express your answer as a mixed number if possible.

a. 2 ft = ____$\frac{2}{3}$____ yd 2 ft = 2 × 1 ft $= 2 × \frac{1}{3}$ yd $= \frac{2}{3}$ yd	b. 6 ft = _____ yd 6 ft = 6 × 1 ft = 6 × _____ yd = _____ yd
c. 5 in = _____ ft	d. 14 in = _____ ft
e. 7 oz = _____ lb	f. 20 oz = _____ lb
g. 1 pt = _____ qt	h. 4 pt = _____ qt

2. Marty buys 12 oz of granola.
    a. What fraction of a pound of granola did Marty buy?

    b. If a whole pound of granola costs $4, how much did Marty pay?

3. Sara and her dad visit Yo-Yo Yogurt again. This time, the scale says that Sara has 14 oz of vanilla yogurt in her cup. Her father's yogurt weighs half as much. How many pounds of frozen yogurt did they buy altogether on this visit? Express your answer as a mixed number.

4. An art teacher uses 1 quart of blue paint each month. In one year, how many gallons of paint will she use?

Lesson 19: Convert measures involving whole numbers, and solve multi-step word problems.
Date: 11/10/13

Lesson 20

Objective: Convert mixed unit measurements, and solve multi-step word problems.

Suggested Lesson Structure

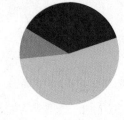

■ Fluency Practice   (12 minutes)
■ Application Problem   (6 minutes)
■ Concept Development   (32 minutes)
■ Student Debrief   (10 minutes)

  Total Time   **(60 minutes)**

Fluency Practice (12 minutes)

- Count by Fractions **5.NF.7**   (3 minutes)
- Convert Measures **4.MD.1**   (3 minutes)
- Multiply Decimals **5.NBT.7**   (3 minutes)
- Find the Unit Conversion **5.MD.2**   (3 minutes)

Count by Fractions (3 minutes)

Note: This fluency prepares students for G5–M4–Lesson 21.

T: Count by ones to 10. (Write as students count.)

S: 1, 2, 3, 4, 5, 6, 7, 8, 9, 10.

T: Count by halves to 10 halves. (Write as students count.)

S: 1 half, 2 halves, 3 halves, 4 halves, 5 halves, 6 halves, 7 halves, 8 halves, 9 halves, 10 halves.

1	2	3	4	5	6	7	8	9	10
$\frac{1}{2}$	$\frac{2}{2}$	$\frac{3}{2}$	$\frac{4}{2}$	$\frac{5}{2}$	$\frac{6}{2}$	$\frac{7}{2}$	$\frac{8}{2}$	$\frac{9}{2}$	$\frac{10}{2}$
$\frac{1}{2}$	1	$\frac{3}{2}$	2	$\frac{5}{2}$	3	$\frac{7}{2}$	4	$\frac{9}{2}$	5
$\frac{1}{2}$	1	$1\frac{1}{2}$	2	$2\frac{1}{2}$	3	$3\frac{1}{2}$	4	$4\frac{1}{2}$	5

T: Let's count by halves again. This time, when we arrive at a whole number, say the whole number. (Write as students count.)

S: 1 half, 1 whole, 3 halves, 2 wholes, 5 halves, 3 wholes, 7 halves, 4 wholes, 9 halves, 5 wholes.

COMMON CORE™

Lesson 20: Convert mixed unit measurements, and solve multi-step word problems.
Date: 11/10/13

4.E.9

T: Let's count by halves again. This time, change improper fractions to mixed numbers. (Write as students count.)

S: 1 half, 1, 1 and 1 half, 2, 2 and 1 half, 3, 3 and 1 half, 4, 4 and 1 half, 5.

Convert Measures (3 minutes)

Materials: (S) Personal white boards, Grade 5 Mathematics Reference Sheet (G5–M4–Lesson 8)

Note: This fluency reviews G5–M4–Lessons 19–20. Allow students to use the conversion reference sheet if they are confused, but encourage them to answer questions without looking at it.

T: (Write 1 ft = __ in.) How many inches are equal to 1 foot?

S: 12 inches.

T: (Write 1 ft = 12 in. Below it, write 2 ft = __ in.) 2 feet?

S: 24 inches.

T: (Write 2 ft = 24 in. Below it, write 4 ft = __ in.) 4 feet?

S: 48 inches.

Continue with the following possible sequence: 1 pint = 2 cups, 7 pints = 14 cups, 1 yard = 3 feet, 6 yd = 18 ft, 1 gal = 4 qt, and 9 gal = 36 qt.

T: (Write 2 c = __ pt.) How many pints are equal to 2 cups?

S: 1 pint.

T: (Write 2 c = 1 pt. Below it, write 4 c = __ pt.) 4 cups?

S: 2 pints.

T: (Write 4 c = 2 pt. Below it, write 10 c = __ pt.) 10 cups?

S: 5 pints.

Continue with the following possible sequence: 12 in = 1 ft, 36 in = 3 ft, 3 ft = 1 yd, 12 ft = 4 yd, 4 qt = 1 gal, and 28 qt = 7 gal.

Multiply Decimals (3 minutes)

Materials: (S) Personal white boards

Note: This fluency reviews G5–M4–Lessons 17–18.

T: (Write 3 × 3 = _____.) Say the multiplication sentence.

S: 3 × 3 = 9.

T: (Write 3 × 0.3 = _____.) On your boards, write the number sentence.

S: (Write 3 × 0.3 = 0.9.)

T: (Write 0.3 × 0.3 = _____.) On your boards, write the number sentence.

S: (Write 0.3 × 0.3 = 0.09.)

3 × 3 = 9	3 × 0.3 = 0.9	0.3 × 0.3 = 0.09	0.03 × 0.3 = 0.009
2 × 8 = 16	2 × 0.8 = 1.6	0.2 × 0.8 = 0.16	0.02 × 0.8 = 0.016
5 × 5 = 25	0.5 × 5 = 2.5	0.5 × 0.5 = 0.25	0.5 × 0.05 = 0.025

Lesson 20:   Convert mixed unit measurements, and solve multi-step word problems.

Date: 11/10/13

4.E.100

Continue this process with the following possible suggestions: 2 × 8, 2 × 0.8, 0.2 × 0.8, 0.02 × 0.8, 5 × 5, 0.5 × 5, 0.5 × 0.5, and 0.5 × 0.05.

Find the Unit Conversion (3 minutes)

Materials: (S) Personal white boards

Note: This fluency reviews G5–M4–Lesson 12.

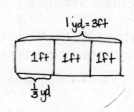

> T: How many feet are in 1 yard?
> S: 3 feet.
> T: (Write 3 ft = 1 yd. Below it, write 1 ft = __ yd.)
>   What fraction of 1 yard is 1 foot?
> S: 1 third.
> T: On your boards, draw a tape diagram to explain your thinking.

Continue with the following possible sequence: 2 ft = __ yd, 5 in = __ ft, 1 in = __ ft, 1 oz = __ lb, 9 oz = __ lb, 1 pt = __ qt, 3 pt = __ qt, 4 days = _____ week, and 18 hours = _____ day.

Application Problem (6 minutes)

A recipe calls for $\frac{3}{4}$ lb of cream cheese. A small tub of cream cheese at the grocery store weighs 12 oz. Is this enough cream cheese for the recipe?

Note: This problem builds on previous lessons involving unit conversions and multiplication of a fraction and a whole number. In addition to the method shown, students may also simply realize that $\frac{3}{4}$ is equal to $\frac{12}{16}$.

Need $\frac{3}{4}$ lb:

$\cdot$ 12oz = ___ lb

$12oz = 12 \times 1oz$

$= 12 \times \frac{1}{16} lb$

$= \frac{12}{16} lb$

$= \frac{3}{4} lb$

There is enough cream cheese for the recipe.

NOTES ON MULTIPLE MEANS OF REPRESENTATION:

Another approach to this Application Problem is to think of it as a comparison problem. (See Table 2 of the Common Core Learning Standards.) Students can draw two bars, one showing the amount needed for the recipe, and another showing the amount sold in the small tub. The tape diagram would help students recognize the need to convert one of the amounts so that like units can be compared.

Concept Development (32 minutes)

Materials: (S) Personal white boards

Problem 1: Conversion of large units to small units.

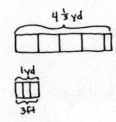

Lesson 20:   Convert mixed unit measurements, and solve multi-step word problems.
Date: 11/10/13

4.E.1

$4\frac{1}{3}$ yd = _____ ft

T: (Write $4\frac{1}{3}$ yd = _____ ft on board.) Which units are larger, yards or feet?

S: Yards.

T: Compare this problem with the conversions we worked on yesterday. What do you notice about the units? Turn and talk.

S: This is starting with larger units and converting to smaller ones. → Yesterday every conversion we did was little to big unit. This is big to little.

T: Let's draw a tape diagram to model this problem. We want to name $4\frac{1}{3}$ yards using feet. (Draw a bar and label $4\frac{1}{3}$ yd.) Let's partition the bar into 4 equal units to represent the 4 whole yards and 1 smaller unit to represent $\frac{1}{3}$ of a yard. $4\frac{1}{3}$ yards is the same as $4\frac{1}{3} \times 1$ yard. (Write on the board.) Think back to our fluency activity. How many feet are in 1 yard?

S: 3 feet.

T: On your boards, draw a tape diagram to explain your thinking.

S: (Draw.)

T: (Show 1 yard equal to 3 feet below tape diagram.) Write a new expression to rename the yard in feet.

S: (Write $4\frac{1}{3} \times 3$ feet.)

T: Before we multiply, let's express $4\frac{1}{3}$ as an improper fraction. How many thirds are in 1?

S: 3 thirds.

T: So how many thirds are in 4?

S: 12 thirds.

T: How many thirds in 4 and 1 third?

S: 13 thirds.

T: Write a new multiplication expression that uses the improper fraction we just found.

S: (Write $\frac{13}{3} \times 3$.)

T: Work with a partner to find the product of 13 thirds and 3.

S: (Work.)

T: (Point to the original problem.) Fill in the blank using a complete sentence.

S: $4\frac{1}{3}$ yd is equal to 13 ft.

Repeat the same process with the following as necessary.

NOTES ON MULTIPLE MEANS OF REPRESENTATION:

The lessons in this topic require students to know basic conversions, such as 16 ounces are combined to make 1 pound. Teachers can provide this background knowledge in the form of posters or other graphic organizers.

Students may also need support with some of the abbreviations used. For example, the abbreviation of pound (lb) and the abbreviation for ounce (oz) may seem confusing to some students. Teachers can post this information in a poster, or provide reference sheets for all students.

COMMON CORE™   Lesson 20:   Convert mixed unit measurements, and solve multi-step word problems.

Date: 11/10/13

4.E.102

$2\frac{1}{4}$ ft = _____ in

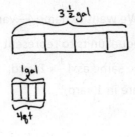

$2\frac{1}{4}$ ft = _____ in

$2\frac{1}{4}$ ft $= 2\frac{1}{4} \times 1$ ft

$= 2\frac{1}{4} \times 12$ in

$= \frac{9}{4} \times 12$ in

$= \frac{9 \times \cancel{12}^{3}}{1 \cancel{4}}$ in

$= 27$ in

$3\frac{1}{2}$ gal = _____ qt

$3\frac{1}{2}$ gal = _____ qt

$3\frac{1}{2}$ gal $= 3\frac{1}{2} \times 1$ gal

$= 3\frac{1}{2} \times 4$ qt

$= \frac{7}{2} \times 4$ qt

$= \frac{7 \times \cancel{4}2}{1 \cancel{2}}$ qt

$= 14$ qt

$1\frac{2}{5}$ hr = _____ min

$1\frac{2}{5}$ hr = _____ min

$1\frac{2}{5}$ hr $= 1\frac{2}{5} \times 1$ hr

$= 1\frac{2}{5} \times 60$ min

$= \frac{7}{5} \times 60$ min

$= \frac{7 \times \cancel{60}^{12}}{1 \cancel{5}}$ min

$= 84$ min.

Problem 2: Conversion of small units to large units.

11 ft = _____ yd

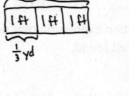

11 ft = _____ yd

11 ft $= 11 \times 1$ ft

$= 11 \times \frac{1}{3}$ yd

$= \frac{11 \times 1}{3}$ yd

$= \frac{11}{3}$ yd

$= 3\frac{2}{3}$ yd

T: (Write 11 ft = ___ yd on the board.) Which units are larger, feet or yards?

S: Yards.

T: Compare this problem to the others we've solved.

S: This one gives us the measurement in small units and wants the amount of large units. → This one goes from little units to big units like the ones we did yesterday.

T: What fraction of 1 yard is 1 foot?

S: 1 third.

T: On your boards, draw a tape diagram to show the relationship between feet and yards.

S: (Draw.)

COMMON CORE™

Lesson 20:   Convert mixed unit measurements, and solve multi-step word problems.

Date: 11/10/13

4.E.1

T: What two whole number of yards will 11 feet fall between? Turn and talk.

S: 9 feet is 3 yards, and 12 ft is 4 yards, so 11 feet must be somewhere between 3 and 4 yards.

T: We know that 11 ft = 11 × 1 ft. (Write on the board.) Write a multiplication sentence that is equivalent to this one using yards.

S: (Work.)

T: Let's record the equivalent expression beneath our first one. (Record as shown.) What is $11 \times \frac{1}{3}$?

S: 11 thirds.

T: Express your answer as yards.

S: 3 and 2 thirds yards.

Repeat the same process with the following as necessary.

$5\frac{1}{2}$ ft = _____ yd $3\frac{1}{3}$ qts = _____ gal

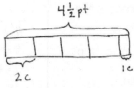

If time permits, the following may be explored with students.

Problem 3: A container can hold $4\frac{1}{2}$ pints of water. How many cups of water can 2 containers hold?

T: (Post the problem on the board, and read it out loud with the students.) How do you solve this problem? Turn and share your idea with a partner.

S: It's a two-step problem. → I first have to convert $4\frac{1}{2}$ pints to cups, and then I'll have to double it.

T: Let's draw a tape diagram for $4\frac{1}{2}$ pt. I'll do it on the board and you draw it on your personal board.

S: (Draw and label.)

T: Say the multiplication expression to convert $4\frac{1}{2}$ pints to cups.

MP.2

S: $4\frac{1}{2} \times 2$ cups.

T: Express $4\frac{1}{2}$ as an improper fraction and restate the expression.

S: $\frac{9}{2} \times 2$ cups.

T: What's the answer?

S: $\frac{18}{2}$ cups.

COMMON CORE™

Lesson 20:   Convert mixed unit measurements, and solve multi-step word problems.

Date: 11/10/13

4.E.104

MP.2

T: How many whole cups is that?

S: 9 cups.

T: Finish by finding the amount of water in two containers. Turn and talk.

S: We have to find the water in 2 containers. → Since 1 container holds 9 cups, then we'll have to double it. 9 cups + 9 cups = 18 cups. → To find the amount 2 containers hold, we have to multiply. 2 × 9 cups = 18 cups.

Problem Set (10 minutes)

Students should do their personal best to complete the Problem Set within the allotted 10 minutes. For some classes, it may be appropriate to modify the assignment by specifying which problems they work on first. Some problems do not specify a method for solving. Students solve these problems using the RDW approach used for Application Problems.

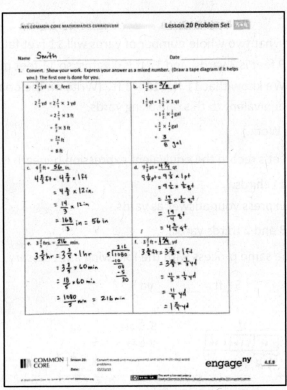

Student Debrief (10 minutes)

Lesson Objective: Convert mixed unit measurements, and solve multi-step word problems.

The Student Debrief is intended to invite reflection and active processing of the total lesson experience.

Invite students to review their solutions for the Problem Set. They should check work by comparing answers with a partner before going over answers as a class. Look for misconceptions or misunderstandings that can be addressed in the Debrief. Guide students in a conversation to debrief the Problem Set and process the lesson.

You may choose to use any combination of the questions below to lead the discussion.

- Share and compare your solutions for Problem 1 with your partner.

- Explain to your partner how to solve Problem 3. Did you have a different strategy than your partner?

- How did you solve for Problem 4? Explain your strategy to a partner.

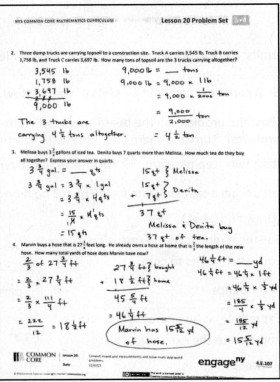

COMMON CORE

Lesson 20:   Convert mixed unit measurements, and solve multi-step word problems.

Date: 11/10/13

Exit Ticket (3 minutes)

After the Student Debrief, instruct students to complete the Exit Ticket. A review of their work will help you assess the students' understanding of the concepts that were presented in the lesson today and plan more effectively for future lessons. You may read the questions aloud to the students.

Lesson 20:   Convert mixed unit measurements, and solve multi-step word
              problems.
Date: 11/10/13

4.E.106

Name _____ Date _____

1. Convert. Show your work. Express your answer as a mixed number. (Draw a tape diagram if it helps you.) The first one is done for you.

a. $2\frac{2}{3}$ yd = __8__ ft $2\frac{2}{3}$ yd $= 2\frac{2}{3} \times 1$ yd $\quad = 2\frac{2}{3} \times 3$ ft $\quad = \frac{8}{3} \times 3$ ft $\quad = \frac{24}{3}$ ft $\quad = 8$ ft	b. $1\frac{1}{2}$ qt = _____ gal $1\frac{1}{2}$ qt $= 1\frac{1}{2} \times 1$ qt $\quad = 1\frac{1}{2} \times \frac{1}{4}$ gal $\quad = \frac{3}{2} \times \frac{1}{4}$ gal $\quad =$
c. $4\frac{2}{3}$ ft = _____ in	d. $9\frac{1}{2}$ pt = _____ qt
e. $3\frac{3}{5}$ hr = _____ min	f. $3\frac{2}{3}$ ft = _____ yd

Lesson 20: Convert mixed unit measurements, and solve multi-step word problems.

Date: 11/10/13

4.E.1

2. Three dump trucks are carrying topsoil to a construction site. Truck A carries 3,545 lb, Truck B carries 1,758 lb, and Truck C carries 3,697 lb. How many tons of topsoil are the 3 trucks carrying all together?

3. Melissa buys $3\frac{3}{4}$ gallons of iced tea. Denita buys 7 quarts more than Melissa. How much tea do they buy all together? Express your answer in quarts.

4. Marvin buys a hose that is $27\frac{3}{4}$ feet long. He already owns a hose at home that is $\frac{2}{3}$ the length of the new hose. How many total yards of hose does Marvin have now?

COMMON CORE™   Lesson 20:   Convert mixed unit measurements, and solve multi-step word problems.

Date: 11/10/13   4.E.108

Name _____   Date _____

1. Convert. Express your answer as a whole number.

    a. $2\frac{1}{6}$ ft = _____ in

    b. $3\frac{3}{4}$ ft = _____ yd

    c. $2\frac{1}{2}$ c = _____ pt

    d. $3\frac{2}{3}$ years = _____ months

COMMON CORE | Lesson 20: | Convert mixed unit measurements, and solve multi-step word problems.
Date: | 11/10/13

4.E.16

Name _____   Date _____

1. Convert. Show your work. Express your answer as a mixed number. The first one is done for you.

a. $2\frac{2}{3}$ yd = __8__ ft $2\frac{2}{3}$ yd $= 2\frac{2}{3} \times 1$ yd $\qquad = 2\frac{2}{3} \times 3$ ft $\qquad = \frac{8}{3} \times 3$ ft $\qquad = \quad \frac{24}{3}$ ft $\qquad = \quad 8$ ft	b. $1\frac{1}{4}$ ft = _____ yd $1\frac{1}{4}$ ft $= 1\frac{1}{4} \times 1$ ft $\qquad = 1\frac{1}{4} \times \frac{1}{3}$ yd $\qquad = \frac{5}{4} \times \frac{1}{3}$ yd $\qquad =$
c. $3\frac{5}{6}$ ft = _____ in	d. $7\frac{1}{2}$ pt = _____ qt
e. $4\frac{3}{10}$ hr = _____ min	f. 33 months = _____ years

Lesson 20:   Convert mixed unit measurements, and solve multi-step word problems.
 Date: 11/10/13

COMMON CORE™

2. Four members of a track team run a relay race in 165 seconds. How many minutes did it take them to run the race?

3. Horace buys $2\frac{3}{4}$ lb of blueberries for a pie. He needs 48 oz of blueberries for the pie. How many more pounds of blueberries does he need to buy?

4. Tiffany is sending a package that may not exceed 16 lb. The package contains books that weigh a total of $9\frac{3}{8}$ lb. The other items to be sent weigh $\frac{3}{5}$ the weight of the books. Will Tiffany be able to send the package?

Lesson 20: Convert mixed unit measurements, and solve multi-step word problems.
Date: 11/10/13

4.E.1

Topic F

Multiplication with Fractions and Decimals as Scaling and Word Problems

5.NF.5, 5.NF.6

Focus Standard:	5.NF.5	Interpret multiplication as scaling (resizing), by:
		a. Comparing the size of a product to the size of one factor on the basis of the size of the other factor, without performing the indicated multiplication.
		b. Explaining why multiplying a given number by a fraction greater than 1 results in a product greater than the given number (recognizing multiplication by whole numbers greater than 1 as a familiar case); explaining why multiplying a given number by a fraction less than 1 results in a product smaller than the given number; and relating the principle of fraction equivalence $a/b = (n×a)/(n×b)$ to the effect of multiplying a/b by 1.
	5.NF.6	Solve real world problems involving multiplication of fractions and mixed numbers, e.g., by using visual fraction models or equations to represent the problem.
Instructional Days:	4	
Coherence -Links from:	G4–M3	Multi-Digit Multiplication and Division
	G5–M2	Multi-Digit Whole Number and Decimal Fraction Operations
-Links to:	G6–M2	Arithmetic Operations Including Division by a Fraction
	G6–M4	Expressions and Equations

Students interpret multiplication in Grade 3 as equal groups, and in Grade 4 students begin to understand multiplication as comparison. Here, in Topic F, students once again extend their understanding of multiplication to include scaling (**5.NF.5**). Students compare the product to the size of one factor, given the size of the other factor (**5.NF.5a**) without calculation (e.g., 486 × 1327.45 is twice as large as 243 × 1327.45, because 486 = 2 × 243). This reasoning, along with the other work of this module, sets the stage for students to reason about the size of products when quantities are multiplied by 1, by numbers larger than 1, and smaller than 1. Students relate their previous work with equivalent fractions to interpreting multiplication by n/n as multiplication by 1 (**5.NF.5b**).

Students build on their new understanding of fraction equivalence as multiplication by *n/n* to convert fractions to decimals and decimals to fractions. For example, 3/25 is easily renamed in hundredths as 12/100 using multiplication of 4/4. The word form of *twelve hundredths* will then be used to notate this quantity as a decimal. Conversions between fractional forms will be limited to fractions whose denominators are factors of 10, 100, or 1,000. Students will apply the concepts of the topic to real world, multi-step problems (**5.NF.6**).

A Teaching Sequence Towards Mastery of Multiplication with Fractions and Decimals as Scaling and Word Problems
Objective 1: Explain the size of the product, and relate fraction and decimal equivalence to multiplying a fraction by 1. (Lesson 21)
Objective 2: Compare the size of the product to the size of the factors. (Lessons 22–23)
Objective 3: Solve word problems using fraction and decimal multiplication. (Lesson 24)

Lesson 21

Objective: Explain the size of the product, and relate fraction and decimal equivalence to multiplying a fraction by 1.

Suggested Lesson Structure

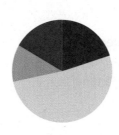

■ Fluency Practice   (12 minutes)
■ Application Problem   (7 minutes)
□ Concept Development   (31 minutes)
■ Student Debrief   (10 minutes)

   Total Time   **(60 minutes)**

Fluency Practice (12 minutes)

- Sprint: Multiply Decimals **5.NBT.7**   (8 minutes)
- Find the Unit Conversion **5.MD.2**   (4 minutes)

Sprint: Multiply Decimals (8 minutes)

Materials: (S) Multiply Decimals Sprint

Note: This fluency reviews G5–M4–Lessons 17–18.

Find the Unit Conversion (4 minutes)

Materials: (S) Personal white boards

Note: This fluency reviews G5–M4–Lesson 20.

T: (Write $2\frac{1}{3}$ yd = _____ ft.) How many feet are in 1 yard?

S: 3 feet.

T: Express $2\frac{1}{3}$ yards as an improper fraction.

S: $\frac{7}{3}$ yards.

T: Write an expression using the improper fraction and feet. Then solve.

S: (Write $\frac{7}{3}$ × 3 feet = 7 feet.)

T: $2\frac{1}{3}$ yards equals how many feet? Answer in a complete sentence.

$2\frac{1}{3}$ yd = __ ft

  $= 2\frac{1}{3} \times 1$ yd

  $= \frac{7}{3} \times 3$ ft

  $= \frac{21}{3}$ ft

  $= 7$ ft

COMMON CORE™

Lesson 21:   Explain the size of the product, and relate fractions and decimal
              equivalence to multiplying a fraction by 1.
Date: 11/10/13

4.F.3

S: $2\frac{1}{3}$ yards equals 7 feet.

Continue with one or more of the following possible suggestions: $2\frac{1}{4}$ gal = ___ qt, $2\frac{3}{4}$ ft = ___ in, and $7\frac{1}{2}$ pt = ___ c.

Application Problem (7 minutes)

Carol had $\frac{3}{4}$ yard of ribbon. She wanted to use it to decorate two picture frames. If she uses half the ribbon on each frame, how many feet of ribbon will she use for one frame? Use a tape diagram to show your thinking.

Note: This Application Problem draws on fraction multiplication concepts taught in earlier lessons in this module.

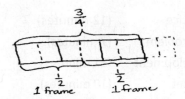

$\frac{3}{4} \times \frac{1}{2} = \frac{3}{8}$ yard for each frame

$= \frac{3}{8} \times 1$ yard

$= \frac{3}{8} \times 3$ feet

$= \frac{9}{8}$ feet

$= 1\frac{1}{8}$ ft of ribbon for each frame.

Concept Development (31 minutes)

Materials: (S) Personal white boards

Problem 1: $\frac{2}{2}$ of $\frac{3}{4}$

T: (Post Problem 1 on the board.) Write a multiplication expression for this problem.

S: (Write $\frac{2}{2} \times \frac{3}{4}$.)

T: Work with a partner to find the product of 2 halves and 3 fourths.

S: (Work and solve.)

T: Say the product.

S: $\frac{6}{8}$.

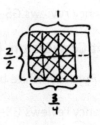

$\frac{2}{2}$ of $\frac{3}{4} = \frac{6}{8}$

T: (Write $= \frac{6}{8}$.) Let's draw an area model to verify our solution. (Draw a rectangle and label it 1.) What are we taking 2 halves of?

S: $\frac{3}{4}$.

T: (Partition model into fourths and shade 3 of them.) How do we show 2 halves?

S: Split each fourth unit into 2 equal parts, and shade both of them.

T: (Partition fourths horizontally, and shade both halves, or 6 eighths.) What is the product?

S: 6 eighths.

T: How does the size of the product, $\frac{6}{8}$, compare to the size of the original fraction, $\frac{3}{4}$? Turn and talk.

S: They're exactly same amount. 6 eighths and 3 fourths are equal. → They're the same. 3 fourths is

Lesson 21:   Explain the size of the product, and relate fractions and decimal equivalence to multiplying a fraction by 1.

Date: 11/10/13

4.F.4

just 6 eighths in simplest form. → Eighths are a smaller unit than fourths but we have twice as many of them, so really the two fractions are equal.

T: I hear you saying that the product, $\frac{6}{8}$, is equal to the amount we had at first, $\frac{3}{4}$. We multiplied. How is it possible that our quantity has not changed? Turn and talk.

S: We multiplied by 2 halves, which is like a whole. So, I'm thinking we showed the whole $\frac{3}{4}$ just using a different name. → 2 halves is equal to 1, so really we just multiplied 3 fourths by 1. Anything times 1 is just itself. → The fraction two-over-two is equivalent to 1. We just created an equivalent fraction by multiplying the numerator and denominator by a common factor.

T: It sounds like you think that our beginning amount (point to $\frac{3}{4}$) didn't change because we multiplied by one. Name some other fractions that are equal to 1.

S: 3 thirds, 4 fourths, 10 tenths, 1 million millionths!

T: Let's test your hypothesis. Work with a partner to find $\frac{3}{3}$ of $\frac{3}{4}$. One of you can multiply the fractions while the other draws an area model.

S: (Share and work.)

MP.3 T: What did you find out?

S: It happened again. The product is 9 twelfths which is still equal to 3 fourths. → We were right: 3 thirds is equal to 1, so we got another product that is equal to 3 fourths. → My area model shows it very clearly. Even though twelfths are a smaller unit, 9 twelfths is equal to 3 fourths.

T: Show some other fraction multiplication expressions involving 3 fourths that would give us a product that is equal in size to 3 fourths.

S: (Show $\frac{3}{4} \times \frac{5}{5}$, $\frac{8}{8} \times \frac{3}{4}$, $\frac{100}{100} \times \frac{3}{4}$.)

T: Is $\frac{3}{4}$ equal to $\frac{18}{24}$? Turn and talk.

S: Yes, if we multiplied 3 fourths by 6 sixths, we'd get $\frac{18}{24}$. → Sure, $\frac{3}{4}$ is $\frac{18}{24}$ in simplest form. I can divide 18 and 24 by 6.

T: Is $\frac{1}{4}$ equal to $\frac{25}{100}$? Work with a partner to write a multiplication sentence and share your thinking.

S: Yes. I know 25 cents is 1 fourth of 100 cents. → It is equal, because if we multiply 1 fourth and 25 twenty-fifths, that renames the same amount just using hundredths. It's like all the others we've done today.

$$\frac{1}{4} \times \frac{25}{25} = \frac{25}{100}$$

Problem 2: Express fractions as an equivalent decimal.

T   (Write $\frac{1}{5} \times \frac{2}{2}$.) Show the product.

$$\frac{1}{5} \times \frac{2}{2} = \frac{2}{10} = 0.2$$

S: $\frac{2}{10}$.

$$\frac{1}{5} = 0.2$$

T: (Write $= \frac{2}{10}$.) What are some other ways to express $\frac{2}{10}$? Turn and talk.

S: We could write it in unit form, like 2 tenths. → One-fifth. → Tenths, that's a decimal. We could write it as 0.2.

COMMON CORE™

Lesson 21:	Explain the size of the product, and relate fractions and decimal equivalence to multiplying a fraction by 1.
Date:	11/10/13

4.F.5

T: Express $\frac{2}{10}$ as a decimal on your board.

S: (Write 0.2.)

T: (Write = 0.2.) We multiplied one-fifth by a fraction equal to 1. Did that change the value of one-fifth?

S: No.

T: So, if $\frac{1}{5}$ is equal to $\frac{2}{10}$, and $\frac{2}{10}$ is equal to 0.2. Can we say that $\frac{1}{5}$ = 0.2? (Write $\frac{1}{5}$ = 0.2.) Turn and talk.

S: They are the same. We multiplied one-fifth by 1 to get to $\frac{2}{10}$, so they must be the same.

T: Let's try 3 fifths. How can we change 3 fifths to a decimal?

S: We could multiply by $\frac{2}{2}$ again. → Since we know one-fifth is equal to 0.2, 3 fifths is just 3 times more than that, so we could triple 0.2.

T: Work with a partner to express 3 fifths as a decimal.

S: (Work and share.)

T: Say $\frac{3}{5}$ as a decimal.

S: 0.6.

T: (Write $\frac{1}{4}$ on the board.) All the fractions we have worked with so far have been related to tenths. Let's think about 1 fourth. We just agreed a moment ago that 1 fourth was equal to 25 hundredths. Write 25 hundredths as a decimal.

S: 0.25.

T: Fourths were renamed as hundredths in this decimal. Could we have easily renamed fourths as tenths? Why or why not? Turn and talk.

S: We can't rename fourths as tenths because 4 isn't a factor of 10. → There's no whole number we can use to get from 4 to 10 using multiplication. → We could name 1 fourth as tenths, but that would be 2 and a half tenths, which is weird.

T: Since tenths are not possible, what unit did we use and how did we get there?

S: We used hundredths. → We multiplied by 25 twenty-fifths.

T: Is 25 hundredths the only decimal name for 1 fourth? Is there another unit that would rename fourths as a decimal? Turn and talk.

S: We could multiply 25 hundredths by 10 tenths, that would be 250 thousandths. So, we could do it in two steps. → If we multiply 1 fourth by 250 over 250, that would get us to 250 thousandths. → Four 250's is a thousand.

T: Work with a neighbor to express $\frac{1}{4}$ as a decimal, showing your work with multiplication sentences. One of you multiply by $\frac{25}{25}$, and the other multiply by $\frac{250}{250}$. Compare your work when you're done.

NOTES ON MULTIPLE MEANS OF REPRESENTATION:

Once students are comfortable renaming fractions using decimal units, make a connection to the powers of 10 concepts learned back in Module 1. Students can be challenged to see that tenths can be notated as $\frac{1}{10^1}$, hundredths as $\frac{1}{10^2}$, and thousandths as $\frac{1}{10^3}$.

Lesson 21: Explain the size of the product, and relate fractions and decimal equivalence to multiplying a fraction by 1.

Date: 11/10/13

4.F.6

S: (Work and share.)

T: What did you find? Are the products the same?

S: Some of us got 25 hundredths, and some of us got 250 thousandths. They look different, but they're equal. I got 0.25, which looks like 25 cents, which is a quarter. Wow, that must be why we call $\frac{1}{4}$ a quarter!

$$\frac{1}{4} \times \frac{250}{250} = \frac{250}{1000} = 0.250$$

$$\frac{1}{4} \times \frac{25}{25} = \frac{25}{100} = 0.25$$

$$\frac{1}{4} = 0.250 = 0.25$$

T: (Write $\frac{1}{4} = 0.250 = 0.25$.) What about $\frac{2}{4}$? How could we express that as a decimal? Tell a neighbor what you think, then show $\frac{2}{4}$ as a decimal.

S: We could multiply by $\frac{25}{25}$ again. → 2 fourths is a half. 1 half is 0.5 → 2 fourths is twice as much as 1 fourth. We could just double 0.25. (Show $\frac{2}{4} = 0.5$.)

T: Think about $\frac{1}{8}$. Are eighths a unit we can express directly as a decimal, or do we need to multiply by a fraction equal to 1 first?

S: We'll need to multiply first.

T: What fraction equal to 1 will help us rename eighths? Discuss with your neighbor.

S: Eight isn't a factor of 10 or 100. I'm not sure. → I don't know if 1,000 can be divided by 8 without a remainder. I'll divide. Hey, it works!

T: Jonah, what did you find out?

S: 1000 ÷ 8 = 125. We can multiply by $\frac{125}{125}$.

T: Work independently, and try Jonah's strategy. Show your work when you're done.

S: (Work and show $\frac{1}{8} = 0.125$.)

T: How would you express $\frac{2}{8}$ as a decimal? Tell a neighbor.

S: We could multiply by $\frac{125}{125}$ again. → We could just double 0.125 and get 0.250. → $\frac{2}{8}$ is equal to $\frac{1}{4}$. We already solved that as 0.250 and 0.25.

T: Work independently to show $\frac{2}{8}$ as a decimal.

S: (Show $\frac{2}{8} = 0.250$ or $\frac{2}{8} = 0.25$.)

T: It's a good idea to remember some of these common fraction–decimal equivalencies, likes fourths and eighths; you will use them often in your future math work.

Follow similar sequence for $\frac{1}{20}$, $1\frac{1}{20}$, $\frac{6}{25}$, and $\frac{51}{50}$.

NOTES ON PROPERTIES OF OPERATIONS:

After completing this lesson, it may be interesting to some students to know the name of the property they've been studying: multiplicative identity property of 1. Consider asking students if they can think of any other identity properties. Hopefully they will say that zero added to any number keeps the same value. This is the additive identity property of 0. (See Table 3 of the Common Core Learning Standards.)

COMMON CORE™

Lesson 21:   Explain the size of the product, and relate fractions and decimal equivalence to multiplying a fraction by 1.

Date: 11/10/13

4.F.7

Problem Set (10 minutes)

Students should do their personal best to complete the Problem Set within the allotted 10 minutes. For some classes, it may be appropriate to modify the assignment by specifying which problems they work on first. Some problems do not specify a method for solving. Students solve these problems using the RDW approach used for Application Problems.

Student Debrief (10 minutes)

Lesson Objective: Explain the size of the product and relate fractions and decimal equivalence to multiplying a fraction by 1.

The Student Debrief is intended to invite reflection and active processing of the total lesson experience.

Invite students to review their solutions for the Problem Set. They should check work by comparing answers with a partner before going over answers as a class. Look for misconceptions or misunderstandings that can be addressed in the Debrief. Guide students in a conversation to debrief the Problem Set and process the lesson.

You may choose to use any combination of the questions below to lead the discussion.

- Share your response to Problem 1(d) with a partner.

- In Problem 2, what is the relationship between Parts (a) and (b), Parts(c) and (d), Parts (e) and (f), Parts (i) and (k), and Parts (j) and (l)? (They have the same denominator.)

- In Problem 2, what did you notice about Parts (f), (g), (h), and (j)? (The fractions are greater than 1, thus the answers will be more than one whole.)

- In Problem 2, what did you notice about Parts (k) and (l)? (The fractions are mixed numbers, thus the answers will be more than one whole.)

- Share and explain your thought process for answering Problem 3.

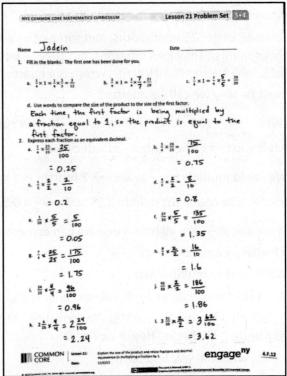

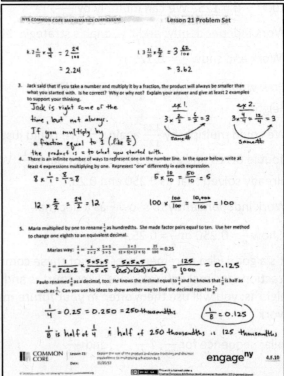

Lesson 21:   Explain the size of the product, and relate fractions and decimal equivalence to multiplying a fraction by 1.

Date: 11/10/13

4.F.8

- In Problem 4, did you have the same expressions to represent one on the number line as your partner's? Can you think of more expressions?
- How did you solve Problem 5? Share your strategy and solution with a partner.

Exit Ticket (3 minutes)

After the Student Debrief, instruct students to complete the Exit Ticket. A review of their work will help you assess the students' understanding of the concepts that were presented in the lesson today and plan more effectively for future lessons. You may read the questions aloud to the students.

Lesson 21: Explain the size of the product, and relate fractions and decimal equivalence to multiplying a fraction by 1.

Date: 11/10/13

4.F.9

A

Multiply.

Correct _____

1	3 x 2 =		23	0.6 x 2 =	
2	3 x 0.2 =		24	0.6 x 0.2 =	
3	3 x 0.02 =		25	0.6 x 0.02 =	
4	3 x 3 =		26	0.2 x 0.06 =	
5	3 x 0.3 =		27	5 x 7 =	
6	3 x 0.03 =		28	0.5 x 7 =	
7	2 x 4 =		29	0.5 x 0.7 =	
8	2 x 0.4 =		30	0.5 x 0.07 =	
9	2 x 0.04 =		31	0.7 x 0.05 =	
10	5 x 3 =		32	2 x 8 =	
11	5 x 0.3 =		33	9 x 0.2 =	
12	5 x 0.03 =		34	3 x 7 =	
13	7 x 2 =		35	8 x 0.03 =	
14	7 x 0.2 =		36	4 x 6 =	
15	7 x 0.02 =		37	0.6 x 7 =	
16	4 x 3 =		38	0.7 x 0.7 =	
17	4 x 0.3 =		39	0.8 x 0.06 =	
18	0.4 x 3 =		40	0.09 x 0.6 =	
19	0.4 x 0.3 =		41	6 x 0.8 =	
20	0.4 x 0.03 =		42	0.7 x 0.9 =	
21	0.3 x 0.04 =		43	0.08 x 0.8 =	
22	6 x 2 =		44	0.9 x 0.08 =	

Lesson 21: Explain the size of the product, and relate fractions and decimal equivalence to multiplying a fraction by 1.

Date: 11/10/13

4.F.10

B

Improvement _____   # Correct _____

Multiply.

1	4 x 2 =		23	0.8 x 2 =	
2	4 x 0.2 =		24	0.8 x 0.2 =	
3	4 x 0.02 =		25	0.8 x 0.02 =	
4	2 x 3 =		26	0.2 x 0.08 =	
5	2 x 0.3 =		27	5 x 9 =	
6	2 x 0.03 =		28	0.5 x 9 =	
7	3 x 3 =		29	0.5 x 0.9 =	
8	3 x 0.3 =		30	0.5 x 0.09 =	
9	3 x 0.03 =		31	0.9 x 0.05 =	
10	4 x 3 =		32	2 x 6 =	
11	4 x 0.3 =		33	7 x 0.2 =	
12	4 x 0.03 =		34	3 x 8 =	
13	9 x 2 =		35	9 x 0.03 =	
14	9 x 0.2 =		36	4 x 8 =	
15	9 x 0.02 =		37	0.7 x 6 =	
16	5 x 3 =		38	0.6 x 0.6 =	
17	5 x 0.3 =		39	0.6 x 0.08 =	
18	0.5 x 3 =		40	0.06 x 0.9 =	
19	0.5 x 0.3 =		41	8 x 0.6 =	
20	0.5 x 0.03 =		42	0.9 x 0.7 =	
21	0.3 x 0.05 =		43	0.07 x 0.7 =	
22	8 x 2 =		44	0.8 x 0.09 =	

Lesson 21: Explain the size of the product, and relate fractions and decimal equivalence to multiplying a fraction by 1.

Date: 11/10/13

4.F.11

Name _____   Date _____

1. Fill in the blanks. The first one has been done for you.

   a. $\frac{1}{4} \times 1 = \frac{1}{4} \times \frac{3}{3} = \frac{3}{12}$

   b. $\frac{3}{4} \times 1 = \frac{3}{4} \times \underline{} = \frac{21}{28}$

   c. $\frac{7}{4} \times 1 = \frac{7}{4} \times \underline{} = \frac{35}{20}$

   d. Use words to compare the size of the product to the size of the first factor.

2. Express each fraction as an equivalent decimal.

   a. $\frac{1}{4} \times \frac{25}{25} =$

   b. $\frac{3}{4} \times \frac{25}{25} =$

   c. $\frac{1}{5} \times \underline{} =$

   d. $\frac{4}{5} \times \underline{} =$

   e. $\frac{1}{20}$

   f. $\frac{27}{20}$

   g. $\frac{7}{4}$

   h. $\frac{8}{5}$

   i. $\frac{24}{25}$

   j. $\frac{93}{50}$

   k. $2\frac{6}{25}$

   l. $3\frac{31}{50}$

COMMON CORE™

Lesson 21:   Explain the size of the product, and relate fractions and decimal
equivalence to multiplying a fraction by 1.
Date: 11/10/13

4.F.12

3. Jack said that if you take a number and multiply it by a fraction, the product will always be smaller than what you started with. Is he correct? Why or why not? Explain your answer and give at least two examples to support your thinking.

4. There is an infinite number of ways to represent 1 on the number line. In the space below, write at least four expressions multiplying by 1. Represent "one" differently in each expression.

5. Maria multiplied by one to rename $\frac{1}{4}$ as hundredths. She made factor pairs equal to 10. Use her method to change one-eighth to an equivalent decimal.

$$\text{Maria's way:} \quad \frac{1}{4} = \frac{1}{2 \times 2} \times \frac{5 \times 5}{5 \times 5} = \frac{5 \times 5}{(2 \times 5) \times (2 \times 5)} = \frac{25}{100} = 0.25$$

$$\frac{1}{8} =$$

Paulo renamed $\frac{1}{8}$ as a decimal, too. He knows the decimal equal to $\frac{1}{4}$, and he knows that $\frac{1}{8}$ is half as much as $\frac{1}{4}$. Can you use his ideas to show another way to find the decimal equal to $\frac{1}{8}$?

COMMON CORE™ | Lesson 21:   Explain the size of the product, and relate fractions and decimal equivalence to multiplying a fraction by 1.   **4.F.13**

Date: 11/10/13

© 2013 Common Core, Inc. All rights reserved. **commoncore.org**

Name _____   Date _____

1. Fill in the blanks to make the equation true.

$$\frac{9}{4} \times 1 = \frac{9}{4} \times - = \frac{45}{20}$$

2. Express the fractions as equivalent decimals:

a. $\frac{1}{4} =$ b. $\frac{2}{5} =$

c. $\frac{3}{25} =$ d. $\frac{5}{20} =$

COMMON CORE | Lesson 21:   Explain the size of the product, and relate fractions land decimal equivalence to multiplying a fraction by 1.   4.F.14

Date: 11/10/13

Name _____ Date _____

1. Fill in the blanks.

   a. $\frac{1}{3} \times 1 = \frac{1}{3} \times \frac{3}{3} = \frac{}{9}$

   b. $\frac{2}{3} \times 1 = \frac{2}{3} \times \frac{}{} = \frac{14}{21}$

   c. $\frac{5}{2} \times 1 = \frac{5}{2} \times \frac{}{} = \frac{25}{}$

   d. Compare the first factor to the value of the product.

2. Express each fraction as an equivalent decimal.

   a. $\frac{3}{4} \times \frac{25}{25} = \frac{3 \times 25}{4 \times 25} = \frac{}{100} =$

   b. $\frac{1}{4} \times \frac{25}{25} =$

   c. $\frac{2}{5} \times \frac{}{} =$

   d. $\frac{3}{5} \times \frac{}{} =$

   e. $\frac{3}{20}$

   f. $\frac{25}{20}$

COMMON CORE™ | Lesson 21: Explain the size of the product, and relate fractions and decimal equivalence to multiplying a fraction by 1.

Date: 11/10/13

4.F.15

g. $\dfrac{23}{25}$ _____

h. $\dfrac{89}{50}$ _____

i. $3\dfrac{11}{25}$ _____

j. $5\dfrac{41}{50}$ _____

3. $\dfrac{6}{8}$ is equivalent to $\dfrac{3}{4}$. How can you use this to help you write $\dfrac{6}{8}$ as a decimal? Show your thinking to solve.

4. A number multiplied by a fraction is not always smaller than what you start with. Explain this, and give at least two examples to support your thinking.

5. Elise has $\dfrac{3}{4}$ dollar. She buys a stamp that costs 44 cents. Change both numbers into decimals, and tell how much money Elise has after paying for the stamp.

COMMON CORE™

Lesson 21:   Explain the size of the product, and relate fractions and decimal
equivalence to multiplying a fraction by 1.

Date: 11/10/13

4.F.16

Lesson 22

Objective: Compare the size of the product to the size of the factors.

Suggested Lesson Structure

■ Fluency Practice   (11 minutes)
■ Application Problem   (7 minutes)
☐ Concept Development   (32 minutes)
■ Student Debrief   (10 minutes)

   Total Time   **(60 minutes)**

Fluency Practice (11 minutes)

- Find the Unit Conversion **5.MD.2**   (5 minutes)
- Multiply Fractions by Whole Numbers **5.NF.4**   (4 minutes)
- Group Count by Multiples of 100 **5.NBT.2**   (2 minutes)

Find the Unit Conversion (5 minutes)

Materials: (S) Personal white boards

Note: This fluency reviews G5–M4–Lesson 20.

> T: (Write $3\frac{1}{4}$ gal = _____ qt and $3\frac{1}{4}$ gal = $3\frac{1}{4}$ × 1 gallon.) many quarts are in 1 gallon?
>
> S: 4 quarts.
>
> T: Write an equivalent multiplication sentence using an improper fraction and quarts.
>
> S: (Write = $\frac{13}{4}$ × 4 qts.)
>
> T: Solve and show.
>
> S: (Work and hold up board.)

$3\frac{1}{4}$ gal = __ qt   How

$3\frac{1}{4}$ gal = $3\frac{1}{4}$ × 1 gallon

$\quad = \frac{13}{4}$ × 4 qts

$\quad = \frac{13}{4}$ × 4

$\quad = 13$ qt

Continue with one or more of the following possible suggestions: $2\frac{2}{3}$ yd = __ ft, $2\frac{5}{6}$ ft = __ yd and $5\frac{1}{2}$ pt = __ c, $\frac{1}{2}$ c = __ pt.

Multiply Fractions by Whole Numbers (4 minutes)

Materials: (S) Personal white boards

Note: This fluency reviews G5–M4–Lesson 21.

    T: (Write $\frac{1}{2} \times 10 = \underline{\hspace{1cm}}$.) Say the multiplication sentence.

    S: $\frac{1}{2} \times 10 = 5$.

    T: (Write $10 \times \frac{1}{2} = \underline{\hspace{1cm}}$.) Say the multiplication sentence.

    S: $10 \times \frac{1}{2} = 5$.

Continue the process with the following possible suggestions: $\frac{1}{3} \times 12$, $12 \times \frac{1}{3}$, $15 \times \frac{1}{5}$, and $\frac{1}{5} \times 15$.

    T: (Write $\frac{1}{2} \times 6 = \underline{\hspace{1cm}}$.) On your boards, write the number sentence.

    S: (Write $\frac{1}{2} \times 6 = 3$.)

    T: (Write $\frac{2}{2} \times 6 = \underline{\hspace{1cm}}$.) On your boards, write the multiplication sentence. Below it, rewrite the multiplication sentence as a whole number times 6.

    S: (Write $\frac{2}{2} \times 6 = \underline{\hspace{1cm}}$. Below it, write $1 \times 6 = 6$.)

    T: (Write $\frac{3}{2} \times 6 = \underline{\hspace{1cm}}$.) On your boards, write the number sentence.

    S: (Write $\frac{3}{2} \times 6 = 9$.)

Continue with the following possible suggestions: $8 \times \frac{1}{4}$, $8 \times \frac{4}{4}$, and $8 \times \frac{5}{4}$.

Group Count by Multiples of 100 (2 minutes)

Note: This fluency prepares students for G5–M4–Lesson 22.

    T: Count by tens to 100. (Extend finger each time a multiple is counted.)

    S: 10, 20, 30, 40, 50, 60, 70, 80, 90, 100.

    T: (Show 10 extended fingers.) How many tens are in 100?

    S: 10.

    T: (Write $10 \times 10 = 100$.) Count by twenties to 100. (Extend finger each time a multiple is counted.)

    S: 20, 40, 60, 80, 100.

    T: (Show 5 extended fingers.) How many twenties are in 100?

    S: 5.

    T: (Write $20 \times 5 = 100$. Below it, write $5 \times \underline{\hspace{0.5cm}} = 100$.) How many fives are in 100?

    S: 20.

Repeat the process with 4 and 25, 2 and 50.

Lesson 22:   Compare the size of the product to the size of the factors.
Date: 11/10/13

Application Problem (7 minutes)

In order to test her math skills, Isabella's father told her he would give her $\frac{6}{8}$ of a dollar if she could tell him how much money that is and what that amount is in decimal form. What should Isabella tell her father? Show your calculations.

$\frac{6}{8} = \frac{3}{4}$

$\frac{3}{4} \times \frac{25}{25} = \frac{75}{100} = .75$

Isabella should tell her father that $\frac{6}{8}$ of a dollar is the same as 75 cents.

Note: This Application Problem reviews G5–M4–Lesson 21's Concept Development. Among other strategies, students might convert the eighths to fourths, and then multiply by $\frac{25}{25}$, or they may remember the decimal equivalent of 1 eighth and multiply by 6.

Concept Development (32 minutes)

Materials: (T) 12-inch string (S) Personal white boards

Problem 1

a. $\frac{4}{4} \times 12$ inches   b. $\frac{3}{4} \times 12$ inches   c. $\frac{5}{4} \times 12$ inches

T: (Post Problem 1(a–c) on the board.) Find the products of these expressions.

S: (Work.)

T: Let's compare the size of the products you found to the size of this factor. (Point to 12 inches.) Did multiplying 12 inches by 4 fourths change the length of this string? (Hold up the string.) Why or why not? Turn and talk.

S: The product is equal to 12 inches. → We multiplied and got 48 twelfths, but that's just another name for 12 using a different unit. → It's 4 fourths of the string, all of it. → Multiplying by 1 means just 1 copy of the number, so it stays the same. → The other factor just named 1 as a fraction, but it is still just multiplying by 1, so the size of 12 won't change.

T: (Write $\frac{4}{4} \times 12$ inches = 12 inches under first expression.) Did multiplying by 3 fourths change the size of our other factor, 12 inches? If so, how? Turn and talk.

S: The string got shorter because we only took 3 of 4 parts of it. → We got almost all of 12, but not quite. We wanted 3 fourths of it rather than 4 fourths, so the factor got smaller after we multiplied. → 12 got smaller. We got 9 this time.

T: (Write $\frac{3}{4} \times 12 < 12$ under the second expression.) I hear you saying that 12 inches was shortened, resized to 9 inches. How can it be that multiplying made 12 smaller when I thought multiplication

NOTES ON
MULTIPLE MEANS OF
REPRESENTATION:

Whenever students are calculating problems involving measurements, they will benefit if they have established mental benchmarks of each increment. For example, students should be able to think about 12 inches not just as a foot, but also as a specific length, perhaps as length just a little longer than a sheet of paper. Although teachers can give benchmarks for specific increments, it is probably better if students discover benchmarks on their own. Establishing mental benchmarks may be essential for English language learners' understanding.

Lesson 22: Compare the size of the product to the size of the factors.
Date: 11/10/13

4.F.19

always made numbers get bigger? Turn and talk.

S: We took only part of 12. When you take just a part of something it is smaller than what you start with. → We ended up with 3 of the 4 parts, not the whole thing. → Adding $\frac{3}{4}$ twelve times is going to be smaller than adding one the same number of times.

T: So, 9 is 3 fourths as much as 12. True or false?

S: True.

T: Let's consider our last expression. How did multiplying by 5 fourths change or not change the size of the other factor, 12? How would it change the length of the string? Turn and talk.

MP.2

S: The answer to this one was bigger than 12 because it's more than 4 fourths of it. → $\frac{5}{4} \times 12 = \frac{60}{4} = 15$. → The product was greater than 12. → We copied a number bigger than 1 twelve times. The answer had to be greater than copying 1 the same number of times. → 5 fourths of the string would be 1 fourth longer than the string is now.

T: (Write $\frac{5}{4} \times 12 > 12$ under the third expression.) So, 15 is 5 fourths as much as 12. True or false?

S: True.

T: 15 is 1 and $\frac{1}{4}$ times as much as 12. True or false?

S: True.

T: We've compared our products to one factor, 12 inches, in each of these expressions. We explained the changes we saw by thinking about the other factor. We can call that other factor a *scaling factor*. A scaling factor can change the size of the other factor. Let's look at the relationships in these expressions one more time. (Point to the first expression.) When we multiplied 12 inches by a scaling factor equal to 1, what happened to the 12 inches?

S: 12 didn't change. → The product was the same size as 12 inches, even after we multiplied it.

T: (Point.) In the second expression, $\frac{3}{4}$ was the scaling factor. Was this scaling factor more than or less than 1? How do you know?

S: Less than 1, because 4 fourths is 1.

T: What happened to 12 inches?

S: It got shorter.

T: And in our last expression, what was the scaling factor?

S: 5 fourths.

T: More or less than 1?

S: More than 1.

T: What happened to 12 inches?

S: It got longer. → The product was larger than 12 inches.

4.F.20

Problem 2

a. $\frac{4}{4} \times \frac{1}{3}$ b. $\frac{3}{4} \times \frac{1}{3}$ c. $\frac{5}{4} \times \frac{1}{3}$

T: (Post Problem 2 (a–c) on the board.) Keeping in mind the relationships that we've just seen between our products and factors, evaluate these expressions.

S: (Work.)

T: Let's compare the products that you found to this factor. (Point to $\frac{1}{3}$.) What is the product of $\frac{1}{3}$ and $\frac{4}{4}$?

S: $\frac{4}{12}$.

T: Did the size of $\frac{1}{3}$ change when we multiplied it by a scaling factor equal to 1?

S: No.

T: (Write $\frac{4}{4} \times \frac{1}{3} = \frac{1}{3}$ under the first expression.) Since we are comparing our product to 1 third, what is the scaling factor in the second expression?

S: $\frac{3}{4}$.

T: Is this scaling factor more than or less than 1?

S: Less than 1.

T: What happened to the size of $\frac{1}{3}$ when we multiplied it by a scaling factor less than 1? Why?

S: The product was 3 twelfths. That is less than 1 third which is 4 twelfths. → We only wanted part of 1 third this time, so the answer had to be smaller than 1 third. → When you multiply by less than 1, the product is smaller than what you started with.

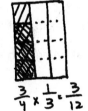

$\frac{3}{4} \times \frac{1}{3} = \frac{3}{12}$

T: (Write $\frac{3}{4} \times \frac{1}{3} < \frac{1}{3}$ on the board.) In the last expression, $\frac{5}{4}$ was the scaling factor. Is the scaling factor more than or less than 1?

S: More than 1.

T: Say the product of $\frac{1}{3} \times \frac{5}{4}$.

S: $\frac{5}{12}$.

T: Is 5 twelfths more than, less than or equal to $\frac{1}{3}$?

S: More than $\frac{1}{3}$.

T: (Write $\frac{5}{4} \times \frac{1}{3} > \frac{1}{3}$ under the third expression.) Explain why product of $\frac{1}{3}$ and $\frac{5}{4}$ is more than $\frac{1}{3}$.

S: (Share.)

Lesson 22:	Compare the size of the product to the size of the factors.
Date:	11/10/13

4.F.21

Problem 3

a. $\frac{1}{2} \times \frac{5}{5}$ b. $\frac{1}{2} \times \frac{3}{5}$ c. $\frac{1}{2} \times \frac{9}{5}$ d. $\frac{1}{2} \times \frac{2}{3}$ e. $\frac{1}{2} \times \frac{1}{2}$ f. $\frac{1}{2} \times \frac{4}{3}$ g. $\frac{1}{2} \times \frac{8}{8}$

T: I'm going to show you some multiplication expressions where we start with $\frac{1}{2}$. The expressions will have different scaling factors. Think about what will happen to the size of 1 half when it is multiplied by the scaling factor. Tell whether the product will be equal to $\frac{1}{2}$, more than $\frac{1}{2}$, or less than $\frac{1}{2}$. Ready? (Show $\frac{1}{2} \times \frac{5}{5}$.)

S: Equal to $\frac{1}{2}$.

T: Tell a neighbor why.

S: The scaling factor is equal to 1.

T: (Show $\frac{1}{2} \times \frac{3}{5}$.)

S: Less than $\frac{1}{2}$.

T: Tell a neighbor why.

S: The scaling factor is less than 1.

T: (Show $\frac{1}{2} \times \frac{9}{5}$.)

S: More than $\frac{1}{2}$.

T: Tell a neighbor why.

S: The scaling factor is more than 1.

Repeat questioning with $\frac{1}{2} \times \frac{2}{3}$, $\frac{1}{2} \times \frac{1}{2}$, $\frac{1}{2} \times \frac{4}{3}$, and $\frac{1}{2} \times \frac{8}{8}$.

Problem 4

At the book fair, Vlad spends all of his money on new books. Pamela spends $\frac{2}{3}$ as much as Vlad. Eli spends $\frac{4}{3}$ as much as Vlad. Who spent the most? The least?

T: (Post Problem 4 on the board, and read it aloud with students.) Read the first sentence again out loud.

S: (Read.)

T: Before we begin drawing, to whose money will we make the comparisons?

S: Vlad's money.

T: What can we draw from the first sentence?

S: We can make a tape diagram. → We should label a tape diagram *Vlad's money*.

T: Vlad spent all of his money at the book fair. I'll draw a tape diagram and label it *Vlad's money* (write *Vlad's $*). Read the next sentence aloud.

COMMON CORE™

Lesson 22:   Compare the size of the product to the size of the factors.
Date: 11/10/13

4.F.2

S: (Read.)

T: What can we draw from this sentence?

S: We can draw another tape that is shorter than Vlad's.

T: Let me record that. (Draw a shorter tape representing Pamela's money.) How will we know how much shorter to draw it? Turn and talk.

S: We know she spent $\frac{2}{3}$ of the same amount. Since Pamela's units are thirds, we can split Vlad's tape into 3 equal units, and then draw a tape below it that is 2 units long and label it *Pamela's money*. → I know Pamela's has 2 units, and those 2 units are 2 out of the 3 that Vlad spent. I'll draw 2 units for Pam, and then make Vlad's 1 unit longer than hers.

T: I'll record that. Thinking of $\frac{2}{3}$ as a scaling factor, did Pamela spend more or less than Vlad? How do you know? Does our model bear that out?

S: Less than Vlad. If you think of $\frac{2}{3}$ as a scaling factor, it's less than 1, so she spent less than Vlad. That's how we drew it. → She spent less than Vlad. She only spent a part of the same amount as Vlad. → Vlad spent all his money or, $\frac{3}{3}$ of his money. Pamela only spent $\frac{2}{3}$ as much as Vlad. You can see that in the diagram.

T: Read the third sentence and discuss what you can draw from this information.

S: (Read and discuss.)

T: Eli spent $\frac{4}{3}$ as much as Vlad. If we think of $\frac{4}{3}$ as a scaling factor, what does that tell us about how much money Eli spent?

S: Eli spent more than Vlad, because $\frac{4}{3}$ is more than 1. → Again, Vlad spent all of his money, or $\frac{3}{3}$ of it. $\frac{4}{3}$ is more than $\frac{3}{3}$, so Eli spent more than Vlad. We have to draw a tape that is one-third more than Vlad's.

T: Since the scaling factor $\frac{4}{3}$ is more than 1, I'll draw a third tape for Eli that is longer than Vlad's money. What is the question we have to answer?

S: Who spent the most and least money at the book fair?

T: Does our tape diagram show enough information to answer this question?

S: Yes, it's very easy to see whose tape is longest and shortest in our diagram. → Even though we don't know exactly how much Vlad spent, we can still answer the question. Since the scaling factors are more than 1 and less than 1, we know who spent the most and least.

T: Answer the question in a complete sentence.

S: Eli spent the most money. Pamela spent the least money.

Problem Set (10 minutes)

Students should do their personal best to complete the Problem Set within the allotted 10 minutes. For some classes, it may be appropriate to modify the assignment by specifying which problems they work on first. Some problems do not specify a method for solving. Students solve these problems using the RDW approach used for Application Problems.

Lesson 22:   Compare the size of the product to the size of the factors.
Date: 11/10/13

4.F.23

Student Debrief (10 minutes)

Lesson Objective: Compare the size of the product to the size of the factors.

The Student Debrief is intended to invite reflection and active processing of the total lesson experience.

Invite students to review their solutions for the Problem Set. They should check work by comparing answers with a partner before going over answers as a class. Look for misconceptions or misunderstandings that can be addressed in the Debrief. Guide students in a conversation to debrief the Problem Set and process the lesson.

You may choose to use any combination of the questions below to lead the discussion.

- In Problem 1, what relationship did you notice between Parts (a) and (b)?

- For Problem 2, compare your tape diagrams with a partner. Are your drawings similar to or different from your partner's?

- Explain to a partner your thought process for solving Problem 3. How did you know what to put for the missing numerator or denominator?

- In Problem 4, did you notice a relationship between Parts (a) and (b)? How did you solve them?

- For Problem 5, did you and your partner use the same examples to support the solution? Can you also give some examples to support the idea that multiplication can make numbers bigger?

- What's the scaling factor in Problem 6? What is an expression to solve this problem?

- How did you solve Problem 7? Share your solution and explain your strategy to a partner.

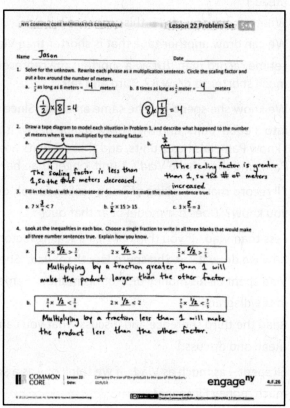

NOTES ON MULTIPLE MEANS OF REPRESENTATION:

Some students may find it helpful to have a physical representation of the tape diagrams as they work to draw these models. Students can use square tiles or uni-fix cubes. For some students, arranging the manipulatives first, and then drawing may be easier, and it may eliminate the need to redraw or erase.

Exit Ticket (3 minutes)

After the Student Debrief, instruct students to complete the Exit Ticket. A review of their work will help you assess the students' understanding of the concepts that were presented in the lesson today and plan more effectively for future lessons. You may read the questions aloud to the students.

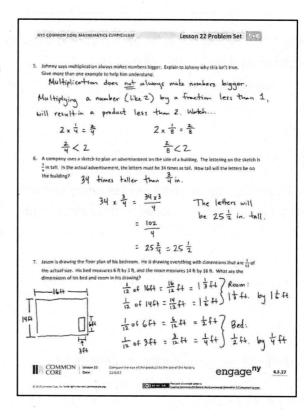

COMMON CORE™

Lesson 22:   Compare the size of the product to the size of the factors.
Date: 11/10/13

4.F.25

Name _____   Date _____

1. Solve for the unknown. Rewrite each phrase as a multiplication sentence. Circle the scaling factor and put a box around the number of meters.

    a. $\frac{1}{2}$ as long as 8 meters = _____ meters   b. 8 times as long as $\frac{1}{2}$ meter = _____ meters

2. Draw a tape diagram to model each situation in Problem 1, and describe what happened to the number of meters when it was multiplied by the scaling factor.

    a.   b.

3. Fill in the blank with a numerator or denominator to make the number sentence true.

    a. $7 \times \dfrac{}{4} < 7$ b. $\dfrac{7}{} \times 15 > 15$ c. $3 \times \dfrac{}{5} = 3$

4. Look at the inequalities in each box. Choose a single fraction to write in all three blanks that would make all three number sentences true. Explain how you know.

    a. | $\frac{3}{4} \times$ ____ $> \frac{3}{4}$ $2 \times$ ____ > 2 $\frac{7}{5} \times$ ____ $> \frac{7}{5}$ |
       | --- |

    b. | $\frac{3}{4} \times$ ____ $< \frac{3}{4}$ $2 \times$ ____ < 2 $\frac{7}{5} \times$ ____ $< \frac{7}{5}$ |
       | --- |

5. Johnny says multiplication always makes numbers bigger. Explain to Johnny why this isn't true.
    Give more than one example to help him understand.

6. A company uses a sketch to plan an advertisement on the side of a building. The lettering on the sketch is
    $\frac{3}{4}$ in tall. In the actual advertisement, the letters must be 34 times as tall. How tall will the letters be on
    the building?

7. Jason is drawing the floor plan of his bedroom. He is drawing everything with dimensions that are $\frac{1}{12}$ of
    the actual size. His bed measures 6 ft by 3 ft, and the room measures 14 ft by 16 ft. What are the
    dimensions of his bed and room in his drawing?

Name _____   Date _____

1. Fill in the blank to make the number sentences true. Explain how you know.

    a. $\dfrac{}{3} \times 11 > 11$

    b. $5 \times \dfrac{}{8} < 5$

    c. $6 \times \dfrac{2}{} = 6$

4.F.29

Name _____   Date _____

1. Solve for the unknown. Rewrite each phrase as a multiplication sentence. Circle the scaling factor and put a box around the number of meters.

   a. $\frac{1}{3}$ as long as 6 meters = _____ meters

   b. 6 times as long as $\frac{1}{3}$ meter = _____ meters

2. Draw a tape diagram to model each situation in Problem 1, and describe what happened to the number of meters when it was multiplied by the scaling factor.

   a.   b.

3. Fill in the blank with a numerator or denominator to make the number sentence true.

   a. $5 \times \dfrac{}{3} > 9$

   b. $\dfrac{6}{} \times 12 < 13$

   c. $4 \times \dfrac{}{5} = 4$

4. Look at the inequalities in each box. Choose a single fraction to write in all three blanks that would make all three number sentences true. Explain how you know.

   a.
$\frac{2}{3} \times$ _____ $> \frac{2}{3}$	$4 \times$ _____ > 4	$\frac{5}{3} \times$ _____ $> \frac{5}{3}$

   b.
$\frac{2}{3} \times$ _____ $< \frac{2}{3}$	$4 \times$ _____ < 4	$\frac{5}{3} \times$ _____ $< \frac{5}{3}$

5. Write a number in the blank that will make the number sentence true.

   $3 \times$ _____ < 1

   a. Explain how multiplying by a whole number can result in a product less than 1.

6. In a sketch, a fountain is drawn $\frac{1}{4}$ yard tall. The actual fountain will be 68 times as tall. How tall will the fountain be?

7. In blueprints, an architect's firm drew everything $\frac{1}{24}$ of the actual size. The windows will actually measure 4 ft by 6 ft and doors measure 12 ft by 8 ft. What are the dimensions of the windows and the doors in the drawing?

Lesson 22: Compare the size of the product to the size of the factors.
Date: 11/10/13

4.F.3

Lesson 23

Objective: Compare the size of the product to the size of the factors.

Suggested Lesson Structure

■ Fluency Practice   (12 minutes)
■ Application Problem   (7 minutes)
  Concept Development   (31 minutes)
■ Student Debrief   (10 minutes)

  Total Time   **(60 minutes)**

Fluency Practice (12 minutes)

- Compare the Size of a Product to the Size of One Factor **5.NF.5**   (5 minutes)
- Compare Decimal Numbers **5.NBT.2**   (2 minutes)
- Write Fractions as Decimals **5.NBT.2**   (5 minutes)

Compare the Size of a Product to the Size of One Factor (5 minutes)

Materials: (S) Personal white boards

Note: This fluency reviews G5–M4–Lesson 21.

T: (Write $1 = \frac{}{6}$.) On your boards, fill in the missing numerator.

S: (Write $1 = \frac{6}{6}$.)

T: (Write $9 \times \underline{\ \ } = 9$.) Say the missing whole number factor.

S: 1.

T: (Write $9 \times \frac{}{2} = 9$.) Fill in the missing numerator to make a true number sentence.

S: (Write $9 \times \frac{2}{2} = 9$.)

T: (Write $9 \times \frac{}{2} < 9$.) Fill in the missing numerator to make a true number sentence.

> **NOTES ON MULTIPLE MEANS OF ACTION AND EXPRESSION:**
>
> It is very helpful for most learners to know and understand the objective of specific lessons. This knowledge helps them make connections to what they already know and what they need to learn. Each lesson in the modules has a stated objective. These objectives should be posted daily. Today's goal, comparing the size of the factors to the size of the product, includes math vocabulary that students should know. For a quick visual review, write an equation below the objective and draw lines showing which number is the factor and which is the product.

Lesson 23:   Compare the size of the product to the size of the factors.
Date: 11/10/13

4.F.31

S: (Write $9 \times \frac{1}{2} < 9$.)

T: (Write $9 \times \frac{\_}{2} > 9$.) Fill in a missing numerator to make a true number sentence.

S: (Write the number sentence filling in a numerator greater than 2.)

Continue this process with the following possible sequence: $\frac{3}{\_} \times 7 = 7$, $\frac{3}{\_} \times 6 < 6$, $\frac{3}{\_} \times 6 > 6$, $\frac{4}{\_} \times 8 < 8$, $\frac{\_}{5} \times 9 = 9$, and $\frac{5}{\_} \times 10 < 10$.

Compare Decimal Numbers (2 minutes)

Materials: (S) Personal white boards

Note: This fluency prepares students for today's lesson.

T: (Write 1 __ 9.) Say the greater number.

S: 9.

T: On your boards, write the symbol to make the number sentence true.

S: (Write 1 < 9.)

Continue this process with the following possible sequence: 1 __ 0.9, 0.95 __ 1, and 0.994 __ 1.

Write Fractions as Decimals (5 minutes)

Materials: (S) Personal white boards

Note: This fluency reviews G5–M4–Lesson 22.

T: (Write $\frac{1}{50} = \frac{}{100}$.) How many fifties are in 100?

S: 2.

T: (Write $\frac{1}{50} \times \frac{2}{2} = \frac{}{100}$.) $\frac{1}{50}$ is the same as how many 1 hundredths?

S: 2 one hundredths.

T: (Write $\frac{1}{50} \times \frac{2}{2} = \frac{2}{100}$. Below it, write $\frac{1}{50} = \_.\_$.) On your boards, write $\frac{1}{50}$ as a decimal.

S: (Write $\frac{1}{50} = 0.02$.)

Continue this process with the following possible sequence $\frac{3}{50}$, $\frac{7}{50}$, $3\frac{7}{50}$, $\frac{1}{20}$, $\frac{3}{20}$, $5\frac{3}{20}$, $\frac{1}{5}$, $\frac{2}{5}$, $\frac{6}{5}$, $\frac{1}{25}$, $\frac{7}{25}$, $4\frac{7}{25}$, $\frac{1}{4}$, $\frac{3}{4}$, and $\frac{11}{4}$.

Application Problem (7 minutes)

Jasmine took $\frac{2}{3}$ as much time to take a math test as Paula. If Paula took 2 hours to take the test, how long did it take Jasmine

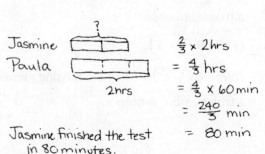

$\frac{2}{3} \times 2 \text{ hrs}$
$= \frac{4}{3} \text{ hrs}$
$= \frac{4}{3} \times 60 \text{ min}$
$= \frac{240}{3} \text{ min}$
$= 80 \text{ min}$

Jasmine finished the test in 80 minutes.

Lesson 23:   Compare the size of the product to the size of the factors.
Date: 11/10/13

4.F.3

to take the test? Express your answer in minutes.

Note: Scaling as well as conversion is required for today's Application Problem. This both reviews G5–M4–Topic E and prepares students to continue a study of scaling with decimals in today's lesson.

Concept Development (31 minutes)

Materials: (S) Personal white boards

Problem 1: $2 \text{ meters} \times \dfrac{97}{100}$ $2 \text{ meters} \times \dfrac{101}{100}$ $2 \text{ meters} \times \dfrac{100}{100}$

- T: (Post Problem 1 on the board.) Let's compare products to the 2 meters in each expression. Let's notice what happens to 2 meters when we multiply, or scale, 2 meters by the other factors. Read the scaling factors out loud in the order they are written.
- S: 97 hundredths, 101 hundredths, 100 hundredths.
- T: Without evaluating them, turn and talk with a neighbor about which expression is greater than, less than, and equal to 2 meters. Be sure to explain your thinking.
- S: $2 \times \dfrac{100}{100}$ would be equal to 2 meters, because it's being scaled by 1. → 2 meters $\times \dfrac{97}{100}$ would be less than 2 meters, because it's being scaled by a fraction less than 1. → 2 meters $\times \dfrac{101}{100}$ would be more than 2 meters, because it's being scaled by a fraction more than 1.
- T: Rewrite the expressions using decimals to express the scaling factors.
- S: (Work and show 2 meters × 0.97, 2 meters × 1.01, and 2 meters × 1.0.)
- T: (Write decimal expressions below the fractional ones.) Which expression is greater than, less than, and equal to 2 meters. Turn and talk.
- S: It's the same as before: 2 times 1 is equal to 1, 2 times 0.97 is less than 2, and 2 times 1.01 is more than 2. → Nothing has changed; we've just expressed the scaling factor as a decimal. We haven't changed the value.

$2 \times \dfrac{97}{100}$ $2 \times \dfrac{101}{100}$ $2 \times \dfrac{100}{100}$

$2 \times 0.97 < 2$ $2 \times 1.01 > 2$ $2 \times 1.00 = 2$

- T: (Write 2 × _____ < 2 on board.) Write three decimal scaling factors that would make this number sentence true.
- S: (Work and show numbers less than 1.0.)
- T: Finish my sentence. To get a product that is *less* than the number you started with, multiply by a scaling factor that is….
- S: Less than 1.
- T: (Write 2 × _____ > 2 on board.) Show me some more decimal scaling factors that would make this number sentence true.
- S: (Work and show numbers more than 1.0.)
- T: Finish this sentence. To get a product that is *more* than the number you started with, multiply by a

scaling factor that is....

S: More than 1.

Problem 2:   **19.4 × 0.96**   **19.4 × 0.02**

T: (Post Problem 2 on the board.) Let's compare our product to the first factor,19.4. Let's consider the other factors the scaling factors. Read the scaling factors out loud in the order they are written.

S: 96 hundredths, 2 hundredths.

T: Look at the first expression. Will the product be more than, less than, or equal to 19.4? Tell a neighbor why.

S: Less than 19.4, because the scaling factor is less than 1.

T: (Write < 19.4 next to the first expression.) Look at the second expression. Will the product be more than, less than, or equal to 19.4? Tell a neighbor why.

S: It's also less than 19.4, because that scaling factor is also less than 1.

T: (Write < 19.4 next to the second expression.) So, we know that both scaling factors will lead to a product that is less than the number we started with. Which expression will give a greater product? Why? Turn and talk.

$$19.4 \times 0.96 < 19.4 \qquad 19.4 \times 0.02 < 19.4$$

S: 19.4 times 96 hundredths. → Even though both scaling factors are less than 1, 96 hundredths is a much bigger scaling factor than 2 hundredths. → 96 hundredths is close to 1. 2 hundredths is almost zero. The first expression will be really close to 19.4 and the second expression will be closer to zero.

T: (Point to first expression.) What is the scaling factor here?

S: 96 hundredths.

T: What would the scaling factor need to be in order for the product to be equal to 19.4?

S: 1.

T: Isn't 1 the same as 100 hundredths?

S: Yes.

T: So this scaling factor, 96 hundredths is *slightly less than* 1. True or false?

S: True.

T: If this is true, what can we say about the product of 19.4 and 0.96? Turn and talk.

S: If we draw a tape diagram of 19.4 × 1 it would be 19.4 units long. Since 96 hundredths is just slightly less than 1, that means that 19.4 × 0.96 is slightly less than 19.4 × 1. The tape diagram should be slightly shorter than the first one we drew. → The expression 19.4 times 96 hundredths is just a little bit less than 19.4.

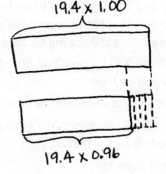

19.4 × 1.00

19.4 × 0.96

19.4 × 0.96 is slightly less than 19.4

T: Imagine partitioning this tape into 100 equal parts. The tape for 19.4 times 96 hundredths should be as long as 96 of those hundredths, or just 4 hundredths less than this whole tape. (Draw a second

Lesson 23:	Compare the size of the product to the size of the factors.
Date:	11/10/13

4.F.3

tape diagram slightly shorter and label it 19.4 × 0.96.)

T: Make a statement about this expression. Is 19.4 times 96 hundredths slightly less than 19.4, or a lot less than 19.4?

S: Slightly less than 19.4.

T: (Write *19.4 × 0.96 is slightly less than 19.4.*) Let's look at the other expression now. Is the scaling factor, 2 hundredths, slightly less than 1 or a lot less than 1? Turn and talk.

S: 1 is 100 hundredths this is only 2 hundredths. It's a lot less than 1. → It's a lot less than 1. In fact, it's only slightly more than zero.

T: This scaling factor is a lot less than 1. Work with a partner to draw two tape diagrams. One should show 19.4, like we did before, and the other should show 19.4 times 2 hundredths.

S: (Work and share.)

T: Make a statement about this expression. Is 19.4 times 2 hundredths slightly less than 19.4, or a lot less than 19.4?

S: It is a lot less than 19.4.

T: (Write *19.4 × 0.02 is a lot less than 19.4.*)

Problem 3:　　　　**1.02 × 1.73**　　　　　　　　**29.01 × 1.73**

T: (Post Problem 3 on the board.) Let's compare our products with the second factor in these expressions. (Point to 1.73 in both expressions.) We'll consider the first factors to be scaling factors. Read the scaling factors out loud in the order they are written.

S: 1 and 2 hundredths, 29 and 1 hundredth.

T: Think about these expressions. Will the products be more than, less than, or equal to the 1.73? Tell your neighbor why.

S: They'll both be more than 1.73, because both scaling factors are more than 1.

T: Let's be more specific. Look at the first expression. Will the product be slightly more than 1.73, or a lot more than 1.73? Tell a neighbor.

S: The product will just be slightly more than 1.73. The scaling factor is just 2 hundredths more than 1. → I can visualize two tape diagrams, and the one showing 1.73 times 1.02 is just a little bit longer, like 2 hundredths longer than the tape showing 1.73. → The product will be slightly more than what we started with because the scaling factor is just slightly more than 1.

T: (Write *1.02 × 1.73 is slightly more than 1.73.*) Think about the second expression. Will its product be slightly more than 1.73, or a lot more than 1.73? Tell a neighbor.

S: The product will just be a lot more than 1.73. The scaling factor is almost 30 times more than 1, so the product will be almost 30 times more too. → I can visualize two tape diagrams, and the one showing 1.73 times 29.01 is a lot longer, like 29 times longer than the tape showing just 1.73. → The product will be a lot more than what we started with because the scaling factor is a lot more than 1.

Problem Set (10 minutes)

Students should do their personal best to complete the Problem Set within the allotted 10 minutes. For some classes, it may be appropriate to modify the assignment by specifying which problems they work on first. Some problems do not specify a method for solving. Students solve these problems using the RDW approach used for Application Problems.

Student Debrief (10 minutes)

Lesson Objective: Compare the size of the product to the size of the factors.

The Student Debrief is intended to invite reflection and active processing of the total lesson experience.

Invite students to review their solutions for the Problem Set. They should check work by comparing answers with a partner before going over answers as a class. Look for misconceptions or misunderstandings that can be addressed in the Debrief. Guide students in a conversation to debrief the Problem Set and process the lesson.

You may choose to use any combination of the questions below to lead the discussion.

- Share your solutions and explain your thought process for solving Problem 1 to a partner. How did you decide which number goes into which expression?

- Compare your solutions for Problem 2 with a partner. Did you have different answers? If so, explain your thinking behind each sorting.

- What was your strategy for solving Problem 3? Share it with a partner.

- How did you solve Problem 4? Did you make a drawing or tape diagram to compare the sprouts? Share it with and explain it to a partner.

- Share your decimal examples for Problem 5 with a partner. Did you have the same or different examples?

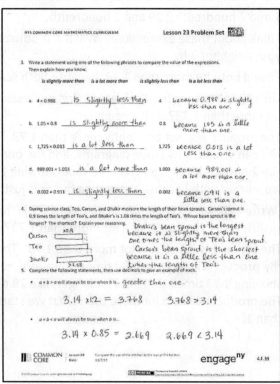

Lesson 23:   Compare the size of the product to the size of the factors.
Date: 11/10/13

4.F.3

Exit Ticket (3 minutes)

After the Student Debrief, instruct students to complete the Exit Ticket. A review of their work will help you assess the students' understanding of the concepts that were presented in the lesson today and plan more effectively for future lessons. You may read the questions aloud to the students.

Lesson 23:   Compare the size of the product to the size of the factors.
Date: 11/10/13

4.F.37

Name _____   Date _____

1. Fill in the blank using one of the following scaling factors to make each number sentence true.

| 1.021 | 0.989 | 1.00 |

   a. 3.4 × _____ = 3.4   b. _____ × 0.21 > 0.21   c. 8.04 × _____ < 8.04

2.

   a. Sort the following expressions by rewriting them in the table.

The product is less than the boxed number:	The product is greater than the boxed number:

   13.89 × 1.004   602 × 0.489   102.03 × 4.015

   0.3 × 0.069   0.72 × 1.24   0.2 × 0.1

   b. Explain your sorting by writing a sentence that tells what the expressions in each column of the table have in common.

COMMON CORE™

Lesson 23:   Compare the size of the product to the size of the factors.
Date: 11/10/13

4.F.3

3. Write a statement using one of the following phrases to compare the value of the expressions. Then explain how you know.

   is slightly more than   is a lot more than   is slightly less than   is a lot less than

   a. 4×0.988 _____ 4

   b. 1.05×0.8 _____ 0.8

   c. $1,725 \times 0.013$ _____ 1,725

   d. 989.001×1.003 _____ 1.003

   e. 0.002×0.911 _____ 0.002

4. During science class, Teo, Carson, and Dhakir measure the length of their bean sprouts. Carson's sprout is 0.9 times the length of Teo's, and Dhakir's is 1.08 times the length of Teo's. Whose bean sprout is the longest? The shortest? Explain your reasoning.

5. Complete the following statements, then use decimals to give an example of each.

   ▪ $a \times b > a$ will always be true when b is...

   ▪ $a \times b < a$ will always be true when b is...

Name _____   Date _____

1. Fill in the blank using one of the following scaling factors to make each number sentence true.

    | 1.009 | 1.00 | 0.898 |

    a. $3.06 \times$ _____ < 3.06 b. $5.2 \times$ _____ $= 5.2$ c. _____ $\times 0.89 > 0.89$

2. Will the product of 22.65×0.999 be greater than or less than 22.65? Without calculating, explain how you know.

Name _____   Date _____

1.

   a. Sort the following expressions by rewriting them in the table.

The product is less than the boxed number:	The product is greater than the boxed number:

   $\boxed{12.5}$ × 1.989 $\boxed{828}$ × 0.921 $\boxed{321.46}$ × 1.26

   $\boxed{0.007}$ × 1.02 $\boxed{2.16}$ × 1.11 $\boxed{0.05}$ × 0.1

   b. What do the expressions in each column have in common?

2. Write a statement using one of the following phrases to compare the value of the expressions. Then explain how you know.

   is slightly more than   *is a lot more than*   *is slightly less than*   *is a lot less than*

   a. 14 × 0.999   _____   14

   b. 1.01 × 2.06   _____   2.06

   c. 1,955 × 0.019   _____   1,955

COMMON CORE™   Lesson 23:   Compare the size of the product to the size of the factors.
Date: 11/10/13

4.F.41

d. Two thousand × 1.0001 _____ two thousand

e. Two-thousandths × 0.911 _____ two-thousandths

3. Rachel is 1.5 times as heavy as her cousin, Kayla. Another cousin, Jonathan, weighs 1.25 times as much as Kayla. List the cousins, from lightest to heaviest, and explain your thinking.

4. Circle your choice.

   a. $a \times b > a$

   For this statement to be true, b must be   **greater than 1**   **less than 1**

   Write two expressions that support your answer. Be sure to include one decimal example.

   b. $a \times b < a$

   For this statement to be true, b must be   **greater than 1**   **less than 1**

   Write two expressions that support your answer. Be sure to include one decimal example.

Lesson 23:	Compare the size of the product to the size of the factors.	
Date:	11/10/13	

4.F.4

Lesson 24

Objective: Solve word problems using fraction and decimal multiplication.

Suggested Lesson Structure

■ Fluency Practice   (12 minutes)

  Concept Development   (38 minutes)

■ Student Debrief   (10 minutes)

   Total Time   **(60 minutes)**

Fluency Practice (12 minutes)

- Compare the Size of a Product to the Size of One Factor **5.NF.5**   (4 minutes)
- Write Fractions as Decimals **5.NBT.2**   (5 minutes)
- Write the Scaling Factor **5.NBT.3**   (3 minutes)

Compare the Size of a Product to the Size of One Factor (4 minutes)

Materials: (S) Personal white boards

Note: This fluency reviews G5–M4–Lesson 21.

  T: How many halves are in 1?

  S: 2.

  T: How many thirds are in 1?

  S: 3.

  T: How many fourths are in 1?

  S: 4.

  T: (Write $1 = \frac{}{10}$.) On your boards, fill in the missing numerator.

  S: (Write $1 = \frac{10}{10}$.)

  T: (Write $6 \times \_\_ = 6$.) Say the missing factor.

  S: 1.

  T: (Write $6 \times \frac{}{3} = 6$.) On your boards, write the equation, filling in the missing numerator.

  S: (Write $6 \times \frac{3}{3} = 6$.)

  T: (Write $6 \times \frac{}{3} < 6$.) On your boards, fill in a numerator to make a true number sentence.

S: (Write $6 \times \frac{1}{3} < 6$ or $6 \times \frac{2}{3} < 6$.)

T: (Write $9 \times \frac{}{6} > 9$.) On your boards, fill in a numerator to make a true number sentence.

S: (Write a number sentence, filling in a numerator greater than 6.)

Continue this process with the following possible sequence: $\frac{2}{} \times 5 = 5$, $\frac{2}{} \times 5 < 5$, $\frac{2}{} \times 5 > 5$, $\frac{4}{} \times 9 < 9$, $\frac{}{6} \times 8 = 8$, and $\frac{5}{} \times 7 < 7$.

Write Fractions as Decimals (5 minutes)

Materials: (S) Personal white boards

Note: This fluency reviews G5–M4–Lesson 23.

T: (Write $\frac{1}{50} = \frac{}{100}$.) How many fifties are in 100?

S: 2.

T: (Write $\frac{1}{50} \times \frac{2}{2} = \frac{}{100}$.) $\frac{1}{50}$ is the same as how many 1 hundredths?

S: 2 one hundredths.

T: (Write $\frac{1}{50} \times \frac{2}{2} = \frac{2}{100}$. Below it, write $\frac{1}{50} = \underline{\ }.\underline{\ }$.) On your boards, write $\frac{1}{50}$ as a decimal.

S: (Write $\frac{1}{50} = 0.02$.)

Continue this process with the following possible sequence: $\frac{3}{50}$, $\frac{9}{50}$, $4\frac{9}{50}$, $\frac{1}{20}$, $\frac{3}{20}$, $4\frac{3}{20}$, $\frac{1}{5}$, $\frac{3}{5}$, $\frac{8}{5}$, $\frac{1}{25}$, $\frac{9}{25}$, $5\frac{9}{25}$, $\frac{1}{4}$, $\frac{3}{4}$, and $\frac{15}{4}$.

Write the Scaling Factor (3 minutes)

Materials: (S) Personal white boards

Note: This fluency reviews G5–M4–Lesson 23.

T: (Write $3 \times \underline{\ } = 3$.) Say the unknown whole number factor.

S: 1.

T: (Write $3.5 \times \underline{\ } = 3.5$.) Say the unknown whole number factor.

S: 1.

T: (Write $4.2 \times 1 = \underline{\quad}$.) Say the product.

S: 4.2.

T: (Write $\underline{\ } \times 0.58 > 0.58$.) Is the unknown factor going to be greater or less than 1?

S: Greater than 1.

T: Fill in a factor to make a true number sentence.

COMMON CORE™

Lesson 24:   Solve word problems using fraction and decimal multiplication.
Date: 11/10/13

4.F.4

S: (Write a number sentence filling in a decimal number greater than 1.)

T: (Write 7.03 × __ < 7.03.) Is the unknown factor greater or less than 1?

S: Less than 1.

T: Fill in a factor to make a true number sentence.

Continue this process with the following possible sequence: 6.07 × __ < 6.07, __ × 6.2 = 6.2, and 0.97 × __ > 0.97.

Concept Development (38 minutes)

Materials: (S) Problem Set

Note: The time normally allotted for the Application Problem has been included in the Concept Development portion of today's lesson.

Suggested Delivery of Instruction for Solving Lesson 24's Word Problems

1. Model the problem.

Have two pairs of student who can successfully model the problem work at the board while the others work independently or in pairs at their seats. Review the following questions before beginning the first problem:

- Can you draw something?
- What can you draw?
- What conclusions can you make from your drawing?

As students work, circulate. Reiterate the questions above. After two minutes, have the two pairs of students share only their labeled diagrams. For about one minute, have the demonstrating students receive and respond to feedback and questions from their peers.

2. Calculate to solve and write a statement.

Give everyone two minutes to finish work on that question, sharing their work and thinking with a peer. All should write their equations and statements of the answer.

3. Assess the solution for reasonableness.

Give students one to two minutes to assess and explain the reasonableness of their solution.

Problem 1

A vial contains 20 mL of medicine. If each dose is $\frac{1}{8}$ of the vial, how many mL is each dose? Express your answer as decimal.

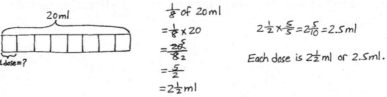

Lesson 24:   Solve word problems using fraction and decimal multiplication.

Date: 11/10/13

4.F.45

In this fraction of a set problem, students are asked to find one-eighth of 20 mL. Since the final answer needs to be expressed as a decimal, students again have some choices in how they solve. As illustrated, some students may choose to multiply $\frac{1}{8}$ by 20 to find the fractional mL in each dose. This method requires the students to then simply express $2\frac{1}{2}$ as a decimal.

Other students may choose to first express $\frac{1}{8}$ as a decimal (0.125), and then multiply that by 20 to find 2.5 mL of medicine per dose. This method is perhaps more direct, but it does require that students recall that 8 is a factor of 1,000 to express $\frac{1}{8}$ as a decimal.

Problem 2

A container holds 0.7 liters of oil and vinegar. $\frac{3}{4}$ of the mixture is vinegar. How many liters of vinegar are in the container? Express your answer as both a fraction and a decimal.

$$\frac{3}{4}\text{ of }0.7l$$
$$=\frac{3}{4}\times\frac{7}{10}$$
$$=\frac{21}{40}l$$

$$\frac{21}{40}\times\frac{25}{25}=\frac{525}{1000}=0.525l$$

There are $\frac{21}{40}l$ or $0.525l$ of vinegar in the container.

In this fraction of a set problem, students are asked to find three-fourths of a set that is expressed using a decimal. Since the final answer needs to be expressed as both a fraction and a decimal, students again have choice in approach. As illustrated, some students may choose to express 0.7 as a fraction, and then multiply by three-fourths to find the fractional liters of vinegar in the container. This method requires the slightly complex step of converting a fraction with denominator of 40 to a decimal. This process is not extremely challenging, but perhaps unfamiliar to students.

Other students may choose to first express $\frac{3}{4}$ as a decimal (0.75), and then multiply that by 0.7 to find 0.525 liters of vinegar are in the container. The decimal 0.525 is easily written $\frac{525}{1000}$ as a fraction. Students may but are not required to simplify this fraction.

Problem 3

Andres completed a 5 km race in 13.5 minutes. His sister's time was $1\frac{1}{2}$ times longer than his time. How long did it take his sister to run the race?

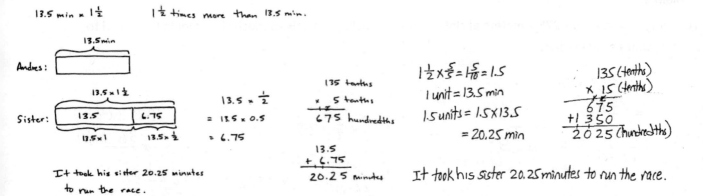

In this problem, Andres' race time (13.5 minutes) is being multiplied by a scaling factor of $1\frac{1}{2}$. Students must interpret both a decimal and fractional factor, thus giving rise to expression of both factors as either decimals or fractions $(13\frac{5}{10} \times 1\frac{1}{2}$ or $\frac{135}{10} \times \frac{3}{2})$. Alternately, students may have chosen to draw a tape diagram showing Andres' sister's time as 1 and a half times more than his. In this manner, students need to multiply to find the value of the half-unit that represents the additional time that his sister spent running, and then add that sum to 13.5 minutes. Student choice of approach provides an opportunity to discuss the efficiency of both approaches during the Student Debrief. In any case, students should find that it took Andres' sister 20.25 (or $20\frac{1}{4}$) minutes to complete the race.

NOTES ON MULTIPLE MEANS OF REPRESENTATION:

Problems 3, 4, and 5 require students to compare quantities. For example, in Problem 3, students are comparing Andres' race time to his sister's time. Typically, when using tape diagrams to solve comparison word problems, at least two bars are used.

There is a strong connection between tape diagrams used with comparison story problems and bar graphs. The bars in bar graphs allow readers to compare quantities, exactly like the bars that are used in comparison word problems. Although tape diagrams are typically drawn horizontally, they can be drawn vertically. Similarly, bar graphs can (and should) be drawn horizontally and vertically. In Problems 3, 4, and 5, it is easy to visualize additional data that would result in additional bars.

Problem 4

A clothing factory uses 1,275.2 meters of cloth a week to make shirts. How much cloth would they need to make $3\frac{3}{5}$ times as many shirts?

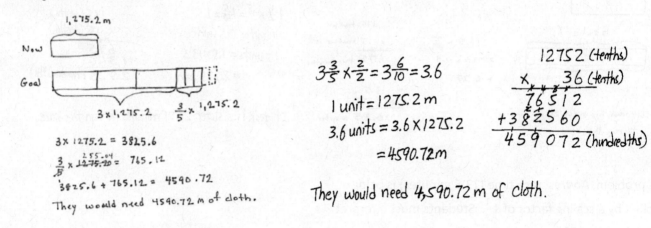

In this scaling problem, a length of cloth (1,275.2 m) is being multiplied by a scaling factor of $3\frac{3}{5}$. Before students solve, ask them to identify the scaling factor and what comparison is being made (that of the initial amount of fabric and the resulting amount). Though students do have the option of expressing both factors as fractions, the method of converting $3\frac{3}{5}$ to a decimal is far simpler. The efficiency of this approach can be a focus during the Student Debrief. Some students may also have chosen to draw a tape diagram showing 1,275.2 meters of cloth being scaled to $3\frac{3}{5}$ times its original length. In this manner, students could have tripled 1,275.2 first, then found three-fifths of it before combining those two totals. In either case, students should find that the factory would need 4,590.72 meters of cloth.

Problem 5

There are $\frac{3}{4}$ as many boys as girls in a class of fifth-graders. If there are 35 students in the class, how many are girls?

What may seem like a simple problem is actually rather challenging, as students are required to work backwards as they solve. The word problem states that there are $\frac{3}{4}$ as many boys as girls in the class, yet the number of girls is unknown. Students should first reason that since the number of boys is a scaled multiple of the number of girls, a tape should first be drawn to represent the girls. From that tape, students can draw a smaller tape (one that is three-fourths the size of the tape representing the girls) to represent the boys in the class. In this way, students can see that 3 units are boys and 4 units are girls. Since there are 35 students in the class and 7 total units, each unit represents 5 students. Four of those

units are girls, so there are 20 girls in the class.

Problem 6

Ciro purchased a concert ticket for $56. The cost of the ticket was $\frac{4}{5}$ the cost of his dinner. The cost of his hotel was $2\frac{1}{2}$ times as much as his ticket. How much did Ciro spend altogether for the concert ticket, hotel, and dinner?

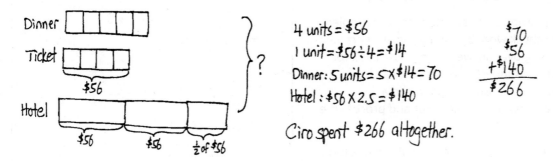

In this problem, students must read and work carefully to identify that the cost of the concert ticket plays two roles. In relation to the cost of the dinner, the ticket cost can be considered the scaling factor as it represents $\frac{4}{5}$ the cost of dinner. However, in relation to the cost of the hotel, the ticket cost should be considered the factor being scaled (as the hotel cost is $2\frac{1}{2}$ times greater.) This understanding is crucial for drawing an accurate model and should be discussed thoroughly as students draw and again in the Student Debrief.

Once the modeling is complete, the steps toward solution are relatively simple. Since the ticket cost represents $\frac{4}{5}$ the cost of dinner, division shows that each unit (or fifth) is equal to $14. Therefore, 5 units (5 fifths), or the cost of dinner, is equal to $70. The model representing the cost of the hotel very clearly shows 2 units of $56 and a half unit of $56, which in total, equals $140. Students must use addition to find the total cost of Ciro's spending.

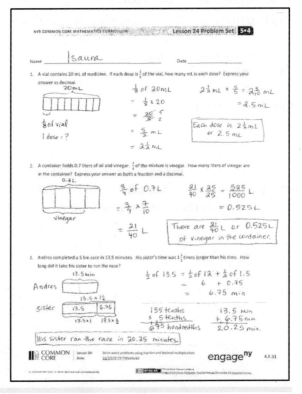

COMMON CORE | Lesson 24: Solve word problems using fraction and decimal multiplication.
Date: 11/10/13

4.F.49

Student Debrief (10 minutes)

Lesson Objective: Solve word problems using fraction and decimal multiplication.

The Student Debrief is intended to invite reflection and active processing of the total lesson experience.

Invite students to review their solutions for the Problem Set. They should check work by comparing answers with a partner before going over answers as a class. Look for misconceptions or misunderstandings that can be addressed in the Debrief. Guide students in a conversation to debrief the Problem Set and process the lesson.

You may choose to use any combination of the questions below to lead the discussion.

- For all the problems in this Problem Set, there are a few ways to solve for the solution. Compare and share your strategy with a partner.

- How did you solve Problem 5? Explain your strategy to a partner. Can you find how many boys there are in the classroom? How many more girls than boys are in the classroom?

- Did you make any drawings or tape diagrams for Problem 6? Share and compare with a partner. Does drawing a tape diagram help you solve this problem? Explain.

Exit Ticket (3 minutes)

After the Student Debrief, instruct students to complete the Exit Ticket. A review of their work will help you assess the students' understanding of the concepts that were presented in the lesson today and plan more effectively for future lessons. You may read the questions aloud to the students.

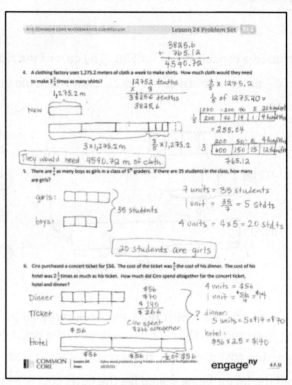

NOTES ON MULTIPLE MEANS OF ENGAGEMENT:

A daily goal for teachers is to get students to talk about their thinking. One possible strategy to achieve this goal is to partner each student with a peer who has a different perspective.

Ask students to separate themselves into groups that solved a specific problem in a similar way. Once these groups are formed, ask each student to partner with a peer in another group. Let these partners describe and discuss their strategies and solutions with each other. It is harder for students to explain different approaches than like approaches.

Lesson 24: Solve word problems using fraction and decimal multiplication.
Date: 11/10/13

4.F.5

© 2013 Common Core, Inc. All rights reserved. commoncore.org

Name _____   Date _____

1. A vial contains 20 mL of medicine. If each dose is $\frac{1}{8}$ of the vial, how many mL is each dose? Express your answer as decimal.

2. A container holds 0.7 liters of oil and vinegar. $\frac{3}{4}$ of the mixture is vinegar. How many liters of vinegar are in the container? Express your answer as both a fraction and a decimal.

3. Andres completed a 5 km race in 13.5 minutes. His sister's time was $1\frac{1}{2}$ times longer than his time. How long did it take his sister to run the race?

4. A clothing factory uses 1,275.2 meters of cloth a week to make shirts. How much cloth would they need to make $3\frac{3}{5}$ times as many shirts?

5. There are $\frac{3}{4}$ as many boys as girls in a class of fifth-graders. If there are 35 students in the class, how many are girls?

6. Ciro purchased a concert ticket for $56. The cost of the ticket was $\frac{4}{5}$ the cost of his dinner. The cost of his hotel was $2\frac{1}{2}$ times as much as his ticket. How much did Ciro spend altogether for the concert ticket, hotel, and dinner?

COMMON CORE

Lesson 24: Solve word problems using fraction and decimal multiplication.
Date: 11/10/13

4.F.5

Name _____   Date _____

1. An artist builds a sculpture out of metal and wood that weighs 14.9 kilograms. $\frac{3}{4}$ of this weight is metal, and the rest is wood. How much does the wood part of the sculpture weigh?

2. On a boat ride tour, there are half as many children as there are adults. There are 30 people on the tour. How many children are there?

Lesson 24:   Solve word problems using fraction and decimal multiplication.
Date: 11/10/13

4.F.53

© 2013 Common Core, Inc. All rights reserved. commoncore.org

Name _____   Date _____

1. Jesse takes his dog and cat for their annual vet visit. Jesse's dog weighs 23 pounds. The vet tells him his cat's weight is $\frac{5}{8}$ as much as his dog's weight. How much does his cat weigh?

2. An image of a snowflake is 1.8 centimeters wide. If the actual snowflake is $\frac{1}{8}$ the size of the image, what is the width of the actual snowflake? Express your answer as a decimal.

3. A community bike ride offers a short ride for children and families, which is 5.7 miles, followed by a long ride for adults, which is $5\frac{2}{3}$ times as long. If a woman bikes the short ride with her children, and then the long ride with her friends, how many miles does she ride altogether?

4. Sal bought a house for $78,524.60. Twelve years later he sold the house for $2\frac{3}{4}$ times as much. What was the sale price of the house?

5. In the fifth grade at Lenape Elementary School, there are $\frac{4}{5}$ as many students who do not wear glasses as those who do wear glasses. If there are 60 students who wear glasses, how many students are in the fifth grade?

6. At a factory, a mechanic earns $17.25 an hour. The president of the company earns $6\frac{3}{4}$ times as much for each hour he works. The janitor at the same company earns $\frac{3}{4}$ as much as the mechanic. How much does the company pay for all three people employees' wages for one hour of work?

Topic G

Division of Fractions and Decimal Fractions

5.OA.1, 5.NBT.7, 5.NF.7

Focus Standard:	5.OA.1	Use parentheses, brackets, or braces in numerical expressions, and evaluate expressions with these symbols.
	5.NBT.7	Add, subtract, multiply, and divide decimals to hundredths, using concrete models or drawings and strategies based on place value, properties of operations, and/or the relationship between addition and subtraction; relate the strategy to a written method and explain the reasoning used.
	5.NF.7	Apply and extend previous understandings of division to divide unit fractions by whole numbers and whole numbers by unit fractions. (Students able to multiple fractions in general can develop strategies to divide fractions in general, by reasoning about the relationship between multiplication and division. But division of a fraction by a fraction is not a requirement at this grade level.)
		a. Interpret division of a unit fraction by a non-zero whole number, and compute such quotients. *For example, create a story context for (1/3) ÷ 4, and use a visual fraction model to show the quotient. Use the relationship between multiplication and division to explain that (1/3) ÷ 4 = 1/12 because (1/12) × 4 = 1/3.*
		b. Interpret division of a whole number by a unit fraction, and compute such quotients. *For example, create a story context for 4 ÷ (1/5), and use a visual fraction model to show the quotient. Use the relationship between multiplication and division to explain that 4 ÷ (1/5) = 20 because 20 × (1/5) = 4.*
		c. Solve real world problems involving division of unit fractions by non-zero whole numbers and division of whole numbers by unit fractions, e.g., by using visual fraction models and equations to represent the problem. *For example, how much chocolate will each person get if 3 people share 1/2 lb of chocolate equally? How many 1/3-cup servings are in 2 cups of raisins?*
Instructional Days:	7	
Coherence -Links from:	G4–M5	Fraction Equivalence, Ordering, and Operations
	G5–M2	Multi-Digit Whole Number and Decimal Fraction Operations
-Links to:	G6–M2	Arithmetic Operations Including Division by a Fraction
	G6–M4	Expressions and Equations

Topic G begins the work of division with fractions, both fractions and decimal fractions. Students use tape diagrams and number lines to reason about the division of a whole number by a unit fraction and a unit fraction by a whole number (**5.NF.7**). Using the same thinking developed in Module 2 to divide whole numbers, students reason about how many *fourths* are in 5 when considering such cases as 5 ÷ 1/4. They also reason about the size of the unit when 1/4 is partitioned into 5 equal parts: 1/4 ÷ 5. Using this thinking as a backdrop, students are introduced to decimal fraction divisors and use equivalent fraction and place value thinking to reason about the size of quotients, calculate quotients, and sensibly place the decimal in quotients (**5.NBT.7**).

A Teaching Sequence Towards Mastery of Division of Fractions and Decimal Fractions
Objective 1: Divide a whole number by a unit fraction. (Lesson 25)
Objective 2: Divide a unit fraction by a whole number. (Lesson 26)
Objective 3: Solve problems involving fraction division. (Lesson 27)
Objective 4: Write equations and word problems corresponding to tape and number line diagrams. (Lesson 28)
Objective 5: Connect division by a unit fraction to division by 1 tenth and 1 hundredth. (Lesson 29)
Objective 6: Divide decimal dividends by non-unit decimal divisors. (Lessons 30–31)

	Topic G:	Division of Fractions and Decimal Fractions	**4.G.2**
	Date:	11/10/13	

Lesson 25

Objective: Divide a whole number by a unit fraction.

Suggested Lesson Structure

■ Fluency Practice   (12 minutes)
■ Application Problem   (7 minutes)
■ Concept Development   (31 minutes)
■ Student Debrief   (10 minutes)
  Total Time   **(60 minutes)**

Fluency Practice (12 minutes)

- Write Fractions as Decimals **5.NBT.2**   (7 minutes)
- Multiply Fractions by Decimals **5.NBT.7**   (5 minutes)

Write Fractions as Decimals (7 minutes)

Materials: (S) Personal white boards

Note: This fluency reviews G5–M4–Lesson 23.

T: (Write $\frac{1}{2} = \frac{}{100}$.) $\frac{1}{2}$ is how many hundredths?

T: (Write $\frac{1}{2} = \frac{50}{100}$.) Write $\frac{1}{2}$ as a decimal.

S: (Write $\frac{1}{2} = 0.5$ or $\frac{1}{2} = 0.50$.)

T: (Write $\frac{1}{4} = \frac{}{100}$.) $\frac{1}{4}$ is how many hundredths?

S: 25 hundredths.

T: (Write $\frac{1}{4} = \frac{25}{100}$.) Write $\frac{1}{4}$ as a decimal.

S: (Write $\frac{1}{4} = 0.25$.)

T: (Write $\frac{3}{4} = \frac{}{100}$.) $\frac{3}{4}$ is how many hundredths?

S: 75 hundredths.

T: (Write $\frac{3}{4} = \frac{75}{100}$.) Write $\frac{3}{4}$ as a decimal.

COMMON CORE™   Lesson 25:   Divide a whole number by a unit fraction.
                   Date: 11/10/13

4.G.3

S: (Write $\frac{3}{4}$ = 0.75.)

T: (Write $1\frac{3}{4}$ = __.__.) Write $1\frac{3}{4}$ as a decimal.

S: (Write $1\frac{3}{4}$ = 1.75.)

Continue the process for $\frac{1}{25}$, $\frac{8}{25}$, $3\frac{8}{25}$, $\frac{1}{5}$, $\frac{2}{5}$, $\frac{7}{5}$, $\frac{1}{20}$, $\frac{9}{20}$, $4\frac{9}{20}$, $\frac{1}{50}$, $\frac{7}{50}$, $\frac{11}{50}$, and $3\frac{11}{50}$.

Multiply Fractions by Decimals (5 minutes)

Materials: (S) Personal white boards

Note: This fluency reviews G5–M4–Lesson 24.

T: (Write $\frac{1}{2} \times \frac{1}{2}$ = _____.) On your boards, write the multiplication sentence.

S: (Write $\frac{1}{2} \times \frac{1}{2} = \frac{1}{4}$.)

T: (Write $\frac{1}{2} \times \frac{1}{2} = \frac{1}{4}$. Beneath it, write $\frac{1}{2} \times 0.\_\_\_ = \frac{1}{4}$.) On your boards, fill in the missing digit.

S: (Write $\frac{1}{2} \times 0.5 = \frac{1}{4}$.)

T: (Write $\frac{1}{2} \times 0.5 = \frac{1}{4}$ = __.__.) Complete the equation.

S: (Write $\frac{1}{2} \times 0.5 = \frac{1}{4}$ = 0.25.)

T: (Write $\frac{1}{2} \times \frac{1}{50}$ = __.__.) On your boards, write the multiplication sentence.

S: (Write $\frac{1}{2} \times \frac{1}{50} = \frac{1}{100}$ = 0.01.)

T: (Write $0.5 \times \frac{1}{50}$ = __.__.)

S: (Write $0.5 \times \frac{1}{50}$ = 0.01.)

T: (Write $\frac{3}{5} \times 0.7$ = __.__.) Rewrite the multiplication sentence as a fraction times a fraction.

S: (Write $\frac{6}{10} \times \frac{7}{10}$ = 0.42.)

T: (Write $0.8 \times \frac{2}{5}$ = __.__ × __.__ = — = __.__.) Rewrite the multiplication sentence, filling in the blanks.

S: (Write $0.8 \times \frac{2}{5} = 0.8 \times 0.4 = \frac{32}{100}$ = 0.32.)

T: (Write $\frac{4}{5} \times 0.9$ = __.__ × __.__ = __.__.) Rewrite the multiplication sentence, filling in the blanks.

S: (Write $\frac{4}{5} \times 0.9 = 0.8 \times 0.9 = 0.72$.)

$$\frac{1}{2} \times \frac{1}{2} = \frac{1}{4}$$

$$\frac{1}{2} \times 0.5 = \frac{1}{4}$$

$$\frac{1}{2} \times 0.5 = \frac{1}{4} = 0.25$$

Lesson 25:   Divide a whole number by a unit fraction.
Date: 11/10/13

4.G.4

Application Problem (7 minutes)

The label on a 0.118-liter bottle of cough syrup recommends a dose of 10 milliliters for children aged 6 to 10 years. How many 10-mL doses are in the bottle?

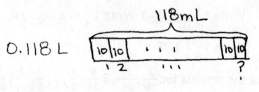

Note: This problem requires students to access their knowledge of converting among different size measurement units—a look back to Modules 1 and 2. Students may disagree on whether the final answer should be a whole number or a decimal. There are only 11 complete 10-mL doses in the bottle, but many students will divide 118 by 10, and give 11.8 doses as their final answer. This invites interpretation of the remainder since both answers are correct.

Concept Development (31 minutes)

Materials: (S) Personal white boards, 4" × 2" rectangular paper (several pieces per student), scissors

Problem 1

Jenny buys 2 pounds of pecans.

a. If Jenny puts 2 pounds in each bag, how many bags can she make?

b. If she puts 1 pound in each bag, how many bags can she make?

c. If she puts $\frac{1}{2}$ pound in each bag, how many bags can she make?

d. If she puts $\frac{1}{3}$ pound in each bag, how many bags can she make?

e. If she puts $\frac{1}{4}$ pound in each bag, how many bags can she make?

NOTES ON MULTIPLE MEANS OF REPRESENTATION:

In addition to tape diagrams and area models, students can also use region models to represent the information in these problems. For example, students can draw circles to represent the apples and divide the circles in half to represent halves.

Note: Continue this questioning sequence to include thirds, fourths, and fifths.

T: (Post Problem 1(a) on the board, and read it aloud with students.) Work with your partner to write a division sentence that explains your thinking. Be prepared to share.

S: (Work.)

T: Say the division sentence to solve this problem.

S: 2 ÷ 2 = 1.

T: (Record on board.) How many bags of pecans can she make?

Lesson 25: Divide a whole number by a unit fraction.
Date: 11/10/13

4.G.5

S: 1 bag.

T: (Post Problem 1(b).) Write a division sentence for this situation and solve.

S: (Solve.)

T: Say the division sentence to solve this problem.

S: $2 \div 1 = 2$.

T: (Record directly beneath the first division sentence.) Answer the question in a complete sentence.

S: She can make 2 bags.

T: (Post Problem 1(c).) If Jenny puts 1 half-pound in each of the bags, how many bags can she make? What would that division sentence look like? Turn and talk.

S: We still have 2 as the amount that's divided up, so it should still be $2 \div \frac{1}{2}$. → We are sort of putting pecans in half-pound groups, so 1 half will be our divisor, the size of the group. → It's like asking how many halves are in 2?

T: (Write $2 \div \frac{1}{2}$ directly beneath the other division sentences.) Will the answer be more or less than 2? Talk to your partner.

S: I looked at the other problems and see a pattern. $2 \div 2 = 1$, $2 \div 1 = 2$, and now I think $2 \div \frac{1}{2}$ will be more than 2. → It should be more, because we're cutting each pound into halves so that will make more groups. → I can visualize that each whole pound would have 2 halves, so there should be 4 half-pounds in 2 pounds.

T: Let's use a piece of rectangular paper to represent 2 pounds of pecans. Cut it into 2 equal pieces, so each piece represents…?

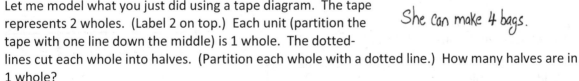

S: 1 pound of pecans.

T: Fold each pound into halves, and cut.

S: (Fold and cut.)

T: How many halves were in 2 wholes?

S: 4 halves.

T: Let me model what you just did using a tape diagram. The tape represents 2 wholes. (Label 2 on top.) Each unit (partition the tape with one line down the middle) is 1 whole. The dotted-lines cut each whole into halves. (Partition each whole with a dotted line.) How many halves are in 1 whole?

S: 2 halves.

T: How many halves are in 2 wholes?

S: 4 halves.

T: Yes. I'll draw a number line underneath the tape diagram and label the wholes. (Label 0, 1, and 2 on the number line.) Now, I can put a tick mark for each half. Let's count the halves with me as I label. (Label $\frac{0}{2}, \frac{1}{2}, \frac{2}{2}, \frac{3}{2}, \frac{4}{2}$.)

S: $\frac{0}{2}, \frac{1}{2}, \frac{2}{2}, \frac{3}{2}, \frac{4}{2}$.

T: There are 4 halves in 2 wholes. (Write $2 \div \frac{1}{2} = 4$.) She can make 4 bags. But how can we be sure 4 halves is correct? How do we check a division problem? Multiply the quotient and the...?

S: Divisor.

T: What is the quotient?

S: 4.

T: The divisor?

S: 1 half.

T: What would our checking expression be? Write it with your partner.

MP.4

S: $4 \times \frac{1}{2}$.

T: Complete the number sentence. (Pause.) Read the complete sentence.

S: $4 \times \frac{1}{2} = 2$ or $\frac{1}{2} \times 4 = \frac{1 \times 4}{2} = \frac{4}{2} = 2$.

T: Were we correct?

S: Yes.

T: Let's remember this thinking as we continue.

Repeat the modeling process with Problem 1(d) and (e), divisors of 1 third and 1 fourth.

Extend the dialogue when dividing by 1 fourth to look for patterns:

T: (Point to all the number sentences in the previous problems: $2 \div 2 = 1$, $2 \div 1 = 2$, $2 \div \frac{1}{2} = 4$, $2 \div \frac{1}{3} = 6$, and $2 \div \frac{1}{4} = 8$.) Take a look at these problems, what patterns do you notice? Turn and share.

S: The 2 pounds are the same, but each time it is being divided into a smaller and smaller unit. → The answer is getting bigger and bigger. → When the 2 pounds is divided into smaller units, then the answer is bigger.

T: Explain to your partner why the quotient is getting bigger as it is divided by smaller units.

S: When we cut a whole into smaller parts, then we'll get more parts. → The more units we split from one whole, then the more parts we'll have. That's why the quotient is getting bigger.

T: Based on the patterns, solve how many bags she can make if she puts $\frac{1}{5}$ pound in each bag. Draw a tape diagram and a number line on your personal board to explain your thinking.

S: (Solve.)

T: Say the division sentence.

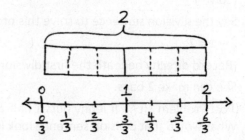

$2 \div \frac{1}{3} = 6$

She can make 6 bags.

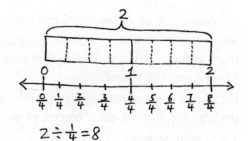

$2 \div \frac{1}{4} = 8$

She can make 8 bags.

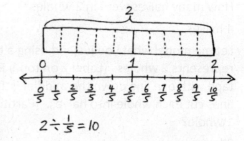

$2 \div \frac{1}{5} = 10$

She can make 10 bags.

Lesson 25: Divide a whole number by a unit fraction.
Date: 11/10/13

4.G.7

S: $2 \div \frac{1}{5} = 10$.

T: Answer the question in a complete sentence.

S: She can make 10 bags.

Problem 2

Jenny buys 2 pounds of pecans.

a.   If this is $\frac{1}{2}$ the number she needs to make pecan pies, how many pounds will she need?

b.   If this is $\frac{1}{3}$ the number she needs to make pecan pies, how many pounds will she need?

c.   If this is $\frac{1}{4}$ the number she needs to make pecan pies, how many pounds will she need?

T: We can also ask different questions about Jenny and her two pounds of pecans. (Post Problem 2(a).) Two is half of what number?

S: 4.

T: Give me the division sentence.

S: It's not division! It's multiplication. → It's 2 twos. That's four.

T: Give me the multiplication number sentence.

S: $2 \times 2 = 4$. → $\frac{1}{2} \times 4 = 2$.

T: Hold on. Stop. Let's try to write a division expression for this whole number situation. (Write $4 \times \underline{\quad} = 8$.)

S: What would the division expression be?

S: $8 \div 4$.

T: Tell me the complete number sentence.

S: $8 \div 4 = 2$.

T: Now try the same process with $\frac{1}{2} \times \underline{\quad} = 2$. Give me the division expression.

S: $2 \div \frac{1}{2}$.

T: Tell me the complete number sentence.

S: $2 \div \frac{1}{2} = 4$.

T: Yes. We are finding how much is in one unit just like we did with $8 \div 2 = 4$. In this case, the whole is the unit.

T: What is the whole unit in this story?

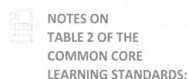

NOTES ON
TABLE 2 OF THE
COMMON CORE
LEARNING STANDARDS:

It is important to distinguish between interpretations of division when working with fractions. When working with fractions, it may be easier to understand the distinction by using the word *unit* rather than *group*.

Number of units unknown (or *number of groups unknown*) is the measurement model of division, for example, for $12 \div 3$ and $3 \div \frac{1}{2}$:

▪   12 cards are put in packs of 3. How many packs are there?

▪   3 meters of cloth are cut into $\frac{1}{2}$ meter strips. How many strips are cut?

Unknown unit (or *group size unknown*) is the partitive model of division, for example, for $12 \div 3$ and $3 \div \frac{1}{2}$:

▪   12 cards are dealt to 3 people. How many cards does each person get?

▪   3 miles is $\frac{1}{2}$ the trip. How far is the whole trip?

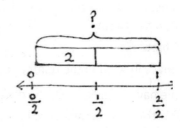

$$2 \div \frac{1}{2} = 2 \times 2 = 4$$

S: The whole amount she needs for pecan pies.

T: Let's go back and answer our question. Jenny buys 2 pounds of pecans. If this is $\frac{1}{2}$ the number she needs to make pecan pies, how many pounds will she need?

S: She will need 4 pounds of pecans.

T: Yes.

T: (Post Problem 2(b) on the board.) The answer is…?

S: 6.

T: Give me the division sentence.

S: $2 \div \frac{1}{3} = 6$.

T: Explain to your partner why that is true.

S: We are looking for the whole amount of pounds. Two is a third, so we divide it by a third. → I still think of it as multiplication though, 2 times 3 equals 6. → But the problem doesn't mention 3, it says a third, so $2 \div \frac{1}{3} = 2 \times 3$. → So, dividing by a third is the same as multiplying by 3.

T: We can see in our tape diagram that this is true. (Write $2 \div \frac{1}{3} = 2 \times 3$.) Explain to your partner why. Use the story of the pecans, if you like.

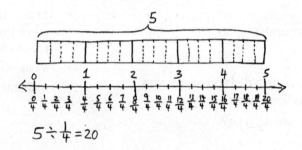

$$2 \div \frac{1}{3} = 2 \times 3 = 6$$

Problem 3

Tien wants to cut $\frac{1}{4}$ foot lengths from a board that is 5 feet long. How many boards can he cut?

$$5 \div \frac{1}{4} = 20$$

Tien can cut 20 boards.

T: (Post Problem 3 on the board, and read it together with the class.) What is the length of the board Tien has to cut?

S: 5 feet.

T: How can we find the number of boards 1 fourth of a foot long? Turn and talk.

S: We have to divide. → The division sentence is $5 \div \frac{1}{4}$. → I can draw 5 wholes, and cut each whole into fourths. Then I can count how many fourths are in 5 wholes.

T: On your personal board, draw and solve this problem independently.

S: (Work.)

T: How many quarter feet are in one foot?

Lesson 25: Divide a whole number by a unit fraction.
Date: 11/10/13

4.G.9

S: 4.

T: How many quarter feet are in 5 feet?

S: 20.

T: Say the division sentence.

S: $5 \div \frac{1}{4} = 20$.

T: Check your work, then answer the question in a complete sentence.

S: Tien can cut 20 boards.

Problem Set (10 minutes)

Students should do their personal best to complete the Problem Set within the allotted 10 minutes. For some classes, it may be appropriate to modify the assignment by specifying which problems they work on first. Some problems do not specify a method for solving. Students solve these problems using the RDW approach used for Application Problems.

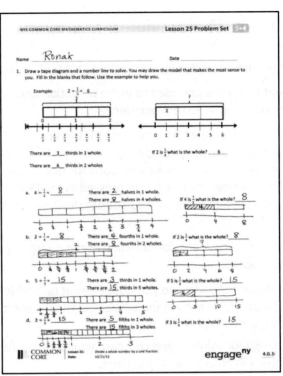

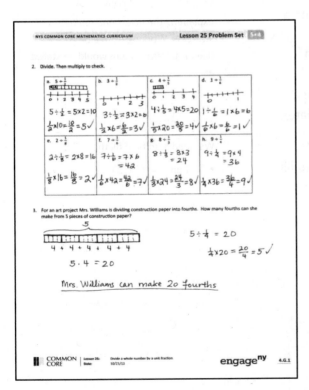

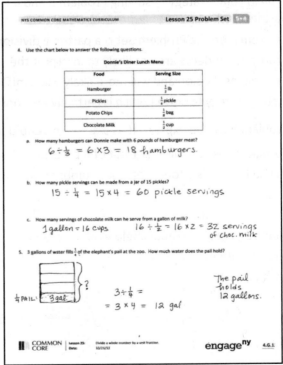

Student Debrief (10 minutes)

Lesson Objective: Divide a whole number by a unit fraction.

The Student Debrief is intended to invite reflection and active processing of the total lesson experience.

Invite students to review their solutions for the Problem Set. They should check work by comparing answers with a partner before going over answers as a class. Look for misconceptions or misunderstandings that can be addressed in the Debrief. Guide students in a conversation to debrief the Problem Set and process the lesson.

You may choose to use any combination of the questions below to lead the discussion.

- In Problem 1, what do you notice about (a) and (b), and (c) and (d)? What are the whole and the divisor in the problems?

- Share your solution and compare your strategy for solving Problem 2 with a partner.

- Explain your strategy of solving Problem 3 and 4 with a partner.

- Problem 5 on the Problem Set is a partitive division problem. Students are not likely to interpret the problem as division and will more likely use a missing factor strategy to solve (which is certainly appropriate).

- Problem 5 can be expressed as $3 \div \frac{1}{4}$. This could be thought of as "3 gallons is 1 out of 4 parts needed to fill the pail" or "3 is 1 fourth of what number?" Asking students to consider this interpretation will be beneficial in future encounters with fraction division. (See UDL box. The model below puts the two interpretations right next to each other.)

NOTES ON
MULTIPLE MEANS OF
ENGAGEMENT:

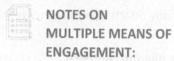

The second to last bullet in today's Debrief brings out an interpretation of fraction division in context that is particularly useful for Grade 6's encounters with non-unit fraction division. In Grade 6, Problem 5 might read:

$\frac{2}{3}$ *gallon of water fills the pail to* $\frac{3}{4}$ *of its capacity. How much water does the pail hold?*

This could be expressed as $\frac{2}{3} \div \frac{3}{4}$. That is, $\frac{2}{3}$ is 3 of the 4 *groups* needed to completely fill the pail. This type of problem can be thought of partitively as *2 thirds is 3 fourths of what number* or $\frac{2}{3} = \frac{3}{4} \times$ ___. This gives rise to explaining the *invert and multiply* strategy. Working from a tape diagram, this problem would be stated as:

- 3 units = $\frac{2}{3}$

- 1 unit = $(\frac{2}{3} \div 3)$

We need 4 units to fill the pail:

- 4 units = $(\frac{2}{3} \div 3) \times 4$

- = $\frac{2}{3} \times \frac{4}{3}$

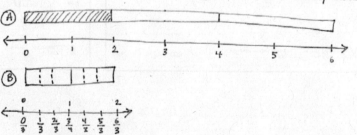

$2 \div \frac{1}{3} = 6$ Ⓐ 2 is a third of what number?
                          Ⓑ 2 contains how many thirds?

COMMON CORE   Lesson 25:   Divide a whole number by a unit fraction.
Date: 11/10/13

© 2013 Common Core, Inc. All rights reserved. commoncore.org

4.G.11

Exit Ticket (3 minutes)

After the Student Debrief, instruct students to complete the Exit Ticket. A review of their work will help you assess the students' understanding of the concepts that were presented in the lesson today and plan more effectively for future lessons. You may read the questions aloud to the students.

Lesson 25:   Divide a whole number by a unit fraction.
Date: 11/10/13

4.G.12

Name _____   Date _____

1. Draw a tape diagram and a number line to solve. You may draw the model that makes the most sense to you. Fill in the blanks that follow. Use the example to help you.

Example: $2 \div \frac{1}{3} =$ __6__

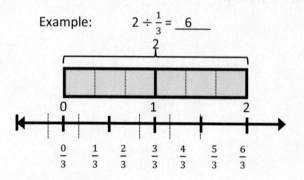   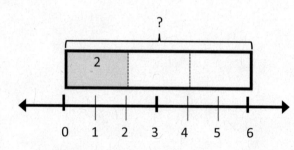

There are __3__ thirds in 1 whole.

There are __6__ thirds in 2 wholes

If 2 is $\frac{1}{3}$, what is the whole? __6__

a. $4 \div \frac{1}{2} =$ _____

There are ____ halves in 1 whole.
There are ____ halves in 4 wholes.

If 4 is $\frac{1}{2}$, what is the whole? _____

b. $2 \div \frac{1}{4} =$ _____

There are____ fourths in 1 whole.
There are ____ fourths in 2 wholes.

If 2 is $\frac{1}{4}$, what is the whole? _____

c. $5 \div \frac{1}{3} =$ _____

There are ____ thirds in 1 whole.
There are ____ thirds in 5 wholes.

If 5 is $\frac{1}{3}$, what is the whole? _____

d. $3 \div \frac{1}{5} =$ _____

There are ____ fifths in 1 whole.
There are ____ fifths in 3 wholes.

If 3 is $\frac{1}{5}$, what is the whole? _____

COMMON CORE | Lesson 25:   Divide a whole number by a unit fraction.
| Date: 11/10/13

4.G.1

2. Divide. Then multiply to check.

a. $5 \div \frac{1}{2}$	b. $3 \div \frac{1}{2}$	c. $4 \div \frac{1}{5}$	d. $1 \div \frac{1}{6}$
e. $2 \div \frac{1}{8}$	f. $7 \div \frac{1}{6}$	g. $8 \div \frac{1}{3}$	h. $9 \div \frac{1}{4}$

3. For an art project, Mrs. Williams is dividing construction paper into fourths. How many fourths can she make from 5 pieces of construction paper?

COMMON CORE™

Lesson 25: Divide a whole number by a unit fraction.
Date: 11/10/13

4.G.14

4. Use the chart below to answer the following questions.

Donnie's Diner Lunch Menu

Food	Serving Size
Hamburger	$\frac{1}{3}$ lb
Pickles	$\frac{1}{4}$ pickle
Potato Chips	$\frac{1}{8}$ bag
Chocolate Milk	$\frac{1}{2}$ cup

a. How many hamburgers can Donnie make with 6 pounds of hamburger meat?

b. How many pickle servings can be made from a jar of 15 pickles?

c. How many servings of chocolate milk can he serve from a gallon of milk?

5. Three gallons of water fills $\frac{1}{4}$ of the elephant's pail at the zoo. How much water does the pail hold?

COMMON CORE Lesson 25: Divide a whole number by a unit fraction.
Date: 11/10/13

4.G.1

Name _____ Date _____

1. Draw a tape diagram and a number line to solve. Fill in the blanks that follow.

    a. $5 \div \frac{1}{2} =$ _____

    There are _____ halves in 1 whole.

    There are _____ halves in 5 wholes.

    5 is $\frac{1}{2}$ of what number? _____

    b. $4 \div \frac{1}{4} =$ _____

    There are _____ fourths in 1 whole.

    There are _____ fourths in _____ wholes.

    4 is $\frac{1}{4}$ of what number? _____

2. Ms. Leverenz is doing an art project with her class. She has a 3-foot piece of ribbon. If she gives each student an eighth of a foot of ribbon, will she have enough for her 22-student class?

Name _____   Date _____

1. Draw a tape diagram and a number line to solve. Fill in the blanks that follow.

    a. $3 \div \frac{1}{3} =$ _____   There are ____ thirds in 1 whole.

                                    There are ____ thirds in __ wholes.

                                    If 3 is $\frac{1}{3}$, what is the whole? _____

    b. $3 \div \frac{1}{4} =$ _____   There are____ fourths in 1 whole.

                                    There are ____ fourths in __ wholes.

                                    If 3 is $\frac{1}{4}$, what is the whole? _____

    c. $4 \div \frac{1}{3} =$ _____   There are ____ thirds in 1 whole.

                                    There are ____ thirds in __ wholes.

                                    If 4 is $\frac{1}{3}$, what is the whole? _____

    d. $5 \div \frac{1}{4} =$ _____   There are____ fourths in 1 whole.

                                    There are ____ fourths in __ wholes.

                                    If 5 is $\frac{1}{4}$, what is the whole? _____

COMMON CORE   Lesson 25:   Divide a whole number by a unit fraction.
                    Date: 11/10/13   **4.G.1**

2. Divide. Then multiply to check.

a. $2 \div \frac{1}{4}$	b. $6 \div \frac{1}{2}$	c. $5 \div \frac{1}{4}$	d. $5 \div \frac{1}{8}$
e. $6 \div \frac{1}{3}$	f. $3 \div \frac{1}{6}$	g. $6 \div \frac{1}{5}$	h. $6 \div \frac{1}{10}$

3. A principal orders 8 sub sandwiches for a teachers' meeting. She cuts the subs into thirds and puts the mini-subs onto a tray. How many mini-subs are on the tray?

4. Some students prepare 3 different snacks. They make $\frac{1}{8}$ pound bags of nut mix, $\frac{1}{4}$ pound bags of cherries, and $\frac{1}{6}$ pound bags of dried fruit. If they buy 3 pounds of nut mix, 5 pounds of cherries, and 4 pounds of dried fruit, how many of each type of snack bag will they be able to make?

COMMON CORE™

Lesson 25:   Divide a whole number by a unit fraction.
Date: 11/10/13

4.G.18

Lesson 26

Objective: Divide a unit fraction by a whole number.

Suggested Lesson Structure

- ■ Fluency Practice   (12 minutes)
- ■ Application Problem   (8 minutes)
- ■ Concept Development   (30 minutes)
- ■ Student Debrief   (10 minutes)
  - **Total Time**   **(60 minutes)**

Fluency Practice (12 minutes)

- Count by Fractions **5.NF.7**   (5 minutes)
- Divide Whole Numbers by Fractions **5.NF.7**   (4 minutes)
- Multiply Fractions **5.NF.4**   (3 minutes)

Count by Fractions (5 minutes)

Note: This fluency reviews G5–M4–Lesson 21.

$\frac{1}{4}$	$\frac{2}{4}$	$\frac{3}{4}$	$\frac{4}{4}$	$\frac{5}{4}$	$\frac{6}{4}$	$\frac{7}{4}$	$\frac{8}{4}$	$\frac{9}{4}$	$\frac{10}{4}$	$\frac{11}{4}$	$\frac{12}{4}$
$\frac{1}{4}$	$\frac{2}{4}$	$\frac{3}{4}$	1	$\frac{5}{4}$	$\frac{6}{4}$	$\frac{7}{4}$	2	$\frac{9}{4}$	$\frac{10}{4}$	$\frac{11}{4}$	3
$\frac{1}{4}$	$\frac{2}{4}$	$\frac{3}{4}$	1	$1\frac{1}{4}$	$1\frac{2}{4}$	$1\frac{3}{4}$	2	$2\frac{1}{4}$	$2\frac{2}{4}$	$2\frac{3}{4}$	3
$\frac{1}{4}$	$\frac{1}{2}$	$\frac{3}{4}$	1	$1\frac{1}{4}$	$1\frac{1}{2}$	$1\frac{3}{4}$	2	$2\frac{1}{4}$	$2\frac{1}{2}$	$2\frac{3}{4}$	3

- T: Count by one-fourth to 12 fourths. (Write as students count.)
- S: 1 fourth, 2 fourths, 3 fourths, 4 fourths, 5 fourths, 6 fourths, 7 fourths, 8 fourths, 9 fourths, 10 fourths, 11 fourths, 12 fourths.
- T: Let's count by one-fourths again. This time, when we arrive at a whole number, say the whole number. (Write as students count.)
- S: 1 fourth, 2 fourths, 3 fourths, 1 whole, 5 fourths, 6 fourths, 7 fourths, 2 wholes, 9 fourths, 10 fourths, 11 fourths, 3 wholes.
- T: Let's count by one-fourths again. This time, change improper fractions to mixed numbers.

Lesson 26:   Divide a unit fraction by a whole number.
Date: 11/10/13

4.G.1

S: 1 fourth, 2 fourths, 3 fourths, 1 whole. 1 and 1 fourth, 1 and 2 fourths, 1 and 3 fourths, 2 wholes, 2 and 1 fourth, 2 and 2 fourths, 2 and 3 fourths, 3 wholes.

T: Let's count by one-fourths again. This time, simplify 2 fourths to 1 half. (Write as students count.)

S: 1 fourth, 1 half, 3 fourths, 1 whole, 1 and 1 fourth, 1 and 1 half, 1 and 3 fourths, 2 wholes, 2 and 1 fourth, 2 and 1 half, 2 and 3 fourths, 3 wholes.

Continue the process, counting by one-fifths to 15 fifths.

Divide Whole Numbers by Fractions (4 minutes)

Materials: (S) Personal white boards

Note: This fluency reviews G5–M4–Lesson 25.

T: (Write $1 \div \frac{1}{2} =$ _____.) Say the division problem.

S: $1 \div \frac{1}{2}$.

T: How many halves are in 1 whole?

S: 2.

T: (Write $1 \div \frac{1}{2} = 2$. Beneath it, write $2 \div \frac{1}{2}$.) How many halves are in 2 wholes?

S: 4.

T: (Write $2 \div \frac{1}{2} = 4$. Beneath it, write $3 \div \frac{1}{2}$.) How many halves are in 3 wholes?

S: 6.

T: (Write $3 \div \frac{1}{2} = 6$. Beneath it, write $8 \div \frac{1}{2}$.) On your boards, write the complete number sentence.

S: (Write $8 \div \frac{1}{2} = 16$.)

Continue with the following possible suggestions: $1 \div \frac{1}{3}, 2 \div \frac{1}{3}, 5 \div \frac{1}{3}, 1 \div \frac{1}{4}, 2 \div \frac{1}{4}, 7 \div \frac{1}{4}, 3 \div \frac{1}{5}, 4 \div \frac{1}{6}$, and $7 \div \frac{1}{8}$.

Multiply Fractions (3 minutes)

Materials: (S) Personal white boards

Note: This fluency reviews G5–M4–Lessons 13–16.

T: (Write $\frac{1}{2} \times \frac{1}{3}$.) Say the multiplication number sentence.

S: $\frac{1}{2} \times \frac{1}{3} = \frac{1}{6}$.

Continue this process with $\frac{1}{2} \times \frac{1}{4}$ and $\frac{1}{2} \times \frac{1}{5}$.

T: (Write $\frac{1}{2} \times \frac{1}{9}$.) On your boards, write the number sentence.

S: (Write $\frac{1}{2} \times \frac{1}{9} = \frac{1}{18}$.)

Lesson 26:   Divide a unit fraction by a whole number.
Date: 11/10/13

4.G.20

T: (Write $\frac{1}{2} \times \frac{5}{9}$.) Say the multiplication sentence.

S: $\frac{1}{2} \times \frac{5}{9} = \frac{5}{18}$.

Repeat this process with $\frac{1}{4} \times \frac{3}{3}$, $\frac{1}{3} \times \frac{3}{2}$, and $\frac{3}{4} \times \frac{1}{5}$.

T: (Write $\frac{2}{3} \times \frac{2}{5} = $____.) Say the multiplication sentence.

S: (Write $\frac{2}{3} \times \frac{2}{5} = \frac{4}{15}$.)

Continue this process with $\frac{3}{4} \times \frac{3}{5}$.

T: (Write $\frac{1}{4} \times \frac{3}{5}$.) On your boards, write the number sentence.

S: (Write $\frac{1}{4} \times \frac{3}{5} = \frac{3}{20}$.)

T: (Write $\frac{3}{4} \times \frac{4}{3} = $____.) On your boards, write the number sentence.

S: (Write $\frac{3}{4} \times \frac{4}{3} = \frac{12}{12} = 1$.)

Application Problem (8 minutes)

A race begins with $2\frac{1}{2}$ miles through town, continues through the park for $2\frac{1}{3}$ miles, and finishes at the track after the last $\frac{1}{6}$ mile. A volunteer is stationed every quarter mile and at the finish line to pass out cups of water and cheer on the runners. How many volunteers are needed?

Note: This multi-step problem requires students to first add three fractions, then divide the sum by a fraction, which reinforces yesterday's division of a whole number by a unit fraction. (How many $\frac{1}{4}$ miles are in 5 miles?) It also reviews adding fractions with different denominators (G5–Module 3).

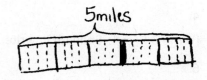

Race: $2\frac{1}{2} + 2\frac{1}{3} + \frac{1}{6} = 2\frac{3}{6} + 2\frac{2}{6} + \frac{1}{6}$
$= 4 + \frac{6}{6}$
$= 5$

Volunteers: $5 \div \frac{1}{4} = 20$

20 volunteers are needed.

Concept Development (30 minutes)

Materials: (S) Personal white boards

Problem 1

Nolan gives some pans of brownies to his 3 friends to share equally.

a. If he has 3 pans of brownies, how many pans of brownies will each friend get?

b. If he has 1 pan of brownies, how many pans of brownies will each friend get?

c. If he has $\frac{1}{2}$ pan of brownies, how many pans of brownies will each friend get?

Lesson 26: Divide a unit fraction by a whole number.
Date: 11/10/13

4.G.2

d. If he has $\frac{1}{3}$ pan of brownies, how many pans of brownies will each friend get?

T: (Post Problem 1(a) on the board, and read it aloud with students.) Work on your personal board and write a division sentence to solve this problem. Be prepared to share.

S: (Work.)

T: How many pans of brownies does Nolan have?

S: 3 pans.

T: The 3 pans of brownies are divided equally into how many friends?

S: 3 friends.

T: Say the division sentence with the answer.

S: $3 \div 3 = 1$.

T: Answer the question in a complete sentence.

S: Each friend will get 1 pan of brownies.

T: (In the problem, erase *3 pans* and replace it with *1 pan*.) Imagine that Nolan has 1 pan of brownies. If he gave it to his 3 friends to share equally, what portion of the brownies will each friend get? Write a division sentence to show how you know.

$$1 \div 3 = \frac{1}{3}$$

OR

1 whole ÷ 3
= 3 thirds ÷ 3
= 1 third

Each friend will get $\frac{1}{3}$ pan of brownie.

S: (Write $1 \div 3 = \frac{1}{3}$ pan.)

T: Nolan starts out with how many pans of brownies?

S: 1 pan.

T: The 1 pan of brownie is divided equally by how many friends?

S: 3 friends.

T: Say the division sentence with the answer.

S: $1 \div 3 = \frac{1}{3}$.

T: Let's model that thinking with a tape diagram. I'll draw a bar and shade it in representing 1 whole pan of brownie. Next, I'll partition it equally with dotted lines into 3 units, and each unit is $\frac{1}{3}$. (Draw a bar and cut it equally into three parts.) How many pans of brownies did each friend get this time? Answer the question in a complete sentence.

S: Each friend will get $\frac{1}{3}$ pan of brownie. (Label $\frac{1}{3}$ underneath one part.)

T: Let's rewrite the problem as thirds. How many thirds are in 1 whole?

S: 3 thirds.

T: (Write 3 thirds ÷ 3 = ___.) What is 3 thirds divided by 3?

S: 1 third. (Write = 1 third.)

NOTES ON MULTIPLE MEANS OF ENGAGEMENT:

While the tape diagramming in the beginning of this lesson is presented as teacher-directed, it is equally acceptable to elicit each step of the diagram from the students through questioning. Many students benefit from verbalizing the next step in a diagram.

Lesson 26: Divide a unit fraction by a whole number.
Date: 11/10/13

T: Another way to interpret this division expression would be to ask, "1 is 3 of what number?" And of course, we know that 3 thirds makes 1.

T: But just to be sure, let's check our work. How do we check a division problem?

S: Multiply the answer and the divisor.

T: Check it now.

S: (Work and show $\frac{1}{3} \times 3 = \frac{3}{3} = 1$.)

T: (Replace *1 pan* in the problem with $\frac{1}{2}$ *pan*.) Now, imagine that he only has $\frac{1}{2}$ pan. Still sharing them with 3 friends equally, how many pans of brownies will each friend get?

T: Now that we have half of a pan instead of 1 whole pan to share, will each friend get more or less than $\frac{1}{3}$ pan? Turn and discuss.

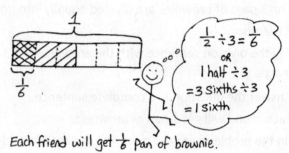

Each friend will get $\frac{1}{6}$ pan of brownie.

S: Less than $\frac{1}{3}$ pan. → We have less to share, but we are sharing with the same number of people. They will get less. → Since we're starting out with $\frac{1}{2}$ pan which is less than 1 whole pan, the answer should be less than $\frac{1}{3}$ pan.

T: (Draw a bar and cut it into 2 parts. Shade in 1 part.) How can we show how many people are sharing this $\frac{1}{2}$ pan of brownie? Turn and talk.

S: We can draw dotted lines to show the 3 equal parts that he cuts the half into. → We have to show the same size units, so I'll cut the half that's shaded into 3 parts and the other half into 3 parts, too.

T: (Partition the whole into 6 parts.) What fraction of the pan will each friend get?

S: $\frac{1}{6}$. (Label $\frac{1}{6}$ underneath one part.)

T: (Write $\frac{1}{2} \div 3 = \frac{1}{6}$.) Let's think again, 1 half is equal to how many sixths? Look at the tape diagram to help you.

S: 3 sixths.

T: So, what is 3 sixths divided by 3? (Write 3 sixths ÷ 3 =____.)

S: 1 sixth. (Write = 1 sixth.)

T: What other question could we ask from this division expression?

S: $\frac{1}{2}$ is 3 of what number?

T: And 3 of what number makes half?

S: Three 1 sixths makes half.

T: Check your work, then answer the question in a complete sentence.

S: Each friend will get $\frac{1}{6}$ pan of brownie.

T: (Erase the $\frac{1}{2}$ in the problem, and replace it with $\frac{1}{3}$.) What if Nolan only has a third of a pan and let 3 friends share equally? How many pans of brownies will each friend get? Work with a partner to

Lesson 26:   Divide a unit fraction by a whole number.
Date: 11/10/13

4.G.2

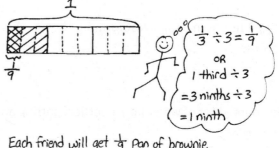

solve it.

S: (Share.)

T: Answer the question in a complete sentence.

S: Each friend will get $\frac{1}{9}$ pan of brownie.

T: (Point to all the previous division sentences: $3 \div 3 = 1$, $1 \div 3 = \frac{1}{3}$, $\frac{1}{2} \div 3 = \frac{1}{6}$, and $\frac{1}{3} \div 3 = \frac{1}{9}$.) Compare our division sentences. What do you notice about the quotients? Turn and talk.

Each friend will get $\frac{1}{9}$ pan of brownie.

S: The answer is getting smaller and smaller because Nolan kept giving his friends a smaller and smaller part of a pan to share. → The original whole is getting smaller from 3 to 1, to $\frac{1}{2}$, to $\frac{1}{3}$, and the 3 people sharing the brownies stayed the same, that's why the answer is getting smaller.

Problem 2

$\frac{1}{5} \div 2 =$ _____

T: (Post Problem 2 on the board.) Work independently to solve this problem on your personal board. Draw a tape diagram to show your thinking.

S: (Work.)

T: What's the answer?

S: $\frac{1}{10}$.

T: How many tenths are in 1 fifth?

S: 2 tenths.

T: (Write 2 tenths ÷ 2 = ___.) What's 2 tenths divided by 2?

S: 1 tenth. (Write = 1 tenth.)

T: Asked another way: (Write $\frac{1}{5}$ = 2 × _____.) Fill in the missing factor.

S: 1 tenth.

T: Let's check our work aloud together. What is the quotient?

S: 1 tenth.

T: The divisor?

S: 2.

T: Let's multiply the quotient by the divisor. What is 1 tenth times 2?

S: 2 tenths.

T: Is 2 tenths the same units as our original whole?

S: No.

T: Did we make a mistake?

S: No, 2 tenths is just another way to say 1 fifth.

Lesson 26: Divide a unit fraction by a whole number.
Date: 11/10/13

4.G.24

T: Say 2 tenths in its simplest form.

S: 1 fifth.

Problem 3

If Melanie pours $\frac{1}{2}$ liter of water into 4 bottles, putting an equal amount in each, how many liters of water will be in each bottle?

Each bottle will have $\frac{1}{8}$ liter of water.

T: (Post Problem 3 on the board, and read it together with the class.) How many liters of water does Melanie have?

S: Half a liter.

T: Half of liter is being poured into how many bottles?

S: 4 bottles.

T: How do you solve this problem? Turn and discuss.

S: We have to divide. → The division sentence is $\frac{1}{2} \div 4$. → I need to divide the dividend 1 half by the divisor, 4. → I can draw 1 half, and cut it into 4 equal parts. → I can think of this as $\frac{1}{2} = 4 \times$ ___.

T: On your personal board, draw a tape diagram and solve this problem independently.

S: (Work.)

T: Say the division sentence and the answer.

S: $\frac{1}{2} \div 4 = \frac{1}{8}$. (Write $\frac{1}{2} \div 4 = \frac{1}{8}$.)

T: Now say the division sentence using eighths and unit form.

S: 4 eighths ÷ 4 = 1 eighth.

T: Show me your checking solution.

S: (Work and show $\frac{1}{8} \times 4 = \frac{4}{8} = \frac{1}{2}$.)

T: If you used a multiplication sentence with a missing factor, say it now.

S: $\frac{1}{2} = 4 \times \frac{1}{8}$.

T: No matter your strategy, we all got the same result. Answer the question in a complete sentence.

S: Each bottle will have $\frac{1}{8}$ liter of water.

Problem Set (10 minutes)

Students should do their personal best to complete the Problem Set within the allotted 10 minutes. For some classes, it may be appropriate to modify the assignment by specifying which problems they work on first. Some problems do not specify a method for solving. Students solve these problems using the RDW approach used for Application Problems.

Lesson 26:   Divide a unit fraction by a whole number.
Date: 11/10/13

4.G.2

Student Debrief (10 minutes)

Lesson Objective: Divide a unit fraction by a whole number.

The Student Debrief is intended to invite reflection and active processing of the total lesson experience.

Invite students to review their solutions for the Problem Set. They should check work by comparing answers with a partner before going over answers as a class. Look for misconceptions or misunderstandings that can be addressed in the Debrief. Guide students in a conversation to debrief the Problem Set and process the lesson.

You may choose to use any combination of the questions below to lead the discussion.

- In Problem 1, what is the relationship between (a) and (b), (c) and (d), and (b) and (d)?

- Why is the quotient of Problem 1(c) greater than Problem 1(d)? Is it reasonable? Explain to your partner.

- In Problem 2, what is the relationship between (c) and (d) and (b) and (f)?

- Compare your drawing of Problem 3 with a partner. How is it the same as or different from your partner's?

- How did you solve Problem 5? Share your solution and explain your strategy to a partner.

- While the invert and multiply strategy is not explicitly taught (nor should it be while students grapple with these abstract concepts of division), discussing various ways of thinking about division in general can be fruitful. A discussion might proceed as follows:

T: Is dividing something by 2 the same as taking 1 half of it? For example, is $4 \div 2 = 4 \times \frac{1}{2}$? (Write this on the board and allow some quiet time for thinking.) Can you think of some examples?

S: Yes. → If 4 cookies are divided between 2 people, each person gets half of the cookies.

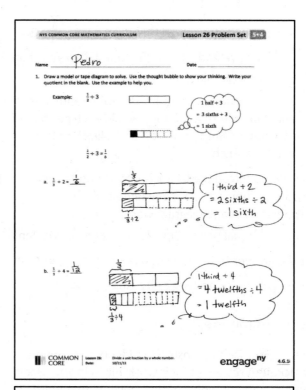

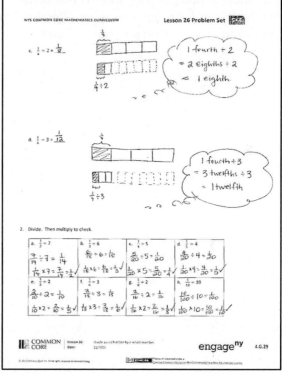

T: So, if that's true, would this also be true: $\frac{1}{4} \div 2 = \frac{1}{4} \times \frac{1}{2}$? (Write and allow quiet time.) Can you think of some examples?

S: Yes. → If there is only 1 fourth of a candy bar and 2 people share it, they would each get half of the fourth. But that would be 1 eighth of the whole candy bar.

Once this idea is introduced, look for opportunities in visual models to point it out. For example, in today's lesson, Problem 3's tape diagram was drawn to show $\frac{1}{2}$ divided into 4 equal parts. But, just as clearly as we can see that the answer to our question is $\frac{1}{4}$ of that $\frac{1}{2}$, we can see that we get the same answer by multiplying $\frac{1}{4} \times \frac{1}{2}$.

Exit Ticket (3 minutes)

After the Student Debrief, instruct students to complete the Exit Ticket. A review of their work will help you assess the students' understanding of the concepts that were presented in the lesson today and plan more effectively for future lessons. You may read the questions aloud to the students.

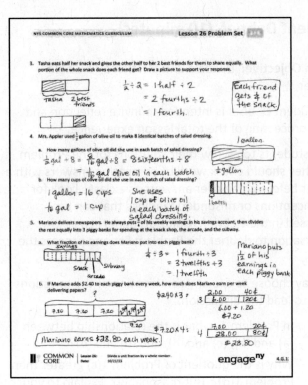

COMMON CORE™

Lesson 26: Divide a unit fraction by a whole number.
Date: 11/10/13

4.G.2

Name _____ Date _____

1. Draw a model or tape diagram to solve. Use the thought bubble to show your thinking. Write your quotient in the blank. Use the example to help you.

Example: $\frac{1}{2} \div 3$

1 half ÷ 3

= 3 sixths ÷ 3

= 1 sixth

$$\frac{1}{2} \div 3 = \frac{1}{6}$$

a. $\frac{1}{3} \div 2 =$ _____

b. $\frac{1}{3} \div 4 =$ _____

c. $\frac{1}{4} \div 2 =$ _____

d. $\frac{1}{4} \div 3 =$ _____

2. Divide. Then multiply to check.

a. $\frac{1}{2} \div 7$	b. $\frac{1}{3} \div 6$	c. $\frac{1}{4} \div 5$	d. $\frac{1}{5} \div 4$
e. $\frac{1}{5} \div 2$	f. $\frac{1}{6} \div 3$	g. $\frac{1}{8} \div 2$	h. $\frac{1}{10} \div 10$

Lesson 26:   Divide a unit fraction by a whole number.
Date: 11/10/13

4.G.2

3. Tasha eats half her snack and gives the other half to her two best friends for them to share equally. What portion of the whole snack does each friend get? Draw a picture to support your response.

4. Mrs. Appler used $\frac{1}{2}$ gallon of olive oil to make 8 identical batches of salad dressing.

   a. How many gallons of olive oil did she use in each batch of salad dressing?

   b. How many cups of olive oil did she use in each batch of salad dressing?

5. Mariano delivers newspapers. He always puts $\frac{3}{4}$ of his weekly earnings in his savings account, then divides the rest equally into 3 piggy banks for spending at the snack shop, the arcade, and the subway.

   a. What fraction of his earnings does Mariano put into each piggy bank?

   b. If Mariano adds $2.40 to each piggy bank every week, how much does Mariano earn per week delivering papers?

Name _____   Date _____

1. Solve. Support at least one of your answers with a model or tape diagram.

    a. $\frac{1}{2} \div 4 =$ _____

    b. $\frac{1}{8} \div 5 =$ _____

2. Larry spends half of his workday teaching piano lessons. If he sees 6 students, each for the same amount of time, what fraction of his workday is spent with each student?

COMMON CORE™

Lesson 26:   Divide a unit fraction by a whole number.
Date: 11/10/13

4.G.

Name _____   Date _____

1. Solve and support your answer with a model or tape diagram. Write your quotient in the blank.

    a. $\frac{1}{2} \div 4 =$ _____

    b. $\frac{1}{3} \div 6 =$ _____

    c. $\frac{1}{4} \div 3 =$ _____

    d. $\frac{1}{5} \div 2 =$ _____

2. Divide. Then multiply to check.

a. $\frac{1}{2} \div 10$	b. $\frac{1}{4} \div 10$	c. $\frac{1}{3} \div 5$	d. $\frac{1}{5} \div 3$
e. $\frac{1}{8} \div 4$	f. $\frac{1}{7} \div 3$	g. $\frac{1}{10} \div 5$	h. $\frac{1}{5} \div 20$

COMMON CORE™   Lesson 26:   Divide a unit fraction by a whole number.

Date: 11/10/13

4.G.32

3. Teams of four are competing in a quarter-mile relay race. Each runner must run the same exact distance. What is the distance each teammate runs?

4. Solomon has read $\frac{1}{3}$ of his book. He finishes the book by reading the same amount each night for 5 nights.

    a. What fraction of the book does he read each of the 5 nights?

    b. If he reads 14 pages on each of the 5 nights, how long is the book?

   Lesson 26:   Divide a unit fraction by a whole number.
    Date: 11/10/13

4.G.

Lesson 27

Objective: Solve problems involving fraction division.

Suggested Lesson Structure

■ Fluency Practice   (12 minutes)
□ Concept Development   (38 minutes)
■ Student Debrief   (10 minutes)
   Total Time   **(60 minutes)**

Fluency Practice (12 minutes)

- Count by Fractions **5.NF.7**   (6 minutes)
- Divide Whole Numbers by Unit Fractions **5.NF.7**   (3 minutes)
- Divide Unit Fractions by Whole Numbers **5.NF.7**   (3 minutes)

Count by Fractions (6 minutes)

Note: This fluency reviews G5–M4–Lesson 25.

   T: Count by sixths to 12 sixths. (Write as students count.)

   S: 1 sixth, 2 sixths, 3 sixths, 4 sixths, 5 sixths, 6 sixths, 7 sixths, 8 sixths, 9 sixths, 10 sixths, 11 sixths, 12 sixths.

   T: Let's count by sixths again. This time, when we arrive at a whole number, say the whole number. (Write as students count.)

   S: 1 sixth, 2 sixths, 3 sixths, 4 sixths, 5 sixths, 1 whole, 7 sixths, 8 sixths, 9 sixths, 10 sixths, 11 sixths, 2 wholes.

   T: Let's count by sixths again. This time, change improper fractions to mixed numbers. (Write as students count.)

   S: 1 sixth, 2 sixths, 3 sixths, 4 sixths, 5 sixths, 1 whole, 1 and 1 sixth, 1 and 2 sixths, 1 and 3 sixths, 1 and 4 sixths, 1 and 5 sixths, 2 wholes.

   T: Let's count by sixths again. This time, simplify 3 sixths to 1 half. (Write as students count.)

   S: 1 sixth, 2 sixths, 1 half, 4 sixths, 5 sixths, 1 whole, 1 and 1 sixth, 1 and 2 sixths, 1 and 1 half , 1 and 4 sixths, 1 and 5 sixths, 2 wholes.

   T: Let's count by 1 sixths again. This time, simplify 2 sixths to 1 third and 4 sixths to 2 thirds. (Write as students count.)

   S: 1 sixth, 1 third, 1 half, 2 thirds, 5 sixths, 1 whole, 1 and 1 sixth, 1 and 1 third, 1 and 1 half, 1 and 2 thirds, 1 and 5 sixths, 2 wholes.

Lesson 27:   Solve problems involving fraction division.
Date: 11/10/13

4.G.34

Continue the process counting by 1 eighths to 8 eighths or, if time allows, 16 eighths.

Divide Whole Numbers by Unit Fractions (3 minutes)

Materials: (S) Personal white boards

Note: This fluency reviews G5–M4–Lesson 25.

T: (Write $1 \div \frac{1}{2}$.) Say the division sentence.

S: $1 \div \frac{1}{2}$.

T: How many halves are in 1 whole?

S: 2.

T: (Write $1 \div \frac{1}{2} = 2$. Beneath it, write $2 \div \frac{1}{2} = $ _____.) How many halves are in 2 wholes?

S: 4.

T: (Write $2 \div \frac{1}{2} = 4$. Beneath it, write $3 \div \frac{1}{2} = $ _____.) How many halves are in 3 wholes?

S: 6.

T: (Write $3 \div \frac{1}{2} = 6$. Beneath it, write $6 \div \frac{1}{2}$.) On your boards, write the division sentence.

S: (Write $6 \div \frac{1}{2} = 12$.)

Continue with the following possible suggestions: $1 \div \frac{1}{3}$, $2 \div \frac{1}{3}$, $7 \div \frac{1}{3}$, $1 \div \frac{1}{4}$, $2 \div \frac{1}{4}$, $9 \div \frac{1}{4}$, $5 \div \frac{1}{5}$, $6 \div \frac{1}{6}$, and $8 \div \frac{1}{8}$.

Divide Unit Fractions by Whole Numbers (3 minutes)

Materials: (S) Personal white boards

Note: This fluency reviews G5–M4–Lesson 26.

T: (Write $\frac{1}{2} \div 2 = $ _____.) Say the division sentence with answer.

S: $\frac{1}{2} \div 2 = \frac{1}{4}$.

T: (Write $\frac{1}{2} \div 2 = \frac{1}{4}$. Beneath it, write $\frac{1}{2} \div 3 = $ _____.) Say the division sentence with the answer.

S: $\frac{1}{2} \div 3 = \frac{1}{6}$.

T: (Write $\frac{1}{2} \div 3 = \frac{1}{6}$. Beneath it, write $\frac{1}{2} \div 4 = $ _____.) Say the division sentence with the answer.

S: $\frac{1}{2} \div 4 = \frac{1}{8}$.

T: (Write $\frac{1}{2} \div 7 = $ _____.) On your boards, complete the number sentence.

S: (Write $\frac{1}{2} \div 7 = \frac{1}{14}$.)

Continue with the following possible sequence: $\frac{1}{3} \div 2$, $\frac{1}{3} \div 3$, $\frac{1}{3} \div 4$, $\frac{1}{3} \div 9$, $\frac{1}{5} \div 3$, $\frac{1}{5} \div 5$, $\frac{1}{5} \div 7$, $\frac{1}{4} \div 4$, and $\frac{1}{8} \div 6$.

Lesson 27: Solve problems involving fraction division.
Date: 11/10/13

4.G.3

Concept Development (38 minutes)

Materials: (S) Problem Set

Note: The time normally allotted for the Application Problem has been reallocated to the Concept Development to provide adequate time for solving the word problems.

Suggested Delivery of Instruction for Solving Lesson 27's Word Problems.

1. Model the problem.

Have two pairs of student work at the board while the others work independently or in pairs at their seats. Review the following questions before beginning the first problem:

- Can you draw something?
- What can you draw?
- What conclusions can you make from your drawing?

As students work, circulate. Reiterate the questions above. After two minutes, have the two pairs of students share only their labeled diagrams. For about one minute, have the demonstrating students receive and respond to feedback and questions from their peers.

2. Calculate to solve and write a statement.

Give everyone two minutes to finish work on that question, sharing his or her work and thinking with a peer. All should write their equations and statements of the answer.

3. Assess the solution for reasonableness.

Give students one to two minutes to assess and explain the reasonableness of their solution.

Problem 1

Mrs. Silverstein bought 3 mini cakes for a birthday party. She cut each cake into quarters, and plans to serve each guest 1 quarter of a cake. How many guests can she serve with all her cakes? Draw a model to support your response.

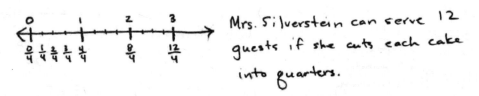

In this problem, students are asked to divide a whole number (3) by a unit fraction ($\frac{1}{4}$), and draw a model. A tape diagram or a number line would both be acceptable models to support their responses. The reference

---

Lesson 27:   Solve problems involving fraction division.
Date: 11/10/13

4.G.36

to the unit fraction as a *quarter* provides a bit of complexity. There are 4 fourths in 1 whole, and 12 fourths in 3 wholes.

Problem 2

Mr. Pham has $\frac{1}{4}$ pan of lasagna left in the refrigerator. He wants to cut the lasagna into equal slices so he can have it for dinner for 3 nights. How much lasagna will he eat each night? Draw a picture to support your response.

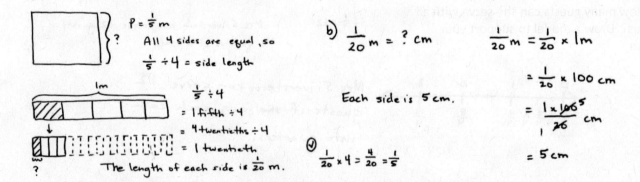

Problem 2 is intentionally similar to Problem 1. Although the numbers used in the problems are identical, careful reading reveals that 3 is now the divisor rather than the dividend. While drawing a supporting tape diagram, students should recognize that dividing a fourth into 3 equal parts creates a new unit, twelfths. The model shows that the fraction $\frac{1}{4}$ is equal to $\frac{3}{12}$, and therefore a division sentence using unit form (3 twelfths ÷ 3) is easy to solve. Facilitate a quick discussion about the similarities and differences of Problems 1 and 2. What do students notice about the division expressions and the solutions?

Problem 3

The perimeter of a square is $\frac{1}{5}$ meter.

   a.   Find the length of each side in meters. Draw a picture to support your response.
   b.   How long is each side in centimeters?

COMMON CORE   Lesson 27:   Solve problems involving fraction division.
   Date: 11/10/13

4.G.3

This problem requires students to recall their measurement work from Grade 3 and Grade 4 involving perimeter. Students must know that all four side lengths of a square are equivalent, and therefore the unknown side length can be found by dividing the perimeter by 4 ($\frac{1}{5}$ m ÷ 4). The tape diagram shows clearly that dividing a fifth into 4 equal parts creates a new unit, twentieths, and that $\frac{1}{5}$ is equal to $\frac{4}{20}$. Students may use a division expression using unit form (4 twentieths ÷ 4) to solve this problem very simply. This problem also gives opportunity to point out a partitive division interpretation to students. While the model was drawn to depict 1 fifth divided into 5 equal parts, the question mark clearly asks "What is $\frac{1}{4}$ of $\frac{1}{5}$?" That is, $\frac{1}{4} \times \frac{1}{5}$.

NOTES ON MULTIPLE MEANS OF ENGAGEMENT:

Perimeter and *area* are vocabulary terms that students often confuse. To help students differentiate between the terms, teachers can make a poster outlining, in sandpaper, the perimeter of a polygon. As he uses a finger to trace along the sandpaper, the student says the word *perimeter*. This sensory method may help some students to learn an often confused term.

Part (b) requires students to rename $\frac{1}{20}$ meters as centimeters. This conversion mirrors the work done in G5–M4–Lesson 20. Since 1 meter is equal to 100 centimeters, students can multiply to find that $\frac{1}{20}$ m is equivalent to $\frac{100}{20}$ cm, or 5 cm.

Problem 4

A pallet holding 5 identical crates weighs $\frac{1}{4}$ ton.

   a. How many tons does each crate weigh? Draw a picture to support your response.
   b. How many pounds does each crate weigh?

1 ton

$\frac{1}{4} \div 5$

$= 1\ \text{fourth} \div 5$

$= 5\ \text{twentieths} \div 5$

$= 1\ \text{twentieth}$

weighs $\frac{1}{20}$ ton.

✓ $\frac{1}{20} \times 5 = \frac{5}{20} = \frac{1}{4}$

b) $\frac{1}{20}$ ton = ? pounds

Each crate weighs 100 pounds.

$\frac{1}{20}$ ton $= \frac{1}{20} \times 1$ ton

$= \frac{1}{20} \times 2,000$ pounds

$= \frac{1 \times 2,000}{20}^{100}$ pounds

$= 100$ pounds

The numbers in this problem are similar to those used in Problem 3, and the resulting quotient is again $\frac{1}{20}$. Engage students in a discussion about why the answer is the same in Problems 3 and 4, but was not the same in Problems 1 and 2, despite both sets of problems using similar numbers. Is this just a coincidence? In addition, Problem 4 presents another opportunity for students to interpret the division here as $\frac{1}{4} = 5 \times$ ___.

Problem 5

Faye has 5 pieces of ribbon each 1 yard long. She cuts each ribbon into sixths.

   a.   How many sixths will she have after cutting all the ribbons?
   b.   How long will each of the sixths be in inches?

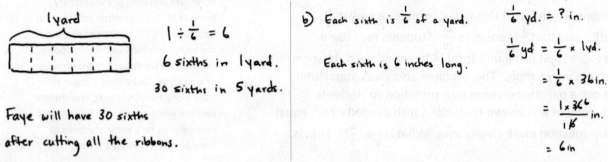

In Problem 5, since Faye has 5 pieces of ribbon of equal length, students have the choice of drawing a tape diagram showing how many sixths are in 1 yard (and then multiplying that number by 5) or drawing a tape showing all 5 yards to find 30 sixths in total.

Problem 6

A glass pitcher is filled with water. $\frac{1}{8}$ of the water is poured equally into 2 glasses.

   a.   What fraction of the water is in each glass?
   b.   If each glass has 3 ounces of water in it, how many ounces of water were in the full pitcher?
   c.   If $\frac{1}{4}$ of the remaining water is poured out of the pitcher to water a plant, how many cups of water are left in the pitcher?

NOTES ON MULTIPLE MEANS OF ENGAGEMENT:

Problem 6 in this lesson may be especially difficult for English language learners. The teacher may wish have students act out this problem in order to keep track of the different questions asked about the water.

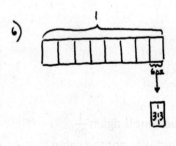

 Lesson 27: Solve problems involving fraction division.
Date: 11/10/13

4.G.3

c) $48\,oz. - 6\,oz. = 42\,oz.$

42oz.

$\frac{3}{4}$ of 42 oz.

$= \frac{3}{4} \times 42\,oz.$

$= \frac{3 \times 42}{4}\,oz.$

$= \frac{126}{24}\,oz.$

$= \frac{63}{2}\,oz. = 31\frac{1}{2}\,oz.$

plant   ?

$31\frac{1}{2}\,oz = ?\ cups$

$31\frac{1}{2}\,oz = 31\frac{1}{2} \times 1\,oz$

$= 31\frac{1}{2} \times \frac{1}{8}c$

$= (31 \times \frac{1}{8}c) + (\frac{1}{2} \times \frac{1}{8}c)$

$= \frac{31}{8}c + \frac{1}{16}c$

$= \frac{62}{16}c + \frac{1}{16}c$

$= \frac{63}{16}c = 3\frac{15}{16}c$

$3\frac{15}{16}$ cups of water are left in the pitcher.

In Part (a), to find what fraction of the water is in each glass, students might divide the unit fraction ($\frac{1}{8}$) by 2 or multiply $\frac{1}{2} \times \frac{1}{8}$. Part (b) requires students to show that since both glasses hold 3 ounces of water each, the 1 unit (or $\frac{1}{8}$ of the total water) is equal to 6 ounces. Multiplying 6 ounces by 8, provides the total amount of water (48 ounces) that was originally in the pitcher. Part (c) is a complex, multi-step problem that may require careful discussion. Since $\frac{1}{8}$ of the water (or 6 ounces) has already been poured out, subtraction yields 42 ounces of water left in the pitcher. After 1 fourth of the remaining water is used for the plant, $\frac{3}{4}$ of the water in the pitcher is $31\frac{1}{2}$ ounces. Students must then rename $31\frac{1}{2}$ ounces in cups.

Student Debrief (10 minutes)

Lesson Objective: Solve problems involving fraction division.

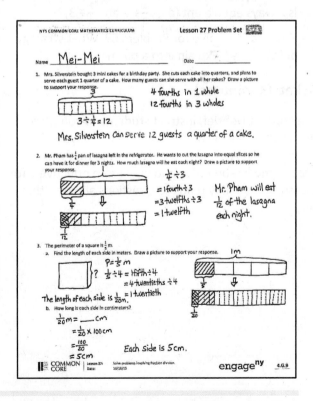

COMMON CORE™   Lesson 27:   Solve problems involving fraction division.
Date: 11/10/13

4.G.40

The Student Debrief is intended to invite reflection and active processing of the total lesson experience.

Invite students to review their solutions for the Problem Set. They should check work by comparing answers with a partner before going over answers as a class. Look for misconceptions or misunderstandings that can be addressed in the Debrief. Guide students in a conversation to debrief the Problem Set and process the lesson.

You may choose to use any combination of the questions below to lead the discussion.

- What did you notice about Problems 1 and 2? What are the similarities and differences? What did you notice about the division expressions and the solutions?

- What did you notice about the solutions in Problems 3(a) and 4(a)? Share your answer and explain it to a partner.

- Why is the answer the same in Problems 3 and 4, but not the same in Problems 1 and 2, despite using similar numbers in both sets of problems? Is this just a coincidence? Can you create similar pairs of problems and see if the resulting quotient is always equivalent (e.g., $\frac{1}{3} \div 2$ and $\frac{1}{2} \div 3$)?

- How did you solve for Problem 6? What strategy did you use? Explain it to a partner.

Exit Ticket (3 minutes)

After the Student Debrief, instruct students to complete the Exit Ticket. A review of their work will help you assess the students' understanding of the concepts that were presented in the lesson today and plan more effectively for future lessons. You may read the questions aloud to the students.

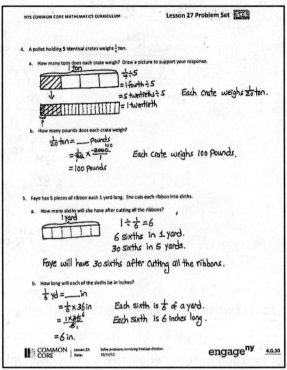

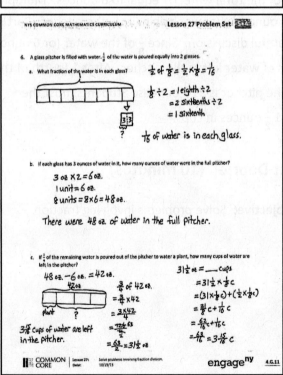

Lesson 27: Solve problems involving fraction division.
Date: 11/10/13

4.G.4

Name _____ Date _____

1. Mrs. Silverstein bought 3 mini cakes for a birthday party. She cut each cake into quarters, and plans to serve each guest 1 quarter of a cake. How many guests can she serve with all her cakes? Draw a picture to support your response.

2. Mr. Pham has $\frac{1}{4}$ pan of lasagna left in the refrigerator. He wants to cut the lasagna into equal slices so he can have it for dinner for 3 nights. How much lasagna will he eat each night? Draw a picture to support your response.

3. The perimeter of a square is $\frac{1}{5}$ meter.
   a. Find the length of each side in meters. Draw a picture to support your response.

   b. How long is each side in centimeters?

Lesson 27: Solve problems involving fraction division.
Date: 11/10/13

4.G.42

4. A pallet holding 5 identical crates weighs $\frac{1}{4}$ ton.
    a. How many tons does each crate weigh? Draw a picture to support your response.

    b. How many pounds does each crate weigh?

5. Faye has 5 pieces of ribbon each 1 yard long. She cuts each ribbon into sixths.
    a. How many sixths will she have after cutting all the ribbons?

    b. How long will each of the sixths be in inches?

Lesson 27:   Solve problems involving fraction division.
Date: 11/10/13

4.G.4

6.   A glass pitcher is filled with water. $\frac{1}{8}$ of the water is poured equally into 2 glasses.

   a.   What fraction of the water is in each glass?

   b.   If each glass has 3 ounces of water in it, how many ounces of water were in the full pitcher?

   c.   If $\frac{1}{4}$ of the remaining water is poured out of the pitcher to water a plant, how many cups of water are left in the pitcher?

Name _____   Date _____

1. Kevin divides 3 pieces paper into fourths. How many fourths does he have? Draw a picture to support your response.

2. Sybil has $\frac{1}{2}$ pizza left over. She wants to share the pizza with 3 of her friends. What fraction of the original pizza will Sybil and her 3 friends each receive? Draw a picture to support your response.

Lesson 27:   Solve problems involving fraction division.
Date: 11/10/13

4.G.4

Name _____ Date _____

1. Kelvin ordered four pizzas for a birthday party. The pizzas were cut in eighths. How many slices were there? Draw a picture to support your response.

2. Virgil has $\frac{1}{6}$ of a birthday cake left over. He wants to share the leftover cake with three friends. What fraction of the original cake will each of the 4 people receive? Draw a picture to support your response.

3. A pitcher of water contains $\frac{1}{4}$ L water. The water is poured equally into 5 glasses.
   a. How many liters of water are in each glass? Draw a picture to support your response.

   b. Write the amount of water in each glass in milliliters.

Lesson 27:   Solve problems involving fraction division.
Date: 11/10/13

4.G.46

4. Drew has 4 pieces of rope 1 meter long each. He cuts each rope into fifths.
   a. How many fifths will he have after cutting all the ropes?

   b. How long will each of the fifths be in centimeters?

5. A container is filled with blueberries. $\frac{1}{6}$ of the blueberries are poured equally into two bowls.
   a. What fraction of the blueberries is in each bowl?

   b. If each bowl has 6 ounces of blueberries in it, how many ounces of blueberries were in the full container?

   c. If $\frac{1}{5}$ of the remaining blueberries are used to make muffins, how many pounds of blueberries are left in the container?

Lesson 28

Objective: Write equations and word problems corresponding to tape and number line diagrams.

Suggested Lesson Structure

■ Fluency Practice   (10 minutes)
▨ Concept Development   (40 minutes)
■ Student Debrief   (10 minutes)
   Total Time   **(60 minutes)**

Fluency Practice (10 minutes)

▪ Count by Fractions **5.NF.7**   (5 minutes)
▪ Divide Whole Numbers by Unit Fractions and Unit Fractions by Whole Numbers **5.NF.7**   (5 minutes)

Count by Fractions (5 minutes)

Materials: (S) Personal white boards

Note: This fluency prepares students for G5–M4–Lesson 29.

   T: Count by tenths to 20 tenths. (Write as students count.)
   S: 1 tenth, 2 tenths,… 20 tenths.
   T: Let's count by tenths again. This time, when we arrive at a whole number, say the whole number.
       (Write as students count.)
   S: 1 tenth, 2 tenths,… 1, 11 tenths, 12 tenths,… 2.
   T: Let's count by tenths again. This time, say the tenths in decimal form. (Write as students count.)
   S: Zero point 1, zero point 2,….
   T: How many tenths are in 1 whole?
   S: 10 tenths.
   T: (Write 1 = 10 tenths. Beneath it, write 2 = _____ tenths.) How many tenths are in 2 wholes?
   S: 20 tenths.
   T: 3 wholes?
   S: 30 tenths.
   T: (Write 9 = __ tenths.) On your boards, fill in the unknown number.
   S: (Write 9 = 90 tenths.)
   T: (Write 10 = __ tenths.) Fill in the unknown number.

Lesson 28:	Write equations and word problems corresponding to tape and number line diagrams.
Date:	11/10/13

4.G.48

S: (Write 10 = 100 tenths.)

Divide Whole Numbers by Unit Fractions and Unit Fractions by Whole Numbers (5 minutes)

Materials: (S) Personal white boards

Note: This fluency reviews G5–M4–Lessons 25–26 and prepares students for today's lesson.

T: (Write $2 \div \frac{1}{3}$.) Say the division sentence.

S: $2 \div \frac{1}{3} = 6$.

T: (Write $2 \div \frac{1}{3} = 6$. Beneath it, write $3 \div \frac{1}{3}$.) Say the division sentence.

S: $3 \div \frac{1}{3} = 9$.

T: (Write $3 \div \frac{1}{3} = 9$. Beneath it, write $8 \div \frac{1}{3} =$ _____.) On your boards, write the division sentence.

S: (Write $8 \div \frac{1}{3} = 24$.)

Continue with $2 \div \frac{1}{4}$, $5 \div \frac{1}{6}$, and $9 \div \frac{1}{6}$.

T: (Write $\frac{1}{2} \div 2$.) Say the division sentence.

S: $\frac{1}{2} \div 2 = \frac{1}{4}$.

T: (Write $\frac{1}{2} \div 2 = \frac{1}{4}$. Beneath it, write $\frac{1}{4} \div 2$.) Say the division sentence.

S: $\frac{1}{4} \div 2 = \frac{1}{8}$.

T: (Write $\frac{1}{4} \div 2 = \frac{1}{8}$. Erase the board and write $\frac{1}{3} \div 2$.) On your boards, write the sentence.

S: (Write $\frac{1}{3} \div 2 = \frac{1}{6}$.)

Continue the process with the following possible sequence: $\frac{1}{6} \div 2$ and $\frac{1}{3} \div 3$.

Concept Development (40 minutes)

Materials: (S) Problem Set, personal white boards

Note: Today's lesson involves creating word problems, which can be time intensive. The time for the Application Problem has been included in the Concept Development.

Note: Students create word problems from expressions and visual models in the form of tape diagrams. In Problem 1, guide students to identify what the whole and the divisor are in the expressions before they start writing the word problems. After about 10 minutes of working time, guide students to analyze the tape diagrams in Problems 2, 3, and 4. After the discussion, allow students to work for another 10 minutes. Finally, go over the answers, and have students share their answers with the class.

Lesson 28:   Write equations and word problems corresponding to tape and
                 number line diagrams.

Date: 11/10/13

4.G.4

Problems 1–2

1. Create and solve a division story problem about 5 meters of rope that is modeled by the tape diagram below.

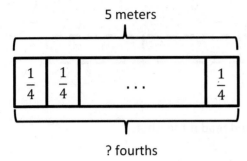

5 meters

$\frac{1}{4}$ | $\frac{1}{4}$ | ... | $\frac{1}{4}$

? fourths

T: Let's take a look at Problem 1 on our Problem Set and read it out loud together. What's the whole in the tape diagram?

S: 5.

T: 5 what?

S: 5 meters of rope.

T: What else can you tell me about this tape diagram? Turn and share with a partner.

S: The 5 meters of rope is being cut into fourths. → The 5 meters of rope is being cut into pieces that are 1 fourth meter long. The question is, how many pieces can be cut? → This is a division drawing, because a whole is being partitioned into equal parts. → We're trying to find out how many fourths are in 5.

T: Since we seem to agree that this is a picture of division, what would the division expression look like? Turn and talk.

S: Since 5 is the whole, it is the dividend. The one-fourths are the equal parts, so that is the divisor. → $5 \div \frac{1}{4}$.

T: Work with your partner to write a story about this diagram, then solve for the answer. (A possible response appears on the student work example of the Problem Set.)

T: (Allow students time to work.) How can we be sure that 20 fourths is correct? How do we check a division problem?

S: Multiply the quotient and the divisor.

T: What would our checking equation look like? Write it with your partner and solve.

S: $20 \times \frac{1}{4} = \frac{20}{4} = 5$.

T: Were we correct? How do you know?

S: Yes. Our product matches the dividend that we started with.

Lesson 28:	Write equations and word problems corresponding to tape and number line diagrams.	
Date:	11/10/13	**4.G.50**

2. Create and solve a story problem about $\frac{1}{4}$ pound of almonds that is modeled by the tape diagram below.

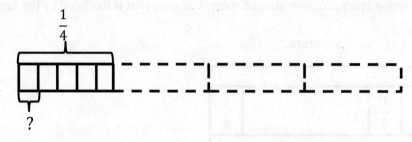

$\frac{1}{4}$

?

T: Let's now look at Problem 2 on the Problem Set, and read it together.

S: (Read aloud.)

T: Look at the tape diagram, what's the whole, or dividend, in this problem?

S: $\frac{1}{4}$ pound of almonds.

T: What else can you tell me about this tape diagram? Turn and share with a partner.

S: The 1 fourth is being cut into 5 parts. → I counted 5 boxes. It means the one-fourth is cut into 5 equal units, and we have to find how much 1 unit is. When you find the value of 1 equal part, that is division. → I see that we could find $\frac{1}{5}$ of $\frac{1}{4}$. That would be $\frac{1}{4} \times \frac{1}{5}$. That's the same as dividing by 5 and finding 1 part.

MP.4

T: We must find how much of a whole pound of almonds is in each of the units. Say the division expression.

S: $\frac{1}{4} \div 5$.

T: I noticed some of you were thinking about multiplication here. What multiplication expression would also give us the part that has the question mark?

S: $\frac{1}{4} \times \frac{1}{5}$.

T: Write the expression down on your paper, then work with a partner to write a division story and solve. (A possible response appears on the student work example of the Problem Set).

T: How can we check our division work?

S: Multiply the answer and the divisor.

T: Check it now.

S: (Write $\frac{1}{20} \times 5 = \frac{5}{20} = \frac{1}{4}$.)

Problem 3

a. $2 \div \frac{1}{3}$

b. $\frac{1}{3} \div 4$

c. $\frac{1}{4} \div 3$

d. $3 \div \frac{1}{5}$

T: (Write the three expressions on the board.) What do all of these expressions have in common?

S: They are division expressions. → They all have unit fractions and whole numbers. → Problems (b) and (c) have dividends that are unit fractions. → Problems (a) and (d) have divisors that are unit fractions.

T: What does each number in the expression represent? Turn and discuss with a partner.

S: The first number is the whole, and the second number is the divisor. → The first number tells how much there is in the beginning. It's the dividend. The second number tells how many in each group or how many equal groups we need to make. → In Problem (a), 2 is the whole and $\frac{1}{3}$ is the divisor. → In Problems (b) and (c), both expressions have a fraction divided by a whole number.

T: Compare these expressions to the word problems we just wrote. Turn and talk.

S: Problems (a) and (d) are like Problem 1, and the other two are like Problem 2. → Problems (a) and (d) have a whole number dividend just like Problem 1. The others have fraction dividends like Problem 2. → Our tape diagram for (a) should look like the one for Problem 1. → The first one is asking how many fractional units in the wholes like Problems (a) and (d). The others are asking what kind of unit you get when you split a fraction into equal parts. → Problems (b) and (c) will look like Problem 2.

T: Work with a partner to draw a tape diagram for each expression, then write a story to match your diagram and solve. Be sure to use multiplication to check your work. (Possible responses appear on the student work example of the Problem Set. Be sure to include in the class discussion all the interpretations of division as some students may write stories that take on a multiplication flavor.)

Problem Set (10 minutes)

The Problem Set forms the basis for today's lesson. Please see the script in the Concept Development for modeling suggestions.

Student Debrief (10 minutes)

Lesson Objective: Write equations and word problems corresponding to tape and number line diagrams.

The Student Debrief is intended to invite reflection and active processing of the total lesson experience.

Invite students to review their solutions for the Problem Set. They should check work by comparing answers with a partner before going over answers as a class. Look for misconceptions or misunderstandings that can be addressed in the Debrief. Guide students in a conversation to debrief the Problem Set and process the lesson.

You may choose to use any combination of the questions below to lead the discussion.

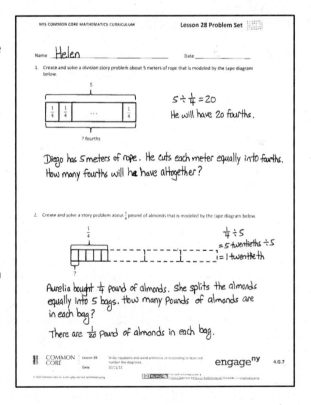

Lesson 28:   Write equations and word problems corresponding to tape and number line diagrams.
Date: 11/10/13

4.G.52

- In Problem 3, what do you notice about (a) and (b), (a) and (d), and (b) and (c)?
- Compare your stories and solutions for Problem 3 with a partner.
- Compare and contrast Problems 1 and 2. What is similar or different about these two problems?
- Share your solutions for Problems 1 and 2 and explain them to a partner.

Exit Ticket (3 minutes)

After the Student Debrief, instruct students to complete the Exit Ticket. A review of their work will help you assess the students' understanding of the concepts that were presented in the lesson today and plan more effectively for future lessons. You may read the questions aloud to the students.

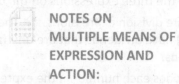

NOTES ON MULTIPLE MEANS OF EXPRESSION AND ACTION:

Comparing and contrasting is often required in English language arts, science, and social studies classes. Teachers can use the same graphic organizers that are successfully used in these classes in math class. Although Venn Diagrams are often used to help students organize their thinking when comparing and contrasting, this is not the only possible graphic organizer. To add variety, charts listing similarities in a center column and differences in two outer columns can also be used.

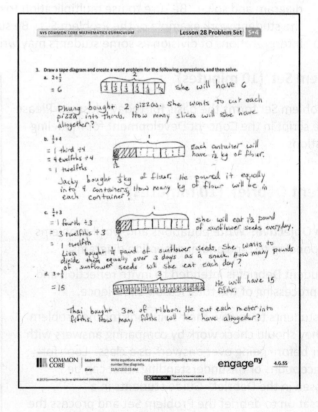

Lesson 28:   Write equations and word problems corresponding to tape and number line diagrams.
Date: 11/10/13

4.G.53

Name _____ Date _____

1. Create and solve a division story problem about 5 meters of rope that is modeled by the tape diagram below.

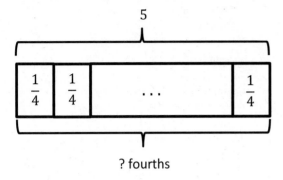

2. Create and solve a story problem about $\frac{1}{4}$ pound of almonds that is modeled by the tape diagram below.

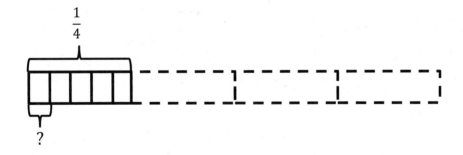

COMMON CORE™ | **Lesson 28:** Write equations and word problems corresponding to tape and number line diagrams.

Date: 11/10/13

4.G.54

3. Draw a tape diagram and create a word problem for the following expressions, and then solve.

   a. $2 \div \frac{1}{3}$

   b. $\frac{1}{3} \div 4$

   c. $\frac{1}{4} \div 3$

   d. $3 \div \frac{1}{5}$

Name _____   Date _____

1. Create a word problem for the following expressions, and then solve.

   a. $4 \div \frac{1}{2}$

   b. $\frac{1}{2} \div 4$

COMMON CORE™ | **Lesson 28:** Write equations and word problems corresponding to tape and number line diagrams.
Date: 11/10/13

4.G.56

Name _____   Date _____

1. Create and solve a division story problem about 7 feet of rope that is modeled by the tape diagram below.

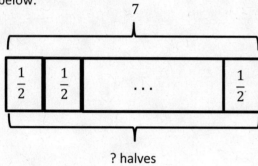

2. Create and solve a story problem about $\frac{1}{3}$ pound of flour that is modeled by the tape diagram below.

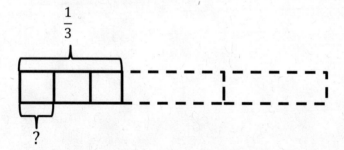

Lesson 28: Write equations and word problems corresponding to tape and
number line diagrams.

Date: 11/10/13

4.G.57

3. Draw a tape diagram and create a word problem for the following expressions. Then solve and check.

   a. $2 \div \frac{1}{4}$

   b. $\frac{1}{4} \div 2$

   c. $\frac{1}{3} \div 5$

   d. $3 \div \frac{1}{10}$

COMMON CORE™

Lesson 28: Write equations and word problems corresponding to tape and number line diagrams.

Date: 11/10/13

4.G.58

Lesson 29

Objective: Connect division by a unit fraction to division by 1 tenth and 1 hundredth.

Suggested Lesson Structure

■ Fluency Practice   (9 minutes)
■ Application Problem   (10 minutes)
■ Concept Development   (31 minutes)
■ Student Debrief   (10 minutes)
  Total Time   **(60 minutes)**

Fluency Practice (9 minutes)

- Count by Fractions **5.NF.7**   (5 minutes)
- Divide Whole Numbers by Unit Fractions and Fractions by Whole Numbers **5.NF.7**   (4 minutes)

Count by Fractions (5 minutes)

Materials: (S) Personal white boards

Note: This fluency prepares students for today's lesson.

T: Count by 1 tenths to 20 tenths. When you reach a whole number, say the whole number. (Write as students count.)

S: 1 tenth, 2 tenths, 3 tenths, 4 tenths, 5 tenths, 6 tenths, 7 tenths, 8 tenths, 9 tenths, 1 whole, 11 tenths, 12 tenths, 13 tenths, 14 tenths, 15 tenths, 16 tenths, 17 tenths, 18 tenths, 19 tenths, 2 wholes.

T: How many tenths are in 1 whole?

S: 10.

T: 2 wholes?

S: 20.

T: 3 wholes?

S: 30.

T: 9 wholes.

S: 90.

T: 10 wholes?

S: 100.

Lesson 29:	Connect division by a unit fraction to division by 1 tenth and 1 hundredth.
Date:	11/10/13

4.G.5

T: (Write 10 = 100 tenths. Beneath it, write 20 = _____ tenths.) On your boards, fill in the unknown.

S: (Write 20 = 200 tenths.)

Continue the process with 30, 50, 70, and 90.

T: (Write 90 = 900 tenths. Beneath it, write 91 = _____ tenths.) On your boards, fill in the unknown.

S: (Write 91 = 910 tenths.)

Continue the process with 92, 82, 42, 47, 64, 64.1, 64.2, and 83.5.

Divide Whole Numbers by Unit Fractions and Fractions by Whole Numbers (4 minutes)

Materials: (S) Personal white boards

Note: This fluency reviews G5–M4–Lessons 25–27 and prepares students for today's lesson.

T: (Write $2 \div \frac{1}{2}$.) Say the division sentence.

S: $2 \div \frac{1}{2} = 4$.

T: (Write $2 \div \frac{1}{2} = 4$. Beneath it, write $3 \div \frac{1}{2}$.) Say the division sentence.

S: $3 \div \frac{1}{2} = 6$.

T: (Write $3 \div \frac{1}{2} = 6$. Beneath it, write $8 \div \frac{1}{2}$.) On your boards, complete the division sentence.

S: (Write $8 \div \frac{1}{2} = 16$.)

Continue the process with $5 \div \frac{1}{4}$, $7 \div \frac{1}{3}$, $1 \div \frac{1}{10}$, $2 \div \frac{1}{10}$, $7 \div \frac{1}{10}$, and $10 \div \frac{1}{10}$.

T: (Write $\frac{1}{2} \div 3$.) Say the division sentence.

S: $\frac{1}{2} \div 3 = \frac{1}{6}$.

T: (Write $\frac{1}{2} \div 3 = \frac{1}{6}$. Beneath it, write $\frac{1}{3} \div 4$.) Say the division sentence.

S: $\frac{1}{3} \div 4 = \frac{1}{12}$.

T: (Write $\frac{1}{3} \div 4 = \frac{1}{12}$. Beneath it, write $\frac{1}{8} \div 5$.) On your boards, write the division sentence.

S: (Write $\frac{1}{8} \div 5 = \frac{1}{40}$.)

T: (Write $\frac{1}{4} \div 3$.) Say the division sentence.

S: $\frac{1}{4} \div 5 = \frac{1}{-20}$.

Continue the process with $7 \div \frac{1}{4}$, $\frac{1}{4} \div 7$, $5 \div \frac{1}{6}$, $\frac{1}{6} \div 5$, $\frac{1}{8} \div 7$, and $9 \div \frac{1}{8}$.

Lesson 29:   Connect division by a unit fraction to division by 1 tenth and 1 hundredth.

Date: 11/10/13

4.G.60

Application Problem (10 minutes)

Fernando bought a jacket for $185 and sold it for $1\frac{1}{2}$ times what he paid. Marisol spent $\frac{1}{5}$ as much as Fernando on the same jacket, but sold it for $\frac{1}{2}$ as much as Fernando sold it for.

How much money did Marisol make? Explain your thinking using a diagram.

Note: This problem is a multi-step problem requiring a high level of organization. Scaling language and fraction multiplication from G5–M4–Topic G coupled with fraction of a set and subtraction warrant the extra time given to today's Application Problem.

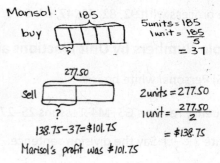

Fernando: $\$185 \times 1\frac{1}{2}$
$= 185 \times \frac{3}{2}$
$= \frac{555}{2}$
$= \$277.50$ selling price

Marisol:
buy   185
5 units = 185
1 unit = $\frac{185}{5}$ = 37

sell   277.50
?
2 units = 277.50
1 unit = $\frac{277.50}{2}$ = $138.75

138.75 − 37 = $101.75
Marisol's profit was $101.75

Concept Development (31 minutes)

Materials: (S) Personal white boards

Problem 1: 7 ÷ 0.1

T: (Post Problem 1 on the board.) Read the division expression using unit form.

S: 7 ones divided by 1 tenth.

T: Rewrite this expression using a fraction.

S: (Write $7 \div \frac{1}{10}$.)

T: (Write $= 7 \div \frac{1}{10}$.) What question does this division expression ask us?

S: How many tenths are in 7? → 7 is one tenth of what number?

T: Let's start with just 1 whole. How many tenths are in 1 whole?

S: 10 tenths.

T: (Write 10 in the blank, then below it, write, *There are _____ tenths in 7 wholes*.) So, if there are 10 tenths in 1 whole, how many are in 7 wholes?

MP.2

S: 70 tenths.

T: (Write 70 in the blank.) Explain how you know. Turn and talk.

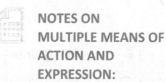

1) $7 \div 0.1 = 7 \div \frac{1}{10} = 70$

There are __10__ tenths in 1 whole.
There are __70__ tenths in 7 wholes.

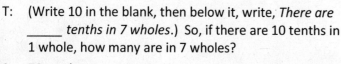

NOTES ON MULTIPLE MEANS OF ACTION AND EXPRESSION:

The same place value mats that were used in previous modules can be used in this lesson to support students who are struggling. Students can start Problem 1 by drawing or placing 7 disks in the ones column. Teachers can follow the same dialogue that is written in the lesson. Have the students physically decompose the 7 wholes into 70 tenths, which can then be divided by one-tenth.

Lesson 29:   Connect division by a unit fraction to division by 1 tenth and 1 hundredth.
Date: 11/10/13

4.G.6

S: There are 10 tenths in 1, 20 tenths in 2, and 30 tenths in 3, so there are 70 tenths in 7.   → Seven is 7 times greater than 1, and 70 tenths is 7 times more than 10 tenths.   → Seven times 10 is 70, so there are 70 tenths in 7.

MP.2

T: Let's think about it another way.   Seven is one-tenth of what number?   Explain to your partner how you know.

S: It's 70, because I think of a tape diagram with 10 parts and 1 part is 7.   7 × 10 is 70.   → I think of place value.   Just move each digit one place to left.   It's ten times as much.

Problem 2:   7.4 ÷ 0.1

T: (Post Problem 2 on the board.)   Rewrite this division expression using a fraction for the divisor.

S: (Write $7.4 \div \frac{1}{10}$.)

T: Compare this problem to the one we just solved.   What do you notice?   Turn and talk.

S: There still are 7 wholes, but now there are also 4 more tenths.   → The whole in this problem is just 4 tenths more than in problem 1.   →
There are 74 tenths instead of 70 tenths.
  → We can ask ourselves, 7.4 is 1 tenth
of what number?

$$7.4 \div 0.1 = 7.4 \div \tfrac{1}{10} = 74$$

There are __70__ tenths in 7 wholes.

There are __4__ tenths in 4 tenths.

$$74 \text{ tenths} \div 1 \text{ tenth} = 74$$

There are __74__ tenths in 7.4.

T: We already know part of this problem. (Write, *There are* _____ *tenths in 7 wholes*.)   How many tenths are in 7 wholes?

S: 70.

T: (Write 70 in the blank, and below it write, *There are* _____ *tenths in 4 tenths*.)   How many tenths are in 4 tenths?

S: 4.

T: (Point to 7 ones.)   So, if there are 70 tenths in 7 wholes, and (point to 4 tenths) 4 tenths in 4 tenths, how many tenths are in 7 and 4 tenths?

S: 74.

T: Work with your partner to rewrite this expression using only tenths to name the whole and divisor.

S: (Write 74 tenths ÷ 1 tenth.)

T: Look at our new expression.   How many tenths are in 74 tenths?

S: 74 tenths.

T: (Write 6 ÷ 0.1.)   Read this expression.

S: 6 divided by 1 tenth.

T: How many tenths are in 6?   Show me on your boards.

S: (Write and show 60 tenths.)

T: 6 is 1 tenth of what number?

S: 60.

T: (Erase 6 and replace with 6.2.)   How many tenths in 6.2?

    Lesson 29:   Connect division by a unit fraction to division by 1 tenth and
                           1 hundredth.   **4.G.62**
    Date: 11/10/13

S: (Write 62 tenths.)

T: 6.2 is 1 tenth of what number?

S: 62.

Continue the process with 9 and 9.8 and 12 and 12.6.

Problem 3:   **a. 7 ÷ 0.01**   **b. 7.4 ÷ 0.01**   **c. 7.49 ÷ 0.01**

T: (Post Problem 3(a) on the board.) Read this expression.

S: 7 divided by 1 hundredth.

T: Rewrite this division expression using a fraction for the divisor.

S: (Write $7 ÷ \frac{1}{100}$.)

a) $7 ÷ 0.01 = 7 ÷ \frac{1}{100} = 700$

There are __100__ hundredths in 1 whole.

There are __700__ hundredths in 7 wholes.

T: We can think of this as finding how many hundredths are in 7. Will your thinking need to change to solve this? Turn and talk.

S: No, because the question is really the same. How many smaller units in the whole? → The units we are counting are different, but that doesn't really change how we find the answer.

T: Will our quotient be greater or less than our last problem? Again, talk with your partner.

S: The quotient will be greater because we are counting units that are much smaller, so there'll be more of them in the wholes. → Not too much. It's the same basic idea but since our divisor has gotten smaller; the quotient should be larger than before.

T: Before we think about how many hundredths are in 7 wholes, let's find how many hundredths are in 1 whole. (Write on the board: *There are _____ hundredths in 1 whole.*) Fill in the blank.

S: 100.

T: (Write 100 in the blank. Write, *There are _____ hundredths in 7 wholes.*) Knowing this, how many hundredths are in 7 wholes?

S: 700.

T: (Write 700 in the blank. Then, post Problem 3(b) on board.) What is the whole in this division expression?

S: 7 and 4 tenths.

T: How will you solve this problem? Turn and talk.

S: It's only 4 more tenths than the one we just solved. We need to figure out how many hundredths are in 4 tenths. → We know there are 700 hundredths in 7 wholes, and this is 4 tenths more than that. There are 10 hundredths in 1 tenth, so there must be 40 hundredths in 4 tenths.

T: How many hundredths are in 7 wholes?

S: 700.

T: How many hundredths in 4 tenths?

NOTES ON MULTIPLE MEANS OF REPRESENTATION:

Generally speaking, it is better for teachers to use unit form when they read decimal numbers. For example, *seven and four-tenths* is generally preferable to *seven point four*. *Seven point four* is appropriate when teachers or students are trying to express what they need to write. Similarly, it is preferable to read fractions in unit form, too. For example, it's better to say *two-thirds*, rather than *two over three* unless referring to how the fraction is written.

Lesson 29:   Connect division by a unit fraction to division by 1 tenth and 1 hundredth.

Date: 11/10/13

4.G.6

S: 40.

T: How many hundredths in 7.4?

S: 740.

T: Asked another way, if 7.4 is 1 hundredth, what is the whole?

S: 740.

T: (Post Problem 4(c) on the board.) Work with a partner to solve this problem. Be prepared to explain your thinking.

S: (Work and show $7.49 \div 0.1 = 749$.)

T: Explain your thinking as you solved.

S: 7.49 is just 9 hundredths more in the dividend than $7.4 \div 0.01$, so the answer must be 749. → There are 700 hundredths in 7, and 49 hundredths in 49 hundredths. That's 749 hundredths all together.

T: Let's try some more. Think first... how many hundredths are in 6? Show me.

S: (Show 600.)

T: Show me how many hundredths are in 6.2?

S: (Show 620.)

T: 6.02?

S: (Show 602.)

T: 12.6?

S: (Show 1,260.)

T: 12.69?

S: (Show 1,269.)

T: What patterns are you noticing as we find the number of hundredths in each of these quantities?

S: The digits stay the same, but they are in a larger place value in the quotient. → I'm beginning to notice that when we divide by a hundredth each digit shifts two places to the left. It's like multiplying by 100.

T: That leads us right into thinking of our division expression differently. When we divide by a hundredth, we can think, "This number is 1 hundredth of what whole?" or "What number is this 1 hundredth of?"

T: (Write $7 \div \frac{1}{100}$ on the board.) What number is 7 one hundredths of?

S: 700.

T: Explain to your partner how you know.

S: It's like thinking 7 times 100 because 7 is one of a hundred parts. → It's place value again but this time we move the decimal point two places to the right.)

T: You can use that way of thinking about these expressions, too.

Problem Set (10 minutes)

Students should do their personal best to complete the Problem Set within the allotted 10 minutes. For some classes, it may be appropriate to modify the assignment by specifying which problems they work on first.

Lesson 29:   Connect division by a unit fraction to division by 1 tenth and 1 hundredth.

Date: 11/10/13

4.G.64

MP.2

Some problems do not specify a method for solving. Students solve these problems using the RDW approach used for Application Problems.

Student Debrief (10 minutes)

Lesson Objective: Connect division by a unit fraction to division by 1 tenth and 1 hundredth.

The Student Debrief is intended to invite reflection and active processing of the total lesson experience.

Invite students to review their solutions for the Problem Set. They should check work by comparing answers with a partner before going over answers as a class. Look for misconceptions or misunderstandings that can be addressed in the Debrief. Guide students in a conversation to debrief the Problem Set and process the lesson.

You may choose to use any combination of the questions below to lead the discussion.

- In Problem 1, did you notice the relationship between (a) and (c), (b) and (d), (e) and (g), (f) and (h)?

- What is the relationship between Problems 2(a) and 2(b)? (The quotient of (b) is triple that of (a).)

- What strategy did you use to solve Problem 3? Share your strategy and explain to a partner.

- How did you answer Problem 4? Share your thinking with a partner.

- Compare your answer for Problem 5 to your partner's.

- Connect the work of Module 1, the movement on the place value chart, to the division work of this lesson. Back then, the focus was on conversion between units. However, it's important to note place value work asks the same question, "How many tenths are in 1 whole?" "How many hundredths in a tenth?" Further, the partitive division interpretation leads naturally to a discussion of multiplication by powers of 10, that is, if 6 is 1 hundredth, what is the whole? (6 × 100 = 600.) This echoes the work students have done on the place value chart.

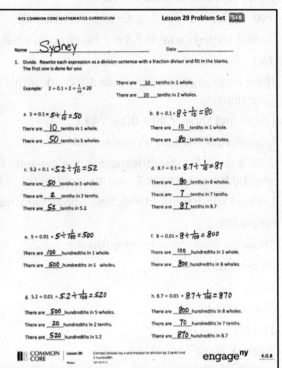

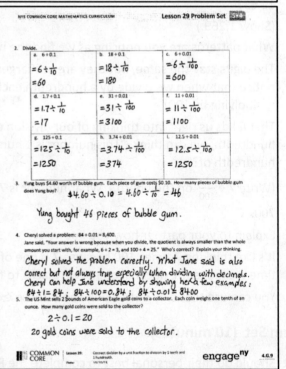

Lesson 29: Connect division by a unit fraction to division by 1 tenth and 1 hundredth.
Date: 11/10/13

4.G.6

Exit Ticket (3 minutes)

After the Student Debrief, instruct students to complete the Exit Ticket. A review of their work will help you assess the students' understanding of the concepts that were presented in the lesson today and plan more effectively for future lessons. You may read the questions aloud to the students.

COMMON CORE™

Lesson 29:   Connect division by a unit fraction to division by 1 tenth and 1 hundredth.
Date: 11/10/13

4.G.66

Name _____   Date _____

1. Divide. Rewrite each expression as a division sentence with a fraction divisor, and fill in the blanks.
    The first one is done for you.

Example: $2 \div 0.1 = 2 \div \frac{1}{10} = 20$

There are ___10___ tenths in 1 whole.

There are ___20___ tenths in 2 wholes.

a. $5 \div 0.1 =$

There are _____ tenths in 1 whole.

There are _____ tenths in 5 wholes.

b. $8 \div 0.1 =$

There are _____ tenths in 1 whole.

There are _____ tenths in 8 wholes.

c. $5.2 \div 0.1 =$

There are _____ tenths in 5 wholes.

There are _____ tenths in 2 tenths.

There are _____ tenths in 5.2

d. $8.7 \div 0.1 =$

There are _____ tenths in 8 wholes.

There are _____ tenths in 7 tenths.

There are _____ tenths in 8.7

e. $5 \div 0.01 =$

There are _____ hundredths in 1 whole.

There are _____ hundredths in 5 wholes.

f. $8 \div 0.01 =$

There are _____ hundredths in 1 whole.

There are _____ hundredths in 8 wholes.

g. $5.2 \div 0.01 =$

There are _____ hundredths in 5 wholes.

There are _____ hundredths in 2 tenths.

There are _____ hundredths in 5.2

h. $8.7 \div 0.01 =$

There are _____ hundredths in 8 wholes.

There are _____ hundredths in 7 tenths.

There are _____ hundredths in 8.7

COMMON CORE

Lesson 29:   Connect division by a unit fraction to division by 1 tenth and
             1 hundredth.
Date: 11/10/13

4.G.6

2. Divide.

a. 6 ÷ 0.1	b. 18 ÷ 0.1	c. 6 ÷ 0.01
d. 1.7 ÷ 0.1	e. 31 ÷ 0.01	f. 11 ÷ 0.01
g. 125 ÷ 0.1	h. 3.74 ÷ 0.01	i. 12.5 ÷ 0.01

3. Yung bought $4.60 worth of bubble gum. Each piece of gum cost $0.10. How many pieces of bubble gum did Yung buy?

4. Cheryl solved a problem: 84 ÷ 0.01 = 8,400.
   Jane said, "Your answer is wrong because when you divide, the quotient is always smaller than the whole amount you start with, for example, 6 ÷ 2 = 3, and 100 ÷ 4 = 25." Who is correct? Explain your thinking.

5. The US Mint sells 2 pounds of American Eagle gold coins to a collector. Each coin weighs one-tenth of an ounce. How many gold coins were sold to the collector?

Name _____ Date _____

1. 8.3 is equal to

   _____ tenths

   _____ hundredths

2. 28 is equal to

   _____ hundredths

   _____ tenths

3. $15.09 \div 0.01 =$ _____

4. $267.4 \div \frac{1}{10} =$ _____

5. $632.98 \div \frac{1}{100} =$ _____

COMMON CORE™   **Lesson 29:**   Connect division by a unit fraction to division by 1 tenth and
1·hundredth.

Date: 11/10/13

4.G.(

Name _____ Date _____

1. Divide. Rewrite each expression as a division sentence with a fraction divisor, and fill in the blanks. The first one is done for you.

Example: $4 \div 0.1 = 4 \div \frac{1}{10} = 40$

There are __10__ tenths in 1 whole.

There are __40__ tenths in 4 wholes.

a. $9 \div 0.1 =$

There are _____ tenths in 1 whole.

There are _____ tenths in 9 wholes.

b. $6 \div 0.1 =$

There are _____ tenths in 1 whole.

There are _____ tenths in 6 wholes.

c. $3.6 \div 0.1 =$

There are _____ tenths in 3 wholes.

There are _____ tenths in 6 tenths.

There are _____ tenths in 3.6.

d. $12.8 \div 0.1 =$

There are _____ tenths in 12 wholes.

There are _____ tenths in 8 tenths.

There are _____ tenths in 12.8.

e. $3 \div 0.01 =$

There are _____ hundredths in 1 whole.

There are _____ tenths in 3 wholes.

f. $7 \div 0.01 =$

There are _____ hundredths in 1 whole.

There are _____ hundredths in 7 wholes.

g. $4.7 \div 0.01 =$

There are _____ hundredths in 4 wholes.

There are _____ hundredths in 7 tenths.

There are _____ hundredths in 4.7.

h. $11.3 \div 0.01 =$

There are _____ hundredths in 11 wholes.

There are _____ hundredths in 3 tenths.

There are _____ hundredths in 11.3.

Lesson 29:   Connect division by a unit fraction to division by 1 tenth and 1 hundredth.

Date: 11/10/13

4.G.70

2. Divide.

a. $2 \div 0.1$	b. $23 \div 0.1$	c. $5 \div 0.01$
d. $7.2 \div 0.1$	e. $51 \div 0.01$	f. $31 \div 0.1$
g. $231 \div 0.1$	h. $4.37 \div 0.01$	i. $24.5 \div 0.01$

3. Giovanna is charged $0.01 for each text message she sends. Last month her cell phone bill included a $12.60 charge for text messages. How many text messages did Giovanna send?

4. Geraldine solved a problem: $68.5 \div 0.01 = 6,850$.

   Ralph said, "This is wrong because a quotient can't be greater than the whole you start with. For example, $8 \div 2 = 4$, and $250 \div 5 = 50$." Who is correct? Explain your thinking.

5. The price for an ounce of gold on September 23, 2013, was $1,326.40. A group of 10 friends decide to share the cost equally on 1 ounce of gold. How much money will each friend pay?

COMMON CORE™

Lesson 29: Connect division by a unit fraction to division by 1 tenth and 1 hundredth.

Date: 11/10/13

4.G.7

Lesson 30

Objective: Divide decimal dividends by non-unit decimal divisors.

Suggested Lesson Structure

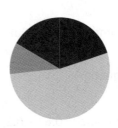

- ■ Fluency Practice   (12 minutes)
- ■ Application Problem   (6 minutes)
- ■ Concept Development   (32 minutes)
- ■ Student Debrief   (10 minutes)
-    **Total Time**   **(60 minutes)**

Fluency Practice   (12 minutes)

- ▪ Sprint: Divide Whole Numbers by Fractions and Fractions by Whole Numbers **5.NBT.7**   (9 minutes)
- ▪ Divide Decimals **5.NBT.7**   (3 minutes)

Sprint: Divide Whole Numbers by Fractions and Fractions by Whole Numbers   (9 minutes)

Materials: (S) Divide Whole Numbers by Fractions and Fractions by Whole Numbers Sprint

Note: This fluency reviews G5–M4–Lessons 26–28.

Divide Decimals   (3 minutes)

Materials: (S) Personal white boards

Note: This fluency reviews G5–M4–Lesson 29.

     T: (Write $1 \div 0.1 =$ ____.)   How many tenths are in 1?
     S: 10.
     T: 2?
     S: 20.
     T: 3?
     S: 30.
     T: 9?
     S: 90.
     T: (Write $10 \div 0.1 =$ ____.)   On your boards, complete the equation, answering how many tenths are in 10.
     S: (Write $10 \div 0.1 = 100$.)

T: (Write 20 ÷ 0.1 = _____.) If there are 100 tenths in 10, how many tenths are in 20?

S: 200.

T: 30?

S: 300.

T: 70?

S: 700.

T: (Write 75 ÷ 0.1 = _____.) On your boards, complete the equation.

S: (Write 75 ÷ 0.1 = 750.)

T: (Write 75.3 ÷ 0.1 = _____.) Complete the equation.

S: (Write 75.3 ÷ 0.1 = 753.)

Continue this process with the following possible sequence: 0.63 ÷ 0.1, 6.3 ÷ 0.01, 63 ÷ 0.1, and 630 ÷ 0.01.

Application Problem (6 minutes)

Alexa claims that $16 \div 4$, $\frac{32}{8}$, and 8 halves are all equivalent expressions. Is Alexa correct? Explain how you know.

$8 \text{ halves} = \frac{8}{2}$ $16 \div 4 = \frac{16}{4}$ $\frac{32}{8} = 32 \div 8$

$\frac{8}{2} \times \frac{4}{4} = \frac{32}{8}$ $\frac{16}{4} \times \frac{2}{2} = \frac{32}{8}$ $32 \div 8 = 4$

$\frac{32}{8} = 4$ $\frac{32}{8} = 4$

Alexa is correct. We can multiply 2 of the expressions by fractions equal to 1 to show that they are all equal to $\frac{32}{8}$. Also, each expression can be simplified & is equal to 4.

Alexa is right.
I can double the whole and the divisor and the quotient doesn't change. $8 \div 2 = 4$
$16 \div 4 = 4$
$32 \div 8 = 4$

$8 : 2 = 4$ $16 : 4 = 4$ $32 \div 8 = 4$

Note: This problem reminds students that when you multiply (or divide) both the divisor and the dividend by the same factor, the quotient stays the same or, alternatively, we can think of it as the fraction has the same value. This concept is critical to the Concept Development in this lesson.

Lesson 30:   Divide decimal dividends by non-unit decimal divisors.
Date: 11/10/13

4.G.7

Concept Development (32 minutes)

Materials: (S) Personal white boards

Problem 1:   **a. 2 ÷ 0.1**   **b. 2 ÷ 0.2**   **c. 2.4 ÷ 0.2**   **d. 2.4 ÷ 0.4**

T: (Post Problem 1(a) on the board.) We did this yesterday. How many tenths are in 2?

S: 20.

T: (Write = 20.) Tell a partner how you know.

S: I can count by tenths. 1 tenth, 2 tenths, 3 tenths,... all the way up to 20 tenths, which is 2 wholes.
→ There are 10 tenths in 1 so there are 20 tenths in 2. → Dividing by 1 tenth is the same as
multiplying by 10, and 2 times 10 is 20.

T: We also know that any division expression can be
rewritten as a fraction. Rewrite this expression as a
fraction.

**NOTES ON
MULTIPLE MEANS OF
REPRESENTATION:**

The presence of decimals in the
denominators in this lesson may pique
the interest of students performing
above grade level. These students can
be encouraged to investigate and
operate with complex fractions
(fractions whose numerator,
denominator, or both contain a
fraction).

S: (Show $\frac{2}{0.1}$.)

T: That fraction looks different from most we've seen
before. What's different about it?

S: The denominator has a decimal point; that's weird.

T: It is different, but it's a perfectly acceptable fraction.
We can rename this fraction so that the denominator is
a whole number. What have we learned that allows us
to rename fractions without changing their value?

S: We can multiply by a fraction equal to 1.

T: What fraction equal to 1 will rename the denominator
as a whole number? Turn and talk.

S: Multiplying by $\frac{2}{2}$ is easy, but that would just make the denominator 0.2. That's not a whole number.
→ I think it is fun to multiply by $\frac{13}{13}$, but then we'll still have 1.3 as the denominator. → I'll multiply
by $\frac{10}{10}$. That way I'll be able to keep the digits the same. → If we just want a whole number, $\frac{20}{20}$ would
work. Any fraction with a numerator and denominator that are multiples of 10 would work, really.

T: I overheard lots of suggestions for ways to rename this denominator as a whole number. I'd like you
to try some of your suggestions. Be prepared to share your results about what worked and what
didn't. (Allow students time to work and experiment.)

S: (Work and experiment.)

T: Let's share some of the equivalent fractions we've created.

S: (Share while teacher records on board. Possible examples include $\frac{20}{1}, \frac{40}{2}, \frac{100}{5}$, and $\frac{200}{10}$.)

T: Show me these fractions written as division expressions with the quotient.

S: (Work and show 20 ÷ 1 = 20, 40 ÷ 2 = 20, 100 ÷ 5 = 20, etc.)

Lesson 30:   Divide decimal dividends by non-unit decimal divisors.
Date: 11/10/13

4.G.74

T: What do you notice about all of these division sentences?

S: The quotients are all 20.

T: Since all of the quotients are equal to each other, can we say then that these expressions are equivalent as well? (Write 2 ÷ 0.1 = 20 ÷ 1 = 40 ÷ 2, etc.)

S: Since the answer to them is all the same, then yes, they are equivalent expressions. → It reminds me of equal fractions, the way they don't look alike but are equal.

T: These are all equivalent expressions. When we multiply by a fraction equal to 1, we create equal fractions and an equivalent division expression.

T: (Post Problem 1(b), 2 ÷ 0.2, on the board.) Let's use this thinking as we find the value of this expression. Turn and talk about what you think the quotient will be.

S: I can count by 2 tenths. 2 tenths, 4 tenths, 6 tenths,… 20 tenths. That was 10. The quotient must be 10. → Two is like 2.0 or 20 tenths. 20 tenths divided by 2 tenths is going to be 10. → The divisor in this problem is twice as large as the one we just did so the quotient will be half as big. Half of 20 is 10.

T: Let's see if our thinking is correct. Rewrite this division expression as a fraction.

S: (Work and show $\frac{2}{0.2}$.)

T: What do you notice about the denominator?

S: It's not a whole number. → It's a decimal.

T: How will you find an equal fraction with a whole number divisor? Share your ideas.

S: We have to multiply it by a fraction equal to 1. → I think multiplying by $\frac{5}{5}$ would work. That will make the divisor exactly 1. → $\frac{10}{10}$ would work again. That would make $\frac{20}{2}$. → This time any numerator and denominator that is a multiple of 5 would work.

T: I heard the fraction 10 tenths being mentioned during both discussions. What if our divisor were 0.3? If we multiplied by $\frac{10}{10}$, what would the new denominator be?

S: 3.

T: What if the divisor were 0.8?

S: 8.

T: What about 1.2?

S: 12.

$$\frac{2}{0.1} \times \frac{10}{10} = \frac{20}{1}$$

$$\frac{2}{0.1} \times \frac{20}{20} = \frac{40}{2}$$

$$\frac{2}{0.1} \times \frac{50}{50} = \frac{100}{5}$$

$$\frac{2}{0.1} \times \frac{100}{100} = \frac{200}{10}$$

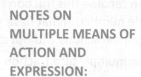

NOTES ON MULTIPLE MEANS OF ACTION AND EXPRESSION:

Place value mats can be used here to support struggling learners. The same concepts that students studied in G5–Module 1 apply here. By writing the divisor and dividend on a place value mat, students can see that 2 ones divided by 2 tenths is equal to 10 since the digit 2 in the ones place is 10 times greater than a 2 in the tenths place.

COMMON CORE™

Lesson 30: Divide decimal dividends by non-unit decimal divisors.
Date: 11/10/13

4.G.

T: What do you notice about the decimal point and digits when we use tenths to rename?

S: The digits stay the same, but the decimal point moves to the right. → The decimal just moves, so that the numerator and the denominator are 10 times as much.

T: Multiply the fraction by 10 tenths.

S: (Show $\frac{2}{0.2} \times \frac{10}{10} = \frac{20}{2}$.)

T: What division expression does our renamed fraction represent?

S: 20 divided by 2.

T: What's the quotient?

S: 10.

T: Let's be sure. To check our division's answer (write $\frac{2}{0.2} = 10$), we multiply the quotient by the...?

S: Divisor.

T: Show me.

S: (Show 10 × 0.2 = 2 or 10 × 2 tenths = 20 tenths.)

T: (Post Problem 1(c), 2.4 ÷ 0.2, on the board.) Share your thoughts about what the quotient might be for this expression.

S: I think it is 12. I counted by 2 tenths again and got 12. → 2.4 is only 4 tenths more than the last problem, and there are two groups of 2 tenths in 4 tenths so that makes 12 altogether. → I'm thinking 24 tenths divided by 2 tenths is going to be 12. → I'm starting to think of it like whole number division. It almost looks like 24 divided by 2, which is 12.

T: Rewrite this division expression as a fraction.

S: (Write and show $\frac{2.4}{0.2}$.)

T: This time we have a decimal in both the divisor and the whole. Remind me. What will you do to rename the divisor as a whole number?

S: Multiply by $\frac{10}{10}$.

T: What will happen to the numerator when you multiply by $\frac{10}{10}$?

S: It will be renamed as a whole number too.

T: Show me.

S: (Work and show $\frac{2.4}{0.2} \times \frac{10}{10} = \frac{24}{2}$.)

T: Say the fraction as a division expression with the quotient.

S: 24 divided by 2 equals 12.

T: Check your work.

S: (Check work.)

T: (Post Problem 1(d) on the board.) Work this one independently.

S: (Work and share.)

$$2.4 \div 0.4 = \frac{2.4}{0.4}$$

$$= \frac{2.4}{0.4} \times \frac{10}{10}$$

$$= \frac{24}{4}$$

$$= 6$$

Lesson 30:   Divide decimal dividends by non-unit decimal divisors.
Date: 11/10/13

4.G.76

Problem 2: a. 1.6 ÷ 0.04   b. 1.68 ÷ 0.04   c. 1.68 ÷ 0.12

T: (Post Problem 2(a) on the board.) Rewrite this expression as a fraction.

S: (Write $\frac{1.6}{0.04}$.)

T: How is this expression different from the ones we just evaluated?

S: This one is dividing by a hundredth. → Our divisor is 4 hundredths, rather than 4 tenths.

T: Our divisor is still not a whole number, and now it's a hundredth. Will multiplying by 10 tenths create a whole number divisor?

S: No, 4 hundredths times 10 is just 4 tenths. That's still not a whole number.

T: Since our divisor is now a hundredth, the most efficient way to rename it as a whole number is to multiply by 100 hundredths. Multiply and show me the equivalent fraction.

S: (Show $\frac{1.6}{0.04} \times \frac{100}{100} = \frac{160}{4}$.)

T: Say the division expression.

S: 160 divided by 4.

T: This expression is equivalent to 1.6 divided by 0.04. What is the quotient?

S: 40.

T: So, 1.6 divided by 0.04 also equals…?

S: 40.

T: Show me the multiplication sentence you can use to check.

S: (Show 40 × 0.04 = 1.6, or 40 × 4 hundredths = 160 hundredths.)

T: (Post Problem 1(b) on the board.) Work with your partner to solve and check.

S: (Work.)

T: (Post Problem 1(c) on the board.) Work independently to find the quotient. Check your work with a partner after each step.

S: (Work and share.)

Problem Set (10 minutes)

Students should do their personal best to complete the Problem Set within the allotted 10 minutes. For some classes, it may be appropriate to modify the assignment by specifying which problems they work on first. Some problems do not specify a method for solving. Students solve these problems using the RDW approach used for Application Problems.

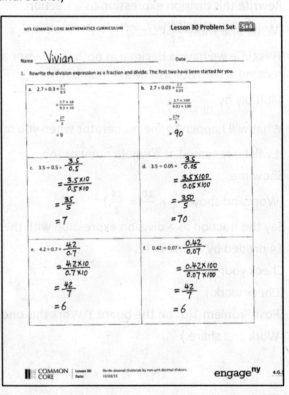

Student Debrief (10 minutes)

Lesson Objective: Divide decimal dividends by non-unit decimal divisors.

The Student Debrief is intended to invite reflection and active processing of the total lesson experience.

Invite students to review their solutions for the Problem Set. They should check work by comparing answers with a partner before going over answers as a class. Look for misconceptions or misunderstandings that can be addressed in the Debrief. Guide students in a conversation to debrief the Problem Set and process the lesson.

You may choose to use any combination of the questions below to lead the discussion.

- In Problem 1, what did you notice about the relationship between (a) and (b), (c) and (d), (e) and (f), (g) and (h), (i) and (j), and (k) and (l)?

- Share your explanation of Problem 2 with a partner.

- In Problem 3, what is the connection between (a) and (b)? How did you solve (b)? Did you solve it mentally or by re-calculating everything?

- Share and compare your solution for Problem 4 with a partner.

- How did you solve Problem 5? Did you use drawings to help you solve the problem? Share and compare your strategy with a partner.

- Use today's understanding to help you find the quotient of 0.08 ÷ 0.4.

Exit Ticket (3 minutes)

After the Student Debrief, instruct students to complete the Exit Ticket. A review of their work will help you assess the students' understanding of the concepts that were presented in the lesson today and plan more effectively for future lessons. You may read the questions aloud to the students.

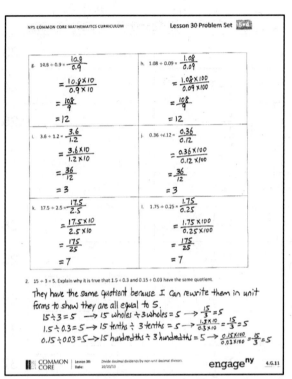

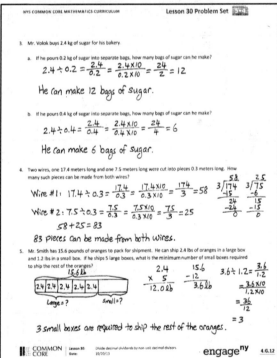

COMMON CORE™

Lesson 30:   Divide decimal dividends by non-unit decimal divisors.
Date: 11/10/13

4.G.78

A

Divide.

Correct _____

1	$\frac{1}{2} \div 2 =$		23	$4 \div \frac{1}{4} =$	
2	$\frac{1}{2} \div 3 =$		24	$\frac{1}{3} \div 3 =$	
3	$\frac{1}{2} \div 4 =$		25	$\frac{2}{3} \div 3 =$	
4	$\frac{1}{2} \div 7 =$		26	$\frac{1}{4} \div 2 =$	
5	$7 \div \frac{1}{2} =$		27	$\frac{3}{4} \div 2 =$	
6	$6 \div \frac{1}{2} =$		28	$\frac{1}{5} \div 2 =$	
7	$5 \div \frac{1}{2} =$		29	$\frac{3}{5} \div 2 =$	
8	$3 \div \frac{1}{2} =$		30	$\frac{1}{6} \div 2 =$	
9	$2 \div \frac{1}{5} =$		31	$\frac{5}{6} \div 2 =$	
10	$3 \div \frac{1}{5} =$		32	$\frac{5}{6} \div 3 =$	
11	$4 \div \frac{1}{5} =$		33	$\frac{1}{6} \div 3 =$	
12	$7 \div \frac{1}{5} =$		34	$3 \div \frac{1}{6} =$	
13	$\frac{1}{5} \div 7 =$		35	$6 \div \frac{1}{6} =$	
14	$\frac{1}{3} \div 2 =$		36	$7 \div \frac{1}{7} =$	
15	$2 \div \frac{1}{3} =$		37	$8 \div \frac{1}{8} =$	
16	$\frac{1}{4} \div 2 =$		38	$9 \div \frac{1}{9} =$	
17	$2 \div \frac{1}{4} =$		39	$\frac{1}{8} \div 7 =$	
18	$\frac{1}{5} \div 2 =$		40	$9 \div \frac{1}{8} =$	
19	$2 \div \frac{1}{5} =$		41	$\frac{1}{8} \div 7 =$	
20	$3 \div \frac{1}{4} =$		42	$7 \div \frac{1}{6} =$	
21	$\frac{1}{4} \div 3 =$		43	$9 \div \frac{1}{7} =$	
22	$\frac{1}{4} \div 4 =$		44	$\frac{1}{8} \div 9 =$	

COMMON CORE™ | **Lesson 30:** Divide decimal dividends by non-unit decimal divisors.
| **Date:** 11/10/13

4.G.

B   Improvement _____   # Correct _____

Divide.

1	$\frac{1}{2} \div 2 =$		23	$3 \div \frac{1}{3} =$	
2	$\frac{1}{5} \div 3 =$		24	$\frac{1}{4} \div 4 =$	
3	$\frac{1}{5} \div 4 =$		25	$\frac{3}{4} \div 4 =$	
4	$\frac{1}{5} \div 7 =$		26	$\frac{1}{3} \div 3 =$	
5	$7 \div \frac{1}{5} =$		27	$\frac{2}{3} \div 3 =$	
6	$6 \div \frac{1}{5} =$		28	$\frac{1}{6} \div 2 =$	
7	$5 \div \frac{1}{5} =$		29	$\frac{5}{6} \div 2 =$	
8	$3 \div \frac{1}{5} =$		30	$\frac{1}{5} \div 5 =$	
9	$2 \div \frac{1}{2} =$		31	$\frac{3}{5} \div 5 =$	
10	$3 \div \frac{1}{2} =$		32	$\frac{3}{5} \div 4 =$	
11	$4 \div \frac{1}{2} =$		33	$\frac{1}{5} \div 6 =$	
12	$7 \div \frac{1}{2} =$		34	$6 \div \frac{1}{5} =$	
13	$\frac{1}{2} \div 7 =$		35	$6 \div \frac{1}{4} =$	
14	$\frac{1}{4} \div 2 =$		36	$7 \div \frac{1}{6} =$	
15	$2 \div \frac{1}{4} =$		37	$8 \div \frac{1}{7} =$	
16	$\frac{1}{3} \div 2 =$		38	$9 \div \frac{1}{8} =$	
17	$2 \div \frac{1}{3} =$		39	$\frac{1}{8} \div 8 =$	
18	$\frac{1}{2} \div 2 =$		40	$9 \div \frac{1}{9} =$	
19	$2 \div \frac{1}{2} =$		41	$\frac{1}{9} \div 8 =$	
20	$4 \div \frac{1}{3} =$		42	$7 \div \frac{1}{7} =$	
21	$\frac{1}{3} \div 4 =$		43	$9 \div \frac{1}{6} =$	
22	$\frac{1}{3} \div 3 =$		44	$\frac{1}{8} \div 6 =$	

Lesson 30: Divide decimal dividends by non-unit decimal divisors.
Date: 11/10/13

4.G.80

Name _____ Date _____

1. Rewrite the division expression as a fraction, and divide. The first two have been started for you.

a. $2.7 \div 0.3 = \dfrac{2.7}{0.3}$ $\qquad = \dfrac{2.7 \times 10}{0.3 \times 10}$ $\qquad = \dfrac{27}{3}$ $\qquad = 9$	b. $2.7 \div 0.03 = \dfrac{2.7}{0.03}$ $\qquad = \dfrac{2.7 \times 100}{0.03 \times 100}$ $\qquad = \dfrac{270}{3}$ $\qquad =$
c. $3.5 \div 0.5 =$	d. $3.5 \div 0.05 =$
e. $4.2 \div 0.7 =$	f. $0.42 \div 0.07 =$

Lesson 30:	Divide decimal dividends by non-unit decimal divisors.
Date:	11/10/13

4.G.&

g. $10.8 \div 0.9 =$	h. $1.08 \div 0.09 =$
i. $3.6 \div 1.2 =$	j. $0.36 \div 0.12 =$
k. $17.5 \div 2.5 =$	l. $1.75 \div 0.25 =$

2. $15 \div 3 = 5$. Explain why it is true that $1.5 \div 0.3$ and $0.15 \div 0.03$ have the same quotient.

COMMON CORE™

Lesson 30:   Divide decimal dividends by non-unit decimal divisors.
Date: 11/10/13

4.G.82

3. Mr. Volok buys 2.4 kg of sugar for his bakery.

   a. If he pours 0.2 kg of sugar into separate bags, how many bags of sugar can he make?

   b. If he pours 0.4 kg of sugar into separate bags, how many bags of sugar can he make?

4. Two wires, one 17.4 meters long and one 7.5 meters long, were cut into pieces 0.3 meters long. How many such pieces can be made from both wires?

5. Mr. Smith has 15.6 pounds of oranges to pack for shipment. He can ship 2.4 lb of oranges in a large box and 1.2 lb in a small box. If he ships 5 large boxes, what is the minimum number of small boxes required to ship the rest of the oranges?

Name _____   Date _____

Rewrite the division expression as a fraction, and divide.

a. 3.2 ÷ 0.8 =	b. 3.2 ÷ 0.08 =
c. 7.2 ÷ 0.9 =	d. 0.72 ÷ 0.09 =

Lesson 30:   Divide decimal dividends by non-unit decimal divisors.
Date: 11/10/13

4.G.84

Name _____   Date _____

1. Rewrite the division expression as a fraction, and divide. The first two have been started for you.

a. $2.4 \div 0.8 = \dfrac{2.4}{0.8}$ $= \dfrac{2.4 \times 10}{0.8 \times 10}$ $= \dfrac{24}{8}$ $=$	b. $2.4 \div 0.08 = \dfrac{2.4}{0.08}$ $= \dfrac{2.4 \times 100}{0.08 \times 100}$ $= \dfrac{240}{8}$ $=$
c. $4.8 \div 0.6 =$	d. $0.48 \div 0.06 =$
e. $8.4 \div 0.7 =$	f. $0.84 \div 0.07 =$
g. $4.5 \div 1.5 =$	h. $0.45 \div 0.15 =$

Lesson 30: Divide decimal dividends by non-unit decimal divisors.
Date: 11/10/13

4.G.8

i. $14.4 \div 1.2 =$	j. $1.44 \div 0.12 =$

2. Leann says $18 \div 6 = 3$, so $1.8 \div 0.6 = 0.3$ and $0.18 \div 0.06 = 0.03$. Is Leann correct? How would you explain how to solve these division problems?

3. Denise is making bean bags. She has 6.4 pounds of beans.

   a. If she makes each bean bag 0.8 pounds, how many bean bags will she be able to make?

   b. If she decides instead to make mini bean bags that are half as heavy, how many can she make?

4. A restaurant's small salt shakers contain 0.6 ounces of salt. Its large shakers hold twice as much. The shakers are filled from a container that has 18.6 ounces of salt. If 8 large shakers are filled, how many small shakers can be filled with the remaining salt?

Lesson 30:	Divide decimal dividends by non-unit decimal divisors.
Date:	11/10/13

4.G.86

Lesson 31

Objective: Divide decimal dividends by non-unit decimal divisors.

Suggested Lesson Structure

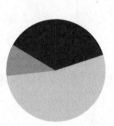

■ Fluency Practice   (12 minutes)
■ Application Problem   (6 minutes)
■ Concept Development   (32 minutes)
■ Student Debrief   (10 minutes)

Total Time   **(60 minutes)**

Fluency Practice (12 minutes)

▪ Multiply Decimals by 10 and 100 **5.NBT.1**   (4 minutes)
▪ Divide Decimals by 1 Tenth and 1 Hundredth **5.NBT.7**   (3 minutes)
▪ Divide Decimals **5.NBT.7**   (5 minutes)

Multiply Decimals by 10 and 100 (4 minutes)

Materials: (S) Personal white boards

Note: This fluency prepares students for G5–M4–Lesson 31.

   T: (Write 3 × 10 = _____.) Say the multiplication sentence.
   S: 3 × 10 = 30.
   T: (Write 3 × 10 = 30. Beneath it, write 20 × 10 = _____.) Say the multiplication sentence.
   S: 20 × 10 = 200.
   T: (Write 20 × 10 = 200. Beneath it, write 23 × 10 = _____.) Say the multiplication sentence.
   S: 23 × 10 = 230.
   T: (Write 2.3 × 10 = _____. Point to 2.3.) How many tenths is 2 and 3 tenths?
   S: 23 tenths.
   T: On your boards, write the multiplication sentence.
   S: (Write 2.3 × 10 = 23.)
   T: (Write 2.34 × 100 = _____. Point to 2.34.) How many hundredths is 2 and 34 hundredths?
   S: 234 hundredths.
   T: On your boards, write the multiplication sentence.
   S: (Write 2.34 × 100 = 234.)

COMMON CORE

Lesson 31:   Divide decimal dividends by non-unit decimal divisors.
Date: 11/9/13

4.G.8

T: (Write 23.4 × 10 = _____. Point to 23.4.) How many tenths is 23 and 4 tenths?

S: 234 tenths.

T: On your boards, write the multiplication sentence.

S: (Write 23.4 × 10 = 234.)

Continue this process with the following possible suggestions: 47.3 × 10, 4.73 × 100, 8.2 × 10, 38.2 × 10, and 6.17 × 100.

Divide Decimals by 1 Tenth and 1 Hundredth (3 minutes)

Materials: (S) Personal white boards

Note: This fluency reviews G5–M4–Lesson 29.

T: (Write 1 ÷ 0.1 = _____.) How many tenths are in 1?

S: 10.

T: 2?

S: 20.

T: 3?

S: 30.

T: 7?

S: 70.

T: (Write 10 ÷ 0.1.) On your boards, write the complete number sentence, answering how many tenths are in 10.

S: (Write 10 ÷ 0.1 = 100.)

T: (Write 20 ÷ 0.1.) If there are 100 tenths in 10, how many tenths are in 20?

S: 200.

T: 30?

S: 300.

T: 90?

S: 900.

T: (Write 65 ÷ 0.1.) On your boards, write the complete number sentence.

S: (Write 65 ÷ 0.1 = 650.)

T: (Write 65.2 ÷ 0.1.) Write the complete number sentence.

S: (Write 65.2 ÷ 0.1 = 652.)

T: (Write $0.08 ÷ 0.1 = \dfrac{}{100} ÷ \dfrac{}{10}$.) On your boards, complete the division sentence.

S: (Write $0.08 ÷ 0.1 = \dfrac{8}{100} ÷ \dfrac{1}{10}$.)

Continue this process with the following possible sequence: 0.36 ÷ 0.1, 3.6 ÷ 0.01, 36 ÷ 0.1, and 360 ÷ 0.01.

Lesson 31:   Divide decimal dividends by non-unit decimal divisors.
Date: 11/9/13

4.G.88

Divide Decimals (5 minutes)

Materials: (S) Personal white boards

Note: This fluency reviews G5–M4–Lessons 29–30.

T: (Write 15 ÷ 5 = _____.) Say the division sentence.

S: 15 ÷ 5 = 3.

T: (Write 15 ÷ 5 = 3. Beneath it, write 1.5 ÷ 0.5 = _____.) Say the division sentence in tenths.

S: 15 tenths ÷ 5 tenths.

T: Write 15 tenths ÷ 5 tenths as a fraction.

S: (Write $\frac{1.5}{0.5}$.)

T: (Beneath 1.5 ÷ 0.5, write $\frac{1.5 \times 10}{0.5 \times 10}$.) On your boards, rewrite the fraction using whole numbers.

S: (Write $\frac{1.5 \times 10}{0.5 \times 10}$. Beneath it, write $\frac{15}{5}$.)

T: (Beneath $\frac{1.5 \times 10}{0.5 \times 10}$, write $\frac{15}{5}$. Beneath it, write = _____.) Fill in your answer.

S: (Write = 3.)

$$1.5 \div 0.5 = 3$$

$$= \frac{1.5 \times 10}{0.5 \times 10}$$

$$= \frac{15}{5}$$

$$= 3$$

Continue this process with the following possible suggestions: 1.5 ÷ 0.05, 0.12 ÷ 0.3, 1.04 ÷ 4, 4.8 ÷ 1.2, and 0.48 ÷ 1.2.

Application Problem (6 minutes)

A café makes ten 8-ounce fruit smoothies. Each smoothie is made with 4 ounces of soy milk and 1.3 ounces of banana flavoring. The rest is blueberry juice. How much of each ingredient will be necessary to make the smoothies?

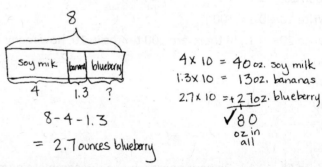

Note: This two-step problem requires decimal subtraction and multiplication, reviewing concepts from G5–Module 1. Some students will be comfortable performing these calculations mentally while others may need to sketch a quick visual model. Developing versatility with decimals by reviewing strategies for multiplying decimals serves as a quick warm-up for today's lesson.

	Lesson 31:	Divide decimal dividends by non-unit decimal divisors.
	Date:	11/9/13

4.G.8

Concept Development (32 minutes)

Materials: (S) Personal white boards

Problem 1:   a. **34.8 ÷ 0.6**   b. **7.36 ÷ 0.08**

T: (Post Problem 1 on the board.) Rewrite this division expression as a fraction.

S: (Work and show $\frac{34.8}{0.6}$.)

T: (Write = $\frac{34.8}{0.6}$.) How can we express the divisor as a whole number?

S: Multiply by a fraction equal to 1.

T: Tell a neighbor which fraction equal to 1 you'll use.

S: I could multiply by 5 fifths, which would make the divisor 3, but I'm not sure I want to multiply 34.8 by 5. That's not as easy. → If we multiply by 10 tenths, that would make both the numerator and the denominator whole numbers. → There are lots of choices. If I use 10 tenths, the digits will all stay the same—they will just move to a larger place value.

T: As always, we have many fractions equal to 1 that would create a whole number divisor. Which fraction would be most efficient?

S: 10 tenths.

T: (Write × $\frac{10}{10}$.) Multiply, then show me the equivalent fraction.

S: (Work and show $\frac{348}{6}$.)

T: (Write = $\frac{348}{6}$.) This isn't mental math like the basic facts we saw yesterday, so before we divide, let's estimate to give us an idea of a reasonable quotient. Think of a multiple of 6 that is close to 348 and divide. (Write ≈ _____ ÷ 6.) Turn and share your ideas with a partner.

S: I can round 348 to 360. → I can use mental math to divide 360 by 6 = 60.

T: (Fill in the blank to get ≈ 360 ÷ 6 = 60.) Now, use the division algorithm to find the actual quotient.

S: (Work.)

T: What is 34.8 ÷ 0.6? How many 6 tenths are in 34.8?

S: 58.

$$34.8 \div 0.6 = \frac{348}{0.6}$$

$$= \frac{34.8}{0.6} \times \frac{10}{10}$$

$$= \frac{348}{6} \qquad \approx 360 \div 6 = 60$$

$$= 58$$

$$\begin{array}{r} 58 \\ 6\overline{)348} \\ -30 \\ \hline 48 \\ -48 \\ \hline 0 \end{array}$$

NOTES ON MULTIPLE MEANS OF ENGAGEMENT:

Some students may require a refresher on the process of long division. This example dialogue might help:

T: Can we divide 3 hundreds by 6, or must we decompose?

S: We need to decompose.

T: Let's work with 34 tens then. What is 34 tens divided by 6?

S: 5 tens.

T: What is 5 tens times 6?

S: 30 tens.

T: How many tens remain?

S: 4 tens.

T: Can we divide 4 tens by 6?

S: Not without decomposing.

T: 4 tens is equal to 40 ones, plus the 8 ones in our whole makes 48 ones. What is 48 ones divided by 6?

S: 8 ones.

Lesson 31:   Divide decimal dividends by non-unit decimal divisors.
Date: 11/9/13

4.G.90

T: Is our quotient reasonable?

S: Yes, our estimate was 60.

T: (Post Problem 1(b), 7.36 ÷ 0.08, on the board.) Work with a partner to find the quotient. Remember to rename your fraction so that the denominator is a whole number.

S: (Work and share.)

T: What is 7.36 ÷ 0.08? How many 8 hundredths are in 7.36?

S: 92.

T: Is the quotient reasonable considering your estimate?

S: Yes, our estimate was 100. → We got an estimate of 90, so 92 is reasonable.

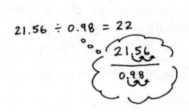

Problem 2:   a. 21.56 ÷ 0.98   b. 45.5 ÷ 0.7   c. 4.55 ÷ 0.7

T: (Post Problem 2(a) on the board.) Rewrite this division expression as a fraction.

S: (Work and show $\frac{21.56}{0.98}$.)

T: We know that before we divide, we'll want to rename the divisor as a whole number. Remind me how we'll do that.

S: Multiply the fraction by $\frac{100}{100}$.

T: Then, what would the fraction show after multiplying?

S: $\frac{2156}{98}$.

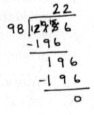

MP.7

T: In this case, both the divisor and the whole become 100 times greater. When we write the number that is 100 times as much, we must write the decimal two places to the…?

S: Right.

T: Rather than writing the multiplication sentence to show this, I'm going to record that thinking using arrows. (Draw a thought bubble around the fraction and use arrows to show the change in value of the divisor and whole.)

T: Is this fraction equivalent to the one we started with? Turn and talk.

S: It looks a little different, but it shows the fraction we got when we multiplied by 100 hundredths. It's equal. → Both the divisor and whole were multiplied by the same amount, so the two fractions are still equal.

T: Because it is an equal fraction, the division will give us the same quotient as dividing 21.56 by 0.98. Estimate 98.

S: 100.

Lesson 31:   Divide decimal dividends by non-unit decimal divisors.
Date: 11/9/13

4.G.9

T: (Write ≈ _____ ÷ 100.) Now estimate the whole, 2,156, as a number that we can easily divide by 100. Turn and talk.

S: 100 times 22 is 2,200. → 2,156 is between 21 hundreds and 22 hundreds. It's closer to 22 hundreds. I'll round to 2,200.

T: Record your estimated quotient, and then work with a partner to divide.

S: (Work and share.)

T: Say the quotient.

S: 22.

T: Is that reasonable?

S: Yes.

T: (Post Problem 2(b), 45.5 ÷ 0.7, on the board.) Rewrite this expression as a fraction and show a thought bubble as you rename the divisor as a whole number.

S: (Work and show $\frac{455}{7}$.)

T: Work independently to estimate, and then find the quotient. Check your work with a neighbor as you go.

S: (Work and share.)

T: (Check student work and discuss reasonableness of quotient. Post Problem 2(c), 4.55 ÷ 0.7, on the board.) Use a thought bubble to show this expression as a fraction with a whole number divisor.

S: (Work and show $\frac{45.5}{7}$.)

T: How is this problem similar to and different from the previous one? Turn and talk.

S: The digits are all the same, but the whole is smaller this time. → The whole still has a decimal point in it. → The whole is 1 tenth the size of the previous whole.

T: We still have a divisor of 7, but this time our whole is 45 and 5 tenths. Is the whole more than or less than it was in the previous problem?

S: Less than.

T: So, will the quotient be more than 65 or less than 65? Turn and talk.

S: Our whole is smaller, so we can make fewer groups of 7 from it. The quotient will be less than 65. → The whole is 1 tenth as large, so the quotient will be too.

T: Divide.

S: (Work.)

T: What is the quotient?

S: 6 and 5 tenths.

T: Does that make sense?

S: Yes.

NOTES ON MULTIPLE MEANS OF ACTION AND EXPRESSION:

Unit form is a powerful means of representing these dividends so that students can more easily see the multiples of the rounded divisor. Expressing 2,156 as 21 hundreds + 56 may allow students to estimate more accurately.

Similarly, students should be using easily identifiable multiples to find an estimated quotient. Remind students about the relationship between multiplication and division so they can think of the following division sentences as multiplication equations:

2,200 ÷ 100 = ___ → 100 × ___ = 2,200

490 ÷ 7 = ___ → 7 × ___ = 490

Problem Set (10 minutes)

Students should do their personal best to complete the Problem Set within the allotted 10 minutes. For some classes, it may be appropriate to modify the assignment by specifying which problems they work on first. Some problems do not specify a method for solving. Students solve these problems using the RDW approach used for Application Problems.

Student Debrief (10 minutes)

Lesson Objective: Divide decimal dividends by non-unit decimal divisors.

The Student Debrief is intended to invite reflection and active processing of the total lesson experience.

Invite students to review their solutions for the Problem Set. They should check work by comparing answers with a partner before going over answers as a class. Look for misconceptions or misunderstandings that can be addressed in the Debrief. Guide students in a conversation to debrief the Problem Set and process the lesson.

You may choose to use any combination of the questions below to lead the discussion.

- Look at the example in Problem 1. What is another way to estimate the quotient? (Students could say 78 divided by 1 is equal to 78.) Compare the two estimated sentences, 770 ÷ 7 = 110 and 78 ÷ 7 = 78. Why is the actual quotient equal to 112? Does it make sense?

- In Problems 1(a) and 1(b), is your actual quotient close to your estimated quotients?

- In Problems 2(a) and 2(b), is your actual quotient close to your estimated quotients?

- How did you solve Problem 4? Share and explain your strategy to a partner.

- How did you solve Problem 5? Did you draw a tape diagram to help you solve? Share and compare your strategy with a partner.

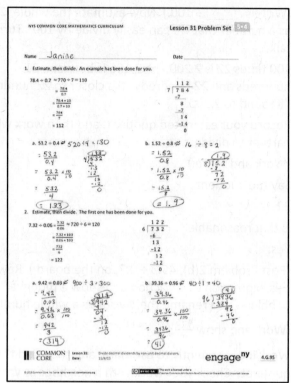

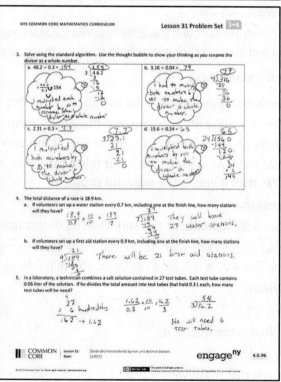

4.G.94

Exit Ticket (3 minutes)

After the Student Debrief, instruct students to complete the Exit Ticket. A review of their work will help you assess the students' understanding of the concepts that were presented in the lesson today and plan more effectively for future lessons. You may read the questions aloud to the students.

Name _____   Date _____

1. Estimate, then divide. An example has been done for you.

$78.4 \div 0.7 \approx 770 \div 7 = 110$

$$= \frac{78.4}{0.7}$$

$$= \frac{78.4 \times 10}{0.7 \times 10}$$

$$= \frac{784}{7}$$

$$= 112$$

```
        1 1 2
    7 | 7 8 4
       -7
        8
       -7
        1 4
       -1 4
          0
```

   a. $53.2 \div 0.4 =$

   b. $1.52 \div 0.8 =$

2. Estimate, then divide. The first one has been done for you.

$7.32 \div 0.06 = \frac{7.32}{0.06} \approx 720 \div 6 = 120$

$$= \frac{7.32 \times 100}{0.06 \times 100}$$

$$= \frac{732}{6}$$

$$= 122$$

```
        1 2 2
    6 | 7 3 2
       -6
        1 3
       -1 2
          1 2
         -1 2
            0
```

   a. $9.42 \div 0.03 =$

   b. $39.36 \div 0.96 =$

COMMON CORE | Lesson 31: | Divide decimal dividends by non-unit decimal divisors.

Date: 11/9/13

4.G.9

3. Solve using the standard algorithm. Use the thought bubble to show your thinking as you rename the divisor as a whole number.

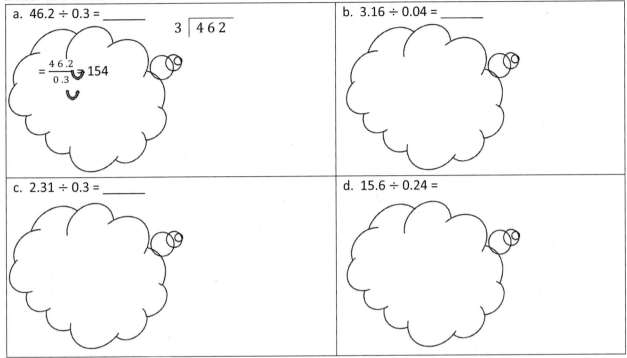

a. 46.2 ÷ 0.3 = _____

3 | 4 6 2

= $\frac{46.2}{0.3}$ → 154

b. 3.16 ÷ 0.04 = _____

c. 2.31 ÷ 0.3 = _____

d. 15.6 ÷ 0.24 =

4. The total distance of a race is 18.9 km.
   a. If volunteers set up a water station every 0.7 km, including one at the finish line, how many stations will they have?

   b. If volunteers set up a first aid station every 0.9 km, including one at the finish line, how many stations will they have?

5. In a laboratory, a technician combines a salt solution contained in 27 test tubes. Each test tube contains 0.06 liter of the solution. If he divides the total amount into test tubes that hold 0.3 liter each, how many test tubes will he need?

COMMON CORE™

Lesson 31: Divide decimal dividends by non-unit decimal divisors.
Date: 11/9/13

4.G.96

Name _____ Date _____

Estimate first, and then solve using the standard algorithm.   Show how you rename the divisor as a whole number.

1. $6.39 \div 0.09$

2. $82.14 \div 0.6$

Name _____   Date _____

1. Estimate, then divide. An example has been done for you.

$78.4 \div 0.7 \approx 770 \div 7 = 110$

$= \dfrac{78.4}{0.7}$

$= \dfrac{78.4 \times 10}{0.7 \times 10}$

$= \dfrac{784}{7}$

$= 112$

```
        1 1 2
    7 | 7 8 4
       -7
        8
       -7
        1 4
       -1 4
          0
```

a. $61.6 \div 0.8 =$

b. $5.74 \div 0.7 =$

2. Estimate, then divide. An example has been done for you.

$7.32 \div 0.06 = \dfrac{7.32}{0.06} \approx 720 \div 6 = 120$

$= \dfrac{7.32 \times 100}{0.06 \times 100}$

$= \dfrac{732}{6}$

$= 122$

```
        1 2 2
    6 | 7 3 2
       -6
        1 3
       -1 2
         1 2
        -1 2
          0
```

a. $4.74 \div 0.06 =$

b. $19.44 \div 0.54 =$

COMMON CORE™

Lesson 31:   Divide decimal dividends by non-unit decimal divisors.
Date: 11/9/13

4.G.98

3. Solve using the standard algorithm. Use the thought bubble to show your thinking as you rename the divisor as a whole number.

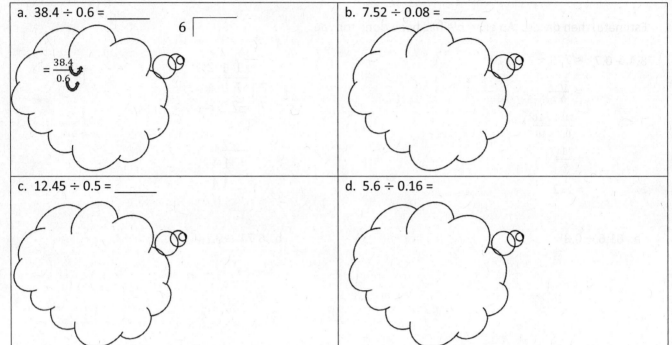

a. 38.4 ÷ 0.6 = _____

$= \dfrac{38.4}{0.6}$

6 |‾‾‾‾‾‾

b. 7.52 ÷ 0.08 = _____

c. 12.45 ÷ 0.5 = _____

d. 5.6 ÷ 0.16 =

4. Lucia is making a 21.6 centimeter beaded string to hang in the window. She decides to put a green bead every 0.4 centimeters and a purple bead every 0.6 centimeters. How many green beads and how many purple beads will she need?

5. A group of 14 friends collects 0.7 pound of blueberries and decides to make blueberry muffins. They put 0.05 pound of berries in each muffin. How many muffins can they make if they use all the blueberries they collected?

Topic H

Interpretation of Numerical Expressions

5.OA.1, 5.OA.2

Focus Standard:	5.OA.1	Use parentheses, brackets, or braces in numerical expressions, and evaluate expressions with these symbols.
	5.OA.2	Write simple expressions that record calculations with numbers, and interpret numerical expressions without evaluating them. *For example, express the calculation "add 8 and 7, then multiply by 2" as 2 × (8 +7). Recognize that 3 × (18932 + 921) is three times as large as 18932 + 921, without having to calculate the indicated sum or product.*
Instructional Days:	2	
Coherence -Links from:	G4–M5	Fraction Equivalence, Ordering, and Operations
	G5–M2	Multi-Digit Whole Number and Decimal Fraction Operations
-Links to:	G6–M2	Arithmetic Operations Including Division by a Fraction
	G6–M4	Expressions and Operations.

The module concludes with Topic H, in which numerical expressions involving fraction-by-fraction multiplication are interpreted and evaluated (**5.OA.1**, **5.OA.2**). Students create and solve word problems involving both multiplication and division of fractions and decimal fractions.

A Teaching Sequence Towards Mastery of Interpretation of Numerical Expressions
Objective 1: Interpret and evaluate numerical expressions including the language of scaling and fraction division. (Lesson 32)
Objective 2: Create story contexts for numerical expressions and tape diagrams, and solve word problems. (Lesson 33)

Lesson 32

Objective: Interpret and evaluate numerical expressions including the language of scaling and fraction division.

Suggested Lesson Structure

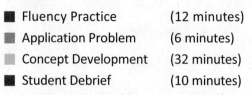

- ■ Fluency Practice   (12 minutes)
- ■ Application Problem   (6 minutes)
- ■ Concept Development   (32 minutes)
- ■ Student Debrief   (10 minutes)
  - **Total Time**   **(60 minutes)**

Fluency Practice (12 minutes)

- Order of Operations **5.OA.1**   (3 minutes)
- Divide Decimals by 1 Tenth and 1 Hundredth **5.NBT.7**   (3 minutes)
- Divide Decimals **5.NBT.7**   (6 minutes)

Order of Operations (3 minutes)

Materials: (S) Personal white boards

Note: This fluency prepares students for today's lesson.

T: (Write $12 \div 3 + 1$.) On your boards, write the complete number sentence.
S: (Write $12 \div 3 + 1 = 5$.)
T: (Write $12 \div (3 + 1)$.) On your boards, copy the expression.
S: (Write $12 \div (3 + 1)$.)
T: Write the complete number sentence, performing the operation inside the parentheses.
S: (Beneath $12 \div (3 + 1) = $ ____, write $12 \div 4 = 3$.)

Continue this process with the following possible suggestions: $20 - 4 \div 2$, $(20 - 4) \div 2$, $24 \div 6 - 2$, and $24 \div (6 - 2)$.

Divide Decimals by 1 Tenth and 1 Hundredth (3 minutes)

Materials: (S) Personal white boards

Note: This fluency reviews G5–M4–Lesson 29.

T: (Write $1 \div 0.1$.) How many tenths are in 1?

COMMON CORE | Lesson 32:   Interpret and evaluate numerical expressions including the language of scaling and fraction division.
    Date: 11/10/13

    4.H.2

S: 10.

T: 2?

S: 20.

T: 3?

S: 30.

T: 6?

S: 60.

T: (Write 10 ÷ 0.1.) On your boards, write the complete number sentence answering how many tenths are in 10.

S: (Write 10 ÷ 0.1 = 100.)

T: (Write 20 ÷ 0.1 = _____.) If there are 100 tenths in 10, how many tenths are in 20?

S: 200.

T: 30?

S: 300.

T: 80?

S: 800.

T: (Write 43 ÷ 0.1.) On your boards, write the complete number sentence.

S: (Write 43 ÷ 0.1 = 430.)

T: (Write 43.5 ÷ 0.1= _____.) Write the complete number sentence.

S: (Write 43.5 ÷ 0.1 = 435.)

T: (Write $0.04 ÷ 0.1 = \frac{}{100} ÷ \frac{}{10}$.) On your boards, complete the division sentence.

S: (Write $0.04 ÷ 0.1 = ÷ \frac{1}{10}$.)

Continue this process with the following possible sequence: 0.97 ÷ 0.1, 9.7 ÷ 0.01, 97 ÷ 0.1, and 970 ÷ 0.01.

Divide Decimals (6 minutes)

Materials: (S) Personal white boards

Note: This fluency reviews G5–M4–Lessons 29–30.

T: (Write $\frac{8}{2}$ = _____.) Say the division sentence.

S: 8 ÷ 2 = 4.

T: (Write $\frac{8}{2}$ = 4. Beneath it, write $\frac{0.8}{0.2}$ = _____.) What is 8 tenths ÷ 2 tenths?

S: 4.

T: On your boards, complete the division sentence.

S: (Write 0.8 ÷ 0.02 = 40.)

Continue this process with 12 ÷ 3, 1.2 ÷ 0.3, 1.2 ÷ 0.03, and 12 ÷ 0.3.

Lesson 32:   Interpret and evaluate numerical expressions including the
language of scaling and fraction division.   4.H.3
Date: 11/10/13

T: (Write 23.84 ÷ 0.2 = ____.) On your boards, write the division sentence as a fraction.

S: (Write $\frac{23.84}{0.2}$.)

T: (Beneath 23.8 ÷ 0.2 = ____, write = $\frac{23.84}{0.2}$.) What do we need to multiply the divisor by to make it a whole number?

S: 10.

T: Multiply your numerator and denominator by 10.

S: (Write $\frac{23.84 \times 10}{0.2 \times 10}$.)

T: (Write $\frac{23.84 \times 10}{0.2 \times 10}$. Use the standard algorithm to solve, then write your answer.

S: (Write 23.8 ÷ 0.2 = 119.2 after solving.)

Continue this process with 5.76 ÷ 0.4, 9.54 ÷ 0.03, and 98.4 ÷ 0.12.

Application Problem (6 minutes)

Four baby socks can be made from $\frac{1}{3}$ skein of yarn. How many baby socks can be made from a whole skein? Draw a number line to show your thinking.

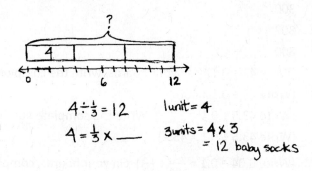

Note: This problem is a partitive fraction division problem intended to give students more experience with this interpretation of division.

Concept Development (32 minutes)

Materials: (S) Personal white boards

Problem 1

Write word form expressions numerically.

a. Twice the sum of $\frac{3}{5}$ and $1\frac{1}{2}$.

b. Half the sum of $\frac{3}{5}$ and $1\frac{1}{2}$.

c. The difference between $\frac{3}{4}$ and $\frac{1}{2}$ divided by 3.

T: (Post Problem 1(a) on the board.) Read the expression aloud with me.

S: (Read.)

T: What do you notice about this expression that would help us translate these words into symbols? Turn and talk.

S: It says *twice*; that means we have to make two copies of something or multiply by 2. → It says *the*

NOTES ON MULTIPLE MEANS OF REPRESENTATION:

The complexity of language in the word form expressions may pose challenges for English language learners. Consider drawing tape diagrams for each expression. Then, have students match each expression to its tape diagram before writing the numerical expression.

Lesson 32: Interpret and evaluate numerical expressions including the language of scaling and fraction division.

Date: 11/10/13

4.H.

sum of, so something is being added. → The part that says *sum of* needs to be added before the multiplying, so we'll need parentheses.

T: Let's take a look at the first part of the expression. Show me on your personal boards how can we write *twice* numerically?

S: (Write 2 ×.)

T: (Write 2 × _____ on the board.) Great, what is being multiplied by 2?

S: The sum of 3 fifths and 1 and one-half.

T: Show me the sum of 3 fifths and 1 and one-half numerically.

S: (Write $\frac{3}{5} + 1\frac{1}{2}$.)

T: (Write $\frac{3}{5} + 1\frac{1}{2}$ in the blank.) Are we finished?
Turn and talk.

$$2 \times \left(\tfrac{3}{5} + 1\tfrac{1}{2}\right) \qquad \left(\tfrac{3}{5} + 1\tfrac{1}{2}\right) \times 2$$

S: (Share.)

T: What else is needed?

S: Parentheses.

T: Why? Turn and talk.

S: You have to have parentheses around the addition expression so that the addition is done before the multiplication. If you don't, the answer will be $\frac{6}{5} + 1\frac{1}{2}$. → Because otherwise, you just go left to right and multiply first.

T: (Draw parentheses around the addition expression.) Work with a partner to find another way to write this expression numerically.

S: (Work and show $(\frac{3}{5} + 1\frac{1}{2}) \times 2$.)

T: (Post Problem 1(b), *half the sum of $\frac{3}{5}$ and $1\frac{1}{2}$*, on the board.) Read this expression out loud with me.

S: (Read.)

T: Compare this expression to the other one. Turn and talk.

S: (Share.)

T: Without evaluating this expression, will the value of this expression be more than or less than the previous one? Turn and talk.

NOTES ON MULTIPLE MEANS OF REPRESENTATION:

Due to the commutativity of addition and multiplication, there are multiple ways of writing expressions involving these operations. Have students be creative and experiment with their expressions. Be cautious, though, that students do not overgeneralize this property and try to apply it to subtraction and division.

S: It's less. The other one multiplied the sum by 2, and this one is one-half of the same sum. → Taking half of a number is less than doubling it.

T: This expression again includes the sum of 3 fifths and 1 and one-half. (Write $\frac{3}{5} + 1\frac{1}{2}$ on the board.) We need to show one-half of it. Tell a neighbor how we can show one-half of this expression.

S: We can multiply it by $\frac{1}{2}$. → We can show $\frac{1}{2}$ times the addition expression, or we can show the addition expression times $\frac{1}{2}$. → Taking a half of something is the same as dividing it by 2, so we could

Lesson 32:   Interpret and evaluate numerical expressions including the
language of scaling and fraction division.
Date: 11/10/13
        4.H.5

divide the addition expression by 2. → We could divide the addition expression by 2, but write it like a fraction with 2 as the denominator.

T: Work with a partner to write this expression numerically in at least two different ways.

S: (Work and share.)

T: (Select students to share their work and explain their thought process.)

Possible student responses:

$$\frac{1}{2} \times \left(\frac{3}{5} + 1\frac{1}{2}\right) \qquad \left(\frac{3}{5} + 1\frac{1}{2}\right) \times \frac{1}{2} \qquad \frac{\frac{3}{5} + 1\frac{1}{2}}{2} \qquad \left(\frac{3}{5} + 1\frac{1}{2}\right) \div 2$$

T: (Post Problem 1(c), *the difference between $\frac{3}{4}$ and $\frac{1}{2}$ divided by 3,* on board.) Read this expression aloud with me.

S: (Read.)

T: Talk with a neighbor about what is happening in this expression.

S: *Difference* means subtract, so one-fourth is being subtracted from 10. → The last part says *divided by 3,* so we can put parentheses around the subtraction expression and then write ÷ 3. → Since it says *divided by 3,* we can write that like a fraction with 3 as the denominator. → Dividing by 3 is the same as taking a third of something, so we can multiply the subtraction expression by $\frac{1}{3}$.

T: Work independently to write this expression numerically. Share your work with a neighbor when you're finished.

S: (Work and share.)

Possible student responses:

$$\left(\frac{3}{4} - \frac{1}{2}\right) \div 3 \qquad\qquad \frac{\frac{3}{4} - \frac{1}{2}}{3} \qquad\qquad \left(\frac{3}{4} - \frac{1}{2}\right) \times \frac{1}{3}$$

T: Look at your numerical expression. Let's evaluate it. Let's put this expression in its simplest form. What is the first step?

S: Subtract one-half from 3 fourths.

T: Why must we do that first?

S: Because it is in parentheses. → Because we need to evaluate the numerator before dividing by 3.

T: Work with a partner, then show me the difference between 3 fourths and one-half.

S: (Work and show $\frac{1}{4}$.)

T: Since we wrote our numerical expressions in different ways, tell your partner what your next step will be in evaluating your expression.

S: I need to multiply one-fourth times one-third. → I need to divide one-fourth by 3.

T: Complete the next step and then share your work with a partner.

Lesson 32:   Interpret and evaluate numerical expressions including the
language of scaling and fraction division.
Date: 11/10/13

4.H.

S: (Work and share.)

T: What is this expression equal to in simplest form?

S: 1 twelfth.

T: Everyone got 1 twelfth?

S: Yes!

T: What does that show us about the different ways to write these expressions? Turn and talk.

S: (Share.)

Problem 2

Write numerical expressions in word form.

    a. $\frac{2}{5} \times \left(\frac{1}{2} - 0.4\right)$ b. $\left(\frac{3}{4} + 1.25\right) \div \frac{1}{3}$ c. $\left(2 \div \frac{1}{5}\right) \times 0.3$

T: (Post Problem 2(a) on the board.) Now we'll rewrite a numerical expression in word form. What is happening in this expression? Turn and talk.

S: In parentheses, there's the difference between one-half and 4 tenths. → The subtraction expression is being multiplied by 2 fifths.

T: Show me a word form expression for the operation outside the parentheses.

S: (Show $\frac{2}{5}$ times.)

T: (Write $\frac{2}{5} \times$ _____ on the board.) We have 2 fifths times what?

S: The difference between one-half and 4 tenths.

T: Exactly! (Write *the difference between* $\frac{1}{2}$ *and 0.4* in the blank, then post Problem 2(b) on the board.) Work with a partner to write this expression using words.

S: (Work and show, *the sum of* $\frac{3}{4}$ *and 1.25 divided by* $\frac{1}{3}$.)

T: Let's evaluate the numerical expression. What must we do first?

S: Add $\frac{3}{4}$ and 1.25.

T: Work with a partner to find the sum in its simplest form.

S: (Work and show 2.)

T: What's the next step?

S: Divide 2 by one-third.

T: How many thirds are in 1 whole?

S: 3.

T: How many are in 2 wholes?

S: 6.

T: (Post Problem 2(c) on the board.) Work independently to rewrite this expression using words. If you finish early, evaluate the expression. Check your work with a partner when you're both ready.

S: (Work and share.)

Lesson 32:   Interpret and evaluate numerical expressions including the language of scaling and fraction division.

Date: 11/10/13

4.H.7

Problem Set (10 minutes)

Students should do their personal best to complete the Problem Set within the allotted 10 minutes. For some classes, it may be appropriate to modify the assignment by specifying which problems they work on first. Some problems do not specify a method for solving. Students solve these problems using the RDW approach used for Application Problems.

Student Debrief (10 minutes)

Lesson Objective: Interpret and evaluate numerical expressions including the language of scaling and fraction division.

The Student Debrief is intended to invite reflection and active processing of the total lesson experience.

Invite students to review their solutions for the Problem Set. They should check work by comparing answers with a partner before going over answers as a class. Look for misconceptions or misunderstandings that can be addressed in the Debrief. Guide students in a conversation to debrief the Problem Set and process the lesson.

You may choose to use any combination of the questions below to lead the discussion.

- For Problems 1 and 2, explain to a partner how you chose the correct equivalent expression(s).

- Compare your answer for Problem 3 with a partner. Is there more than one correct answer?

- What's the relationship between Problems 5(a) and 5(c)?

- Share and compare your solutions for Problem 7 with a partner. Be care with the order of operations; calculate the parenthesis first.

- Share and compare your answers for Problem 8 with a partner. For the two expressions that did not match the story problems, can you think of a story problem for them? Share your ideas with a partner.

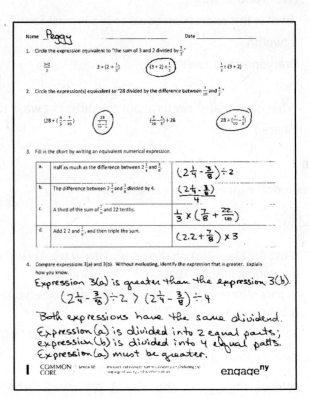

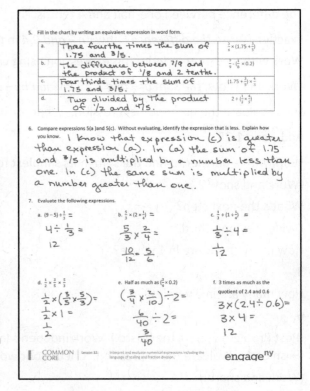

Lesson 32: Interpret and evaluate numerical expressions including the language of scaling and fraction division.

Date: 11/10/13

4.H.8

Exit Ticket (3 minutes)

After the Student Debrief, instruct students to complete the Exit Ticket. A review of their work will help you assess the students' understanding of the concepts that were presented in the lesson today and plan more effectively for future lessons. You may read the questions aloud to the students.

a. Farmer Green picked 20 carrots. He cooked $\frac{2}{3}$ of them and then gave 5 to his rabbits. Write the expression that tells how many carrots he had left.

Expression: $\left(\frac{2}{3} \times 20\right) - 5$

b. Farmer Green picked 20 carrots. He cooked 5 of them and then gave $\frac{2}{3}$ to his rabbits. Write the expression that tells how many carrots the rabbits will get.

Expression: $\frac{2}{3} \times (20 - 5)$

COMMON CORE   Lesson 32: Interpret and evaluate numerical expressions including the language of scaling and fraction division.
Date: 10/19/13

engage^ny   4.H.10

COMMON CORE™   Lesson 32:   Interpret and evaluate numerical expressions including the language of scaling and fraction division.
Date: 11/10/13

4.H.9

Name _____ Date _____

1. Circle the expression equivalent to "the sum of 3 and 2 divided by $\frac{1}{3}$."

$$\frac{3+2}{3} \qquad\qquad 3 + (2 \div \frac{1}{3}) \qquad\qquad (3 + 2) \div \frac{1}{3} \qquad\qquad \frac{1}{3} \div (3 + 2)$$

2. Circle the expression(s) equivalent to "28 divided by the difference between $\frac{7}{10}$ and $\frac{4}{5}$."

$$(28 \div (\frac{4}{5} - \frac{7}{10})) \qquad \frac{28}{\frac{7}{10} - \frac{4}{5}} \qquad (\frac{7}{10} - \frac{4}{5}) \div 28 \qquad 28 \div (\frac{7}{10} - \frac{4}{5})$$

3. Fill in the chart by writing an equivalent numerical expression.

a.	Half as much as the difference between $2\frac{1}{4}$ and $\frac{3}{8}$.	
b.	The difference between $2\frac{1}{4}$ and $\frac{3}{8}$ divided by 4.	
c.	A third of the sum of $\frac{7}{8}$ and 22 tenths.	
d.	Add 2.2 and $\frac{7}{8}$, and then triple the sum.	

4. Compare expressions 3(a) and 3(b). Without evaluating, identify the expression that is greater. Explain how you know.

COMMON CORE™ | **Lesson 32:** Interpret and evaluate numerical expressions including the language of scaling and fraction division.
Date: 11/10/13

4.H.

5. Fill in the chart by writing an equivalent expression in word form.

a.		$\frac{3}{4} \times (1.75 + \frac{3}{5})$
b.		$\frac{7}{9} - (\frac{1}{8} \times 0.2)$
c.		$(1.75 + \frac{3}{5}) \times \frac{4}{3}$
d.		$2 \div (\frac{1}{2} \times \frac{4}{5})$

6. Compare the expressions in 5(a) and 5(c). Without evaluating, identify the expression that is less. Explain how you know.

7. Evaluate the following expressions.

a. $(9-5) \div \frac{1}{3}$

b. $\frac{5}{3} \times (2 \times \frac{1}{4})$

c. $\frac{1}{3} \div (1 \div \frac{1}{4})$

d. $\frac{1}{2} \times \frac{3}{5} \times \frac{5}{3}$

e. Half as much as $(\frac{3}{4} \times 0.2)$

f. 3 times as much as the quotient of 2.4 and 0.6

COMMON
CORE™

Lesson 32:   Interpret and evaluate numerical expressions including the
language of scaling and fraction division.
Date: 11/10/13

4.H.11

8. Choose an expression below that matches the story problem, and write it in the blank.

$\frac{2}{3} \times (20 - 5)$ $(\frac{2}{3} \times 20) - (\frac{2}{3} \times 5)$ $\frac{2}{3} \times 20 - 5$ $(20 - \frac{2}{3}) - 5$

a. Farmer Green picked 20 carrots. He cooked $\frac{2}{3}$ of them and then gave 5 to his rabbits. Write the expression that tells how many carrots he had left.

Expression: _____

b. Farmer Green picked 20 carrots. He cooked 5 of them and then gave $\frac{2}{3}$ to his rabbits. Write the expression that tells how many carrots the rabbits will get.

Expression: _____

COMMON CORE™   **Lesson 32:**   Interpret and evaluate numerical expressions including the language of scaling and fraction division.

Date: 11/10/13

4.H.1

Name _____ Date _____

1. Write an equivalent expression in numerical form.

   A fourth as much as the product of two-thirds and 0.8

2. Write an equivalent expression in word form.

   a. $\frac{3}{8} \times (1 - \frac{1}{3})$

   b. $(1 - \frac{1}{3}) \div 2$

3. Compare the expressions in 2(a) and 2(b). Without evaluating, determine which expression is greater, and explain how you know.

Name _____   Date _____

1. Circle the expression equivalent to "the difference between 7 and 4, divided by a fifth."

$7 + (4 \div \frac{1}{5})$ $\qquad$ $\frac{7-4}{5}$ $\qquad$ $(7 - 4) \div \frac{1}{5}$ $\qquad$ $\frac{1}{5} \div (7 - 4)$

2. Circle the expression(s) equivalent to "42 divided by the sum of $\frac{2}{3}$ and $\frac{3}{4}$."

$(\frac{2}{3} + \frac{3}{4}) \div 42$ $\qquad$ $(42 \div \frac{2}{3}) + \frac{3}{4}$ $\qquad$ $42 \div (\frac{2}{3} + \frac{3}{4})$ $\qquad$ $\frac{42}{\frac{2}{3} + \frac{3}{4}}$

3. Fill in the chart by writing the equivalent numerical expression or expression in word form.

	Expression in word form	Numerical expression
a.	A fourth as much as the sum of $3\frac{1}{8}$ and 4.5	
b.		$(3\frac{1}{8} + 4.5) \div 5$
c.	Multiply $\frac{3}{5}$ by 5.8, then halve the product	
d.		$\frac{1}{6} \times (4.8 - \frac{1}{2})$
e.		$8 - (\frac{1}{2} \div 9)$

4. Compare the expressions in 3(a) and 3(b). Without evaluating, identify the expression that is greater. Explain how you know.

COMMON CORE™

Lesson 32:   Interpret and evaluate numerical expressions including the language of scaling and fraction division.

Date: 11/10/13

4.H.

© 2013 Common Core, Inc. All rights reserved. commoncore.org

5. Evaluate the following expressions.

a. $(11 - 6) \div \frac{1}{6}$

b. $\frac{9}{5} \times (4 \times \frac{1}{6})$

c. $\frac{1}{10} \div (5 \div \frac{1}{2})$

d. $\frac{3}{4} \times \frac{2}{5} \times \frac{4}{3}$

e. 50 divided by the difference between $\frac{3}{4}$ and $\frac{5}{8}$

6. Lee is sending out 32 birthday party invitations. She gives 5 invitations to her mom to give to family members. Lee mails a third of the rest, and then she takes a break to walk her dog.

a. Write a numerical expression to describe how many invitations Lee has already mailed.

b. Which expression matches how many invitations still need to be sent out?

$32 - 5 - \frac{1}{3}(32 - 5)$ $\frac{2}{3} \times 32 - 5$ $(32 - 5) \div \frac{1}{3}$ $\frac{1}{3} \times (32 - 5)$

COMMON CORE™   Lesson 32:   Interpret and evaluate numerical expressions including the language of scaling and fraction division.   4.H.15

Date: 11/10/13

Lesson 33

Objective: Create story contexts for numerical expressions and tape diagrams, and solve word problems.

Suggested Lesson Structure

■ Fluency Practice   (12 minutes)
■ Concept Development   (38 minutes)
■ Student Debrief   (10 minutes)
  Total Time   **(60 minutes)**

Fluency Practice (12 minutes)

▪ Sprint: Divide Decimals **5.NBT.7**   (9 minutes)
▪ Write Equivalent Expressions **5.OA.1**   (3 minutes)

Sprint: Divide Decimals (9 minutes)

Materials: (S) Divide Decimals Sprint

Note: This fluency reviews G5–M4–Lessons 29–32.

Write Equivalent Expressions (3 minutes)

Materials: (S) Personal white boards

Note: This fluency reviews G5–M4–Lesson 32.

   T: (Write $2 \div \frac{1}{3} =$ _____.) What is $2 \div \frac{1}{3}$?

   S: 6.

   T: (Write $2 \div \frac{1}{3} + 4$.) On your boards, write the complete number sentence.

   S: (Write $2 \div \frac{1}{3} + 4$. Beneath it, write $= 6 + 4$. Beneath it, write $= 10$.)

Continue this process with the following possible suggestions: $\frac{5+3}{5}$, $\frac{1}{3} \div (2 + 2)$, $(4 + 3) \div \frac{1}{4}$, and $(\frac{2}{5} - \frac{3}{10}) \div 5$.

Lesson 33:	Create story contexts for numerical expressions and tape diagrams, and solve word problems.
Date:	11/10/13

4.H.

Concept Development (38 minutes)

Materials: (S) Problem Set

Note: The time normally allotted for the Application Problem has been included in the Concept Development portion of today's lesson in order to give students the time necessary to write story problems.

Suggested Delivery of Instruction for Solving Lesson 32's Word Problems

1. Model the problem.

Have two pairs of student work at the board while the others work independently or in pairs at their seats. Review the following questions before beginning the first problem:

- Can you draw something?
- What can you draw?
- What conclusions can you make from your drawing?

As students work, circulate. Reiterate the questions above. After two minutes, have the two pairs of students share only their labeled diagrams. For about one minute, have the demonstrating students receive and respond to feedback and questions from their peers.

2. Calculate to solve and write a statement.

Give everyone two minutes to finish work on that question, sharing their work and thinking with a peer. All should write their equations and statements of the answer.

3. Assess the solution for reasonableness.

Give students one to two minutes to assess and explain the reasonableness of their solution.

**NOTES ON
MULTIPLE MEANS OF
ENGAGEMENT:**

When selecting students to work at the board, teachers typically choose their top students to model their thinking. Consider asking students who may struggle to work at the board, being sure to support them as necessary but also praising their effort and perseverance as they work. This approach can help improve the classroom climate and reinforce the notion that math work is often more about determination and persistence than it is sheer math skill.

Problem 1

Ms. Hayes has $\frac{1}{2}$ liter of juice. She distributes it equally to 6 students in her tutoring group.

a. How many liters of juice does each student get?

b. How many more liters of juice will Ms. Hayes need if she wants to give each of the 24 students in her class the same amount of juice found in Part (a)?

Lesson 33:	Create story contexts for numerical expressions and tape diagrams, and solve word problems.	4.H.17
Date:	11/10/13	

1a) $\frac{1}{2}$ liter ÷ 6

= 1 half ÷ 6

= 6 twelfths ÷ 6

= 1 twelfth

Each student gets $\frac{1}{12}$ liter of juice.

1b) $24 \times \frac{1}{12}\ell$

= $\frac{24 \times 1}{1 \times 12}\ell$

= 2ℓ

2ℓ of juice needed for 24 students

$2\ell - \frac{1}{2}\ell = 1\frac{1}{2}\ell$

Ms. Hayes will need $1\frac{1}{2}\ell$ more.

In this problem, Ms. Hayes is sharing equally, or dividing, one-half liter of juice among six students. Students should recognize this problem as $\frac{1}{2} \div 6$. A tape diagram shows that when halves are partitioned into 6 equal parts, twelfths are created. Likewise, the diagram shows that 1 half is equal to 6 twelfths, and when written in unit form, 6 twelfths divided by 6 is a simple problem. Each student gets one-twelfth liter of juice. In Part (b), students must find how much more juice is necessary to give a total of 24 students $\frac{1}{12}$ liter of juice. Some students may choose to solve by multiplying 24 by one-twelfth to find that a total of 2 liters of juice is necessary. Encourage interpretation as a scaling problem. Help students see that since 24 students is 4 times more students than 6, Ms. Hayes will need 4 times more juice as well. Four times one-half is, again, equal to 2 liters of juice. Either way, Ms. Hayes will need $1\frac{1}{2}$ more liters of juice.

Problem 2

Lucia has 3.5 hours left in her workday as a car mechanic. Lucia needs $\frac{1}{2}$ of an hour to complete one oil change.

a. How many oil changes can Lucia complete during the rest of her workday?
b. Lucia can complete two car inspections in the same amount of time it takes her to complete one oil change. How long does it take her to complete one car inspection?
c. How many inspections can she complete in the rest of her workday?

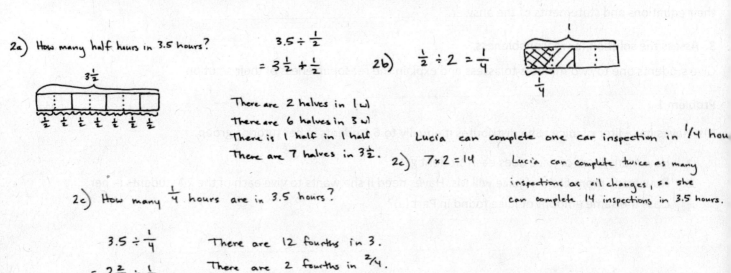

2a) How many half hours in 3.5 hours?

$3\frac{1}{2}$

$\frac{1}{2}$ $\frac{1}{2}$ $\frac{1}{2}$ $\frac{1}{2}$ $\frac{1}{2}$ $\frac{1}{2}$

$3.5 \div \frac{1}{2}$

= $3\frac{1}{2} + \frac{1}{2}$

There are 2 halves in 1 w.
There are 6 halves in 3 w.
There is 1 half in 1 half.
There are 7 halves in $3\frac{1}{2}$.

2b) $\frac{1}{2} \div 2 = \frac{1}{4}$

$\frac{1}{4}$

Lucia can complete one car inspection in $\frac{1}{4}$ hour.

2c) $7 \times 2 = 14$

Lucia can complete twice as many inspections as oil changes, so she can complete 14 inspections in 3.5 hours.

2c) How many $\frac{1}{4}$ hours are in 3.5 hours?

$3.5 \div \frac{1}{4}$

= $3\frac{2}{4} \div \frac{1}{4}$

There are 12 fourths in 3.
There are 2 fourths in $\frac{2}{4}$.
There are 14 fourths in $3\frac{2}{4}$.

Lucia can complete 14 inspections in 3.5 hours.

Lesson 33: Create story contexts for numerical expressions and tape diagrams, and solve word problems.

Date: 11/10/13

4.H.1

In Part (a), students are asked to find how many half-hours are in a 3.5 hour period. The presence of both decimal and fraction notation in these problems adds a layer of complexity. Students should be comfortable choosing which form of fractional number is most efficient for solving. This will vary by problem and, in many cases, by student. In this problem, many students may prefer to deal with 3.5 as a mixed number ($3\frac{1}{2}$). Then a tape diagram clearly shows that $3\frac{1}{2}$ can be partitioned into 7 units of $\frac{1}{2}$. Others may prefer to express the half hour as 0.5. Still others may begin their thinking with, "How many halves are in 1 whole?" and continue with similar prompts to find how many halves are in 3 wholes and 1 half.

In Part (b), students reason that since Lucia can complete 2 inspections in the time it takes her to complete just one oil change, $\frac{1}{2}$ may be divided by 2 to find the fraction of an hour that an inspection requires. Students may also reason that there are two 15-minute units in one half-hour period, and therefore, Lucia can complete an inspection in $\frac{1}{4}$ hour.

In Part (c), a variety of approaches is also possible. Some may argue that since Lucia can work twice as fast completing inspections, they need only to double the number of oil changes she could complete in 3.5 hours to find the number of inspections done. This type of thinking is evidence of a deeper understanding of a scaling principle. Other students may solve Part (c), just as they did Part (a), but using a divisor of $\frac{1}{4}$. In either case, Lucia can complete 14 inspections in 3.5 hours.

NOTES ON MULTIPLE MEANS OF ENGAGEMENT:

Challenge high achieving students (who may also be early finishers) to solve the problems more than one way. After looking at their work, challenge them by specifying the operation they must use to begin, or change the path of their approach by requiring a certain operation within their solution.

Challenge them further by asking them to use the same general context but to write a different question that results in the same quantity as the original problem.

Problem 3

Carlo buys $14.40 worth of grapefruit. Each grapefruit cost $0.80.

a. How many grapefruit does Carlo buy?

b. At the same store, Kahri spends one-third as much money on grapefruit as Carlo. How many grapefruit does she buy?

3a) $14.40 ÷ 0.80 $= \frac{14.4}{0.8} \times \frac{10}{10}$

$= \frac{144}{8}$

$= 18$

Carlo buys 18 grapefruit.

$$\begin{array}{r} 18 \\ 8\overline{)144} \\ -8 \\ \hline 64 \\ -64 \\ \hline 0 \end{array}$$

3b) $18 ÷ 3 = 6$

Kahri buys 6 grapefruit.

Students divide a decimal dividend by a decimal divisor to solve Problem 3. This problem is made simpler by showing the division expression as a fraction. Then, multiplication by a fraction equal to 1 ($\frac{10}{10}$ or $\frac{100}{100}$, depending on whether 80 cents is expressed as 0.8 or 0.80) results in both a whole number divisor and

Lesson 33: Create story contexts for numerical expressions and tape diagrams, and solve word problems.

Date: 11/10/13

4.H.19

dividend. From here, students must divide 144 by 8 to find a quotient of 18. Carlo buys 18 grapefruit with his money.

In Part (b), since Kahri spends one-third of her money on equally priced grapefruit, students should reason that she would be buying one-third the number of fruit. Therefore, 18 ÷ 3 shows that Kahri buys 6 grapefruit. Students may also choose the far less-direct method of solving a third of $14.40 and dividing that number ($4.80) by $0.80, to find the number of grapefruit purchased by Kahri.

Problem 4

Studies show that a typical giant hummingbird can flap its wings once in 0.08 of a second.

    a. While flying for 7.2 seconds, how many times will a typical giant hummingbird flap its wings?

    b. A ruby-throated hummingbird can flap its wings 4 times faster than a giant hummingbird. How many times will a ruby-throated hummingbird flap its wings in the same amount of time?

4a) $7.2 \div 0.08 = \dfrac{7.2}{0.08} \times \dfrac{100}{100}$

$= \dfrac{720}{8}$

$= 90$

A Giant Hummingbird can flap its wings 90 times in 7.2 seconds.

4b) $90 \times 4 = 360$

A Ruby Throated Hummingbird can flap its wings 360 times in 7.2 seconds.

Problem 4 is another decimal divisor/dividend problem. Similarly, students should express this division as a fraction, and then multiply to rename the divisor as a whole number. Ultimately, students should find that the giant hummingbird can flap its wings 90 times in 7.2 seconds. Part (b) is another example of the usefulness of the scaling principle. Since a ruby-throated hummingbird can flap its wings 4 times faster than the giant hummingbird, students need only to multiply 90 by 4 to find that a ruby-throated hummingbird can flap its wings a remarkable 360 times in 7.2 seconds. Though not very efficient, students could also divide 0.08 by 4 to find that it takes a ruby-throated hummingbird just 0.02 seconds to flap its wings once. Then division of 7.2 by 0.02 (or 720 by 2, after renaming the divisor as a whole number) yields a quotient of 360.

Problem 5

Create a story context for the following expression.

$\frac{1}{3} \times (\$20 - \$3.20)$

5) Jamis had a $20 bill. He spent $3.20 of it on breakfast & one-third of the remaining money on a book. How much did Jamis spend on the book?

5) Wilma promises to share her change equally among her 3 children. She pays her $3.20 bill with a $20. How much does each child receive?

   **Lesson 33:**   Create story contexts for numerical expressions and tape diagrams, and solve word problems.

Date: 11/10/13   4.H.2

Working backwards from expression to story may be challenging for some students. Since the expression given contains parentheses, the story created must first involve the subtraction of $3.20 from $20. For students in need of assistance, drawing a tape diagram first may be of help. Note that the story of Jamis interprets the multiplication of $\frac{1}{3}$ directly, whereas the story of Wilma interprets the expression as division by 3.

Problem 6

Create a story context about painting a wall for the following tape diagram.

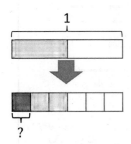

6) Ariel is painting her room & she finishes half of it before lunch. While painting she spends equal time kneeling, standing, & climbing a ladder. What portion of the job was painted while kneeling?

Again, students are asked to create a story problem, this time using a given tape diagram and the context of painting a wall. The challenge here is that this tape diagram implies a two-step word problem. The whole, 1, is first partitioned into half, and then one of those halves is divided into thirds. The story students create should reflect this two-part drawing. Students should be encouraged to share aloud and discuss their stories and thought process for solving.

6) One-half of a wall is painted white. The other half is painted to look like a Romanian flag, having equal parts blue, yellow, & red. What fraction of the wall is painted yellow?

Student Debrief (10 minutes)

Lesson Objective: Create story contexts for numerical expressions and tape diagrams, and solve word problems.

NOTES ON
MULTIPLE MEANS OF
ENGAGEMENT:

Challenge early finishers in this lesson by encouraging them to go back to each problem and provide an alternate means for solution or an additional model to represent the problem. Students could discuss how their interpretation of each problem led them to solve it the way they did, and how and why alternate interpretations could lead to a differing solution strategy.

Lesson 33:   Create story contexts for numerical expressions and tape
               diagrams, and solve word problems.
Date: 11/10/13

4.H.21

The Student Debrief is intended to invite reflection and active processing of the total lesson experience.

Invite students to review their solutions for the Problem Set. They should check work by comparing answers with a partner before going over answers as a class. Look for misconceptions or misunderstandings that can be addressed in the Debrief. Guide students in a conversation to debrief the Problem Set and process the lesson.

You may choose to use any combination of the questions below to lead the discussion.

- For Problems 1 to 5, did you draw a tape diagram to help solve the problems? If so, share your drawings and explain them to a partner.

- For Problems 1 to 4, there are different ways to solve the problems. Share and compare your strategy with a partner.

- For Problems 5 and 6, share your story problem with a partner. Explain how you interpreted the expression in Problem 5, and the tape diagram in Problem 6.

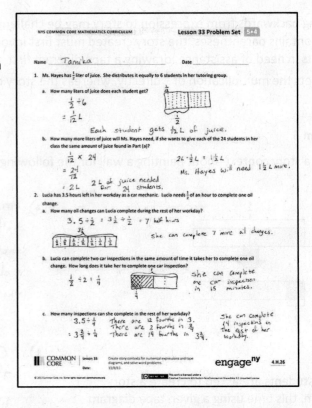

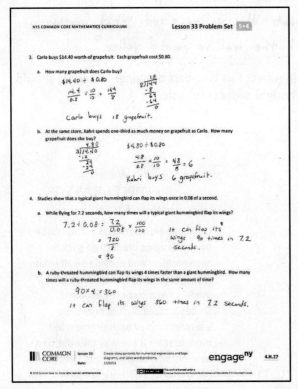

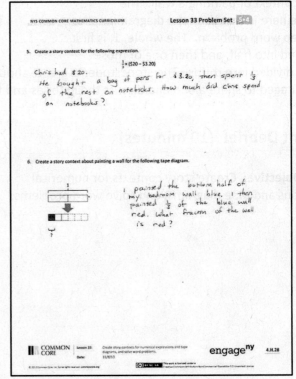

COMMON CORE

Lesson 33: Create story contexts for numerical expressions and tape diagrams, and solve word problems.

Date: 11/10/13

4.H.2

Exit Ticket (3 minutes)

After the Student Debrief, instruct students to complete the Exit Ticket. A review of their work will help you assess the students' understanding of the concepts that were presented in the lesson today and plan more effectively for future lessons. You may read the questions aloud to the students.

Lesson 33:	Create story contexts for numerical expressions and tape diagrams, and solve word problems.	4.H.23
Date:	11/10/13	

A

Divide.

Correct _____

1	1 ÷ 1 =		23	5 ÷ 0.1 =	
2	1 ÷ 0.1 =		24	0.5 ÷ 0.1 =	
3	2 ÷ 0.1 =		25	0.05 ÷ 0.1 =	
4	7 ÷ 0.1 =		26	0.08 ÷ 0.1 =	
5	1 ÷ 0.1 =		27	4 ÷ 0.01 =	
6	10 ÷ 0.1 =		28	40 ÷ 0.01 =	
7	20 ÷ 0.1 =		29	47 ÷ 0.01 =	
8	60 ÷ 0.1 =		30	59 ÷ 0.01 =	
9	1 ÷ 1 =		31	3 ÷ 0.1 =	
10	1 ÷ 0.1 =		32	30 ÷ 0.1 =	
11	10 ÷ 0.1 =		33	32 ÷ 0.1 =	
12	100 ÷ 0.1 =		34	32.5 ÷ 0.1 =	
13	200 ÷ 0.1 =		35	25 ÷ 5 =	
14	800 ÷ 0.1 =		36	2.5 ÷ 0.5 =	
15	1 ÷ 0.1 =		37	2.5 ÷ 0.05 =	
16	1 ÷ 0.01 =		38	3.6 ÷ 0.04 =	
17	2 ÷ 0.01 =		39	32 ÷ 0.08 =	
18	9 ÷ 0.01 =		40	56 ÷ 0.7 =	
19	5 ÷ 0.01 =		41	77 ÷ 1.1 =	
20	50 ÷ 0.01 =		42	4.8 ÷ 0.12 =	
21	60 ÷ 0.01 =		43	4.84 ÷ 0.4 =	
22	20 ÷ 0.01 =		44	9.63 ÷ 0.03 =	

COMMON CORE | **Lesson 33:** | Create story contexts for numerical expressions and tape diagrams, and solve word problems.
| **Date:** | 11/10/13

4.H.2

B

Improvement _____   # Correct _____

Divide.

1	10 ÷ 1 =		23	4 ÷ 0.1 =	
2	1 ÷ 0.1 =		24	0.4 ÷ 0.1 =	
3	2 ÷ 0.1 =		25	0.04 ÷ 0.1 =	
4	8 ÷ 0.1 =		26	0.07 ÷ 0.1 =	
5	1 ÷ 0.1 =		27	5 ÷ 0.01 =	
6	10 ÷ 0.1 =		28	50 ÷ 0.01 =	
7	20 ÷ 0.1 =		29	53 ÷ 0.01 =	
8	70 ÷ 0.1 =		30	68 ÷ 0.01 =	
9	1 ÷ 1 =		31	2 ÷ 0.1 =	
10	1 ÷ 0.1 =		32	20 ÷ 0.1 =	
11	10 ÷ 0.1 =		33	23 ÷ 0.1 =	
12	100 ÷ 0.1 =		34	23.6 ÷ 0.1 =	
13	200 ÷ 0.1 =		35	15 ÷ 5 =	
14	900 ÷ 0.1 =		36	1.5 ÷ 0.5 =	
15	1 ÷ 0.1 =		37	1.5 ÷ 0.05 =	
16	1 ÷ 0.01 =		38	3.2 ÷ 0.04 =	
17	2 ÷ 0.01 =		39	28 ÷ 0.07 =	
18	7 ÷ 0.01 =		40	42 ÷ 0.6 =	
19	4 ÷ 0.01 =		41	88 ÷ 1.1 =	
20	40 ÷ 0.01 =		42	3.6 ÷ 0.12 =	
21	50 ÷ 0.01 =		43	3.63 ÷ 0.3 =	
22	80 ÷ 0.01 =		44	8.44 ÷ 0.04 =	

Lesson 33:   Create story contexts for numerical expressions and tape diagrams, and solve word problems.

Date: 11/10/13

4.H.25

Name _____   Date _____

1. Ms. Hayes has $\frac{1}{2}$ liter of juice. She distributes it equally to 6 students in her tutoring group.

    a. How many liters of juice does each student get?

    b. How many more liters of juice will Ms. Hayes need, if she wants to give each of the 24 students in her class the same amount of juice found in Part (a)?

2. Lucia has 3.5 hours left in her workday as a car mechanic. Lucia needs $\frac{1}{2}$ of an hour to complete one oil change.

    a. How many oil changes can Lucia complete during the rest of her workday?

    b. Lucia can complete two car inspections in the same amount of time it takes her to complete one oil change. How long does it take her to complete one car inspection?

    c. How many inspections can she complete in the rest of her workday?

Lesson 33:   Create story contexts for numerical expressions and tape
               diagrams, and solve word problems.
Date: 11/10/13

4.H.2

3. Carlo buys $14.40 worth of grapefruit. Each grapefruit cost $0.80.

   a. How many grapefruit does Carlo buy?

   b. At the same store, Kahri spends one-third as much money on grapefruit as Carlo. How many grapefruit does she buy?

4. Studies show that a typical giant hummingbird can flap its wings once in 0.08 of a second.

   a. While flying for 7.2 seconds, how many times will a typical giant hummingbird flap its wings?

   b. A ruby-throated hummingbird can flap its wings 4 times faster than a giant hummingbird. How many times will a ruby-throated hummingbird flap its wings in the same amount of time?

Lesson 33:   Create story contexts for numerical expressions and tape diagrams, and solve word problems.

Date: 11/10/13

4.H.27

5. Create a story context for the following expression.

$$\frac{1}{3} \times (\$20 - \$3.20)$$

6. Create a story context about painting a wall for the following tape diagram.

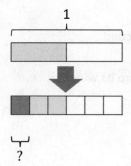

COMMON CORE™

Lesson 33: Create story contexts for numerical expressions and tape
diagrams, and solve word problems.
Date: 11/10/13

4.H.2

Name _____   Date _____

1. An entire commercial break is 3.6 minutes.

    a. If each commercial takes 0.6 minutes, how many commercials will be played?

    b. A different commercial break of the same length plays commercials half as long. How many commercials will play during this break?

COMMON CORE™ | Lesson 33: | Create story contexts for numerical expressions and tape diagrams, and solve word problems.   **4.H.29**
                     | Date: | 11/10/13

© 2013 Common Core, Inc. All rights reserved. **commoncore.org**

Name _____   Date _____

1. Chase volunteers at an animal shelter after school, feeding and playing with the cats.

    a. If he can make 5 servings of cat food from a third of a kilogram of food, how much does one serving weigh?

    b. If Chase wants to give this same serving size to each of 20 cats, how many kilograms of food will he need?

2. Anouk has 4.75 pounds of meat. She uses a quarter pound of meat to make one hamburger.

    a. How many hamburgers can Anouk make with the meat she has?

    b. Sometimes Anouk makes sliders. Each slider is half as much meat as is used for a regular hamburger. How many sliders could Anouk make with the 4.75 pounds?

COMMON CORE   **Lesson 33:**   Create story contexts for numerical expressions and tape
diagrams, and solve word problems.   4.H.3

Date: 11/10/13

3. Ms. Geronimo has a $10 gift certificate to her local bakery.

   a. If she buys a slice of pie for $2.20 and uses the rest of the gift certificate to buy chocolate macaroons that cost $0.60 each, how many macaroons can Ms. Geronimo buy?

   b. If she changes her mind and instead buys a loaf of bread for $4.60 and uses the rest to buy cookies that cost $1\frac{1}{2}$ times as much as the macaroons, how many cookies can she buy?

4. Create a story context for the following expressions.

   a. $(5\frac{1}{4} - 2\frac{1}{8}) \div 4$

   b. $4 \times \left(\frac{4.8}{0.8}\right)$

5. Create a story context for the following tape diagram.

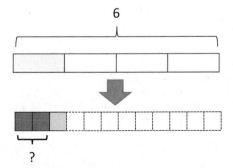

COMMON CORE™

Lesson 33: Create story contexts for numerical expressions and tape diagrams, and solve word problems.

Date: 11/10/13

4.H.31

Name _____ Date _____

1. Multiply or divide. Draw a model to explain your thinking.

   a. $\frac{1}{2} \times 6$

   b. $\frac{1}{2} \times 7$

   c. $\frac{3}{4} \times 12$

   d. $\frac{2}{5} \times 30$

   e. $\frac{1}{3}$ of 2 ft = _____ inches

   f. $\frac{1}{6}$ of 3 yds = _____ feet

   g. $\left(3 + \frac{1}{2}\right) \times 14$

   h. $4\frac{2}{3} \times 13$

2. If the whole bar is 3 units long, what is the length of the shaded part of the bar? Write a multiplication equation for the diagram, and then solve.

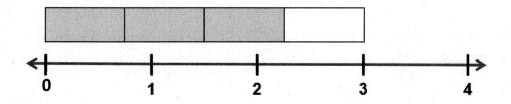

3. Circle the expression(s) that are equal to $\frac{3}{5} \times 6$. Explain why the others are *not* equal using words, pictures, or numbers.

    a. $3 \times (6 \div 5)$

    b. $3 \div (5 \times 6)$

    c. $(3 \times 6) \div 5$

    d. $3 \times \frac{6}{5}$

4. Write the following as expressions.

 a. One-third the sum of 6 and 3.

 b. Four times the quotient of 3 and 4.

 c. One-fourth the difference between $\frac{2}{3}$ and $\frac{1}{2}$.

5. Mr. Schaum used 10 buckets to collect rainfall in various locations on his property. The following line plot shows the amount of rain collected in each bucket in gallons. Write an expression that includes multiplication to show how to find the total amount of water collected in gallons. Then solve your expression.

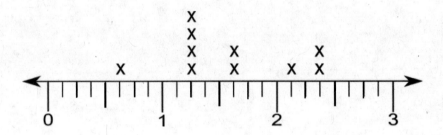

6. Mrs. Williams uses the following recipe for crispy rice treats. She decides to make $\frac{2}{3}$ of the recipe.

    2 cups melted butter
    24 oz marshmallows
    13 cups rice crispy cereal

a. How much of each ingredient will she need? Write an expression that includes multiplication. Solve
    by multiplying.

b. How many fluid ounces of butter will she use? (Use your measurement conversion chart if you wish.)

c. When the crispy rice treats have cooled, Mrs. Williams cuts them into 30 equal pieces. She gives two-
    fifths of the treats to her son and takes the rest to school. How many treats will Mrs. Williams take to
    school? Use any method to solve.

Mid-Module Assessment Task	Topics A–D
Standards Addressed	

Write and interpret numerical expressions.

5.OA.1 Use parentheses, brackets, or braces in numerical expressions, and evaluate expressions with these symbols.

5.OA.2 Write simple expressions that record calculations with numbers, and interpret numerical expressions without evaluating them. *For example, express the calculation "add 8 and 7, then multiply by 2" as 2 × (8 +7). Recognize that 3 × (18932 + 921) is three times as large as 18932 + 921, without having to calculate the indicated sum or product.*

Apply and extend previous understandings of multiplication and division to multiply and divide fractions.

5.NF.3 Interpret a fraction as division of the numerator by the denominator (*a/b = a ÷ b*). Solve word problems involving division of whole numbers leading to answers in the form of fractions or mixed numbers, e.g., by using visual fraction models or equations to represent the problem. *For example, interpret 3/4 as the result of dividing 3 by 4, noting that 3/4 multiplied by 4 equals 3, and that when 3 wholes are shared equally among 4 people each person has a share of size 3/4. If 9 people want to share a 50-pound sack of rice equally by weight, how many pounds of rice should each person get? Between what two whole numbers does your answer lie?*

5.NF.4 Apply and extend previous understandings of multiplication to multiply a fraction or whole number by a fraction.

   a. Interpret the product (*a/b*) × *q* as *a* parts of a partition of *q* into *b* parts; equivalently, as the result of a sequence of operations *a* × *q* ÷ *b*. *For example, use a visual fraction model to show (2/3) × 4 = 8/3, and create a story context for this equation. Do the same with (2/3) × (4/5) = 8/15. (In general, (a/b) × (c/d) = ac/bd.)*

5.NF.6 Solve real world problems involving multiplication of fractions and mixed numbers, e.g., by using visual fraction models or equations to represent the problem.

Convert like measurement units within a given measurement system.

5.MD.1 Convert among different-sized standard measurement units within a given measurement system (e.g., convert 5 cm to 0.05 m), and use these conversions in solving multi-step, real world problems.

Represent and interpret data.

5.MD.2 Make a line plot to display a data set of measurements in fractions of a unit (1/2, 1/4, 1/8). Use operations on fractions for this grade to solve problems involving information presented in line plots. *For example, given different measurements of liquid in identical beakers, find the amount of liquid each beaker would contain if the total amount in all the beakers were redistributed equally.*

Evaluating Student Learning Outcomes

A Progression Toward Mastery is provided to describe steps that illuminate the gradually increasing understandings that students develop *on their way to proficiency.* In this chart, this progress is presented from left (Step 1) to right (Step 4). The learning goal for each student is to achieve Step 4 mastery. These steps are meant to help teachers and students identify and celebrate what the student CAN do now and what they need to work on next.

A Progression Toward Mastery

Assessment Task Item and Standards Assessed	STEP 1 Little evidence of reasoning without a correct answer. (1 Point)	STEP 2 Evidence of some reasoning without a correct answer. (2 Points)	STEP 3 Evidence of some reasoning with a correct answer or evidence of solid reasoning with an incorrect answer. (3 Points)	STEP 4 Evidence of solid reasoning with a correct answer. (4 Points)
1 **5.NF.4a** **5.MD.1**	The student draws valid models and/or arrives at the correct product for two or more items.	The student draws valid models and/or arrives at the correct product for at least four or more items.	The student draws valid models and/or arrives at the correct product for at least six or more items.	The student correctly answers all eight items, and draws valid models: a. 3 b. 3 1/2 c. 9 d. 12 e. 8 inches f. 1 1/2 feet g. 49 h. 60 2/3
2 **5.NF.4a** **5.NF.3**	The student's work shows no evidence of being able to express the length of the shaded area.	The student approximates the length of the shaded bar, but does not write a multiplication equation.	The student is able to write the correct multiplication equation for the diagram, but incorrectly states the length of the shaded part of the bar.	The student correctly: ▪ Writes a multiplication equation: 3/4 × 3. ▪ Finds the length of the shaded part of the bar as 9/4 or 2 1/4.
3 **5.OA.1**	The student is unable to identify any equal expressions.	The student correctly identifies one correct expression.	The student correctly identifies two equal expressions.	The student correctly: ▪ Identifies (a), (c), and (d) as equal to 3/5 × 6. ▪ Explains why (b) is not equal.

A Progression Toward Mastery

4 **5.OA.2**	The student is unable to write expressions for (a), (b), or (c).	The student correctly writes one expression.	The student correctly writes two expressions.	The student correctly writes three expressions: a. $1/3 \times (6 + 3)$ b. $4 \times (3 \div 4)$ or $\quad 4 \times 3/4$ c. $1/4 \times (2/3 - 1/2)$
5 **5.NF.4a** **5.NF.6** **5.MD.2**	The student is neither able to produce a multiplication expression that identifies the data from the line plot, nor is able to find the total gallons of water collected.	The student is either able to write a multiplication expression that accounts for all data points on the line plot, or is able to find the total gallons of water collected.	The student's multiplication expression correctly accounts for all the data points on the line plot when finding the total gallons of water collected, but makes a calculation error.	The student correctly: ■ Accounts for all data points in the line plot in the multiplication expression. ■ Finds the total gallons of water collected as 15 6/8 gallons or 15 3/4 gallons.
6 **5.NF.4a** **5.NF.6** **5.MD.1**	The student correctly calculates two correct answers.	The student is able to correctly calculate three correct answers.	The student is able to correctly calculate four correct answers.	The student correctly: a. Calculates: 1 1/3 c butter; 16 oz of marshmallows; 8 2/3 c of cereal b. Converts 1 1/3c butter to 10 2/3 fluid ounces. c. Uses an equation or model and finds the number of treats taken to school as 18 treats.

Name _Hayley_   Date _1-25_

1. **Multiply or divide. Draw a model to explain your thinking.**

a) $\frac{1}{2} \times 6 = 6 \div 2 = 3$

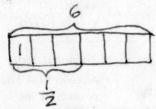

b) $\frac{1}{2} \times 7 = 7 \div 2 = 3\frac{1}{2}$

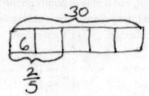

c) $\frac{3}{4} \times 12 = 9$

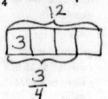

d) $\frac{2}{5} \times 30 = 12$

e)

$\frac{1}{3}$ of 2 ft = ___8___ inches

2 ft × 12 = 24 inches

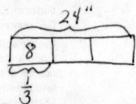

f)

$\frac{1}{6}$ of 3 yds = _1½_ feet

3 yd

$\frac{1}{2}$ of a yard = $\frac{1}{2}$ of 3 ft

3 ft

1½ ft

g) $\left(3 + \frac{1}{2}\right) \times 14 =$

$(3 \times 14) + \left(\frac{1}{2} \times 14\right) =$

$42 + 7 =$

49

h) $4\frac{2}{3} \times 13 =$

$(4 \times 13) + \left(\frac{2}{3} \times 13\right) =$

$52 + \frac{2 \times 13}{3} =$

$52 + \frac{26}{3} = 52 + 8\frac{2}{3} =$

$60\frac{2}{3}$

2. If the whole bar is 3 units long, what is the length of the shaded part of the bar? Write a multiplication equation for the diagram and then solve.

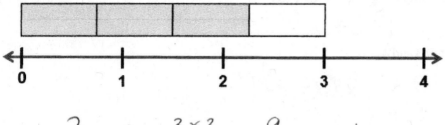

$$\frac{3}{4} \times 3 = \frac{3 \times 3}{4} = \frac{9}{4} = 2\frac{1}{4}$$

3. Circle the expression(s) that are equal to $\frac{3}{5} \times 6$. Explain why the others are *not* equal using words, pictures or numbers.

    a. $3 \times (6 \div 5)$

    b. $3 \div (5 \times 6)$ $= 3 \div 30 = 0.1$

    c. $(3 \times 6) \div 5$

    d. $3 \times \frac{6}{5}$

4. Write the following as expressions.

   a. One-third the sum of 6 and 3.

   $$\frac{1}{3} \times (6+3)$$

   b. Four times the quotient of 3 and 4.

   $$4 \times (3 \div 4)$$

   c. One-fourth the difference between $\frac{2}{3}$ and $\frac{1}{2}$.

   $$\frac{1}{4} \times \left(\frac{2}{3} - \frac{1}{2}\right)$$

5. Mr. Schaum used 10 buckets to collect rainfall in various locations on his property. The following line plot shows the amount of rain collected in each bucket in gallons. Write an expression that includes multiplication to show how to find the total amount of water collected in gallons. Then solve your expression.

$$\frac{5}{8} + \left(4 \times 1\frac{2}{8}\right) + \left(2 \times 1\frac{5}{8}\right) + 2\frac{1}{8} + \left(2 \times 2\frac{3}{8}\right) =$$

$$\frac{5}{8} + 4 + \frac{4\times2}{8} + 2 + \frac{2\times5}{8} + 2\frac{1}{8} + 4 + \frac{2\times3}{8} =$$

$$12 + \frac{5}{8} + \frac{8}{8} + \frac{10}{8} + \frac{1}{8} + \frac{6}{8} =$$

$$13 + \frac{22}{8} = 15\frac{6}{8} = 15\frac{3}{4} \text{ gallons}$$

6. Mrs. Williams uses the following recipe for crispy rice treats. She decides to make $\frac{2}{3}$ of the recipe.

      2 cups melted butter
      24 oz marshmallows
      13 cups rice crispy cereal

a. How much of each ingredient will she need? Write an expression that includes multiplication. Solve by multiplying.

$$\frac{2}{3} \times 2 \text{ cups} = \frac{2 \times 2}{3} = \frac{4}{3} = 1\frac{1}{3} \text{ cups of butter}$$

$$\frac{2}{3} \times 24 \text{ oz} = \frac{2 \times 24}{3} = \frac{48}{3} = 16 \text{ oz of marshmellows}$$

$$\frac{2}{3} \times 13 \text{ cups} = \frac{2 \times 13}{3} = \frac{26}{3} = 8\frac{2}{3} \text{ cups of cereal}$$

b. How many fluid ounces of butter will she use? (Use your measurement conversion chart if you wish.)

$$1 \text{ cup} = 8 \text{ oz}$$

$$1\frac{1}{3} \times 8 = (1 \times 8) + (\frac{1}{3} \times 8) = 8\frac{8}{3} = 10\frac{2}{3} \text{ fluid oz}$$

c. When the rice crispy treats have cooled, Mrs. Williams cuts them into 30 equal pieces. She gives two-fifths of the treats to her son and takes the rest to school. How many treats will Mrs. Williams take to school? Use any method to solve.

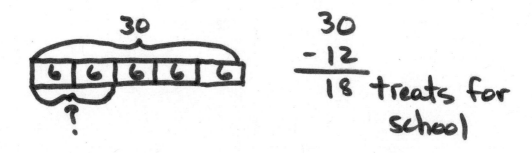

$$\begin{array}{r} 30 \\ -12 \\ \hline 18 \end{array} \text{ treats for school}$$

Name _____   Date _____

1. Multiply or divide. Draw a model to explain your thinking.

a. $\frac{1}{3} \times \frac{1}{4}$

b. $\frac{3}{4}$ of $\frac{1}{3}$

c. $2\frac{3}{4} \times \frac{8}{9}$

d. $4 \div \frac{1}{3}$

e. $5 \div \frac{1}{4}$

f. $\frac{1}{4} \div 5$

2. Multiply or divide using any method.

a. 1.5×32

b. 1.5×0.32

c. $12 \div 0.03$

d. $1.2 \div 0.3$

e. $12.8 \times \frac{3}{4}$

f. $102.4 \div 3.2$

3. Fill in the chart by writing an equivalent expression.

a.	One-fifth of the sum of one-half and one-third	
b.	Two and a half times the sum of nine and twelve	
c.	Twenty-four divided by the difference between $1\frac{1}{2}$ and $\frac{3}{4}$	

4. A castle has to be guarded 24 hours a day. Five knights are ordered to split each day's guard duty equally. How long will each knight spend on guard duty in one day?

   a. Record your answer in hours.

   b. Record it in hours and minutes.

   c. Record your answer in minutes.

5. On the blank, write a division expression that matches the situation.

a. _____   Mark and Jada share 5 yards of ribbon equally. How
                                  much ribbon will each get?

b. _____   It takes half of a yard of ribbon to make a bow. How many bows
                                  can be made with 5 yards of ribbon?

c. Draw a diagram for each problem and solve.

d. Could either of the problems also be solved by using $\frac{1}{2} \times 5$? If so, which one(s)? Explain your thinking.

6. Jackson claims that multiplication always makes a number bigger. He gave the following examples:

    ▪   If I take 6, and I multiply it by 4, I get 24, which is bigger than 6.
    ▪   If I take $\frac{1}{4}$, and I multiply it by 2 (whole number), I get $\frac{2}{4}$, or $\frac{1}{2}$ which is bigger than $\frac{1}{4}$.

    Jackson's reasoning is incorrect. Give an example that proves he is wrong, and explain his mistake using pictures, words, or numbers.

7. Jill is collecting honey from 9 different beehives, and recorded the amount collected, in gallons, from each hive in the line plot shown:

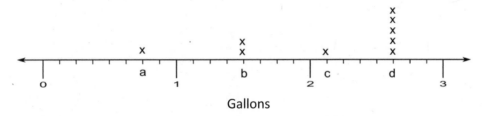

Gallons

    a. She wants to write the value of each point marked on the number line above (Points a–d) in terms of the largest possible whole number of gallons, quarts, and pints. Use the line plot above to fill in the blanks with the correct conversions. (The first one is done for you.)

        a.   ___0___ gal ___3___ qt ___0___ pt

        b.   _____ gal _____ qt _____ pt

        c.   _____ gal _____ qt _____ pt

        d.   _____ gal _____ qt _____ pt

b. Find the total amount of honey collected from the five hives that produced the most honey.

c. Jill collected a total of 19 gallons of honey. If she distributes all of the honey equally between 9 jars, how much honey will be in each jar?

d. Jill used $\frac{3}{4}$ of a jar for baking. How much honey did she use baking?

e. Jill's mom used $\frac{1}{4}$ of a gallon of honey to bake 3 loaves of bread. If she used an equal amount of honey in each loaf, how much honey did she use for 1 loaf?

f. Jill's mom stored some of the honey in a container that held $\frac{3}{4}$ of a gallon. She used half of this amount to sweeten tea. How much honey, in cups, was used in the tea? Write an equation and draw a tape diagram.

g. Jill uses some of her honey to make lotion. If each bottle of lotion requires $\frac{1}{4}$ gallon, and she uses a total of 3 gallons, how many bottles of lotion does she make?

Write and interpret numerical expressions.

5.OA.1   Use parentheses, brackets, or braces in numerical expressions, and evaluate expressions with these symbols.

5.OA.2   Write simple expressions that record calculations with numbers, and interpret numerical expressions without evaluating them. *For example, express the calculation "add 8 and 7, then multiply by 2" as 2 × (8 +7). Recognize that 3 × (18932 + 921) is three times as large as 18932 + 921, without having to calculate the indicated sum or product.*

Perform operations with multi-digit whole numbers and with decimals to hundredths.

5.NBT.7   Add, subtract, multiply, and divide decimals to hundredths, using concrete models or drawings and strategies based on place value, properties of operations, and/or the relationship between addition and subtraction; relate the strategy to a written method and explain the reasoning used.

Apply and extend previous understandings of multiplication and division to multiply and divide fractions.

5.NF.3   Interpret a fraction as division of the numerator by the denominator ($a/b = a \div b$). Solve word problems involving division of whole numbers leading to answers in the form of fractions or mixed numbers, e.g., by using visual fraction models or equations to represent the problem. *For example, interpret 3/4 as the result of dividing 3 by 4, noting that 3/4 multiplied by 4 equals 3, and that when 3 wholes are shared equally among 4 people each person has a share of size 3/4. If 9 people want to share a 50-pound sack of rice equally by weight, how many pounds of rice should each person get? Between what two whole numbers does your answer lie?*

5.NF.4   Apply and extend previous understandings of multiplication to multiply a fraction or whole number by a fraction.

   a.   Interpret the product of $(a/b) \times q$ as a parts of a partition of q into b equal parts; equivalently, as the result of a sequence of operations $a \times q \div b$. *For example, use a visual fraction model to show (2/3 × 4 = 8/3, and create a story context for this equation. Do the same with (2/3) × (4/5) = 8/15. (In general, (a/b) × (c/d) = ac/bd.)*

5.NF.5   Interpret multiplication as scaling (resizing) by:

   a.   Comparing the size of a product to the size of one factor on the basis of the size of the other factor, without performing the indicated multiplication.

   b.   Explaining why multiplying a given number by a fraction greater than 1 results in a product greater than the given number (recognizing multiplication by whole numbers greater than 1 as a familiar case); explaining why multiplying a given number by a fraction less than 1 results in a product smaller than the given number; and relating the principle of fraction equivalence $a/b = (n\times a)/(n\times b)$ to the effect of multiplying a/b by 1.

**COMMON
CORE**™   Module 4:   Multiplication and Division of Fractions and Decimal Fractions
             Date: 11/10/13

4.S.1

5.NF.6   Solve real world problems involving multiplication of fractions and mixed numbers, e.g., by using visual fraction models or equations to represent the problem.

5.NF.7   Apply and extend previous understandings of division to divide unit fractions by whole numbers and whole numbers by unit fractions. (Students able to multiple fractions in general can develop strategies to divide fractions in general, by reasoning about the relationship between multiplication and division. But division of a fraction by a fraction is not a requirement at this grade level.)

   a.   Interpret division of a unit fraction by a non-zero whole number, and compute such quotients. *For example, create a story context for (1/3) ÷ 4, and use a visual fraction model to show the quotient. Use the relationship between multiplication and division to explain that (1/3) ÷ 4 = 1/12 because (1/12) × 4 = 1/3.*

   b.   Interpret division of a whole number by a unit fraction, and compute such quotients. *For example, create a story context for 4 ÷ (1/5), and use a visual fraction model to show the quotient. Use the relationship between multiplication and division to explain that 4 ÷ (1/5) = 20 because 20 × (1/5) = 4.*

   c.   Solve real world problems involving division of unit fractions by non-zero whole numbers and division of whole numbers by unit fractions, e.g., by using visual fraction models and equations to represent the problem. *For example, how much chocolate will each person get if 3 people share 1/2 lb of chocolate equally? How many 1/3-cup servings are in 2 cups of raisins?*

Convert like measurement units within a given measurement system.

5.MD.1   Convert among different-sized standard measurement units within a given measurement system (e.g., convert 5 cm to 0.05 m), and use these conversions in solving multi-step, real world problems.

Represent and interpret data.

5.MD.2   Make a line plot to display a data set of measurements in fractions of a unit (1/2, 1/4, 1/8). Use operations on fractions for this grade to solve problems involving information presented in line plots. *For example, given different measurements of liquid in identical beakers, find the amount of liquid each beaker would contain if the total amount in all the beakers were redistributed equally.*

Evaluating Student Learning Outcomes

A Progression Toward Mastery is provided to describe steps that illuminate the gradually increasing understandings that students develop *on their way to proficiency.* In this chart, this progress is presented from left (Step 1) to right (Step 4). The learning goal for each student is to achieve Step 4 mastery. These steps are meant to help teachers and students identify and celebrate what the student CAN do now and what they need to work on next.

Name __Seth__   Date __2/15__

1. Multiply or divide. Draw a model to explain your thinking.

a) $\frac{1}{3} \times \frac{1}{4} = \frac{1}{12}$

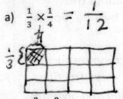

b) $\frac{3}{4}$ of $\frac{1}{3} = \frac{3}{12}$

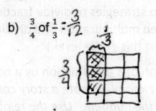

c) $2\frac{3}{4} \times \frac{8}{9} =$

$\frac{4}{4} \times \frac{8}{9} = \frac{8}{4} \times \frac{11}{9} =$

$\frac{2}{1} \times \frac{11}{9} = \frac{22}{9} = 2\frac{4}{9}$

d) $4 \div \frac{1}{3} = 4 \times 3 = 12$

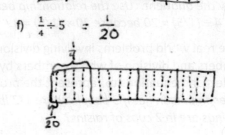

e) $5 \div \frac{1}{4} = 20$

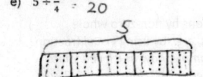

f) $\frac{1}{4} \div 5 = \frac{1}{20}$

2. Multiply or divide using any method.

a) $1.5 \times 32 = 48.0$

   15 tenths
   $\times 32$
   ———
   30
   $+450$
   ———
   480 tenths

b) $1.5 \times 0.32 = 0.48$

   $(1 \times .32) + (.5 \times .32) =$
   $.32 + .16 =$
   $.48$

c) $12 \div 0.03 =$

   $(12 \times 100) \div (0.03 \times 100) =$
   $1200 \div 3 =$
   400

d) $1.2 \div 0.3 =$

   $(1.2 \times 10) \div (0.3 \times 10) =$
   $\frac{12 \div 3}{4}$

e) $12.8 \times \frac{3}{4} =$

   $(12 \times \frac{3}{4}) + (\frac{8}{10} \times \frac{3}{4}) =$

   $9 + \frac{24}{40} = 9\frac{24}{40} = 9\frac{3}{5}$

f) $102.4 \div 3.2 = (102.4 \times 10) \div (3.2 \times 10) =$

   $1,024 \div 32 = 32$

   $\begin{array}{r} 32 \\ 32\overline{)1,024} \\ -96 \\ \hline 64 \\ -64 \\ \hline 0 \end{array}$

A Progression Toward Mastery

Assessment Task Item and Standards Assessed	STEP 1 Little evidence of reasoning without a correct answer. (1 Point)	STEP 2 Evidence of some reasoning without a correct answer. (2 Points)	STEP 3 Evidence of some reasoning with a correct answer or evidence of solid reasoning with an incorrect answer. (3 Points)	STEP 4 Evidence of solid reasoning with a correct answer. (4 Points)
1 5. NF.4 5. NF.7	The student draws valid models and/or arrives at the correct answer for two or more items.	The student draws valid models and/or arrives at the correct answer for three or more items.	The student draws valid models and/or arrives at the correct answer for four or more items.	The student correctly answers all eight items, and draws valid models: a. $\frac{1}{12}$ b. $\frac{3}{12}$ c. $2\frac{4}{9}$ d. 12 e. 20 f. $\frac{1}{20}$
2 5.NBT.7	The student has two or fewer correct answers.	The student has three correct answers.	The student has four correct answers.	The student correctly answers all six items: a. 48 b. 0.48 c. 400 d. 4 e. 9.6 or 924/40 or any equivalent fraction f. 32
3 5.OA.2	The student has no correct answers.	The student has one correct answer.	The student has two correct answers.	The student correctly answers all three items: a. $\frac{1}{5} \times (\frac{1}{2} + \frac{1}{3})$ b. $(9 + 12) \times 2\frac{1}{2}$ or $2\frac{1}{2} \times (9 + 12)$

A Progression Toward Mastery

				c. $24 \div (1\frac{1}{2} - \frac{3}{4})$
4 **5.NF.3** **5.NF.6** **5.MD.1**	The student has no correct answers.	The student has one correct answer.	The student has two correct answers.	The student correctly answers all three items: a. 4.8 hours b. 4 hours, 48 minutes c. 288 minutes
5 **5.NF.6** **5.NF.7**	The student gives one or fewer correct responses among Parts (a), (b), (c), and (d).	The student gives at least two correct responses among Parts (a), (b), (c), and (d).	The student gives at least three correct responses among Parts (a), (b), (c), and (d).	The student correctly answers all four items: a. $5 \div 2$ b. $5 \div 1/2$ c. Draws a correct diagram for both expressions and solves. d. Correctly identifies $5 \div 2$, and offers solid reasoning.
6 **5.NF.5**	The student gives both a faulty example and a faulty explanation.	The student gives either a faulty example or explanation.	The student gives a valid example or a clear explanation.	The student is able to give a correct example and clear explanation.

7
 	
5.NF.3
 	
5.NF.4
 	
5.NF.6
 	
5.NF.7
 	
5.MD.1
 	
5.MD.2
	The student has two or fewer correct answers.	The student has three correct answers.	The student has five correct answers.	The student correctly answers all seven items:
				
				a. 1 gal, 2 qts
				   2 gal, 1 pt
				   2 gal, 2 qt, 1 pt
				
				b. 13 gal, 1 pt
				
				c. 2 1/9 gal
				
				d. 1 7/12 gal
				
				e. 1/12 gal
				
				f. 6 c
				
				g. 12 bottles

Module 4:	Multiplication and Division of Fractions and Decimal Fractions
Date:	11/10/13

3. Fill in the chart by writing an equivalent expression.

a)	One fifth of the sum of one-half and one-third	$\frac{1}{5} \times \left(\frac{1}{2} + \frac{1}{3}\right)$
b)	Two and a half times the sum of nine and twelve	$2\frac{1}{2} \times (9 + 12)$
c)	Twenty-four divided by the difference between $1\frac{1}{2}$ and $\frac{3}{4}$	$24 \div \left(1\frac{1}{2} - \frac{3}{4}\right)$

4. A castle has to be guarded 24 hours a day. Five knights are ordered to split each day's guard duty equally. How long will each knight spend on guard duty in one day?

a. Record your answer in hours.

$$\begin{array}{r} 4.8 \\ 5 \overline{)24.0} \\ -20 \\ \hline 4.0 \\ 4.0 \\ \hline 0 \end{array}$$

4.8 hours

b. Record it in hours and minutes.

$\frac{1}{10}$ of 60 min = 6 min

6 min × 8 = 48 min

4.8 hours = 4 hours 48 minutes

c. Record your answer in minutes.

$$\begin{array}{r} 6\overset{0}{0} \\ \times 4 \\ \hline 240 \end{array} \text{ minutes}$$

$$\begin{array}{r} 240 \\ + 48 \\ \hline 288 \end{array}$$

4.8 hours = 288 minutes

5. On the blank, write a division expression that matches the situation.

a. ____ $5 \div 2$ ____   Mark and Jada share 5 yards of ribbon equally. How much ribbon will each get?

b. ____ $5 \div \frac{1}{2}$ ____   It takes half of a yard of ribbon to make a bow. How many bows can be made with 5 yards of ribbon?

c. Draw a diagram for each problem and solve.

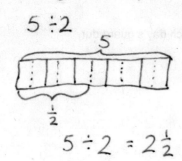

$5 \div 2$

$5 \div 2 = 2\frac{1}{2}$

$5 \div \frac{1}{2}$

$5 \div \frac{1}{2} = 10$

d. Could either of the problems also be solved by using $\frac{1}{2} \times 5$? If so, which one(s)? Explain your thinking.

$5 \div 2 = 5 \times \frac{1}{2}$. Dividing by 2 is the same as taking $\frac{1}{2}$ of something, which means multiplying. $\frac{1}{2} \times 5$ is the same as $5 \times \frac{1}{2}$.

6. Jackson claims that multiplication always makes a number bigger. He gave the following examples:

    ▪ If I take 6, and I multiply it by 4, I get 24, which is bigger than 6.
    ▪ If I take $\frac{1}{4}$, and I multiply it by 2 (whole number), I get $\frac{2}{4}$, or $\frac{1}{2}$ which is bigger than $\frac{1}{4}$.

    Jackson's reasoning is incorrect. Give an example that proves he is wrong, and explain his mistake using pictures, words or numbers.

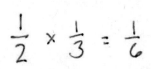 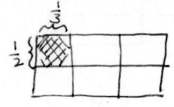 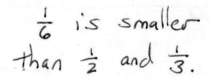

7. Jill is collecting honey from 9 different beehives, and recorded the amount collected, in gallons, from each hive in the line plot shown:

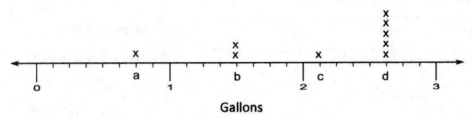

Gallons

a. She wants to write the value of each point marked on the number line above (points a-d) in terms of the largest possible whole number of gallons, quarts, and pints. Use the line plot above to fill in the blanks with the correct conversions (the first one is done for you).

    a) ___0___ gal ___3___ qt ___0___ pt

    b) ___1___ gal ___2___ qt ___0___ pt

    c) ___2___ gal ___0___ qt ___1___ pt

    d) ___2___ gal ___2___ qt ___1___ pt

e.   Jill's mom used $\frac{1}{4}$ of a gallon of honey to bake 3 loaves of bread. If she used an equal amount of honey in each loaf, how much honey did she use for 1 loaf?

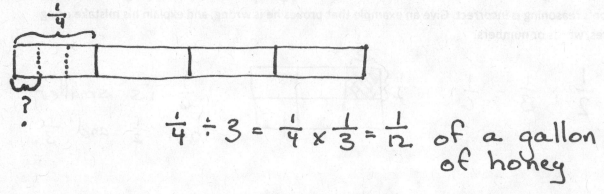

$$\frac{1}{4} \div 3 = \frac{1}{4} \times \frac{1}{3} = \frac{1}{12} \text{ of a gallon of honey}$$

f.   Jill's mom stored some of the honey in a container that held ¾ of a gallon. She used half of this amount to sweeten tea. How much honey, in cups, was used in the tea? Write an equation and draw a tape diagram.

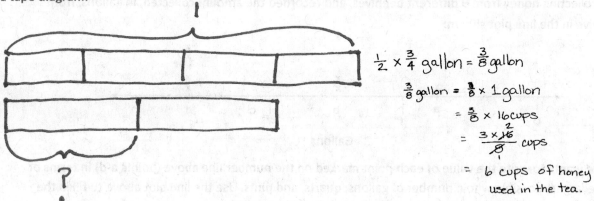

$$\frac{1}{2} \times \frac{3}{4} \text{ gallon} = \frac{3}{8} \text{ gallon}$$

$$\frac{3}{8} \text{ gallon} = \frac{3}{8} \times 1 \text{ gallon}$$

$$= \frac{3}{8} \times 16 \text{ cups}$$

$$= \frac{3 \times \overset{2}{\cancel{16}}}{\underset{1}{\cancel{8}}} \text{ cups}$$

$$= 6 \text{ cups of honey used in the tea.}$$

g.   Jill uses some of her honey to make lotion. If each bottle of lotion requires $\frac{1}{4}$ gallon, and she uses a total of 3 gallons, how many bottles of lotion does she make?

$$3 \div \frac{1}{4} = 3 \times 4 = 12 \text{ bottles of lotion}$$